JMLS

THRONE OF GOLD

THRONE OF GOLD

The Lives of the Aga Khans

Anne Edwards

HarperCollins*Publishers*

HarperCollins*Publishers*
77–85 Fulham Palace Road,
Hammersmith, London W6 8JB

Published by HarperCollins*Publishers* 1995
3 5 7 9 8 6 4 2

Copyright © Anne Edwards 1995

The Author asserts the moral right to
be identified as the author of this work

A catalogue record for this book is
available from the British Library

ISBN 0 00 215196 0

Set in Linotron Galliard by
Rowland Phototypesetting Ltd,
Bury St Edmunds, Suffolk

Printed in Great Britain by
HarperCollinsManufacturing Glasgow

For Robert Jorgen with love

CONTENTS

LIST OF ILLUSTRATIONS

AUTHOR'S NOTE

The name *Khan* is very common in Muslim countries where it translates as 'chief'. There is no relationship between the Aga Khans and Kublai Khan (1214–94) or Genghis Khan (1162–1227), founder of the Mongol dynasty; nor to any other families with the name Khan. In Iran or Indo-Pakistan through-out the centuries, the word *Khan* has been used before the tribal name (for example, *Khushhal Khan Khatak, Muhammad Khan Jamali*). In more recent times the tribal name was dropped, which explains the enormous number of people with the family name of Khan.

From about 1859, when it first appeared in official papers of the Bombay Government, the Aga Khans I–IV have enjoyed the style of 'His Highness'. It has been ratified (sometimes with reluctance) by the British Government to each successive Aga and it is not hereditary. (It should be remembered that the family holds British citizenship.)

But Great Britain did not recognize the title of 'Prince' for the Aga Khan III's two sons, Aly and Sadruddin Khan. The justification for such an honorific was based on the claim that the Aga Khan's grandmother was a Persian princess with hereditary rights (and the same holds true for the current Aga Khan IV and his two sons, Rahim and Hussain). The elder son, Aly Khan, was allowed the courtesy title of Prince by the British Government in 1938 after an incident the previous year (see chapter nine).

The Ismailis call their prayers *duas*. Though like all Muslims they have prayer meetings every Friday, they do not do so in a mosque, meeting instead in what is called a *jamaat khana*. Today, in London, this *jamaat khana* is 5 Palace Gate W8, Aly Khan's former residence. The Ismaili Centre in the Cromwell Road has been the main gathering-point for Ismaili Muslims in London since 1984.

In the present book, names and terms taken from Arabic and other non-European languages have been transliterated using the most familiar or easy forms; no accents or diacriticals have been used.

AGA KHAN MEHALATEE ——— **SARV-I JAHAN KHANUM**
(His Highness Aga Khan I)
also called Hasan Ali Shah.
Born in Persia *c*. 1800.
Appointed Governor-General of Kerman
by his father-in-law.
Style of His Highness in use by Bombay
Govt. from *c*. 1859.
Died 12 April 1881 at Bombay.
Buried at Mazagoan.

daughter of
FATH ALI, SHAH OF PERSIA

Principal wife

ALI SHAH ——— **SHAMS AL-MULUK** (Lady Ali Shah
(His Highness Aga Khan II)
Born *c*. 1830 at Mahallat.
Confirmed in the title of His Highness
9 August 1882.
Died August 1885 aged 54.

niece of
NASR-ed-DIN, SHAH OF PERSIA
Recipient of the Imperial Order of the
Crown of India.
Died 7 February 1938 at Baghdad, Iraq

Sir SULTAN MOHAMMED ——— **SHAHAZDA BEGUM**
(His Highness Aga Khan III)
Born 2 November 1877 at Karachi, British
India.
Confirmed in his father's titles 1885.
Created K.C.I.E. (1898) and promoted
G.C.I.E. (1902), G.C.S.I. (1911),
G.C.V.O. (1923) and G.C.M.G. (1955).*
Accorded status of First Class Chief of the
Bombay Presidency (with 11 gun salute)
1916 and sworn of The Privy Council 1934.
Died 11 July 1957 at Versoix, Switzerland,
aged 79.
Buried 1 February 1959 at Aswan, Egypt.

daughter of
AGA JANGISHAH
Married at Poona 1896.
Marriage dissolved by decree of divorce
8 December 1926.

First wife. No issue.

MOHAMMED MAHDI KHAN   **ALY SOLOMAN KHAN** ——— The Honourable **JOAN BARBARA**
Born 1909.
Died 1910 at Monte Carlo.

(Prince Aly Khan)
Born 17 June 1911 at Turin, Italy.
Recipient of the Croix de Guerre (with
palms) and the Bronze Star Medal (US).
Lieutenant-Colonel in the British Army
(Wiltshire Regiment). Head of the Pakistan
Delegation to the United Nations and a
vice-president of the General Assembly
(1958) and vice-chairman of the Peace
Observation Commission (1959).
Died 12 May 1960 at Paris, France.
Buried (temporarily at the Château de
l'Horizon) at Damascus, Syria, 11 July 1972.

YARDE-BULLER
daughter of
JOHN 3rd BARON CHURSTON
(and formerly the wife of THOMAS
LOEL EVELYN BULKELEY
GUINNESS).
Married 18 May 1936 at Paris, France.
Marriage dissolved by decree of divorce
at Paris, France, 7 April 1949.

KARIM ——— **SARAH FRANCES**
(His Highness Aga Khan IV)
Born 13 December 1936 at Geneva,
Switzerland.
Succeeded to the Imamate under the will
of his grand-father. Granted the style and
title of His Highness by Queen Elizabeth
II in 1957 and that of Royal Highness by
Shah of Iran 1959.
Installed as Imam 19 October 1957 at Dar
es Salaam.
Bachelor of Arts of Harvard University.

daughter of Lt. Col. A.E. CROKER-
POOLE
(and formerly the wife of Lord JAMES
CRICHTON-STUART).
Married 28 October 1969 at
Ile de la Cité, Paris.

RAHIM   **HUSSAIN**   **ZAHRA**
(Prince Rahim)   (Prince Hussain)   (Princess Zahra)
Born 1971.   Born 1974.   Born 1970.

The Family Tree of the Aga Khans

(2) THERESA MAGLIANO
(GINETTA)
of Monte Carlo, Monaco.
'Muta Marriage' 1908, actual
marriage 23 January 1923
at Bombay.
Died November 1926 aged 38.

(3) ANDRÉE JOSEPHINE
CARRON
Married 7 December 1929
at Aix-les-Bains, France.
Marriage dissolved by
decree of divorce 1943 at
Geneva, Switzerland.

(4) YVETTE BLANCHE
LABROUSSE
(variously Larbousse and
Lebrusse) of Cannes.
Married 9 October 1944 at
Vevey, Switzerland.

(2) MARGARITA CANSINO
(RITA HAYWORTH)
(formerly the wife of ORSON
WELLES
Marriage dissolved by decree of
divorce 12 November 1948).
Married 27 May 1949 at Vallauris,
France.
Marriage dissolved by decree of
divorce on 26 January 1953 at
Reno, Nevada, USA, and on
22 May 1957 at Geneva,
Switzerland.
Died 1987.

SADRUDDIN KHAN
(Prince Sadruddin Aga Khan)
Born 17 January 1933 at Neuilly,
France.
Bachelor of Arts of Harvard University.
Consultant to the Secretary-General of
the United Nations.

NINA DYER
Married 27 August 1957.
Marriage dissolved by decree
of divorce 1962.
Died 1966.

(2) CATHERINE ALEYA
SURSOCK
Married 1972.

YASMIN KHAN
(Princess Yasmin)
Born 28 December 1949 at Lausanne,
Switzerland.

BASIL EMBIRICOS
Married 1985.
Marriage dissolved by decree of divorce
1986.

(2) CHRISTOPHER
JEFFERIES
Married 1989
Marriage dissolved by
decree of divorce 1993.

issue.

AMYN
(Prince Amyn Aga Khan)
Born December 1937.

*K.C.I.E. is the abbreviation for Knight Commander of the Most Eminent Order of the Indian Empire.
G.C.I.E. represents a Knight Grand Commander of the Order.
G.C.S.I. stands for Knight Grand Commander of the Most Exalted Order of the Star of India,
G.C.V.O. Knight Grand Cross of the Royal Victorian Order and G.C.M.G. Knight Grand Cross of
the Most Distinguished Order of St Michael and St George.

Family Tree © Terence McCarthy

ACKNOWLEDGEMENTS

In the view of this writer biography should do more than focus on one figure (or, as in this book, on several figures in one family), exploring the events and significance of his or her life. It must also include an account of the subject's (or subjects') times. This need for context is especially important to comprehend such exotic and commanding lives as those of the Aga Khans. It would be impossible to understand Aga Khan III, for example, without grasping the difficulties of being the religious leader of a Muslim sect based in India at the time of Queen Victoria's reign at the height of the British Empire and during the struggle for Indian independence. In writing a dynastic biography, the biographer's task becomes even more complicated. The scene must be set for all the major players in the family.

Aga Khan III cast a wide, intimidating shadow over his entire family, but the son he passed over in the succession, Aly Khan, and the grandson, Karim, who succeeded as Aga Khan IV had the greatest struggle to be their own persons. In telling the story of these three fascinating and multi-faceted men I have had much encouragement and dedicated assistance.

I am particularly grateful to my two English researchers. I owe a great debt to Terence McCarthy who, with tremendous perseverance, took on the extensive and often complex research involved, which included comprehensive study of the Ismailis, interviews and many hours going through archival material at the India Office Library. My association with Sally Slaney goes back over a number of years – and books. Once again her unerring eye for photographs has helped to make my biographer's task a good deal easier. The writing of this book has never been a lonely job because of these two marvellous people.

I have also been fortunate to have had Richard Johnson as my editor at HarperCollins. My appreciation as well to Daniel Easterman, an expert on Muslim affairs, for his careful study of the final manuscript, and to Betty Palmer, whose manuscript editing skills were much valued.

I owe a personal debt of gratitude to Terrence Kennedy (former brother-in-law of Aga Khan III), Mme Lawrence Moschietto Sihol (a close friend of Aga Khan III), John Henderson and David LeVine (Harvard alumni), Michael Korda, the late William Shirer, Peter Townsend, Barbro Ek (Director, Aga Khan Program, MIT), Liz Andrews (Archivist, Reference Library, MIT),

Katie Poole (Director, Roach Visual Library, MIT), Dana Loytved (United Nations Archives), Danielle M. Green (Curatorial Assistant, Harvard University), Ms Doris Jean Waren (Librarian, Keeneland Association Inc.), Paul Arbor (*Life* Research), Kristine Kreuger (American Academy of Motion Picture Arts and Sciences), Tamara Nijinsky (Nijinsky Archives), and all the good people at the India Office who helped with this project.

My thanks to Lisa Queen at William Morrow who came to my rescue just when most needed and who has always worn her regal name with proper majesty.

Finally, I once again pay tribute to my husband, Stephen Citron, who was with this book, as he has been with so many of my other endeavours, my prime source of encouragement, constructive criticism and patient companionship. A fine writer in his own right, he has never hesitated in taking time from his work to advise or help me on mine.

ANNE EDWARDS
Blandings Way, Connecticut
1995

As far as the eye can see thousands are streaming across the countryside. At dawn the great pilgrimage began . . . Old men, young men, poor men and rich men, the lame, the halt and the blind. Some barefoot and in filthy rags, others on mules and those who are very sick in rough tatters. They have come at the bidding of their High Priest. Presently a huge limousine slides silently between the waiting thousands and from it steps an imposing figure in flowing Kashmir shawl, robes and a Persian lamb headdress. A sigh, as soft as an evening breeze, runs through the immense throng who fall on their knees, their lips moving in silent prayer. Rose petals thrown by devoted worshipping hands fall like gentle rain, and slowly the broad figure lifts one arm above his head to bless them. Then, as suddenly as he came, he is gone and behind him he leaves the multitudes rejoicing; for have they not fulfilled the life dream of every true Ismaili? Have they not been privileged to set their humble eyes on the mighty . . . Aga Khan, direct descendant of Allah's greatest Prophet?

Ibn Dhul Quarnain

BOMBAY
19 JANUARY 1936

Intense sunlight made a blaze of the magnificent spectacle of His Highness Aga Khan III's Golden Jubilee procession. A platform, with a divan upholstered in spun gold and studded with hundreds of diamonds and rubies, had been erected in a large open square in the section of Bombay often referred to as the 'Ismaili Vatican'. The vast throng of over thirty thousand of the Aga Khan's followers were crushed together waiting to be blessed by their divine ruler and to see him receive his weight in gold in the style of moguls of an ancient time. The ceremony, *tula-vidhi*, is supposed to bring peace, health and prosperity to the person weighed.

Directly descended from Mohammed through the Prophet's daughter Fatima, the Aga Khan was the Imam (the spiritual leader, or Pope) to over fifteen million Ismaili Muslims. Yet, though recognized as an important linchpin in oriental politics, and an influence in the lives of many factions of Islam not directly under his jurisdiction, he possessed no political territories. To the world at large he was known for his fabulous wealth and his thoroughbred horses, and as a representative in the Anglo-Western politics of the Indian people. He felt a close alliance to Great Britain and to Europe. In fact he spent more time in his luxurious suite at the Ritz Hotel in London and his several homes in France than at his princely estate in the élite Bombay suburb of Malabar.

Like China's last emperor Pu Yi and Rama V, the former king of Siam, both his near contemporaries, as a boy the Aga Khan had been placed under the care of an English tutor. By now he was a dedicated Anglophile; he had been a great admirer of Queen Victoria and became a close friend of the current occupants of Windsor Castle, King George V and his consort Queen Mary.

The Aga Khan had been married three times. The third Begum, his wife of seven years, red-haired, green-eyed Andrée Carron, a French-woman who had worked in a confectioner's shop before their liaison, sat beside him on the raised seat of the open limousine, her green and gold sari thickly embroidered with diamonds. The hefty, bespectacled, 59-year-old Aga Khan (thirty years the Begum's senior) wore flowing purple robes decorated with more than a dozen glittering medals, and on his balding head a jewel-encrusted green silk turban.

As the open car and its occupants turned the corner into the square at precisely the appointed hour of 11 AM, along with several other limousines carrying Ismaili nobles and security guards, there were deafening shouts of enthusiasm. Then, all at once, the enormous crowd pushed forward to get a glimpse of their Imam and his Begum. Pandemonium followed. People were knocked to the ground; many were trampled underfoot. Shouts turned to screams of panic and terror. Bombay's chief of police, who was in the first vehicle of the motorcade, started out of his car in an attempt to quell the mob and was seriously injured in the crush.

Finally, the police and the security guards managed to clear a path for the Aga Khan's car to proceed. The screech of ambulance sirens added to the clamour in the square. The Imam, his face inscrutable, his posture erect, held up his right arm in a gesture of blessing. He grasped the Begum's hand so tightly with his free hand that the 61-carat diamond ring she wore made a small gash in his palm; she immediately bound it surreptitiously with her white linen handkerchief.

By the time the open car reached the platform a semblance of order had been restored and the injured were on their way to hospital (miraculously, no one had been killed). Standing with regal dignity on one side of the raised dais was Lady Ali Shah, the Aga Khan's frail, elderly mother, her dark-hooded eyes revealing nothing of the drama that surrounded her. At her elbow stood the Aga Khan's younger son, three-year-old Prince Sadruddin, his glowing brown eyes opened wide with terror as he stared out at the enormous crowds which thronged the square. (The Aga Khan's elder son, Aly Khan, was attending to his studies in England.) Nearby was a giant set of scales with a chair counterpoised by a huge pan in which gold bullion would be placed to balance the Imam's weight. As he stepped up on the dais, he glanced at the large structure, smiling, and then took his place on the divan, his mother and son standing on his right, the Begum on his left.

Once the Aga Khan was seated the shouts of his followers rose again. He stood up so that they could see him better and raised both arms for silence, a gesture which the crowd mistook for a salutation and cheered vigorously.

Despite the advice of his close associates, the Aga Khan intended to announce a change in the prearranged plans for his Golden Jubilee. Only an hour before his arrival in the square, he had received a telegram informing him that King George V was critically ill. Unless the King's condition took a turn for the better, he had decided to cancel all but the religious activities that were scheduled to follow the weighing ceremony. He lowered his arms and raised them again as he began to speak. But the loudspeaker system was poor and his words so unintelligible above the acclamation of the crowd that he was forced to abandon any attempt to continue.

Nearly fifteen minutes passed before the shouting subsided. Gulamali Merchant, an Ismaili official, helped the Aga Khan to the scale, and then said: 'On behalf of Your Highness' followers, I most reverently and respectfully request that Your Highness allow yourself to be weighed in gold on this happy and auspicious occasion and to accept the gold as a humble token of our love, devotion, and gratitude for all the unbounded bounty and benefits that Your Highness' followers have derived during your Imamate in the last fifty years.'

The Aga Khan sank heavily on to the weighing-chair. His eyes narrowed behind the round gold rims of his thick glasses as he watched three Ismaili nobles load bars of gleaming gold bullion on to the counterpan until the scale was finally balanced to rousing cheers from the spectators. The Aga Khan tipped the scale at 220.3 pounds (he was barely five feet five inches tall). The value of his weight in gold was 335,000 rupees, about $125,000, a vast fortune in 1936 in either America or Europe, but almost beyond imagining in India where even thirty years later, according to V. S. Naipaul, the poverty was *quivering*; it was a nation of 'poor fields, those three-legged dogs, those sweating red-coated railway porters carrying heavy tin trunks on their heads . . . the rickshaw puller . . . beast of burden more degrading than degraded'; an India where it was cheaper to use men than machines, where parents lopped off a child's hand or crippled him to make him a more poignant beggar, where great masses of people spent their entire lives on the streets of the country's overpopulated cities, and where here in Bombay you had to pick your way at night because so many thousands upon thousands of homeless people slept in the gutters.

The extremes in Bombay were jarring. There was the English Yacht Club – proper and elegant – whose members boasted of 'never having an Indian enter' (as a guest, for Indians served in all menial capacities);[1] the sumptuous grounds and estates in the suburbs where the richest Indians had their homes and where the Aga Khan lived, when in India, in regal splendour attended by over a hundred servants. Yet, despite the poverty of so many contrasted to the overwhelming wealth of a very few, the city was the most cosmopolitan in the country; the centre of India's film industry and said to be Hollywood, New York and Chicago rolled into one. But none of those American cities, strapped as they were by the hardness of the times, suffered the appalling, degrading impoverishment that pervaded Bombay.

These same extremes were evident among the Aga Khan's admirers and followers; there were princes and maharajahs, prosperous businessmen and many, like those who had come to pay him homage on this day, who were so desperately poor they had walked barefoot, often from great distances, some to pay their respects and some to see their Imam being honoured on his Golden Jubilee.

After the weighing, personal and valuable gifts were presented to the Aga Khan; a gold-bordered robe and one thousand rupees in silver from the Maharajah of Kutch, silver and jewels from other rich men. Passages of the Quran were read to the crowd by the Aga Khan, after which a path was once again cleared. The immense throng fell to their knees. Rose petals, to scent the air, were thrown 'like gentle rain' before the Aga Khan's gilt palanquin as it moved through the streets of Bombay. The oversized litter, borne by twelve men, was lined in

[1] About this time the English novelist W. Somerset Maugham was travelling in India and on his journey from Bombay to Calcutta had lunch with the Crown Prince of Hyderabad. 'Do you know the difference between the Club at Bombay and the Club at Calcutta?' the Prince asked him. Maugham shook his head. 'In one they don't allow either dogs or Indians; in the other they do allow dogs,' the Prince bitterly explained.

gold cloth. A matching canopy was raised on intricately carved mahogany posts, and beneath it their Imam was seated on a pile of enormous, gold, tasselled pillows.

The Aga Khan was not blind or hardened to the poverty in India or of his poorest followers. The gold he received was symbolic, on loan (well but discreetly guarded) from several banks. An equivalent amount in cash was to be raised by donations from Ismaili communities to found a Golden Jubilee Fund, some of the capital to be invested in various businesses to create income for the betterment of their communities, especially in the areas of education, health provision and housing.

The Aga Khan was especially devoted, as he said in his Jubilee speech, to the cause of education and to the 'evolution of all legitimate freedom and legitimate equality between men and women. The responsibility before God for prayers, for action, and for moral decisions is the same for men and women, according to the Prophet's holy message. Pious and believing Muslims who really wish to understand the holy message of the Prophet . . . should immediately set to work with the object of bringing about the full and legitimate evolution of Muslim women in Islamic society so that they can honestly hold their own with the men.'

Education was segregated in India at this time and schools for girls rare. The Aga Khan's most driving ambition was to change this situation in the communities of his followers. 'If a man had two children,' he explained, 'and if he could only afford to give education to one, I would say that he must give preference to the girl. The boy can go and labour but the girl cannot. Even in the upliftment of the country the education of girls is more important than the education of boys. The male can bend his energies to manual effort for reward, but the girl's function is the maintenance of home life and the bringing up of the children. Her influence in the family circle is, therefore, enormous and the future of the generations depends upon her ability to lead the young along the right paths and instruct them in the rudiments of culture and civilization.'

He also believed sincerely that Great Britain and its King-Emperor (be it the current gravely ill George V, or his eldest son and heir, the Prince of Wales) would come to the rescue of India's poor masses. He had little time for India's present political struggle to gain independence. His alliance was with Great Britain and he made no secret of this.

Just four days after his *tula-vidhi* word was received of King George V's death. He called for an immediate end to the Jubilee celebrations, ordered all Ismaili shops in Bombay (where his word was taken as law by a great percentage of the population) to be closed and business suspended for three days. He put on mourning clothes, telling his followers to do likewise. His grieving was deep; his ties with the British royal family went back to the old queen, Victoria, whom he had much revered. This close relationship with Great Britain did not set well with many of India's political leaders.

'The Aga Khan,' India's future prime minister, Jawaharlal Nehru, wrote in a letter detailing the Imam's past to his daughter Indira (who would also one day become prime minister of India), 'was the special agent of the English; he lived in England, was chiefly interested in English horseracing, and was always hobnobbing with English politicians. He was not even an orthodox Muslim, as he was head of a special sect. It was further pointed out that during the World War [I] the English had used him as a kind of counterpoise to the Sultan-Caliph in the East, and had increased his prestige by propaganda and otherwise had tried to make him the leader of the Indian Muslims, so that they might be kept in hand [not an unfair accusation, but it is doubtful that the Aga Khan was completely aware of the duplicity of the British in this case].' And, Nehru continued: 'If the Aga Khan was so solicitous about the Caliph, why had he not supported the Caliph in wartime when a *jihad* or holy war had been declared against the English?'

Some claimed the Aga Khan's steadfast allegiance to Great Britain was motivated by his extensive financial ties to that country. At the time, his income was estimated to be $10 million a year, only a portion of which came from the eight to ten per cent tax on the incomes of his followers, special levies, and countless gifts. His great wealth was due to shrewd investment of his inherited fortune. At the same time his scale of living was fabulous.

There were his estates in India, France, Switzerland and Egypt (nine in all), luxurious private hotel suites in London, Paris and Cannes; his thousands of servants; his collections of jewels, the rubies alone having been estimated by an expert as worth more than two hundred million dollars; the twelve racing stables he maintained in England, Ireland, France and India.

He was proud that he was the first Oriental admitted to the exclusive Jockey Club and took great pleasure when it was said that (because he was so light-skinned) he looked like a prosperous Englishman when dressed in a suit and a bowler hat, although his Eastern roots would have been hard to deny. But it was not the Aga Khan's intention to disavow his heritage, for he was extremely proud of his race. What he had always wished for was an equality that would erase any colour prejudice. By self-appointment he had gone from Indian prince to ambassador without portfolio between East and West. *The Times* said that 'he was condemned to be the Canute of Muslim India,' and that he had been 'born to worship Queen Victoria and an Empire upon which the sun would never set'.

But by 1936, the time of his Golden Jubilee, that Empire was already beginning to wane. The Second World War would soon toll its end. For the next decade the Aga Khan was a man caught between two worlds, preferring the old; not knowing how he could adjust to the new if it came to that.

VIVAT REGINA!
AGA KHAN III AND
QUEEN VICTORIA
1882–1901

Prince Sultan Mohammed, his colourful brocade outfit and turban fitting splendour for an Indian prince, even one just three years old, sat beside his elderly, fiercely-moustached grandfather, the first Imam to bear the title of Aga Khan; he was too thrilled to notice the parched fields they passed as the dashing coach and four sped through the sun-baked countryside on its way to the Bombay racetrack in the late summer of 1880. The young prince was born in Karachi (then part of India) on a grand estate overlooking the Arabian Sea on 2 November 1877, but now lived in Bombay near his grandfather.

India in the 1880s was the exotic land of Rudyard Kipling's stories: 'gentlemen officers wearing plumed shakos and riding at the head of their turbaned sepoys; of district magistrates lost in the torrid wastes of the Deccan; of sumptuous imperial balls . . . of cricket matches on the manicured lawns of Calcutta's Bengal Club; of polo games on the sunburnt plains of Rajputana; of tiger hunts in Assam . . . of officers in scarlet tunics, scaling the rock defiles of the Khyber Pass.'

This was India's romantic legend. But it was also a country of unbearable heat, widespread disease and the acrid, nauseating smell of urine and decaying flesh clinging in the airless heat of the sun. Bombay, the home of the Aga Khan and his family, was not spared the inhuman conditions of other cities and states in the country. Children brutally deformed by their parents thrust out their stunted limbs to beg and emaciated men, protected from the harsh whip of the sun only by a loincloth, died in the gutters with little attention paid until the stench grew too powerful to ignore.

For over two years India had suffered drought and famine during which some ten million people had died. The Aga Khan and his Indian followers had been more fortunate than others. Largely merchants, they did not rely on the land, a contributory factor to their somewhat arrogant attitude to other Indians. Their self-regard was also bolstered by their faith in their generous and clever leader. The old Aga Khan, friend of the British and much in Queen Victoria's good graces, had guided them through the bad times with a modicum of travail. Food could be brought by railway from other parts of the country, but could only be had by those with money; and the majority of the Aga Khan's followers, thanks to his acumen and the grace of the British Crown, had enough to feed their families.

Prince Sultan Mohammed was protected from ugly sights. He seldom left the well-kept, lushly planted grounds of the palace where he lived with his parents, his grandfather's son and heir Prince Ali Shah and the daughter of a rich Persian, Nizam-ud-Daulah, and niece of Persia's ruling Shah. Ali Shah's first marriage had produced two sons; his second had been childless. He remarried for the third time at forty-six, bewitched, it was said, by the much younger new Lady Ali Shah's luminous dark eyes (partially hidden behind her veil). Two sons were born and died in the first two years of their union. Their third son, Prince Sultan Mohammed, was born in 1877, just a few months after Queen Victoria was crowned Empress of India. Throughout his life, this coincidence was to have a great influence on him.

Effectively, India had been under British rule and a part of the Empire since the famous defeat of the Nawab of Bengal at Plassey by Robert Clive in 1757. The country was divided into large states or provinces, two-thirds of them, including Bombay (of which the city of Bombay was a major port), under the direct government of the British, headed by a Viceroy. An English official, called the Resident, lived in each of the larger states and exercised control over the administration and there were crowds of government functionaries and civil servants. In many of the states, Indian princes and religious leaders, like the Aga Khan, who had ruled before the arrival of the British, still remained. Some retained their internal authority and were given protection if they agreed to let Britain control foreign policy. Others, the Aga Khan among them, received pensions from the British who were in effective control.[1]

[1] Aga Khan I was given a pension of 1000 rupees a month (then about $500) by the British in acknowledgement of his help in the war in Afghanistan. The modesty of the amount was to become an issue with him, and he continued to write to successive

British domination brought peace to the warring princedoms of India, but this meant little to the families immured in crushing poverty. Great Britain looked to India for food and raw materials, not manufactured goods, and so the country continued as an agricultural society and was not propelled into the machine age. As a result, India's social system began to stagnate. None the less, the British conferred one great benefit on India: English education, intended to produce a competent civil service, also put Indians in touch with current Western thought. Jawaharlal Nehru, one of India's greatest statesmen, wrote: 'A new class began to arise, the English-educated class, small in numbers and cut off from the masses, but still destined to take the lead in new nationalist movements.'

As an infant, Prince Sultan Mohammed was in the care of an Indian ayah and Lady Ali Shah, who held the strictest views on how her son should be educated. He would be well-versed in several languages, a scholar of Asian literature and made aware at an early age of the responsibilities of his elevated position. A week before the boy's third birthday the ayah was dismissed and a squad of tutors arrived in the little prince's grand apartments, richly hung with silken tapestries. There was an Indian Ismaili tutor to help him in his theological studies; others to teach him Urdu and Persian. Lady Ali Shah was also determined that her son should never forget the ties, begun by Aga Khan I, that bound his family to the British Empire. And so Mrs Elizabeth Glyn, who was distantly related to a former British Viceroy, Lord Ellenborough, became the boy's main tutor, teaching him English (which he spoke fluently though with a trace of an Oriental accent), reading to him from Scott and Dickens, retelling British history in accordance with her Victorian concepts.

Viceroys over the years requesting an increase and including among his reasons the much greater pensions awarded to Indian princes. Shortly after his wife, the Begum Sarv-i Jehan Khanum, arrived in Bombay, he had her write to the Viceroy, Lord Falkland: 'The inadequate pension of 1000 rupees per month which His Highness receives from your government is . . . barely enough to meet his expenses . . . and I find myself now in a forlorn state, in a foreign land, and in want of sufficient means to maintain myself suitably to my rank . . . Several Persian refugees though far inferior in rank and position to what appertains in my place have liberally shared in the bounty of your government and enjoy pensions. I trust I appeal not in vain for suitable assistance from your Lordship's Government.'(Aga Khan I Archive, India Office Library) Her plea was rejected.

Mrs Glyn, a woman of both great compassion and discipline, lived in the palace, her sitting-room dominated by a giant portrait of Queen Victoria above which was hung the sword belonging to her husband, Colonel Glyn, who had fought and died in the Indian Mutiny of 1857–8. If Prince Sultan Mohammed had done his lessons exceptionally well, he was permitted to have tea with Mrs Glyn there and to listen to her stories about the great mother queen and the glory she had brought to the world.

Like his grandfather, the boy came to love horses and racing. The stables of the Aga Khan were filled with the finest thoroughbreds – Arabian, French and English. He had won many cups and proudly told his grandson about the visit of Edward, Prince of Wales, to his stables in 1877 and the admiration Queen Victoria's heir, a great aficionado of the sport, had expressed for his horses.[1] The old man was now nearly blind and on one memorable day when Prince Sultan Mohammed visited his grandfather's famous stables, he helped to lead him to where his favourite charger waited. Once mounted, the Aga Khan had the boy lifted by servants on to a pony of his own and they rode round the course together.

He was only four when his grandfather died and his father, Prince Ali Shah, a large, handsome man with piercing black eyes and a thick black beard, became Aga Khan II. The boy saw very little of his father, a crack shot who spent most of his time on lengthy tiger hunts when not touring the many Ismaili communities in Asia and Africa. With his father so often away and his older half-brothers living at a distance in Poona with their own families, young Prince Sultan Mohammed grew up in a house of women, run by the strong hand of his mother.

Lady Ali Shah was a determined, imposing woman. She rarely appeared in public, wore long, baggy black trousers, tight at the ankle, and over them (displaying an inward need for self-expression) a distinc-

---

[1] Aga Khan II also entertained the Prince of Wales at Aga Hall. Noticing the abundance of tiger skins displayed, the Prince enquired what method had been used to bag them – from the back of a specially trained elephant or from a *machan*, the platform constructed in a tree for that purpose? Being stout, the Prince had 'rueful memories of being pushed and pulled up trees' on recent tiger shoots. 'No,' said his host, whose girth, though considerable, was not as great as Edward's. 'I am too fat for tree work (and unsure on an elephant). I stand up and shoot.'

tive long, loose dress of brilliant hues topped by an all-enveloping *chador* – black for outdoor wear, vibrantly coloured indoors. Her eyes were large and expressive; her skin a rich nut colour; her hands long and slender. She spoke English, Urdu and Persian in a deep, staccato voice that demanded and received attention. (Years later Sultan Mohammed, by then Aga Khan III, was to admit, 'My mother is the only woman of whom I have ever been afraid.')

The young prince had only two friends near his age, his cousins Shamsuddin and his younger brother Abbas, whom he loved but saw infrequently. He lived in what one biographer aptly called 'perfumed isolation', his rooms heavily scented by custom more than need, for street odours never reached his windows. It is true that at the time Indians defecated wherever nature dictated: on city streets; by the river banks where the women washed the clothes; beneath the windows on the grounds of the estates that they tended or the universities at which they studied or taught. Even eighty years later, according to V. S. Naipaul, without warning a man would raise his dhoti (a loose cotton loincloth), 'revealing a backside bare save for what appears to be a rope-like G-string; he squats, pisses [or defecates] on the pavement, leisurely rises; the dhoti still raised, he rearranges his G-string, lets the dhoti fall, and continues [with his walk or work] . . . These squatting figures . . . are never spoken of; they are never written about . . . the truth is that *Indians do not see these squatters* [italics his] and might even, with complete sincerity, deny they exist.'

The acrid stench of dung and urine clung to the pavements of the cities and the dry earth of the land, invading even the finest homes through open windows. For this reason rose petals were thrown in the path of princes and religious figures and a heady, sweet scent permeated the rooms of their homes. But Mrs Glyn, the English governess, demanded that Western standards be enforced among those who lived or came and went in the various palaces of the Aga Khan as the family moved with the seasons from Bombay to Poona, south to Mahabaleshwar and then back to Bombay again. Fouling the grounds with human waste was strictly forbidden and fines were imposed on servants and staff if the rules were not heeded.

Despite their toilet habits, Indians are required by their religions to bathe daily, usually in the river; to use only their left hand for unclean purposes; to eat with their right hand only. Mrs Glyn's determination to introduce Western ways into the palaces of the Aga Khan brought sharp comment. 'The habits of Europe — the right hand used for love-making, toilet paper and food, the weekly bath in a tub of water contaminated by the body of the bather, the washing in a wash-basin that has been spat and gargled into — make it clear which culture is really the more sanitary,' a palace staff member responded when told the latest edict issued by the Englishwoman.

In the first three years of his father's reign, Prince Sultan Mohammed's two older stepbrothers died suddenly; one in a fall from a horse, the other of a fever. The little prince would now become his father's heir. In view of this a new staff was placed in charge of his education. Mrs Glyn was replaced by a male English tutor, Mr Kenny, a stern man who believed a seven-year-old boy was old enough to behave like a man. There were two other new tutors to help with the boy's education in English, French, literature, mathematics, science and history, a Mr Gallagher and a Mr Lawrence (both of whom were Irish). All three men, although not Jesuits, had been found by the Jesuit order in Bombay at Lady Ali Shah's request. They were not in the least narrow-minded as one might assume. Although strict in their methods, they were broadminded men 'with a zest for knowledge and the ability to impart it'.

Mr Kenny quickly recognized his student's greatly impaired vision and insisted that he be prescribed with proper glasses both for reading and for distance, finally overcoming the objections of his mother, who appeared to believe that such a visible artificial aid would convey an impression of weakness. Spectacles opened up a new world to the boy. Books became his passion, but he was not given much free time to satisfy it, his entire day almost always being occupied with studies. He saw even less of his two beloved cousins, Shamsuddin and Abbas. His life was now filled with adults.

For Persian and Arabic and in all matters Islamic — literature, history and religion — he was tutored every afternoon for three hours by 'a bigoted sectarian' whose mind, the Aga Khan was later to say, 'was one of the darkest and narrowest' that he was ever to encounter. 'It was saddening and in a sense frightening to listen to him talk. He gave one the feeling that God had created men solely to send them to hell and eternal damnation.'[1]

After dinner came the boy's most hated lesson — two hours of calligraphy in the classical Arabic and Persian script which his mother was convinced was of the highest importance to becoming a learned man. Lady Ali Shah was a demanding overseer. Daydreaming was discouraged, idle time filled with added studies. She ordered his tutors to reprimand him at any sign of disobedience. On one occasion, when he was not prepared for a lesson, his hated Islamic teacher thrashed him so fiercely that a servant pleaded with his mother to intervene.

'No,' she replied. 'It is better that he should be punished than grow up ignorant. He must learn to fulfil his destiny.'

Despite glasses, his poor eyesight inhibited him in most sports. This physical inactivity caused him to become plump and pudgy and was the source of great distress because the weight and slackness of muscle made it even more difficult for him to play tennis or handball, sports his Western tutors considered obligatory. His awkwardness at them was a constant source of embarrassment to him. And though he loved horses and liked nothing better than to lead them around the vast grounds attached to the stables, he was not fond of riding either.

His daily regime was geared for the time when he would one day become the Imam. His mother hovered over him, never allowing him far from her sight; several dozen servants hastened noiselessly to do his bidding, padding in slippers across the deep plush carpets. He seldom saw his father and was to remember little about him. For in August 1885, just four years after Ali Shah became Imam and Aga Khan II, he caught a fever after a long day's water-fowling in heavy rain. Pneumonia developed and he died in Poona (a distance of 75 miles from Bombay) eight days later. After the embalming, his coffin was

[1] In his memoirs, Aga Khan III wrote: 'The vast majority of Muslim believers all over the world are charitable and gently disposed to those who hold other faiths, and they pray for divine forgiveness and compassion for all. There developed, however, in Iran and Iraq a school of doctors of religious law whose outlook and temper — intolerance, bigotry, and spiritual aggressiveness — resembled my old teacher's, and . . . who ardently and ostentatiously sing the praises of the Lord, and yet are eager to send to hell and eternal damnation all except those who hold precisely their own set of opinions.'

taken on a week-long journey by horse-drawn carriage to Kufa, and then across seven miles of desert to Najaf, a holy place for all Shia Muslims, where he was buried near his saintly ancestor Ali, the first Imam and son-in-law of Mohammed.[1]

Prince Sultan Mohammed, at eight years of age, was now Aga Khan III. Whatever childhood he had enjoyed was at an end, for his exalted position as hereditary Imam, or spiritual chief of the Ismaili sect of the Shia Muslims, and a direct descendant of Mohammed, made him a supremely holy figure in the eyes of his millions of followers, invested with mystical powers and uncommon wisdom. Grown men now kneeled in his presence, brought him gifts, sought his blessings and heeded his words.

Since the sixth century a cloud of mystery and secrecy has enveloped the sect of the Ismailis of which the young Aga Khan was now Imam. The story began in the desolate Bedouin region of al-Hijaz by the Red Sea, bordered by the cities of Mecca, where the Prophet Mohammed was born in 571, and Medina, the City of the Prophet, where he later lived.

Mohammed was a wealthy merchant until the age of forty, when in a cave on Mount Hira he had a vision in which he was chosen to preach Allah's word. The Arabs, unlike other nations, had hitherto had no prophets.[2] Thereafter Mohammed continued to have revelations, which were recorded in the Quran. His earliest teachings were: there is but one God, man must in all things submit to him, there is a heaven and a hell, and the world will come to an end with a great judgement. He included as religious duties frequent prayers and almsgiving.

---

[1] Kufa is a town on the River Euphrates, 90 miles south of Baghdad. Founded in 638, on the site of an ancient Mesopotamian city, it grew quickly and became a great educational and cultural centre. Repeatedly plundered by the Karmathians in the 9th and 10th centuries, it lost its importance, but its tombs, its history, its proximity to Najaf and the shrine of the Imam Ali still attract large numbers of pilgrims.

[2] All Islamic schools of thought accept the principle that thousands of years before Mohammed's lifetime there had been prophets or messengers of God, who appeared in other parts of the world to cultures intellectually able to comprehend the messages they brought. Islam universally accepts Abraham, Moses and Jesus.

When Mohammed died in 632 he left his succession fiercely contested by two factions. Only one of Mohammed's seven children, his daughter Fatima, survived into adulthood. Fatima, her father's close companion as a young woman, married his first cousin, Ali, who was expected to succeed the Prophet. But during the last hours of his fatal illness, Mohammed had delegated another close friend, Abu-Bakr, a prosperous merchant and the father of Mohammed's favourite of his twelve wives, Aisha (a child of eight at the time of their marriage), to lead the daily prayers. This dying gesture was interpreted by a large group of the Prophet's followers as meaning that Mohammed had chosen the staid, conservative Abu-Bakr for his successor. It was this faction that won and Abu-Bakr became the first of the orthodox Caliphs whose followers are called Sunnis.

Ali emerged as the leader of the Shia, 'the party of the House of Ali'. For a century the Shia were cruelly persecuted, but remained loyal to Ali's descendants as Imams. During the mid-years of the eighth century a new dynasty, the Abbasids, descending from a brother of Mohammed, contested the succession of the Shia. Fearing his eldest son and heir, Ismail, would be murdered, the Shia Imam Jafar al-Sadiq smuggled him out of the country and then staged a mock funeral claiming he had died. Jafar himself was murdered and, with Ismail still in hiding, his younger brother Musa al-Kazim claimed the Imamate.

Forced to remain in hiding, Ismail and his followers, the Ismailis, practised their faith in secret, fearing death and the seizure of their books and religious works by their enemies. They met in hidden lodges. Novices were obliged to swear an oath of secrecy. They believed that 'the esoteric truth that reposed in the living Imam, descendant of the Prophet and God-inspired leader, was inaccessible to the ordinary man.' Ismaili doctrine differs to some extent from that of other Shi'ites in the description of the Imam's nature: he is believed to have two – one 'speaking', one 'silent'.

The covert life that was forced upon them might well have spawned the secret order for which the Ismailis are best remembered by the Western world. In 1094 the Ismailis split into two factions, the Mustalis (the smaller group) and the Nizaris of which the Aga Khans were later Imams. The Nizaris were distinguished by their blind obedience to their spiritual leader and by their ruthless use of murder to eliminate opponents. The order spread across Persia and Syria and soon inspired terror throughout the Muslim world. Hasan and the grand master who ruled after him wielded great political power until 1256 when the Mongols, headed by Hulagu Khan, attacked and destroyed their fortress and massacred most of the Persian branch of the sect. It was said that the Nizari killers acted under the influence of hashish, and so they entered European folklore via the writings of Marco Polo as the Assassins (from *hashshashin*), giving rise to the English term for one who kills for political motives. It has been claimed that scattered groups still exist in northern Syria.

Decimated in numbers, the Ismailis were now the minority of the three major Muslim groups, the Sunnis, the Twelver Shia, and the Ismailis. They sent members of their faith to foreign shores – Egypt, Africa and China – to find converts, mastering languages before 'proceeding to break down rival beliefs and to substitute, step by step, their own credo'. The converts were called Khojas (an Indian term of some complexity meaning 'lord'). It was these converts who became the main body of the future Aga Khan's international followers and who were to come from all over the sub-continent, from Burma, Ceylon, Malaya and the Middle East, to Nairobi in East Africa and far-flung places like Madagascar, Mauritius, Zanzibar and Abyssinia.

The young Aga Khan's early forefathers ruled with great splendour over Egypt and North Africa during the tenth and eleventh centuries. When they were forced by plundering armies to move down to Persia (renamed Iran in 1935) and joined the already established Ismaili community there, they left behind lasting monuments of culture and enlightenment in the shape of institutions of learning and works of great art. The most famous university of Islam, al-Azhar, as well as the city of Cairo were founded by them in 970.

There had been forty-five Imams in direct line of descent before the first Aga Khan, the young Imam's grandfather, whose given name was Hasan Ali Shah, and who had succeeded as Imam in 1817, when his father, Shah Khalil Allah, was murdered in a village disturbance. The Persian ruler, Fath Ali Shah, fearful that the Ismailis would hold him responsible, appointed Hasan Ali governor of the rich province of

Mahallat, granted him the title of 'Aga Khan' (Lord Chief), and gave him permission to marry his daughter, Princess Sarv-i Jehan Khanum. It was from this Persian princess that the sons of all the Aga Khans claimed the right to the title of Prince.

The newly named Aga Khan resembled a court dandy more than a religious leader. Striking in appearance, light-skinned with a gallant manner and a great lust for battle and beautiful women, he was to claim that he had fathered three thousand children (only three legitimately) and that 'every man in his household cavalry of eight hundred could rightly claim him as father.'

But his charm was a façade for his tremendous ambition. With Fath Ali Shah's death in 1834, the Aga Khan found his position precarious. In 1837 the prime minister of Persia, with whom he had strong political differences, requested the hand of one of the Aga Khan's daughters for a person of low birth who had previously been in the minister's service and had become a favourite of his. The Aga Khan deeply resented the insult and sent his troops against the government. Defeated in battle with severe losses to his army, he escaped Persia with his surviving cavalry into the province of Sind in Afghanistan where there was a large community of Ismailis who gave him their prayers, emptied their pockets, and with their swords remanned his forces.

By 1838, the British were at war with Afghanistan and they saw in this warlike religious leader a welcome ally. The Aga Khan and his cavalry regiment assisted the British in routing 20,000 of the enemy with only 3000 men. This victory enabled the Governor-General Lord Ellenborough, to annex the border province of Sind and send Whitehall the famous telegraphic quip in Latin, PECCAVI – 'I have sinned (Sind)'.

The Aga Khan visited Bombay briefly in 1846 and established himself there two years later, maintaining his religious leadership and, a keen businessman, building up a great personal fortune in horses and real estate.[1] He had left his children, his principal wife Sarv-i Jehan

---

[1] Eighteen years earlier, when he was still in Persia, the Ismaili community in Bombay (estimated at that time as about 1400 families) refused to hand over the compulsory

continued overleaf

Khanum and his harem in Persia (multiple wives then being acceptable to Ismailis), and once more turned to the British, this time to see that his family was given safe passage to Bombay. The British complied but then backed down on honouring Sarv-i Jehan Khanum with a gun salute on her arrival, a tribute made to Indian princes and their families. After much negotiating they agreed only to have the Princess met by government officials. Following this snub, the Aga Khan in 1859 was granted by the British the non-hereditary title of 'His Highness' which seemed to satisfy his injured pride.

Life in Bombay was not smooth. In 1864 the Aga Khan was forced to take legal action to establish his descent when the Khoja Reform Party, a liberal branch of the sect, in an attempt to discredit him as Imam, vigorously attacked his morals, alleging that 'although seventy years of age he insisted on maintaining his *droit du seigneur*.' With so many illegitimate children the Aga Khan could hardly defend himself against the accusation; nor did he need to, because his position as the rightful heir to the Imamate was unimpeachable.

He never quite understood or enjoyed the company of his eldest son and heir, Prince Ali Shah. A man with conflicting character traits, the Aga Khan was able to kill in battle as he had done in Persia and Sind without a show of conscience and was said to be responsible for the assassination of numbers of his dissenters. Yet he was violently against the slaughter of animals (although his method of training horses by putting a leather muzzle over the animal's mouth and then tying a handkerchief over it to keep it from breathing for as long as possible to strengthen its lungs, was considered 'gross cruelty' by the British). Distant and cold toward Prince Ali Shah, he was a most affectionate and proud grandfather to Sultan Mohammed.

He was mainly responsible for reorganizing his sect to revolve around offerings of money through *das-sondh* (tithing) to the Imam,

---

tithe or *das-sondh* to the Aga Khan. Desperate for funds to raise an army, he sent his strong, militant, maternal grandmother Marie Bibi to extract the *das-sondh* from them. Marie Bibi turned to the British courts for help, claiming that a moral contract existed between the members of the sect and their Imam. In the end only twelve families persisted in their refusal to pay. The obdurate individuals were excommunicated, considered by the sect a fate worse than death, but were later reinstated.

which quickly became the foundation of the sect. There are other contributions to the Imam: gifts for special occasions, and the ritual of the *kahada-khuaraki* where food and drink are given to him. In fact whenever Ismailis have a large meal part of the food is set aside to be auctioned at the meeting-house or *jamaat khana*, the cash proceeds being awarded to the Imam.

And now eight-years-old Sultan Mohammed was Imam and had to be prepared to take over all the tasks required of him. His father's younger brother Jangi Shah became his guardian and Lady Ali Shah supervised his financial empire. But the young boy was expected to fill the role that was his destiny from the day of his succession.

It is doubtful that the still childlike Aga Khan III had even a vague concept of his great wealth. (Although records were not kept, *das-sondh*, which was technically ten per cent but went as high as one-eighth of their earnings given to the Aga Khan by those followers whose income was considered sufficient for their needs, was estimated to bring him $10 million annually.) But he could recite the names and histories of the 47 Imams who preceded him and what their relationship was to him and to Mohammed. He knew he was descended from the Prophet and that, now that he was Imam, he was seen to be endowed with great wisdom and treated as a holy figure. Later he was to say that his father's death and his elevation to Imam was 'the first big emotional and spiritual crisis of my life'. Any chance he might have had of a childhood was gone. For weeks he saw no one but his tutors and the religious men of his sect while he was being groomed for his new role.

In September 1885, a month after his father's death, he entered the cavernous room of Aga Hall, the enormous stone palace in Bombay built by his grandfather, to be installed as the 48th Imam. Leading his attendants, his step was even, his head high, eyes straight ahead as he walked in his gold Oriental slippers past the bearded, turbaned, barefoot Ismaili nobles who knelt on the hard stone floor in veneration of him. He was dressed in rich brocade, a robe called a *sherwani* which had been specially made for the occasion, and a tall black astrakhan hat. He appeared self-assured but solemn as he sat down on the Gadi of Imams, a divan-like throne, and glanced at his elderly, patriarchal disciples who now stood waiting for him to speak.

'Why are you looking so sad?' he said in Urdu with mature irritation. 'Isn't your Imam among you doing your work?'

He then mounted the many steps to the white tower that dominated the coldly impressive Aga Hall and stood in the open niche, a magnificent, brightly-embroidered cloak around his shoulders, and called his people to prayer, raising his arms to bless them in the name of Allah with startling authority.

Life was never the same after that. It was not so much that his responsibilities were too heavy or his studies too intense; he had been under a strict, demanding regime since the departure of Mrs Glyn. The difficulty was that he had no one of his own age as a companion and that all the adults he came in contact with treated him as a saint or a supremely religious person, and always he was viewed as an adult and expected to say and do wise things. It was hard for him to understand the change in the attitude of people towards him and to assess who he was: a boy who would have liked to have been playing games, or a much revered religious leader.

In his free time away from his duties as Imam and his studies, he trailed through the rooms of the palaces that he now owned looking at his possessions, a child of eight who would have much preferred toy soldiers to golden urns and jewels. As he grew a little older he would go out into his many fragrant gardens (where few were permitted to enter) to sit in a shady spot and read, preferably in English, biographies and memoirs of great men, histories and poetry. To his relief his mother got rid of his father's hawks and hounds, for – like his grandfather – Sultan Mohammed hated the sport of hunting. (Actually, no one called him by his given name any longer, not even his mother. He was referred to always by family, staff and followers as 'Your Highness', having had the title officially conferred upon him by Queen Victoria a year after his father's death.)

His greatest joy around the age of eleven were the afternoons when he and his mother were invited for tea at Viceregal Lodge by Lady Dufferin, wife of the Viceroy, Frederick Hamilton-Temple-Blackwood, 1st Marquis of Dufferin and Ava. There, in shuttered elegance and before a massive portrait of Queen Victoria, he drank tea from crested English china and devoured giant portions of seedcake and jam and bread.

Only on such carriage excursions as those to Viceregal Lodge which took him through parched streets where naked, pot-bellied children, the stain of betel-leaves (which they chewed to alleviate their hunger) marking their gaunt faces, clung to their emaciated mothers, was he awakened to India's extreme poverty. A rug was placed across the path from his carriage to the door of the Lodge. He walked upon it beneath a gold-fringed umbrella to protect him from the cruel heat of the afternoon, servants throwing rose petals before him and bowing as they backed away.

With Lady Ali Shah's constant diligence, in 1885–90 he was worth, at a conservative estimate, about £20 million. His financial matters were handled by ministers, his guardian and his mother (who had shown an amazing talent in finding high-yield investments) and as a religious figure his Ismaili investments were exempt from taxation.

Her husband's death, contrary to Indian custom, liberated Lady Ali Shah to the extent that she took an active interest in her son's financial affairs (the Hindu ritual of suttee, a widow being sacrificed in her husband's funeral pyre, was fairly commonplace in India at this time and some Khojas practised it). But it was the young Aga Khan who, once he reached his teens, insisted she come out of purdah, 'the imprisonment of half the nation,' he called it. The women he most admired were Western: Mrs Glyn, Lady Dufferin, and, of course, Queen Victoria. But once her son reached puberty, Lady Ali Shah allowed herself to mellow and a new, more nurturing relationship was begun. Although she could never be called affectionate, the two shared many interests – poetry, history and politics – and a greater understanding between them was reached.

Shortly after his sixteenth birthday, his uncle Jangi Shah and his younger son, the Aga Khan's friend Abbas, were ambushed and stabbed to death in Jeddah. Rumour spread that the young Aga Khan had hired assassins to do the deed. The culprits, who appeared to be bandits, were found and arrested, but were discovered poisoned in their cells twenty-four hours later. Further speculation circulated outside the Ismailis that they had been killed by the Aga Khan's order so as not to incriminate him. There was no proof of a plot by Jangi Shah to usurp his nephew's Imamate for either himself or his son, and he had grown very rich in the years he had been his nephew's guardian. As he was known to carry large sums on his person, and no money was found on the bodies, robbery seems the likely cause of the crime.

The double murder greatly affected the Aga Khan. His uncle had been perhaps more of a father to him than his own, and Abbas one of his few childhood friends. The accusations cut him deeply. Also, he was now in charge of his own affairs (although his mother remained, and would continue to be, a dominant figure) and undertook the administration of the Imamate. Since his installation at eight years of age he had conducted prayers and been responsible for the final decision in all serious disputes between his followers that were submitted to him, particularly in matters pertaining to excommunication. Now, he opened up the doors of Aga Hall to any of his people who sought spiritual guidance.

For two weeks every year members of his sect made the pilgrimage to Aga Hall to see him from as far away as Egypt and East Africa. It was his duty to advise them about their spiritual welfare and to feed and house them. The first year more than ten thousand people came and a tent city had to be set up in the grounds of Aga Hall. The next year the figure doubled. Before going out to preside over them in prayer, he was bathed in a huge silver bowl scented with rose petals, dressed by numerous servants in a richly-embroidered robe of brocade worn over silk pyjamas, a gold fez on his head, and then was led into the cavernous Throne Room where he was seated on the Gadi of Imams and read aloud passages from the Quran.

He had come to believe that he had superhuman powers, '. . . could forgive sins, sanctify marriage with a sprinkling of holy water, cure illness with a flick of the hand and banish the wicked from all community rights, including that of sacred burial. The faithful touched the rose-petalled floor of Aga Hall with their foreheads and did not rise until their Imam gave the signal.'

They all brought tributes which they placed reverently at his feet. The very poor came as supplicants, not as donors, and usually left well satisfied simply to have been blessed by their Imam (although most received small gifts of charity).

He frequently travelled throughout India to meet his *mukhis*, the local leaders of Ismaili communities where, dressed in magnificent brocade robes trimmed in jewels and gold, he would be carried on a brilliant palanquin to their prayer-house, listen to the problems of his disciples and gravely settle disputes. When he returned to Bombay from one of these journeys in the summer of 1893, he found people not only dying of famine but from a widespread plague that had taken the lives of over a million people. Out of fear, most of them refused to submit to an inoculation that could have saved them. In one large gathering of his followers in Aga Hall he attempted to convince them of the virtues of the vaccine. When he saw he was failing, he seized the syringe that a doctor had been explaining and plunged it into his own arm. His followers immediately agreed to be inoculated.

He was succeeding in his task as Imam, but he was lonely, conscious always of who he was and what was expected of him, overweight, his eyesight worse than ever. He retained from his grandfather a true love of horses and learned to ride well. His mother had sold many of the racing thoroughbreds and there were now thirty horses where once there had been eighty. He bought Arabians and brought in well-known trainers, having decided to enter racing with yellow and green as his colours; and he won the Nizam Gold Cup, India's most prestigious race, four times in succession (1893–6).

He had taken his life into his own hands. He blamed his former state of melancholy on having to live at Aga Hall when he was in Bombay. Like other cities of the raj, Bombay was divided into Indian and European sections. Most of the Ismailis lived in the congested inner-city area of Mazagoan where Aga Hall, the centre of their world, was located amid narrow streets, many shops, noise, dirt, milling crowds and the sort of Indian anarchy that tended to frighten the British. The population of Mazagoan was ten times what it had been when his grandfather held court at Aga Hall.

Overruling his mother's wishes, in 1895 the Aga Khan moved out of Mazagoan and into a sprawling estate in the prestigious European part of Bombay – Malabar Hill. Built very much in the colonial tradition of the time with wide verandas, vast high-ceilinged rooms, and courtyards filled with exotic plants, the house (named Land's End) was set on the top of the hill overlooking the Arabian Sea with a magnificent panoramic view of Bombay as well. The air was cool, the area quiet and dignified. He travelled back and forth each day to Aga Hall for prayers and to minister to his followers. But he had taken, whether aware of it or not, his first steps into crossing over into a European lifestyle.

3

The Aga Khan III was raised during the heyday of British paternalism in India, a time when relations between British and Indian were in general relaxed, agreeable, without rancour or conspicuous bigotry. Nationalism was only in its first stirring. During this period the Bombay army commander was Queen Victoria's third son, Arthur, Duke of Connaught, who took an early interest in the boy-Imam, having him frequently to tea and accepting invitations to Aga Hall in return. Visits to Viceregal Lodge and to Government House where there was in the Aga Khan's later recall, 'unstrained social mixing at receptions, on the race course, or on the polo ground,' were greatly anticipated by the young Imam.

As the century moved into its last decade a radical change took place. The Indian Congress, tolerantly encouraged at the time of its first formation in the 1880s, had grown swiftly and was suddenly looked upon by the British as a dangerous political organization whose ultimate aim was to help India break loose from its bond to Britain. To add to the fears of the British living in India, the educated classes in the country had grown in great numbers, threatening (the British believed) their position as an imperial, governing race. It was not long before Indians were regarded by many of the British as a second-class race, and the pernicious idea that white men possessed some intrinsic and unchallengeable superiority began to spread.

Europeans invited Indians to their homes less and less as the acceptance of a colour bar became more evident. The Aga Khan attributed this change to the return to England in 1890 of the Duke of Connaught, whom he considered a strong influence on race relations in India at that time. This theory skims over a problem that had become deeply ingrained and widespread long before the Queen's son returned home.

The Aga Khan now found himself in the most impressionable years of his life in an alien world. He had always regarded the British as his friends and felt a great loyalty and awe for the Crown. Despite his position, his great wealth and all his years of pro-British allegiance, he too became a victim of the colour bar as very few invitations came for him to visit the homes of Bombay's influential and affluent white population. He was deeply hurt. From some old acquaintances 'there was frigidity where there had been warmth', he wrote.

His life was more solitary than ever. There were, of course, the trips to see his Indian followers, which often meant difficult journeys across desert regions and precipitous mule-back trips to reach Ismaili mountain communities. His arrival was always heralded with much excitement and activity. The Imam was considered the final judge in arbitration between families and neighbours and grievances were often held in abeyance until his arrival. He would also meet community leaders to discuss their problems. Some issues, like the lack of water in desert areas or the absence of medical assistance in the smaller and more inaccessible communities, he could not solve at once. But they awoke in him a resolve to place into action educational facilities enabling Ismailis to become engineers and doctors and so help themselves.

On his tours, prayer meetings and various Ismaili celebrations were attended by huge crowds of people and he always travelled with a large staff. Still, he had few personal friends. Mr Kenny and the other tutors had departed from the time of his eighteenth birthday. He could no longer sit at the luncheon or dinner table with Lady Ali Shah and her ladies in waiting and discuss poetry and philosophy as he had once done. And although he quite approved of the European idea of a mistress, the thought of establishing a harem was not only disagreeable to him, it went against everything he had been taught was right by his British tutors and would have been strongly condemned by the Western women, like Lady Dufferin and Mrs Glyn, whom he admired – concubinage and polygamy were totally unacceptable. When he became noticeably melancholy, his mother proposed a cure.

In the early 1890s, Bombay was run by a paternal bureaucratic government with a generally contented population, few politicians and an income tax equivalent to sixpence in the pound (2.5 per cent). Then came 1896, a year in which thousands perished from the plague. Panic ensued. Masses of people took to the roads to escape death and not only spread the monstrous disease but headed straight into the brutal Muslim–Hindu racial clashes that were on the rise throughout India. Lady Ali Shah, with the Aga Khan's full agreement, believed his followers needed a joyous celebration to counterbalance the difficulties of the times.

Her son, Lady Ali Shah recalled, had spoken quite warmly about his sixteen-year-old cousin Shahzada, daughter of his murdered uncle and sister of his trusted childhood friend Shamsuddin. In fact the Aga Khan had found himself very drawn to Shahzada when he was last in Poona where she lived. Shahzada possessed a quiet beauty, eloquent eyes, and a voice with a seductive lilt. She had occupied his thoughts many times since then. Yes, marriage could well be the remedy for his depression. A married Imam would give his followers great peace of mind knowing that his line, with the blessing of Allah, would continue, and the match would put an end to any remaining doubts about Jangi Shah's assassination.

Protocol demanded that an intermediary approach Shahzada on his behalf and that the details of a wedding settlement be worked out in advance if she accepted his offer, which indeed she did. They would be married on his nineteenth birthday, 2 November 1896, in Poona, where he had an enormous estate (the journey was a tedious half-day carriage ride from Bombay). As Shamsuddin was also engaged to be married, a spectacular double ceremony was planned. A guest list of 25,000 included an unending line of Indian princes, British dignitaries and Ismaili delegations from all over the globe. The wedding festivities lasted for sixteen days with daily entertainment: music, acrobats, tumblers, sword dancers and horse shows. There were banquets every night although, according to the laws of the religion, no alcohol was served.

Special guests were housed in the 300-room Yarovda palace set on the crest of a hill, which Ali Shah had recently had built for half a million rupees – constructed, it was said at the time, for no other purpose than to provide employment for the Aga Khan's followers after their great losses from the hardship of the plague and the famine that ensued. For other guests of high note, hundreds of elaborate tents with Persian rugs and commodious furniture had been raised on the highest grounds while below them was a tent city where poorer followers and servants camped. A great platform had been built adjacent to the palace; here, with honoured guests able to see a good deal better than others, the long double ceremony, the two grooms and their brides seated side by side, the *mukhi* chanting his prayers, was held. There were great cheers when the Aga Khan and Shahzada were at last pronounced man and wife; Shahzada was now the Begum Aga Khan.

Neither was prepared for the unhappiness that followed. In his memoirs, written in English and published more than a half a century later, the Aga Khan takes the blame for the disaster of their sexual union and the resulting estrangement. Shahzada was simply not prepared for intercourse, he implies. 'Tenderness and diffused affection – and my wife had all that I could give – were no use for our forlorn plight . . . Mine, I thought, was the blame for the grief and misunderstanding that embroiled us; and this deepened my affection for my wife; but for her, baffled and bewildered as she was, the affection I offered was no substitute nor atonement.' But there have been others who said that Shahzada married the Aga Khan and withheld her favours out of revenge for the deaths of her father and younger brother.

The months that followed his unfortunate marriage were difficult. Violent rioting began anew between Muslims and Hindus. The Aga Khan ordered his followers not to join in attacks on Hindus, and even offered sanctuary to them on his estates. Plague and famine continued in some areas where the Ismailis lived. He brought in medical authorities, gave them laboratory space in the house in Malabar, provided modern equipment and supplied food for as many as he could from the kitchens of his many homes.

Privately, his life was in as much chaos as his Imamate. His marriage was a dismal failure. A rumour was later to circulate that Shahzada suffered some physical problem that made her incapable of consummating a sexual union. On his part the Aga Khan always spoke well of his Begum. But it was impossible to deny that the marriage was a sham. After their first few nights together he was not known to have entered her bedroom again and by the following spring it appeared obvious that there would be no heir.

In truth, he was drawn to European women, their appearance, outspokenness and vivacity. They had strongly influenced his thinking as a youth. Though he could easily have divorced Shahzada, it would have been a disastrous political move, especially so soon after the marriage. And so he accepted the situation as it was, left Shahzada to herself, and surrounded her with all the comforts she could wish for.

With Lady Ali Shah's keen foresight, the Aga Khan was now many times richer than he had been upon his succession. Besides newly-acquired mining interests, increased holdings of land, and wisely invested securities, he owned nine palaces scattered all over India so that he could follow the sun and take his choice of sea, desert, city or country pleasures. Although he spent only a few weeks a year in any one of them, each of these grand homes was filled with valuable furnishings and the gardens were magnificently cared for. He had thousands of servants, a valuable stable and enough jewels to fill the vaults at Cartier's Paris store. All the Aga Khan wanted was to visit Europe, socialize with the rich, titled and famous, and perhaps be presented to Queen Victoria. And so he decided that he would embark on a European tour.

He set off from Bombay for Marseilles in the last week of February 1897, on a new French ocean liner of the Messageries Maritimes, with only two servants, dressed in Indian attire. From Marseilles he took the train to Nice. His plan was to spend several weeks on the Riviera which Queen Victoria visited around that time every year, with the hope that he might get the opportunity to be presented to her.

Queen Victoria (who travelled incognito as the Comtesse de Balmoral) much enjoyed her annual spring sojourns on the Riviera, where she stayed in the Hotel Excelsior Regina at Cimiez, near Nice, for it seemed to her a great change from her life in England. In reality, little was altered for her household other than the locale.

The royal entourage of more than thirty people, including her Indian servants in gold-striped turbans and full Indian dress, arrived in Nice on the Queen's *train spécial*, its interior elegantly upholstered and tasselled in dove blue, soft rose, and pearl grey; the Royal Arms displayed on each carriage. It was a moment at which English people were not much liked by the French owing to territorial rivalries in Africa which culminated in a diplomatic dispute known as the Fashoda Incident.[1] Despite this fractious situation, quantities of people lined the route to catch a glimpse of the royal train as it passed. And in Boulogne where it stopped and in Nice, when the Queen disembarked, there were crowds of cheering people. Victoria had become a kind of icon of the monarchical form of government which France had abolished but still admired.

The Queen appeared quite affable despite the ardours of such a long journey. The winter of 1896 had been filled with great unhappiness, for her much-loved son-in-law, Prince Henry of Battenberg, husband of her youngest daughter Beatrice, had died in January. The Battenbergs lived with the Queen at Windsor and Henry's death threw a terrible gloom over the old castle. Then there was the matter of the Munshi.

The Munshi (from the Urdu for tutor) was Queen Victoria's former attendant Abdul Karim, who had started by waiting at the royal table and had been promoted ten years earlier by Victoria to teacher of Urdu and Hindustani to the Queen. So successful was he in his task that the Queen addressed her Indian troops 'in what they were assured was their own language'. The Queen greatly liked the Munshi but her household, the court and her ministers were frosty in their attitude towards him.

On the Munshi's behalf, partly as a protest against prejudice and partly because she had come to rely upon him, the Queen had challenged two Viceroys, two Prime Ministers, two Secretaries of State, and most of her Court, who not only regarded him as a 'jumped-up

[1] While Britain was preparing the conquest of the Sudan the French tried to forestall them and occupy the upper Nile region, which would have extended their vast West and Central African empire to the Red Sea and given them control of the Nile. Major Jean-Baptiste Marchand (1863–1934), in command of a small force, raised the tricolour in the village of Fashoda on the White Nile on 10 July 1898. The French left Fashoda four months later after Lord Kitchener tactfully convinced Marchand of the hopelessness of his position. These events caused deep resentment in France and a Franco-British war seemed inevitable: only the skilful diplomacy of the prime minister, Lord Salisbury, achieved a peaceful settlement on 21 March 1899 in which in return for giving up Fashoda (renamed Kodok), France obtained the western Sudan (now Mali).

footman' but also 'believed him to be a low-class impostor, supplying Afghanistan . . . with State secrets extracted from her Majesty's boxes.' The Queen fought these allegations with promotions to show her belief in the Munshi. In 1894 she had made him her Indian Secretary with an office, clerks under him and the appropriate title of Hafiz ('one who knows the Quran by heart') and ordered that all photographs showing him in his former vocation as a domestic in the royal household be destroyed. Her ministers were horrified and, to undermine his credibility, wrote her a devastating report casting doubt on the Munshi's claim that his father was a doctor.

The Queen was furious. '. . . to make out that the poor good Munshi is so *low* is really *outrageous* and in a country like England quite out of place . . . She has known 2 Archbishops . . . sons respectively of a Butcher & a Grocer,' she wrote in the royal third person to Lord Salisbury. 'Abdul's father saw good & honourable service as a Dr & he [Abdul] feels cut to the heart at being thus spoken of. It probably comes from some low jealous Indians or Anglo-Indians . . . The Queen is so sorry for the poor Munshi's sensitive feelings.'

No one could persuade Victoria to get rid of the Munshi, whom the court and her ministers believed to be a threat to the throne although no direct allegations were made. More than the Munshi's subversive threat, his closeness to the Queen at a time of great racial intolerance in the country was thought to jeopardize national sentiment toward her.

Ignoring her ministers' advice, the Queen built several cottages for the Munshi at Windsor so that he could bring his wife, nephew and aunts from India, and gave him a handsome landau after she learned he had been made to ride in a hired carriage instead of one from the royal stables. She appeared to depend on him even more after Prince Henry of Battenberg's death and his presence at court remained a matter of great derision. There had been a terrible row over the Munshi in the royal household before the Queen departed for France. Against her wishes but to bring peace, the Munshi had been left behind. However, the Queen finally had her way and on 1 April he arrived in Cimiez amid much grumbling in her household.

While abroad, Victoria kept to the exact schedule that she maintained at Windsor. Every detail of the installation of the court was carefully supervised. She had a large drawing room and private dining room, with an extremely luxurious suite for her private use along with many others for the use of her household. The Riviera sun was elusive in March, which did not deter the Queen from taking her daily ride in an open carriage with one of her attendants or a member of her family; the Prince and Princess of Wales and their daughters, as well as the Duchess of York (the future Queen Mary), were also in the South of France. During these outings the Queen would have her travelling companion throw one-franc pieces to the beggars ('some such awful frights too, with horrible disfigurements!' the Duchess of York wrote to her husband, later King George V; while others 'lined the way bowing politely when GrandMaMa [the Queen] had passed').

At 8.30 every evening the Queen's guests were assembled in a brightly lit anteroom, shepherded into the drawing room, lined up, and uneasily awaited Victoria's entry on the arm of one of her Indian servants. After dinner she would sit in the centre of the drawing room, receiving guests each in turn for a short talk. At eleven o'clock precisely, she retired. The evening was at an end.

She had been told that the young Aga Khan was nearby early in her stay. But it was not until the Munshi had arrived that she considered summoning him to one of these evenings. The Aga Khan was, after all, a very highly-placed Indian and she was certain that he would recognize the Munshi's own high caste and back her in supporting him.

Not realizing the difficulty of finding suitable living arrangements at the height of the season, the Aga Khan was confronted by a dilemma on his arrival. Queen Victoria was at the Hotel Excelsior Regina in Cimiez, Austria's Emperor Franz Josef at Cap Martin and all their royal relatives and their staffs had to be accommodated. There was also a plethora of Balkan kings, Russian grand dukes, and German princes who were occupying the best hotel space available on the Riviera. Finally, to his delight, he was offered the rooms at the Hotel Excelsior Regina that had been occupied by the Princess of Wales when she rather suddenly decided to return to England.

The Aga Khan could not have been more pleased. He avidly followed all the news about Victoria and her entourage and attempted to time his comings and goings with hers so that he might see her.

He sent her a note with his regards and his hope that they could meet, which – to his great disappointment – was passed off with a card embossed with a crown, stating that the Queen appreciated his attention and kind regards and would see what could be done about a meeting. A week passed without further word. Finally, on the day that the Munshi arrived, a note was delivered to him from the Queen summoning him to dine in her suite that evening. He was greeted by the Munshi, exchanged only a few words with Victoria (who he noted spoke with a German accent and had the habit of frequently inserting 'tso' ['so'] in her conversation). Although seated at the far end of the table from her, he was much dazzled by her presence. He was not greatly impressed by the Munshi or his colleagues. Later he wrote that he and his two personal attendants were dismayed by the low quality of the Queen's Indian staff: 'They were distinctly second-class servants, of the kind you find around hotels and restaurants, the kind that the newly-arrived or transient European is apt to acquire in the first hotel in which he stays – very different from and very inferior to the admirable, trustworthy, and very high-grade men whom, throughout the years of British rule in India, you would encounter at Viceregal Lodge or at Government House in any of the provinces . . .'

He wore full Indian regalia at his meeting with the Queen, but before long his rooms were filled with extravagant purchases of European clothes. He was thrilled by the display of the opulence on the Riviera: 'I stared at the shop windows, and what shop windows, the jewellers especially!' he later recalled, adding that the streets of Monte Carlo in the fashionable hours were packed with 'the carriages of the great and the wealthy, handsome landaus and victorias with fine, high-stepping horses and coachmen and footmen in dashing liveries.'

He entertained himself while waiting for a second royal invitation, which never did come, by visiting Monte Carlo for the first *Concours d'Élégance* (a motorcar exhibition) and spent several evenings in the Casino there playing roulette. He was to admit that the only people to whom he spoke after the queen's dinner, other than his own staff, were the officials at the Casino.

A photograph of one of those visits reveals the Aga Khan, his black moustache curled upward, wearing a straw hat, European suit and spats buttoned over his leather shoes. Other pictures taken the same year show an extraordinary number of royal personages and celebrities present that season: Grand Duke Serge of Russia, the bearded Grand Duke of Luxembourg (wearing a homburg hat), the King of Württemburg, the Duchess of Roxburghe and the Duchess of Marlborough, wearing enormous hats and long feather boas, Prince Hohenlohe, Ignace Paderewski (red hair sprouting wildly beneath his white panama), the actress and former mistress of the Prince of Wales, Lillie Langtry (heavily veiled, as she tended to be as she aged), Grand Duke Nicholas of Russia, Prince Kotchoubey (a pet dachshund in his arms), Prince Radziwill of Poland, the King of Sweden, the Prince of Denmark, Prince Albert of Monaco and a trio of American millionaires: Pierpont Morgan, W. K. Vanderbilt and Anthony Drexel (along with some very lovely unidentified ladies).

The Queen would have nothing to do with Monte Carlo and only reluctantly allowed a brief meeting at her hotel with the Prince and Princesse de Monaco (she was the former Alice Heine from New Orleans and the widow of the Duc de Richelieu). It had not helped that members of Victoria's entourage related stories to her about a local Russian pawnbroker 'who lends money to the miserable [Russian royal] wretches on their way to Monte Carlo and they are generally unable to redeem their pledges, so he acquires splendid jewels for next to nothing . . .'

Despite the distraction of the high life in Monte Carlo, once the Queen and her entourage had left Cimiez, the Aga Khan saw no reason to remain on the Riviera. He travelled to Paris, staying in a suite at the Hotel Bristol, attended the Comédie française, dined with the star, Madame Bartet (who he believed was a greater actress than Sarah Bernhardt), met numerous European beauties, and discovered the pleasure of good wine and, one suspects, passionate women. Although alcohol was forbidden in his religion, he managed to rationalize his enjoyment of it.

There was a large Khoja community in Paris, and while the Aga Khan was there they came to the Bristol with their problems and requests, or simply to pay homage to their Imam. The management was not too pleased by the many prostrate forms outside the Aga

Khan's suite 'face down, shoes off' and asked him to see his faithful by appointment only. He obliged, but a week later he departed for London. To his great joy he had received a letter from the Duke of Connaught explaining that the Queen would be pleased if he would dine with her at Windsor Castle and possibly discuss his presence at the Queen's Diamond Jubilee in July.

Wearing his stylish new European clothes, the Aga Khan left Paris immediately after buying a solid gold elephant adorned with diamonds and encased in a jewelled casket as a gift to the Queen for her Jubilee. An equerry from Buckingham Palace, representing the Queen, and Sir Gerald Fitzgerald from the India Office were sent to meet him off the boat train at Waterloo Station. He was driven in a royal carriage to the Albemarle Hotel in Piccadilly, where he had engaged a suite to use as his base throughout the summer.

The young Imam was greatly impressed by the splendour of London in what were the halcyon days of the Victorian age. Britain was at the height of Empire and London in the 1890s was the financial centre of the world. The wealth and political power was held by a small, closed circle of aristocrats and by the increasing numbers of the immensely wealthy *nouveaux riches* who had, somewhat reluctantly, been allowed in. The Aga Khan was accepted into that clique, his 'own rank and august connections' gaining him immediate entry, he was to claim. There was little doubt that the Queen's invitation to Windsor opened most doors of society for him and as the London season had just begun he found himself 'in a glittering, superbly organized round and ritual'.

He had himself fitted for the formal attire – frock coats, morning coats, stiff collars, silk hats, patent leather shoes and gloves – that were *de rigueur* for a gentlemen caught up in such a heady whirl of social activities: balls and garden parties at great ducal mansions, racing at Epsom, Ascot and Newcastle, country-house weekends, dinners at the finest tables in London, and the opera. He was also much enamoured of the European women he had met who wore gowns that flattered their figures and sat at dinner tables with men and spoke their minds. There had been an orchestra at one reception and he would have liked to have danced with some of the beautiful women who attended, but he did not know how to.

At one dinner party he was introduced to Florence Nightingale, who commented afterwards that he was 'a most interesting man, but one is never likely to teach him sanitation' – apparently a reference to his table manners, for during the course of the dinner he had used the corner of the tablecloth to wipe his mouth and had belched quite loudly (in his country a compliment on the meal) before leaving the table.

Unaware that he might not be perceived in the way he saw himself, he was euphoric. This was a life that he could once only have imagined. He was greatly stimulated by the role women played in European society and he found he enjoyed their company as friends as well as lovers. There was a long list of women – actresses and ballet dancers, as well as young socialites who were attracted to his exotic background and his generous nature. He had an eye for beauty and liked his lady friends to be slim and dark-eyed. Discretion was the key word in any relationship that moved to the bedroom. He was not seen alone with a woman in public. Private dinners were arranged in his rooms.

At long last came the day he was to be received at Windsor Castle. Once again the Queen sent a carriage and an equerry to the station to meet him and he was driven to the castle where the Duke of Connaught, Lord Salisbury, the prime minister (who had formerly been Secretary of State for India), and Lord George Hamilton, the current Secretary of State, greeted him on behalf of the Queen. A short time later he was received by the Queen in the audience room. Her short, thick form was 'enfolded in voluminous black wraps and shawls' and she sat on a red brocade and carved mahogany sofa. She extended her hand to be kissed and then informed him that she was now going to knight him, but that since he was the 'descendant of kings' (his quotation) he would not be asked to kneel before her. With that, she handed him the order with her signature which made him a knight of the realm. Lord George, who had accompanied him, tapped him slightly on the shoulder signalling the end of the audience and he left her presence.

The interior of Windsor Castle disappointed him. Although he was given a fine suite, and did comment on the grandeur of the building, even in early summer a damp chill penetrated the rooms and the corridors were almost glacial. Also, a sombre atmosphere brooded over the castle, an aura of mourning; pages had dour faces, maids in dowdy black uniforms moved on hushed feet and there was a smell that he could not identify – old furniture polished to a sheen and a dampness that clung to everything – all so different from the perfumed and sun-filled rooms with windows looking out to magnificent vistas to which he was accustomed.

This depressing introduction to the home life of Queen Victoria was instantly dispelled when he went in to dinner that evening. He was seated between the newly-widowed Princess Beatrice of Battenberg and the Queen. Victoria was dressed as usual in black but wore numerous large rings on her stubby white fingers and a wide diamond bracelet, set in the centre with a miniature of her dead husband. A platter of white lace sat on top of her wispy grey hair. Her deep blue eyes were failing but as she and the Aga Khan were both rather short, she looked directly into his eyes as they spoke, quite unnerving him.

The Victorians were extremely hearty eaters and the quantity of the food – twelve courses that night – was amazing. Halfway through the meal a dish of sorbet was served so the stomach could be cooled and rested before the really solid part of the meal – four choices of meat that had followed consommé, thick soup, salmon, cutlets of chicken and roast pigeons – was tackled. Green salad, asparagus in white sauce, a mousse of ham, fresh fruit in champagne and cheese was served before the final touch – a choice of four extraordinary desserts, one flaming.

The dinner guests seemed to relax during the sorbet course, the conversation becoming more spirited during the pause before the rest of the meal continued. The Queen was interested in hearing about the Aga Khan's life in India and recalled being told how well her son, the Prince of Wales, had been received by her guest's grandfather. She asked if medical men were well thought of in his country.

'By the educated, of course,' he replied. 'But we have fine hospitals.'

The subject was changed by Lord Salisbury (for fear of mention of the Munshi and his father), a keen amateur scientist who was among the first to have electrical wiring in his house, at Hatfield in

Hertfordshire, which it seems sometimes set the panels in the Marble Hall smouldering. Lord Salisbury ('his eyes . . . red . . . the pouches beneath them purple') was a gigantic man who ate with an enormous appetite, and had to be helped in and out of his seat because his legs were not strong enough to support his weight.

After dinner everyone adjourned to the Corridor, a long, narrow, gloomy room where the Queen sat while protocol required her guests to stand (an exception being made for Lord Salisbury) and for them to remain until her departure. During this time each guest was presented to the Queen to exchange a few words. When the Aga Khan's turn came she handed him a fair-sized portrait of herself in a frame decorated with the rose of England in rubies, the thistle of Scotland in topazes, and the harp of Ireland in emeralds. Finally, the Queen rose to retire for the night and the group dispersed.

The next morning the Munshi came to his room with a note from the Queen that she herself had written in Urdu and Arabic characters. It contained some simple sentences on the beauty of India and was not very well constructed although the lettering was good. He dismissed the Munshi as he would have a servant. The man glared at him and left the room. It was only then that the Aga Khan realized that the Queen had sent her Indian secretary expressly so that the two should meet on a more personal basis, and that perhaps her gift of the previous night had been more in the nature of a bribe.

The Aga Khan was introduced to the cornucopia of breakfast at Windsor, with almost as many courses as the banquet the previous night: there were huge platters of chops, cutlets, steaks, sausages, chickens and woodcock, rashers of bacon 'a quarter inch thick for grilling', tureens of egg dishes, kidneys, kippers and sweetbreads. The Queen did not join her guests; she rose early and was out in her pony-chair, despite the unseasonable chill of the late May day, being drawn around the grounds by a white donkey, a regime she followed daily in all seasons, wrapped in layers and layers of clothes if need be to protect her from the elements.

Later in the day the Aga Khan met the Queen (Victoria addressed him as Prince Sultan Mohammed; he reverently called her 'Your Majesty'), and was surprised to find the Munshi standing by her side. The Munshi did not acknowledge his presence and turned his gaze aside. The Queen introduced the subject of the building of a Mohammedan College that the Munshi was championing and which she had given her promise to subscribe to. There was no doubt that the Munshi was an intelligent man, but the Aga Khan was certain that he was posing as someone above his actual birth. Besides, he found the man not only rude but unsavoury. The Munshi had not greeted him with the respect due from an Indian to a man of his rank, either that morning or now. There was no way to make sure whether he was being deliberately insulting or was merely ignorant of the courtesy extended to a man of his position. (He entirely dismissed the fact that in the morning he himself had been rude to the man.)

That afternoon, Lord George Hamilton travelled back to London on the train with the Aga Khan and asked for his opinion of the Munshi. The Aga Khan rather reluctantly (for he did not want to offend the Queen) said he was obviously a man of low caste who was self-educated. When this was reported to her the Queen was furious; first that the Aga Khan had not requested a private meeting with her Indian secretary in London and second, because she was certain that Lord George Hamilton had poisoned his mind. 'How dared [he] say her Munshi was not a gentleman,' stormed the Queen, 'when the Gaekwar of Baroda was raised to a prince from a goatherd?'

By June 1897, Queen Victoria had ruled longer than any monarch in British history and could count more than 350 million people in her domains. Her Empire seemed to have no bounds, her reign, now in its sixtieth year, no end. Even as more and more colonies established their own legislatures, she retained the veneration longevity inspires and the devotion of her colonial subjects. The Aga Khan remained one of her staunch devotees and was much excited at the prospect of attending her Diamond Jubilee.

The plan for the Jubilee was to produce a magnificent pageant which would surpass all previous celebrations and demonstrate to all who watched or read of the procession 'the sublime vision of peoples of different races and religions, drawn together from all parts of the world, celebrating as one great family, their common loyalty to the Queen.' On a heroic scale the Diamond Jubilee was to be 'a masterpiece of imperial propaganda'.

In fact, Great Britain had reached its apogee. Imperialism was now a habit. The English had overflowed their shores and sailed across the world to plant their ideas, culture and language. Through this they had produced an imperial élite whose true vocation was Empire. To England and the world the indomitable old Queen symbolized the true might of that empire, unchanging, unwavering, bowing to no man.

India was one of the great jewels in the Queen's crown. At her coronation, sixty years earlier, it had been governed by the East India Company, a private trading concern. Now the august Queen-Empress was its ruler. Prayers on Victoria's behalf, asking God to protect her, were offered in mosques and in Buddhist pagodas, and in Bombay the poor were fed and children given treats in celebration of her long reign. The Aga Khan had been chosen by the Muslims of Western India to represent them at the Jubilee and to give an address on their behalf at a banquet held a few days before the great procession. He stood, dressed (by his choice and in defiance of his advisers) in finely-tailored Savile Row clothes, and proudly declared that he was 'as loyal to the English throne as his grandfather who had fought on the battle-fields of Afghanistan and Sind.'

There was a pervading prejudice against people of colour at court and in social circles, a fact that did not seem greatly to affect the Aga Khan whose station and wealth appeared to place him above such bigotry. He was light-skinned, of course, and he now dressed in Western clothes. All of these things had a cumulative effect.

The sun, after an overcast morning, blazed high in the heavens as he started on his way to Buckingham Palace to join the procession on the day of the Jubilee, 22 June 1897. He had been awakened shortly before six AM by the grinding sound of the local council carts as they freshly-gravelled the roadways, a custom, according to the *Daily Telegraph*, 'which prevailed since the good, old days of Samuel Pepys'. The streets had been thronged with celebrating citizens since the previous night, when Big Ben sounded the last stroke of twelve and a peal of bells throughout London had proclaimed Diamond Jubilee Day. Beneath his hotel windows crowds were cheering, 'God Save the Queen!' above the cacophony of blaring horns and cornets.

It was just as well the Aga Khan had risen early, for he was to ride in an open coach in the procession and had to be in the courtyard of Buckingham Palace by ten o'clock. He joined the splendid gathering to form the procession where uniforms, carriages, medals and sabres made a blazing mass of colour. Never had there been such a glittering array of royalty and foreign emissaries, and the sun, as if by the Queen's command, now pierced sharply through the clouds.

The procession was headed by a cavalcade of officers, military attachés, and representatives of all the courts of Europe, followed by the Kaiser's regiments and a deputation from the Prussian dragoon guards. The Aga Khan rode in a carriage before the most brilliant group of all: the officers of the Imperial Service troops from India, 'swarthy, mostly bearded men wearing a rare collection of wondrously twisted turbans in bright colours trimmed in gold. Their tunics (or

kirtas) were scarlet and peacock blue and jade green, laced and inter-
laced with gold or silver, broadly and vividly sashed.' Although dressed
in formal English attire, the Aga Khan wore all the ribbons and medals
of his rank and massive diamond rings that split the sun's rays into
thousands of dazzling facets as he tipped his black silk hat to the
crowds.

The display of pageantry and its international extent were unprecedented. There were the gaily-dressed Fijians, their hair trained upward
and dyed bright red, regiments of Canadians, Australians, New Zealan-
ders, Africans, *Zaptiehs* from Cyprus, Dyaks from Borneo. The Indian
princes, in their native costumes, rode at the back of Queen Victoria's
carriage, the Prince of Wales astride a magnificent black horse and
resplendent in his field marshal's uniform rode on her left side, on the
other side Lord Wolseley, commander-in-chief of the British army.

The Queen sat in her ornate, gilded, open carriage drawn by eight
of the royal stable's finest cream-coloured horses ridden by elaborately
uniformed postilions with scarlet-coated footmen walking at their
sides. Though nearly eighty, Victoria appeared undaunted by the
uncommon heat and the strenuous demands of the long procession.
Her customary black silk moiré dress (after nearly forty years, she
remained in mourning for her beloved husband, Prince Albert) was
embroidered with silver emblems of her reign. An aigrette of diamonds
trimmed her black lace bonnet, and her white lace parasol, which she
used to protect herself from the hot sun, bobbed up and down as the
carriage made its way slowly along the Jubilee route, a tedious three-
hour journey through the centre of London and its outlying districts.
At the end of it, the Aga Khan, who was exhausted, was stunned by
how radiant the elderly Queen appeared.

He stayed on in London for several weeks before returning to
Bombay. Short of stature, somewhat corpulent, he had acquired a
pince-nez and a neat black moustache, and looked quite fashionable
in his Savile Row suit, a cravat with a jewelled pin at his neck, a silk
hat dandyishly brimmed, when he boarded the ocean liner that would
take him home. His esteem for the Queen had settled into true reverence. (Twenty years later he wrote of his memory of this visit: 'Victoria
in the course of her long reign, came nearer to the hearts of the Indian
subjects she loved so well than any of the emperors the great peninsula

had in the last thousand years of her chequered history. The many [Indian] princes who visited the Court of Windsor during Her Majesty's reign took back to their territories . . . memories of her sincere and maternal affection for her Indian subjects. Her consideration and kindness for such ordinary Indians as came near the presence, her employment of Indian personal servants, the pains she took to acquire a working knowledge of Hindustani – all this became widely known and appreciated in India. To cold casuists, hair-splitting in their studies, the Indian feeling of warm affection for the Sovereign may seem illogical; but it is one of the great formative forces of the world.')

There could not have been a greater contrast to the celebrations in England which the Aga Khan had just attended than the deadly pall that enveloped Bombay, its neighbouring cities and the countryside upon his return in late September 1897. While he had been in Europe, the state of Bombay had suffered a new outbreak of bubonic plague. Although the epidemic was under control, thousands had died from the disease.

He stepped off the liner from Europe dressed once again in the robes and trappings of his Muslim rank, a grey astrakhan fez on his head, his feet encased in Oriental slippers. The Savile Row suits, silk top hats and shining patent leather shoes were packed away, but he had not so easily disposed of his need to belong to the world he left behind as surely as he did to the one to which he had returned.

His love affair with the Western world was always to be a magnet pulling him away from the Oriental world. Lady Ali Shah was alarmed when she saw the clothes that he had brought back with him: cut-away coats and evening suits, striped waistcoats, stove-pipe hats and shirts with starched fronts, several gold watches with fobs and chains, and no sooner had he arrived than he hired a young Englishman to teach him how to dance.

During his absence, Hashim Shah, the son of one of his father's younger brothers, had been murdered in Poona by a gunshot to his head by a *fida'i* (the Aga Khan's most fanatical followers). The reason for the murder was never ascertained, but there were unfounded rumours that Hashim Shah had plans to challenge the Aga Khan's leadership. The assassin, Jiva Jooma, was arrested, tried and sentenced to excommunication from the faith and life imprisonment.

Much was made of the fact that the assassin's defence was paid for by the Aga Khan, although it was not unusual for him to pay legal costs for indigent followers in serious trouble from the vast sums subscribed to him. There were other adversaries who complained that he had spent too much time in Europe away from his wife; still more who carped that his household was immense and contained hundreds of seemingly unnecessary retainers.

The feudal nature of his sect had always presented difficulties for him. He had inherited an unwieldy number of dependants of his grand-father's horsemen and of Ismaili pilgrims taken in as retainers including entire families from as far away as East Africa. The bigger the families grew, the smaller their allowances became as the money was split among them. The Aga Khan fed and housed them, but to supplement their dwindling incomes many had turned to unsavoury occupations, as beggars, race-tipsters, selling contraband or just idling. Others were unruly and got into trouble with the law. The Aga Khan came to their defence, but the Jiva Jooma incident brought the situation to the attention of his followers, who were not pleased about the money they were contributing to their Imam being used on such people.

Getting rid of these charges occupied the Aga Khan for the next few months. Those who were foreign born he insisted return to their native countries. He paid lump sums to others to leave his protection. For the children he provided funds for schooling and job-training. When the purge was over he still retained a domestic staff of well over a thousand employed between his nine residences. With this problem fairly behind him, he turned his attention to the sham of his marriage.

Entirely separate quarters for Shahzada were devised, built and lav-ishly decorated at Malabar Hill, to make it less likely that the two would need to see one another. Shahzada was filled with bitterness; according to him she sadly drifted into 'a private purgatory of resent-ment and reproach'.

He was now twenty-one, full of vigour, powerful, rich and, although dedicated to his responsibility as Imam, not satisfied to live either a celibate life or to take on a harem. In India there seemed to be no other alternative for him. In Europe it was another matter.

The lure to return was strong. Five months later he was back in England.

He had cultivated a reputation as a wildly extravagant host, in the habit of giving expensive jewels and other impressive gifts to beautiful women whom he desired. London society once again opened its doors to him. The Prince of Wales made him a member of his select Marlborough Club, and then, as the Aga Khan's success as an owner and breeder of racehorses in India was known, Queen Victoria, in a gesture he was never to forget, presented him with a Royal Household badge for the Royal Enclosure at Ascot, a courtesy extended to him by the Crown throughout his life.

He visited the Prince of Wales's breeding stable at Sandringham and Lord Marcus Beresford, racing adviser to the Prince, agreeably surprised him by taking steps to register the Aga Khan's colours at Ascot. Because his traditional colours were unavailable in England at that time (being employed by another racing stable), green and chocolate were given him. This meant he could, if he wished, race one of his horses at Ascot. He attended the Derby, cheering the winner, the 100–1 outsider Jeddah, and told the Duke of Connaught that one day he hoped he might win the Derby. But for the time being he decided to remain a spectator in European racing.

From England he travelled to Germany to meet Queen Victoria's grandson, Kaiser Wilhelm II, at Sanssouci, his palace in Potsdam a short distance from Berlin. This was to be a political, not a social visit. He was entertained during his stay, but not in the grand style he had experienced in London. The Aga Khan had many Khoja followers in German East Africa, who for years had been seeking rice-growing concessions along the banks of the River Rufiji near Dar es Salaam which had been denied by the Germans. After two discussions on the matter with the Kaiser, the Aga Khan won these concessions for his people. The Kaiser apparently made a good impression upon him, for he commented to the press that he was 'certainly a great man'.

He left Europe with much reluctance, his attraction to Western culture stronger than ever, and his fascination with European women fired. It would, in fact, continue throughout his life. If he had been able to do so he would have remained and visited Paris and Monte

Carlo before returning to India. But Lady Ali Shah, fearing he might stay away for many months, and worse, enter into an alliance with a European woman, had persuaded him to return. (Never a day went by when he was away that she did not write to him, and he replied almost as often.)

For the next year, at his mother's urging and that of his other financial advisers, his travel was concentrated on Ismaili communities, first to East Africa where many rich and prominent Ismailis lived. In Zanzibar, which was the Ismaili headquarters for Africa, an angry dispute raged between the Ismailis and the local Africans over valuable land which both claimed needed settling, and in the German colony of Dar es Salaam, Ismailis were being accused of hostile activities and violence seemed about to erupt.

'I was staying in Bagamoyo [separated from Zanzibar by the narrow Zanzibar Channel] in August of 1899,' a former German colonial official wrote, 'when His Highness the Aga Khan set foot on the African continent for the first time. His Highness arrived in his own yacht which was anchored about four miles from shore. Thousands of Indians, natives and also Europeans were waiting on the beach to see His Highness and welcome him . . . the enthusiasm . . . during his whole stay was tremendous . . . an Indian from Zanzibar sent a cab with a white horse so that [he] could move about with great speed. Ovations of the highest veneration took place everywhere . . .' Obviously not from the German officials, however, for although the Aga Khan did help to mediate the delicate situation, he came away feeling very cold towards the Germans, whom he found arrogant and difficult to work with. He went from East Africa to Egypt, spent a week in Cairo, where he was struck by the 'all-pervading presence of the English', and then returned to Bombay for another week before leaving for Burma.

His plan was to visit the Riviera in March 1900, at the time of Queen Victoria's annual stay. But on 12 October 1899 the Transvaal and the Orange Free State went to war against Great Britain. Because the Boer War aroused so much hostility against the British abroad, the Queen cancelled her holiday to the Riviera and remained at Windsor. The Aga Khan cut short his stay in the South of France and went to Paris, then decided to return to Bombay as it seemed an inopportune time (although his feelings were entirely pro-British) to impose on royal hospitality. He was never to see the Queen again.

Queen Victoria suffered a mild stroke on 17 January 1901 while at Osborne House, her home on the Isle of Wight where from her bedroom window you could see far across the waters of the Solent to the distant shore of Spithead and the soft curves of the Downs beyond. The Prince of Wales and her other children and grandchildren (Kaiser Wilhelm among them) were sent for. On 20 January, apart from some breathing difficulty, she seemed to be holding her own. By the next morning her mind was wandering, but she gained consciousness long enough to ask her doctor, Sir James Reid, whether she was better. He assured her she was. Eagerly she replied, 'Then may I have Turi [her small dog]?' The pet was brought to her room and allowed to lie on the bed beside her. On the afternoon of 22 January, her condition much deteriorated, she came to long enough to recognize the Prince of Wales standing by her bedside. 'Bertie!' she cried and weakly raised her arms towards him. He embraced her and then, unable to contain his emotion, hurried from the room.

One by one each member of her family, who had all crowded into the room, called out their names in solemn succession to let her know they were all there. She died that evening, and the Prince of Wales, now an ageing man of sixty, became King Edward VII.

The old Queen's death was a terrible blow to the magic of the British Empire. With her 'went the Imperial virtue,' James Morris eloquently wrote. 'She was like a great old oak, whose roots run deep into a parkland, whose branches shade half a meadow, and when she died some old instinct died too, the British lost some sense of favour, the world a sense of awe.'

Perhaps no one beyond Queen Victoria's family, household and ministers would feel a greater loss than the Aga Khan. From the time of his childhood, the Queen had been a symbol to him of majesty and mystery. He had wanted to be accepted by her almost as a child might wish to be favoured by its mother. And she had stood as a reminder throughout his life of the world beyond his own, a culture other than his; the forbidden and the desired. Her impact on him had been tremendous. Because of her, he would always feel an integral part of him belonged to her world.

A HOME
AWAY FROM HOME

Great Britain now had a King-Emperor. Edward VII's entrance on to the world stage as a head of state, after so many decades of waiting in the wings, came when the Empire was at the height of its glory and India was truly Britain's most prized possession.

For over two hundred years the British had been in India and they no longer saw as inequitable the spectacle of a few of their appointed administrators governing so vast and populous a country. They viewed the Indians with a mixture of paternalism and arrogance, deliberately capitalizing on the country's love of colour and pageantry, its ingrained caste system, the masses' veneration of the few hundreds of Indian princes, and the mystique of monarchy as devices to sustain their rule.

For Western visitors, India was an exotic and strange world filled with mystery and adventure. Travellers were intoxicated with its charms and dazed by its kaleidoscopic display. So dazzled were they that they did not see or care that Indians were given little say in the governing of their own country, were often treated as second-class citizens, and that there was very little social exchange between the British and the Indians. In fact, India was a conquered country, ruled by Great Britain and the King-Emperor, separated by two social worlds, with most British viewing Indians, however rich, titled or sophisticated, as members of an alien and subordinate race.

The Aga Khan found himself in a somewhat different position from any of his countrymen. He was not just a rich Indian prince with a degree of jurisdiction over the masses under his leadership. He was the Imam of a large Muslim sect that spread its branches over many of the lands where the British did not have as strong a hold as they did in India and where his influence could be helpful. He was also well positioned to influence other Muslim groups if need be, to sway them towards ideas and attitudes beneficial to Great Britain. It did much for his acceptance by the British that he was fabulously rich and would not need to come to them for handouts, that he was lighter-skinned than most Indians, being of Persian descent, and so more socially acceptable, and that when abroad he had quickly adapted to European dress and social demeanour and shared with King Edward a great sporting interest in horses.

The Viceroy of India in 1901, the year Edward ascended the throne, was the 42-year-old George Nathaniel Curzon, educated at Eton and Oxford, British statesman and brilliant political strategist. Curzon offered the Aga Khan a seat on the Legislative Council in Bombay. It was a popular choice, for the young Imam was well-liked by the British, Hindus and Muslims. He was the youngest man on the Council, which handled civil disputes and whose approval had to be gained for most civic projects. Of the Indians who served with him, he was the only one who had spent so much time in Europe.

His most recent trip to England, where he had attended the Queen's funeral, had fired him with ideas on how to help the widespread poverty in India and reduce the large numbers of early deaths. Social activities were at a standstill in Britain during the mourning period, and on more private occasions he had met Lytton Strachey and other British intellectuals and engaged in discussions of what he called, 'serious matters . . . the human condition'.

Illiteracy, he counselled all who would listen on his return to Bombay, was the root cause of the extreme poverty and devastating disease in India, which – with education – could be turned around. It was not an entirely popular cause. What was expounded in upper-class and intellectual English social circles was not a true picture of the British attitude towards India and its people. With education, of course, would come a driving ambition and dedication to self-rule.

The Aga Khan wanted an educated India that would become an independent member of the British Commonwealth. This caused him to fall out with the country's most potent voice, the Indian National Party, which itself was about to split into two factions; a moderate group led by Gopal Krishna Gokhale, who sought dominion status for India, and a militant bloc under Bal Gangadhar Tilak, who demanded complete independence. By aligning himself with Gokhale, the Aga Khan drew the animosity of Tilak and his followers. But his pro-British views further ingratiated him with Curzon and with Lord Kitchener, fresh from his victories in the South African war and the new commander-in-chief of the British army in India.

Lord Curzon was more feared than loved, but there is no doubt that it was his energy that contributed to India's growing strength. He started co-operative credit societies whose aim was to rescue the farmer from the clutches of the moneylender, and set up a research institute intended to promote improved methods of agriculture. He was responsible for the construction of 6000 miles of railway track and a management board to oversee the train system, and he planned the irrigation of 6.5 million acres of land. Industry grew under his viceroyalty. So did order, for in 1903 he carried out an important police reform. He was also diligent about fostering the preservation of Indian artistic treasures and the discovery of the Indian past. And though it was not his aim, he contributed more than any other Englishman to turn nationalism from a set of individual opinions into a nationwide movement.

Although Curzon dared 'to approach the civilization of India with a respect rare among the pig-stickers and box-wallahs,' James Morris wrote, 'and tried to convince the Indians themselves that they should not wish to be brown Britons,' his contribution to later Indian independence was diametrically opposed to his intention.

At the time that Curzon became Viceroy, he was the rising hope of the imperialist wing of the British Conservative Party. The Viceroyalty, he once said, was 'the dream of my childhood, the fulfilled ambition of my manhood, and my highest conception of duty to the State'. Immensely industrious, eloquent, arrogant, an autocrat, a connoisseur with a taste for lordliness, he believed that the idea of trusteeship meant developing one's ward without expectation of ever handing it over, and he did not conceive, even when he saw the changes being made during his seven-year tenure as Viceroy, that the Indians could take over their own country in any time in the foreseeable future. He was an imposing figure, an absolute but paternal Governor-General, a symbol of Empire, and one of its most astute conjurors.

Perhaps no country other than Great Britain was capable of producing such dazzling displays of panoply, and no other nation enjoyed them more than India. Owing to the ill-health of King Edward VII (during the first year of his reign, surgery for appendicitis had followed unrelated but exhausting bouts of pleurisy, bronchitis and a slow recovery from severe knee injuries suffered in a fall down a spiral staircase while a guest at Waddesdon Manor, the house of Baron de Rothschild), his Coronation was postponed from early June to 9 August 1902. Even with this two-month delay, the festivities and the Coronation procession were somewhat curtailed so as not to impede the sixty-year-old King's recovery.

The Aga Khan was in London for the Coronation and found the event disappointing when compared with the magnificent spectacle of Queen Victoria's Diamond Jubilee. King Edward loved pomp, and Great Britain longed for it. The Boer War – the worst war England had suffered, with more than 100,000 casualties – ended on 31 May 1902, only weeks before the originally scheduled Coronation. Then a spate of unseasonably cold weather put an extra damper on celebrations. The sun, however, miraculously came out on the day itself and Queen Alexandra was ablaze with the refractions of light from her jewelled crown – the Koh-i-noor diamond (the largest in the world at that time) at its centre, glittering pavé diamonds so closely covering the frame that they appeared to be one spectacular stone. None the less, there was a sense that things were somehow less than before, and in India her son's Coronation did little to assuage the deep sadness felt at Victoria's death.

Lord Curzon was concerned that India's enthusiasm for the Crown was eroding with the loss of the old Queen, and that Indians felt far removed from a Coronation that was being held in London. Indians were seduced by the aura of grand and ostentatious spectacle and equated it with power. And so in January 1903 he staged a Grand Durbar at Delhi that had never been equalled, personally supervising everything down to the smallest detail. (At the last minute he decided that the rousing hymn 'Onward Christian Soldiers' should be omitted, not in recognition that most of those present would be Hindus or Muslims, but because the line 'Crowns and thrones may perish' might be taken too literally.)

A massive tent city was erected on a vast brown plain outside Delhi. And it was there that feudatories first gathered: 'the bewhiskered Maharajahs of Punjab, the bold soldier-princes of Rajasthan, royalty of Nepal in peculiar hats, sleek Bengalis and beautiful Tamils, Sikhs, with gilded scimitars, gaunt Baluchis with ceremonial camels, Burmese and Sikkimese and Madrasis and wonderful rustic potentates from Gujarat or Kerala.'

The grand procession to the amphitheatre past the hundreds of thousands who had made the pilgrimage to Delhi was led by Curzon himself, dressed in the flamboyant trappings of his rank, riding (no doubt in severe pain: he had a serious spinal dislocation and wore a steel corset to keep him erect) a massive elephant draped in silver and gold cloth and frontlet pieces of jewels that blazed in the bright Delhi sun. Behind Curzon's elephant came fifty more, equally bedecked and bedizened. They were followed by the cavalry and riders in full army regalia on 120 more gaily decorated elephants.

As the grand procession headed for Kashmir Gate where they would enter the amphitheatre and where 8000 of the privileged (including the American-born Lady Curzon, dressed in blue and gold and wearing a diamond tiara) were waiting for a further display, 'trumpets sounded, guns fired, soldiers presented arms, plumes waved, elephants snorted, jewels glittered, cameras clicked, ["nearly everyone had a Kodak," wrote one participant, "even many of the natives themselves"] . . . Here were standard-bearers and heralds in tabards carrying the King-Emperor's Proclamation, and High Court judges in their wigs. Here were the twelve State trumpeters and the twelve military bands, and the 40,000 parading soldiers . . . The trumpets sound. The drums roll . . . the vast polychromatic crowd rises thunderously to its feet [to sing] the first solemn notes of the British National Anthem – so dignified, so old, so far from home, so simple in that exotic setting, so touching, so profound, that the very soul of India seems to [have been] stirred.'

The most popular group in the procession was the surviving British and Indian veterans of the Mutiny, '. . . old tottering fellows . . .' said a spectator; 'the people shouted till they were hoarse.' Forgotten was the cost of Empire – over two million British graves scattered throughout India.

The Aga Khan was not entirely comfortable in the full costume Curzon requested he wear. The maharajahs were similarly in full regalia and later confessed that they were ashamed of the ridiculous garb they wore on the occasion but were fearful they could lose their wealth and titles if they did not accede to Curzon's wishes. Still, to the Aga Khan, this pageant would remain a burning memory, one that seared the idea of Empire ever deeper in his heart.

Not long after the Durbar, the Aga Khan was off again to Europe. Lady Ali Shah found it difficult to conceal her unhappiness over her son's long absences from Bombay and his lack of an heir. The Riviera had become his home away from home. His mistresses were many and beautiful. Without exception, the women were all unmarried, European and extremely low profile: a young woman who managed a boutique, a novice ballerina, a supporting actress in a theatre company – women whose names even linked with his would not attract the press.

He played hard, gambled heavily, and spent much time at the various racecourses in England and France. Still, he did not neglect his duties as a religious leader or as a spokesman for Muslim causes.

He was seriously grieved when Lord Curzon, in a historic quarrel with Lord Kitchener over the degree to which the civil government should control the Indian Army, was obliged to resign in 1905. The Aga Khan much admired Curzon and was working closely with his Viceroy's Council on a plan to resettle in Africa large numbers of Indian Muslims (Ismailis included) whose small farms had been devastated by drought and who needed a new start. Curzon's replacement, Lord Minto, the recent governor-general of Canada, was more moderate, an amiable man, well-liked and well-experienced for his new post. He lacked Curzon's charismatic presence and dynamic energy, but he understood the colonial mind and was patient, yet persistent, in winning his goals, one of which was to bring Indian Muslims and Hindus to a peaceful accord. He considered the Aga Khan a strong mediating hand in this purpose and made a concentrated effort to win his confidence.

'We all feel,' Lord Minto wrote in his diary about the British in India, 'that we are mere sojourners in the land, that we are camping, and on the march.'

When the Aga Khan reached Africa in the summer of 1905 to discuss the resettling in Zanzibar of several hundred Indian Ismailis, he was shocked by the high increase in tuberculosis among the Africans, and their apathy towards work, progress and religion. Taking matters into his own hands he decided that what Ismailis everywhere needed was a written constitution. Working with local leaders he laid the ground-work of the Worldwide Ismaili Organization of Territorial, Provincial, and Local Councils, the leaders to be selected by him from local candidates.

The cornerstone of the Constitution was 'a personal law to govern the lives of Ismailis from cradle to grave. Antiquated Muslim practices were discarded [the poor treatment of women, schools for boys only among them], contamination with local tribal customs [from such extremes as the immolation of widows and the killing of female children to bathing or washing clothes in unclean river water] shunned. Polygamy was out, as were child marriages [before the age of fifteen]. Engagements would be registered and could not be lightly broken off. Divorces were a matter for the *mukhi*, perhaps even the Council; among grounds for divorce were a partner's renunciation of the Ismaili faith, a husband's impotence, or a disease that made married life dangerous for the other partner.' As written in the Constitution, at weddings, Ismailis were to: 'Avoid ostentation, limit the number of wedding guests (to two hundred in Africa), no extravagant wedding gowns, no alcoholic drinks.' The severest punishment to be meted out to any Ismaili found guilty of a serious crime was excommunication, which meant that no Ismaili other than a member of the immediate family could speak to or have any social, business or sexual association with the person. Apostates were regarded as enemies and no Ismaili was to marry a defector from the faith.

By 1906 the Aga Khan was regarded by India's Muslims as their titular leader (Muslims totalled about 25 per cent of the country's then 294 million population), and in October was chosen to head a deputation to ask the current Viceroy, Lord Minto, for guarantees against the Hindu majority, the Muslims to have their own representatives as a community. Three months later the All-India Muslim League was founded. Unlike the Indian National Party, which, though Hindu-dominated, claimed to represent all sects and beliefs, the All-India Muslim League, with the Aga Khan as president, was concerned only with Muslim rights. Its formation led to separate constituencies for Muslims and Hindus and lasting opprobrium for the well-meaning Minto, who was unfairly accused of trying to divide Muslims from Hindus and so perpetuate British rule.

But Hindus and Muslims had distrusted and disparaged each other
since the collapse of the Mughal empire at the beginning of the eighteenth century. Hindus regarded all Muslims as descendants of
Untouchables and believed that a Muslim would contaminate a Hindu
kitchen if allowed to enter it; the touch of a Muslim's hand would
cause an orthodox Hindu to rush off to purify himself with hours of
ritual ablutions. Intermarriage was entirely condemned on both sides,
and almost unheard of.

The differences of the two religions created a great barrier. Hindus
worshipped God in a multiplicity of forms: in animals (the cow was
venerated and allowed to wander through city and village streets, and
they refused to kill the sacred animal even in time of great famine),
the sea, the sun, divine incarnations, ancestors and sages. Muslims
believed there was one God, Allah, and the Quran forbade the faithful
to represent him in any shape or form.

Unlike the Hindus, Muslims abhor idols and idolatry and consider
paintings and statues blasphemous. Their mosques are adorned only
with abstract designs and the repeated calligraphic representation of the
ninety-nine names of God, while Hindu temples have been described as
'a kind of spiritual shopping centre, a clutter of goddesses with snakes
coiling from their heads, six-armed gods with fiery tongues, elephants
with wings talking to the clouds, jovial little monkeys, dancing maidens
and squat phallic symbols'. If they wanted to taunt the Hindus,
Muslims drove their own cows past the front doors of temples on the
way to the slaughterhouse. To retaliate, the Hindus would incite the
Muslims by playing music (forbidden in their austere service) outside
a mosque during their solemn time for prayers.

Economic rivalry was also a problem between the two communities.
The Hindus had quickly seized upon the opportunities that British
education brought to India. Although they felt more comfortable
socially with the Muslims, whose beliefs were not as foreign to them
as those of the Hindus, the British had employed Hindus to administer
India for them. The Aga Khan was much aware that lack of education
was a serious hindrance to the advancement of Muslims: he built
schools for his young followers and stressed the importance of education at every opportunity to members of his own sect and other
Muslim communities alike. More politically oriented and socially aware

than any of his predecessors, he had become a strong force in the larger Muslim population.

Lady Minto wrote in her diary for 9 February 1910: 'The Aga Khan arrived to stay with us today [at their home, Spring Tower, in the Kurrum Valley]. He seems to have made a triumphal progress through India amongst the Muslims. He says the only real way to appeal to the feelings of the Natives is by means of the superstitions of their religion and consequently he has instructed the priests in every mosque to issue a decree that any Mohammedans who incite to rebellion, or go about preaching sedition, will be eternally damned. He suggested that a similar manifesto should be issued by the Hindus, as if doubts were thrown upon their prospects of happiness in a future state it might have a deterring effect.'

As the Aga Khan's power among the Muslim population grew, his relationship to Great Britain and the Crown strengthened. The India Office's correspondence files on the Aga Khan closely followed his progress with the All-India Muslim League, albeit with a rather arrogant attitude that often reveals itself in inter-office memos but of which he seemed to be unaware. He retained his great awe of the Crown. King Edward admired his knowledge of racehorses and his daughter-in-law, the former Duchess of York, now the Princess of Wales (and the future Queen Mary), was impressed with his stand on women's rights.

Shortly after the great Durbar to celebrate Edward's coronation, the Prince and Princess of Wales visited India. The Aga Khan bought an estate in Calcutta in the hope that the royal couple might stay there. They did not, but they did receive him, and Lady Ali Shah as well. Curzon (just weeks before his resignation and Lord Minto's arrival to replace him as Viceroy in 1905) believed India's many princes would be personally offended that they had not been similarly singled out as hosts to the royal visitors, and there was already fear of a rise in anti-British sentiments.

'Would the people of India be happier if you ran the country?' Prince George asked Gopal Krishna Gokhale (whose power on the Legislative Council was fast growing) during a private meeting at the time of this visit.

'No, sir,' Gokhale replied, 'I do not say they would be happier, but they would have more self-respect.'

'That may be,' the Prince snapped back, 'but I cannot see how there can be real self-respect while the Indians treat their women as they do now,' and he was caught glancing over at his wife for her approval, for they had been thoroughly shocked by the poor treatment of women in India, the stories of immolation of widows and of the killing of female children, even though the Aga Khan had told them of these appalling customs in an earlier meeting.

The Prince of Wales was as sensitive to the problem of caste as he was to the plight of the Indian woman. In his diary he wrote: 'I could not help being struck by the way in which all salutations by the Natives were disregarded by the persons to whom they were given. Evidently we are too much inclined to look upon them as a conquered and down-trodden race and the Native, who is becoming more and more educated, realizes this. I could not help but notice that the general bearing of the European towards the Native was to say the least unsympathetic. In fact not the same as that of superiors to inferiors at home.' (The Prince seemed unaware that very word 'Native' was already considered offensive by the Aga Khan and most enlightened Indians.)

In a short time the Muslim League, with the Aga Khan as its head, became a political force. His object was twofold – to help unite Muslims in a common cause and to establish himself as a liaison between the Muslim world and Europe. His work for the league caused him to travel even more regularly between India and Europe, with frequent trips elsewhere: Malaya, Singapore, China, Japan, Russia (where he met Tsar Nicholas II), Hawaii and the United States. He maintained the habit of dressing in European attire when abroad. He was now an extremely sophisticated man, taken seriously by world leaders.

In the autumn of 1907 his health broke down; his stressful pace, the amount of travelling he was doing, and the concern he had for his people had taken their toll. He struggled with a severe bout of bronchitis and the doctors were worried about his lungs and his heart. They suggested a total rest. He went back to the Riviera, deciding to stay in Monte Carlo, with his large suite of servants, two secretaries and a private physician, at the luxurious Hotel de Paris, famous for its cuisine.

*　　　*　　　*

Monte Carlo was at the height of its golden age in 1907, spun into glittering orbit during the previous decade through the efforts of Princess Alice of Monaco who had recently left her husband, Prince Albert, to live in London with her lover, the opera composer Isidore de Lara. The scandal did not apparently damage the momentum of the social scene in this postage-stamp country, which relied heavily upon its Casino for its financial security. Princess Alice, who had as her close personal friends not only royalty and society's *crème de la crème* but some of the most shining luminaries of the theatre, literature, art, music and dance, had contributed much in her tenure to the cultural attractions – opera, theatre, ballet and seasonal charity galas – that gave Monte Carlo a touch of class.

The resort was also a magnet for gamblers, conmen and opportunists – male and female. Rich American heiresses and poor but titled foreigners increasingly used it as a mating ground. (To an unwed heiress, a title was worth anywhere from $200,000 to $4 million. To a needy noble, the price tag was his ticket to a life of plenty and was not forfeited if the marriage was brief or the lady felt short-changed.) There were also many beautiful women happy to exchange their favours for jewels, carriages and clothes, and more astute ones (perhaps more talented) who demanded fine art, antiques, real estate and solid annuities from the titled and rich men who frequented the tables and shared their beds.

Many profitable liaisons were sealed in Monte Carlo. When a man such as the Aga Khan with both a high title and great wealth arrived, he received unusual attention. Edward VII, not in good health, missed that season (which followed Easter), but King Leopold II of Belgium, Grand Duke Michael of Russia, and the Prince of Nepal made an imposing royal trio. Needless to say the Aga Khan did not lack for female companionship. For one thing, he was notorious for the generosity of his gifts; for another, he was genuinely liked. But he had suddenly found himself in need of a deeper relationship. He liked women and found them often wise and good companions and companionship was something that he felt missing from his life.

Although still married to Shahzada, he never saw her. He remained devoted to his mother and continued to write to her almost daily when he was abroad. He relied greatly on her judgement in matters of finance. Lady Ali Shah, however, was critical of certain aspects of his life. And there was much he could not discuss with her, that she could not – being an Eastern woman, and dedicated to him as Imam – possibly understand. She would have had him divorce Shahzada to marry another Ismaili with high connections and get busy on the task of producing an heir. He wanted a woman he could respect and talk to, who shared some of his interests, spoke languages, would travel with him and could hold her own at a royal or society dinner. As Indian princesses seldom travelled or were educated abroad, it seemed to him that only a European woman would fit that bill.

He had recently spent a month in New York where he found American women 'grating' and the city too noisy. Even so the trip aroused a great interest in opera and ballet, which he attended for the first time. Once back in Monte Carlo he became friendly with King Edward VII's former mistress Lillie Langtry, who maintained a villa there, attending her salons which never failed to include visiting artists – performers, composers, writers, painters. This was a fresh, new world for the Aga Khan, and although not gifted in any of the arts, he found great pleasure in meeting those who were.

The Monte Carlo Opera House, where theatre, ballet and opera were performed, was part of the same building that housed the Casino. The first ballet that season was *Giselle*. Making her solo debut in the company at the age of nineteen in the supporting role of Princess Bathilde was Theresa Magliano, a lithe, dark-eyed Italian beauty, called Ginetta by her friends and family. The Aga Khan could not keep his eyes off her and was greatly moved in the scene where Giselle kneels at Bathilde's feet and wonderingly touches the rich fabric of her skirt. Ginetta rose with elegant grace and regally lifted the kneeling girl to her feet. There was something about the way in which she did this, her posture and demeanour, that so impressed him that he returned the following evening to see the ballet again. He then sought out a journalist he knew in Monte Carlo, to arrange a meeting.

'We little dancers,' Gina Lamy, another ballerina at the Opera House reminisced fifty years later, 'when we had finished dancing, we would go and sit on the benches in the Casino garden. One evening this English journalist came to Ginetta in the garden and said, "I know a gentleman who is very much in love with you. He is very rich. He can give you everything. Tomorrow morning, if you are by the kiosk outside the Casino, he will make himself known to you."'

Ballerinas during that period did not enjoy a good reputation. Many rich and titled men found them charming mistresses, but the taint of the theatre and the fact that they were *dancers* seemed to preclude marriage. Ginetta was the eldest child of Rosa, a former vaudeville performer, and Giovanni Magliano, an ironworker in Turin, who had taught himself to paint when in his mid-thirties and was now a restorer of church frescoes. Ginetta had been her mother's favourite of their four children, two sons – Antonio and Mario – and two daughters – Ginetta and Emmy, who was five years younger than her sister. Rosa was desperate to raise her own station in life and she saw her older daughter, who she believed was the talented member of the family, as the way this could come about.

Rosa was undoubtedly ambitious for Ginetta. Emmy, then only fourteen, was also studying for a career in ballet. '[My father] was never rich enough,' Emmy later recalled. 'My mother had extravagant habits. She loved luxury and display. She had got from her grand-mother a chinchilla coat – imagine, chinchilla! And she cut it up into little coats for my sister and myself. She wanted us to be fine ladies.'

The Aga Khan wrote in his memoirs that he and Ginetta fell almost immediately in love. Certainly, Ginetta was smitten with this exotic young man, ten years her senior, prince and leader of over 15 million people. 'My sister', said Emmy, 'was a pure young girl when she met the Aga. She knew nothing of life and men. Naturally, she had idealized everything. It was to be a story from *A Thousand and One Nights*.'

Rosa had allowed Ginetta to go to Monte Carlo on the condition that she stay with family friends, the Moschiettos originally from Turin, who had a home there. The Moschietto household included three boys and a young daughter, Lorenza – who, adopting the French spelling, changed her name to Laurence when she matured. 'Well, it was very difficult in our busy house for Ginetta to meet with the Aga Khan,' Laurence told this author. The Aga Khan wooed Ginetta with some fabulous jewels from Cartier. Finally Ginetta agreed to take an apart-ment by herself, paid for by the ardent Aga, so that they could meet privately.

He was known in Monte Carlo for spending a night with a beautiful young woman, sending her a gleaming new sports car or an extravagant piece of jewellery and not seeing her again. With Ginetta it was another matter. He thought he was truly in love and he agreed before they were ever sexually involved, that if Ginetta should decide against going to bed with him once they were alone he would still settle a comfortable amount on her. But he also added that if she bore him a son he would divorce his wife and marry her.

Whatever Ginetta's true feelings were for the Aga Khan (and there is no reason not to believe that she cared sincerely for him), she was pregnant within a month. The Aga Khan was elated. Rosa was sent for to look after her daughter. Young Emmy came with her. Rosa's moral outrage was quickly appeased by the new affluence she realized she could have with Ginetta's liaison and possible marriage. The Aga Khan, deciding he wanted to marry Ginetta whether their child was male or female, returned to Bombay to confront his mother with his decision to divorce Shahzada, marry a European woman and to make his home on the Continent.

These were not the only obstacles he had to overcome.

Ginetta was a Roman Catholic whose religion and country did not recognize marriage to a divorced person. She would have to convert and cast aside her own religion, which she had not yet agreed to do.

The Aga Khan arrived in Bombay in the spring of 1908 just as a sensational court case brought by Shahzada's sister, Haji Bibi, was laid against him. Further, from the wording of the brief it could be assumed that Shahzada was a plaintiff, although not technically named. Haji Bibi claimed that as a daughter of the murdered Jangi Shah, she and other relatives with blood ties to the Aga Khan and his ancestors were entitled to a share of the community's property and the Imam's income as of their hereditary right. For an Ismaili to sue the Imam was shocking enough; for the Imam's sister-in-law (and cousin) to do so was stunning.

Animosity between Shahzada's family and the Aga Khan and Lady Ali Shah had grown steadily in the decade since Jangi Shah's assassination, exacerbated by the poor fashion in which Shahzada was believed by her relatives to have been treated. The Aga Khan had always been generous to his wife, providing her with a most luxurious way of life, denying her nothing that she might request. But it was quite clear by now that Shahzada would never be the mother of his children. There was also the humiliation of being cast aside by the Imam and the possibility of having to live a solitary life until his death, because remarriage – although acceptable for a man – was not looked upon favourably for the divorced wife. The likelihood that the Aga Khan would divorce Shahzada also raised the possibility that whatever benefits his wife's family now had might cease. Had there been a child of the union it would have been a different matter, for then they would have remained in direct blood line with the Imam.

It is doubtful that many outside the family were aware of these internecine complications. They knew, of course, that there had yet been no child born to the Imam and his Begum. Shahzada remained

71

in the houses at Malabar Hill and at Poona in separate quarters. Such private problems, in any event, were never brought into the trial which quickly became entangled in daily discussions about the Imam's financial relations with his Imamate. Newspapers, other than Ismaili publications, carried sensational banner stories about how the Aga Khan came by his great wealth which were so exaggerated that readers not of his faith were quick to equate him with the Indian princes and British colonists who exploited the poor for personal gain. This was far from the reality. True, his wealth was enormous, but because of his (or perhaps Lady Ali Shah's) combined business acumen and concern for his followers, a sizeable amount of the monies he made from his investments and collected from Ismailis was reinvested in the betterment of their living conditions and in their future. Housing, health and educational facilities were all being improved.

The practice of Ismaili tithing, previously a private tenet of the religion, was publicly revealed in the course of the trial along with an accounting of the fees the Imam received for all weddings, funerals (to ensure the departed's soul rested in peace), at the naming of a child, at all special prayer assemblies, and at the *jamaat khana* on the seventh day of the month, when followers fasted from six in the evening until ten the next morning. There was even a frequent ceremony, the public was told, called *sir bundi*, in which a wealthy follower was expected to hand over the deeds of his property to the Imam, the elders then fixing a price at which it could be bought back from him.

Mr Justice Russell, the representative from the Bombay High Court who was hearing the case, requested and was granted permission to attend a *jamaat khana* so that he could judge more fairly. 'We sat on chairs in front of a raised seat or throne on which the Aga Khan sits,' he later recalled. 'The whole room was filled with Khojas seated or kneeling on the ground, in another room the women of the community . . . a most impressive sight owing to the reverence with which the whole proceedings were conducted.'

The veneration that was so openly displayed towards the Aga Khan at the ceremony greatly influenced Judge Russell's view of the proceedings. He had known little of the Ismaili faith when the case was first brought before him, and had assumed that the Aga Khan functioned much like any Indian prince, his followers being his subjects or servants. He now saw him in more of a papal light, as a religious figure, and he began to question his assumptions in regard to the Aga Khan's income and his expenditures.

As the trial progressed, Haji Bibi on behalf of her family went into detail about the cost of every home belonging to the Aga Khan, the jewellery he possessed, his horses, the expensive clothes he wore, his yacht and carriages, his staff of a thousand servants. Several female cousins followed her to the stand to inform the court how much money the Aga Khan lavished on the European women he befriended. The idea was to inflame Europeans and Indians alike. One woman came very close to calling the Aga Khan intolerant towards his own brown brothers and Judge Russell had to clear the courtroom to restore order.

His final decision was that the offerings and presents made to the previous Aga Khans I and II and their current heir were their absolute property and that no other member of their family was entitled to any interest in such income or gifts. Haji Bibi was completely defeated in her claim and she left the court, along with several female members of her family, extremely bitter. She insinuated to the press who surrounded her that Judge Russell could not, after all, be expected to hand down a fair verdict when he was a friend of the Aga Khan's and had even dined with him. That was the truth as far as it went: the two men were acquainted and had both attended several large functions in Bombay. But it is doubtful if this fact influenced the judge, for such social interchange between Indian and British dignitaries was common and much encouraged by both. What swayed Judge Russell was his revisionist view of the Aga Khan as religious leader and a lack of belief in what the parade of women witnesses had to say.

'As regards the ladies [who were witnesses],' he commented when later goaded, 'I could not see their faces as they were covered from head to foot in black dominoes with white pieces of muslin let in across the face. But one has only to read the evidence . . . to see how full of inconsistencies and untruths it is.'

Despite the Aga Khan's having won the case, to divorce Shahzada at this juncture could well have led to more unpleasant publicity and gossip. His decision was to let things rest for a time. He returned almost immediately to Monte Carlo where Ginetta waited for him, bought a house overlooking the Casino in the rue Bel Respiro, named it Villa Ginetta and gave it to her as a present. A few months later, although he did not make a public statement or file for it in any court, he privately declared himself divorced from Shahzada and made arrangements for her to have a financially secure future and an estate in Poona. (A letter was sent to Shahzada to this effect.)

His wish was to marry Ginetta as soon as he could. This was not a simple matter. In Europe his self-decreed divorce from Shahzada was not considered legal and binding. He could have returned to be remarried in India, but the validity of the union would still be questioned. And, of course, in Ginetta's condition a trip of that difficulty was not advisable. On Ginetta's part, she remained torn as to whether she wanted to divest herself of her faith and place herself in the position of never being able to return to her home in Italy: it was against the law there for a Catholic to marry a divorced person, who would be regarded as a bigamist.

But neither did Ginetta want to remain (as she called him) 'Aggy's' mistress and have her child remain illegitimate, a loathsome idea for a young woman with her strict Catholic upbringing. She was also truly besotted with the Aga Khan. Without doubt, he was the most exotic and exciting man she had ever known. He seemed to be acquainted with almost everyone famous in the world, was rich beyond her wildest fantasies, told her endless, fascinating stories of an alien culture that mesmerized her. Also, her mother was anxious for her to marry the exotic prince. Rosa, in fact, was enjoying the first financial bonanza of her life and had discovered the excitement of the gambling tables at Monte Carlo.

Her brother Mario joined Ginetta, Emmy and their mother at the Villa Ginetta while the Aga Khan struggled to find a way for him and his beautiful ballerina to marry. In the meantime the dance company moved on without her. And then Ginetta miscarried. Everything she had worked so hard to achieve seemed to have escaped her and what she wanted – marriage, a real home, children – was, for the moment at least, beyond her grasp. She was terribly unhappy, not sure what she should do, and fearful that the loss of the child she had been carrying would end her affair with the Aga Khan.

But never in his thirty years had the Aga Khan been this desperately in love. He, too, was in a serious quandary, and just as fearful that he would lose Ginetta. She only had to look at him with her large, dark, soulful eyes and he melted. He was as keen to have a family as she was. Finally, in the late spring of 1908 he made arrangements for a Muslim ceremony to be performed in Egypt and Ginetta agreed to marry him and to convert. Emmy and Mario accompanied her to Cairo.

Only six people (the others were members of the Aga Khan's entourage) were present at the wedding, which was a *muta* marriage (first practised early in the history of Islam, to allow Muslim warriors, separated from their wives for lengthy periods, to enter into temporary associations with one or more other women for a contracted, specified period of time and to legitimize the children of such marriages). Doubts still remain that this marriage was legal. When that same year the Aga Khan bought some land in Cimiez and on it, as a wedding gift to Ginetta, built the magnificent Villa Terpischore, the deed was written in the name *Theresa Magliano*, her situation listed as *nubile* (unmarried).[1]

In March 1909, Ginetta gave birth at home in Monte Carlo to a son, Mohammed Mahdi Khan, whom she called Giuseppe. Ginetta

[1] It has been suggested that the bride's maiden name was used on the deeds because the land was purchased before their marriage, but the dates on file contradict this.

The civil legality of their marriage was always a problem for the Aga Khan and Theresa Magliano. In his will the Aga Khan wrote: 'In the year 1908 I was married to Cleope Theresa Magliano according to the Muta form of marriage as recognized by Shia Law. The period and dowry were fixed at fifty years and ten thousand francs, respectively. Previously to the said marriage my wife . . . became a convert to Mohammedism, adopting the tenets of the Shia sect and thereafter continued to be a Muslim by religion . . .' Shia Law accepted the Muta marriage of a man to a second wife (without legal divorce); thus the children of the union were held to be legitimate.

Never satisfied with this arrangement, Theresa Magliano and the Aga Khan were married again in Bombay on 23 January 1923 (fifteen years after their *muta* marriage) in 'a permanent form of marriage . . . observing the ceremonials which are customary among Shia Muslims'. Even this did not satisfy the Aga Khan, and on 8 December 1926, a week *after* Theresa died, he secured a proper divorce from his first wife Shahzada, *who in fact was also dead*, in accordance with Shia Law. The exact purpose of this bizarre legal action was never made clear: it may have been intended to secure his heirs from any claims made by Shahzada's litigious family.

was ecstatic and insisted on staying in Monte Carlo to care for her son and supervise the decoration of the newly completed house in Cimiez while the Aga Khan took numerous trips to see his followers and to meet foreign leaders.

Turkey, where there was a large group of Ismailis, was in a state of serious upheaval. The Young Turk movement, a reformist and strongly nationalistic group, had recently forced through a liberal constitution and overthrown Turkey's despotic sultan, Abd-al-Hamid II. His brother, Muhammad V, was placed on the throne, but with no actual power. What worried the Aga Khan was Germany's growing role in Turkey's domestic affairs. The Kaiser was becoming more and more patently anti-British. The Aga Khan met Muhammad V, but realized how little power the sultan had over his country and of what little consequence were any promises he made to protect the Khojas. He left Turkey heavy-hearted, conscious of Europe's deteriorating political situation and Germany's increasing power, fearful of its international repercussions and in regard to Ismailis who lived in many of the troubled regions. They were too often regarded as nomads, outsiders, and could be the first to suffer displacement in a time of unrest and upheaval.

On 6 May 1910, Edward VII died, increasing the Aga Khan's uneasiness about the stability of the Empire. Edward had not shown the strength that Victoria exhibited, but he was a constant reminder of the glory that was Great Britain and to a large extent this aura of mightiness seemed a safeguard for the rest of Europe. It was not that the new King George possessed less character – indeed, he could boast of more. But the death of Victoria's son seemed to spell a final end to the grandeur of the age in which she reigned. The Aga Khan, with most of the world, sensed this was the case. He attended the funeral along with the sovereigns of nine countries – Germany, Denmark, Sweden, Greece, Norway, Portugal, Spain, Belgium and Bulgaria; the ex-President of the United States, Theodore Roosevelt, the French foreign minister, Stéphen Pichon, Grand Duke Michael of Russia, and the Duke of Aosta representing the King of Italy.

Kaiser Wilhelm had travelled to England for the funeral on his private yacht, the *Hohenzollern*, escorted by four British destroyers.

The vessel was anchored in the Thames estuary and Wilhelm then boarded the royal train for London, where he was met at Victoria Station by his cousin, the new King George, whom he kissed on both cheeks. He had never been able to win over his uncle, Edward VII, and despite a show of seeming emotion – kneeling with the new king in silent prayer, grasping his hand in a warm handshake, a tearful sigh for newsmen – he was not in the least reticent about exposing his hostilities to his fellow sovereigns and their representatives.

He told the Duke of Aosta: 'All the long years of my reign my colleagues the Monarchs of Europe, have paid no attention to what I have to say. Soon, with my great Navy to endorse my words, they will be more respectful.'

He bitterly reported to Theodore Roosevelt that King Edward, his mother's brother, had never visited Berlin, but had always gone to Paris and he considered this an unpardonable snub. He added that King George 'was a thorough Englishman and hates all foreigners but I do not mind that as long as he does not hate Germans more than other foreigners'.

Still, no matter what Wilhelm's personal grievances, he ordered the German army and navy to wear mourning for eight days and the German fleet in home waters to fly its flags at half-mast. And in the funeral procession Wilhelm II, Emperor of Germany, grandson of Queen Victoria, mounted on a grey horse, wore the scarlet uniform of a British field marshal and carried the baton of that rank as he rode beside King George. The Duke of Connaught, Queen Victoria's only surviving son, was on the other side – the three men led the procession and set the pace for the cavalcade of regal mourners they led through the streets of grim London. Behind them in a glass coach rode the widowed Queen Alexandra and her sister the Empress Marie of Russia, followed by the new Queen Mary and her children (two would be future kings of Great Britain) and Alexandra's two brothers, King Frederick VIII of Denmark and King George I of Greece, and her nephew King Haakon VII of Norway.

The remaining monarchs that attended the funeral came after them, seven queens and a dazzlement of 'splendidly mounted princes', as *The Times* called them: Prince Fushimi, brother of the Emperor of Japan; Prince Carl, brother of the King of Sweden; Prince Henry, consort of the Queen of Holland; and the Crown Princes of Germany, Austria, Serbia, Rumania and Montenegro; the princes of Siam and of Persia, five princes of the former French royal house of Orléans, Prince Tsia-tao of China in traditional dress, the heir to Muhammad V of Turkey and a brother of the Khedive of Egypt wearing gold-tasselled fezzes. The Indian princes wore full ceremonial dress, but the Aga Khan walked with them in a newly acquired, finely-tailored Savile Row morning suit and silk hat.

The black-clad crowds that lined the path of the funeral cortège on the hot, sultry morning of 20 May were hushed and orderly until that moment when the glorious spectacle passed by them. Jewelled orders and gold-and-silver scabbards and helmets glittered in the harsh sun; their brilliantly hued uniforms trimmed in gold braid and their crimson sashes were a shocking contrast to the mourning of some of the partici-pants and of the spectators. Seventy nations were represented in this last and greatest gathering of royalty and rank. Only a few years later some of them would disappear from the map and many of the royalty would be either dead or deposed.

The procession, accompanied by the music of several army bands combined to play Handel's 'Dead March' from *Saul* and Chopin's 'Funeral March', ended at Paddington Station where the coffin was lifted on to the royal train for the half-hour journey to Windsor, accom-panied by the royal family and all the dignitaries. At Windsor, the Aga Khan watched as it was placed on a waiting gun carriage. Blue-jackets dragged it slowly uphill to St George's Chapel, all of the long funeral procession following on foot except for one coach carrying Queen Alexandra and the Empress Marie. The most touching sight was the dead King's dog Caesar (on his collar were engraved the words: 'I am Caesar, the King's dog'), his lead held securely by a Highlander as he trotted behind the coffin, and Edward's favourite horse Kildare, with empty saddle and boots reversed in the stirrups in the traditional manner, led by two grooms.

Nobody in Europe knew what tragedy lay before them. The newly federated German Empire under Wilhelm II was emerging as a poten-tial enemy to European peace. There was, James Morris wrote, 'war in the air . . . All the symptoms were brewing; economic rivalries, patriotic frustrations, the ambitions of leaders, dynastic squabbles, the general sense that an epoch was disintegrating and could only be cleared away by violence.'

The Aga Khan felt the tension that was as thick as the English fog. He was staying as usual in his private suite at the Ritz Hotel (decorated with his own growing collection of fine European antiques) and as Great Britain was in mourning there were no social gatherings, but he met friends for dinner and the talk centred on Kaiser Wilhelm and the threat he posed.

Just a few days after the funeral, the Aga Khan received a telegram from Ginetta. Giuseppe was running a high fever and the doctors thought he had spinal meningitis. The Aga Khan hurried to Monte Carlo as quickly as he could but arrived too late. Mohammed Mahdi, age one, was dead. He was buried quietly in a small cemetery in Monaco and in the presence of only a few family members. The Aga Khan was much grieved, but Ginetta was so distraught that he remained with her for several months until her melancholy eased, her recovery helped by finding herself pregnant again.

The Aga Khan agreed that Ginetta should be in Turin with her family, where she could receive the top medical care that was not yet available in Monte Carlo. He accompanied her to see that she was well installed with a considerable staff and a private nurse in a large, cheerful apartment in a fashionable section of the city near her parents and then left for a tour of Ismaili communities. He returned in May to see that she was well. Assured that she was, he travelled to London to be present at the Coronation of George V. He was invited as an honoured guest of the King, not merely to the ceremony but to all the state banquets and receptions. He would sit in the Royal Box at the gala performances at the Royal Opera House, as well.

All his life the Aga Khan had been drawn to Great Britain by its magnificent ceremonial displays, which were later to influence his own exalted celebrations. Once again he watched from his windows in his Ritz suite as the crowds gathered for a royal procession. Everywhere he looked he saw the gleam of exotic raiment – gold braid, turbans, fezzes and uniforms from Africa, the Orient and India dispersing the greyness of the day: 22 June 1911. London was a feast of colour and a panorama of marvellous diversity among the races of mankind, and the Aga Khan was as mesmerized by the spectacle as any one of the crowds of people on the packed street below him. He arrived at Westminster Abbey by limousine at ten AM and was pleased to find his seat, one of 7000 in the fully-occupied Abbey, was directly behind the peers of the realm.

The Coronation was far grander than any living person might have witnessed. There were more troops, a greater gathering of representatives from the far reaches of the Empire, and a longer procession through the streets than there had been at Queen Victoria's Golden and Diamond Jubilees or King Edward's Coronation and funeral. The decision to go all out was made in an attempt to dispel any private fear that, with King Edward gone, the country might lose its awesome, regal presence.

Once Queen Mary, in a brilliant tiara entirely of diamonds, entered the Abbey, these apprehensions were entirely dismissed. Her deep purple velvet robes, six yards long, were dotted with ermine tails; and her gown of white satin was embroidered with gold, as were her shoes and gloves. What made her coronation robes even more spectacular was the majesty with which she wore them. Moments later King George's procession entered the Abbey, and even the grandeur of Queen Mary's entrance was surpassed for, dressed in a crimson robe of state with an ermine cape over his shoulders, he was flanked by twenty gentlemen-at-arms and his train was borne by eight scarlet-uniformed pages.

The week that followed the Coronation was filled with festivities and the Aga Khan enjoyed a great many of them. One lasting impression was a gala performance of the ballet *Pavillon d'Armide* at Covent Garden with Nijinsky and Karsavina. That evening the German Emperor sat on Queen Mary's right. 'I saw that she engaged him in earnest conversation,' the Aga Khan was to recall in his memoirs, 'and that her courtesy to him was not formal or chilly.'

The ultra-fashionables of King Edward's court and his racing set had disappeared almost entirely in the year since his death. George and Mary surrounded themselves with old and tried friends, conservatives with strong family values. The Aga Khan was not sure how he would fit in, but he held the King in high regard.

King George had none of his father's bonhomie or polished charm, although his most regal Queen more than made up for this deficiency.

And the King did have a continuing sense of Empire; he confided to the Aga Khan that he looked forward to the possibility of going with Queen Mary to India to hold a Coronation Durbar at Delhi. The Aga Khan was elated at this news, although unaware that the information had been leaked rather than confided. The King had written to Lord Morley, Secretary of State for India, several months earlier, 'I . . . trust & believe that if the proposed visit could be made known sometime before, it would tend to allay unrest & I am sorry to say, seditious spirit which unfortunately exists in some parts of India.'

While the Aga Khan was in London attending the Coronation and the social occasions spawned by it, Ginetta gave birth to a son, Aly Soloman Khan, on 17 June 1911. There was no notice in any of Turin's newspapers. With the Aga Khan still in London, four days later, as required by law, Dr Alfredo Pozzi, the obstetrician who delivered the baby, arranged for a city official to come to the house on Corso Oporto to prepare the birth certificate. Because the *muta* marriage was not accepted as legal in Italy, the boy's birth certificate stated that his mother was 'Theresa Magliano, unmarried, twenty-two years old, living on independent means'. The Aga Khan was listed as the father.[1]

The ambiguity of their situation greatly disturbed Ginetta far more than it did the Aga Khan, for she had not cast aside her European concepts when she became a Muslim. Then too, spending such a great span of time in Italy with her family brought back much of the lifelong influence of Catholic doctrine.

The Aga Khan arrived in Turin when the child was three weeks

---

[1] The birth certificate in the archives of Turin's town hall reads as follows (translated from the Italian): 'In the year 1911, 17th of June, 5 p.m. before me, Piere Carossa, acting vice-secretary of the delegation [December 31, 1909], officer of the civil government of the city of Turin, has come Dr Alfredo Pozzi, 39 years old, obstetrician, living in Turin, who declared that at 2 p.m. of the 13th of June, same year, in this house, 17 Corso Oporto, from the union of Teres [*sic*] Magliano, unmarried, 22 years old, living on independent means, here in person, as a co-declarant with His Highness the Aga Khan, son of the late Aga Ali Shah, 34 years old, born at Karachi (British India), living at Monte Carlo, was born a male baby who is not present and to whom are given the names Aly Salomone [*sic*]. To this are present as witnesses Francesca Crescio, 28 [the nurse], living on independent means, and Rosa Magliano, 39, living on independent means, both residents of Turin. The child has not been shown owing to hygienic reasons.'

old. Ginetta's brother Mario met him at the railway station. It was a hot summer day and the two white horses that pulled the carriage were shedding. The Aga Khan glowered as he brushed the hairs from his dark suit. 'Never white horses in summertime,' he said before making his way into the house to see his infant son.

Villa Terpsichore, the red-tiled Florentine mansion which he had built in Cimiez, had been ready for occupation for many months and the Aga Khan decided that Ginetta would be more contented if he could settle her and the baby there. He wrote later that he felt a great spiritual closeness to Ginetta, that it was, perhaps, the strongest love of his life. He knew she was unhappy even now that she had a healthy son and there was nothing she could want materially.

Ginetta was like a beautiful butterfly, the Aga Khan once remarked to a friend. She needed freedom but could not soar very high or fly very far. She missed her career and her family and found the Oriental approach to marriage – the man having two lives, independent and married, the wife having only the latter – difficult to accept.

Some of her conflict was resolved when she became acquainted with members of the art colony on the Riviera. After attending a sculpture exhibition she decided she would like to take lessons. Within a year she had become a promising sculptor and had built a studio in the grounds at Cimiez. Cold stone seemed a curious exchange for an attentive husband, for the Aga Khan was now occupied with a younger mistress (a pattern that would follow throughout his life). But Ginetta was markedly more cheerful, and when the Aga Khan was absent – which was more often than not – her house was filled at weekends with artists and artisans.

The Aga Khan seldom took her with him on a trip, never on a tour of Ismaili communities, and although he visited India and his mother every year, it would not be until 1923 that Ginetta would see India for the first time. This was not attributable to neglect on his part. The legality of their marriage remained clouded as long as he did not have a divorce from Shahzada that was recognized in Europe. He also fostered a nagging fear that his European wife might not be appreciated by Ismailis and his mother as he would want her to be. None the less, Ginetta was accepted as the Begum in England and on the Continent and her exclusion from his travels to the Middle East and India was a thorn in her side. She had especially wanted to travel with him to India at the time of King George and Queen Mary's visit there. Not only was she to miss the grandeur of the royal couple's Coronation Durbar, but also the investiture of the Aga Khan as Knight Grand Commander of the Order of the Star of India.

There were five days of ceremonies, processions, and tournaments before the Coronation Durbar in Delhi on 12 December 1911, at noon, with a relentless midday sun beating down on two concentric amphitheatres, the larger one constructed to accommodate 100,000 spectators, the smaller and grander one the princes, rulers and notables – the Aga Khan included – of the Indian Empire. The two amphitheatres were joined by a dais 200 feet wide. In the very centre of this construction was a series of marble step-like platforms. On the top stood two solid silver thrones encased in gold, placed (with a sense of theatre that Curzon would have appreciated) upon a cloth-of-gold carpet and beneath a golden cupola 68 feet from the ground, which ensured that the royal couple, resplendent in Imperial robes of velvet and ermine, would be seen by all.

The investiture was held that evening in an enormous, brilliantly lit state reception tent, Oriental rugs on the ground, gold cloth covering the walls and several hundred candles burning. The King-Emperor and his consort sat enthroned, a superb assemblage gathered about them. The Aga Khan looked regal in white and gold with a gold turban, which appeared to be *de rigueur* for young maharajahs or sons of maharajahs. Shortly after his investiture the electricity flickered. Suddenly one of the lights high up in the canvas canopy exploded. Whistles blew, fire engines were heard cranking up outside, officers drew their swords and hacked at the fabric hangings. The tent did not catch fire, but if it had it would have blazed like a sheet of celluloid.

The day after the Coronation Durbar, the Aga Khan presided over the Mohammedan Educational Conference (of which he was President) in Delhi. It was on this occasion that he began his lifelong commitment to Muslim education. He spoke earnestly for reform of the terrible position of Muslim women, calling the system of purdah 'the permanent imprisonment and enslavement of half the nation. How can we expect prayers from the children of mothers who have never shared, or even seen, the free, social intercourse of modern mankind?' he asked. 'This terrible cancer must either be cut out, or the body of Muslim society will be poisoned to death by the permanent waste of all the women of the nation.'

'Education, education, *education*,' he stressed. 'A great, but silent crisis has come in the fortunes of Islam, and unless this class wake up to the altered conditions of life and to the necessity of superintending and educating the rising generation, the very existence of Islam is at stake . . . an effort must now be made for the foundation of a University where Muslim youths can get . . . a knowledge of their glorious past and religion and where the whole atmosphere of the place, it being a residential University, may, like Oxford, give more attention to character than to mere examinations.'

And, as always, he was the Empire's champion. 'We have the advantage of living under a Government which administers justice evenly between rich and poor and between persons of different breed and class . . . we enjoy a complete freedom to devise plans for the amelioration of our people. We have no reason to fear that our deliberations will be abruptly closed if we propose schemes of education other than those approved by the Government. We know that no book and no branch of knowledge will be forbidden to us by official command; and lastly, we know that, under the protection of British rule, we shall be allowed to work out to the end any plans for social and economic salvation which we may devise.'

He travelled back to Bombay shortly after. King George, Queen Mary and their huge suite also returned to Bombay, where they had originally docked. The Aga Khan was among the dignitaries to see them off on the royal ship *Medina* on 29 December. Two days later, after a long visit to his mother (whom Queen Mary had met in India, commenting at the time that the old Begum's court was the grandest she had ever seen), he stood on the deck of the ship that was returning him to Europe and his wife and son. He was dressed as an English gentleman, and raised a silver-handled cane in a gesture of farewell.

7

Tucked into the Aga Khan's waistcoat pocket, no matter where he travelled, was a watch with a compass on its reverse side. With this instrument he always knew the time and the direction of Mecca. Every Friday – whether in Cimiez, any one of his three newly acquired homes (Villa Popea in Deauville, a town house in the rue de Prony in Paris or Maisons-Lafitte, an estate on the outskirts of the city), or his personal suites at the Ritz in London and at many of the most elegant hotels in Europe – he would allow one hour for meditation and prayer and, using his small watch-compass, would turn towards the holy city of Islam.

'My way of life,' he wrote at this time, 'has taken me from the slowly changing East to the West, which is ever-swiftly changing. The work I have to do keeps me, for the most time, in Europe and on the move. I am a pacifist and an internationalist. Yet I belong to no country in the West but only to many people in the East. My skin, my religion, my taste in food, my way of thinking – all these make me differ profoundly from the people among whom I move.'

As Europe in 1914 drifted toward war he became deeply concerned about Britain's security. Not only could war in Europe endanger his considerable financial interests there, but should Britain become weakened by a protracted conflict it might also cut Ismaili communities off from his guidance and block the transfer of his revenues from them to Europe where he chose to reside.

He was equally troubled over the instability of these communities. Because of their nomadic past and their insistence on holding to old customs, they continued to be outsiders in countries where they had been living for decades. As such, they were often harassed and stood in danger of becoming the butt of fanatical bigotry in times of stress.

To safeguard Ismaili communities against such violations he asked his followers to adopt the nationality of the country of their residence, adapt to local custom in dress, speak the language, and become assimilated in all but their religious beliefs. His advice could well have been born of his own experience. He continued to dress as a fashionable European and spoke the local language of the country he was in whenever possible. Now fluent in French, Italian, Spanish, German, English and several Asian languages, he was convinced that his success in social, business and political areas was due to this accomplishment. He also felt great pride in the intelligence of the Ismaili people, their superior education (due to his constant goading on this score), and their ability to change when conditions called for it.

Deciding he must carry this message personally to his people, he set out on an extensive tour of Ismaili communities in his far-spread religious realm. He left Ginetta and Aly in the luxury and park-like beauty of Maisons-Lafitte and departed on an extended itinerary in the third week of June 1914, Burma scheduled as his first stop. While on the high seas he learned that Austria's Archduke Franz Ferdinand had been assassinated on 28 June at Sarajevo in Bosnia-Herzegovina. The diplomatic manoeuvres that were to end in war had been set in motion. War talk was heard everywhere he went in Burma. He met Ismaili leaders and *mukhis* in Rangoon. They enthusiastically approved of his new policies and committed themselves to work for their fulfilment.

Despite war clouds overhead, he was in high spirits as he stepped aboard a ship for Zanzibar, his next port of call. He arrived on 4 August, the day England declared war on Germany. His first move was to meet the British Resident and offer his services to the British Government. His next was to pack up the German decorations given to him by the Kaiser (and which he often wore when in full regalia) and return them by messenger to the German representative in Zanzibar. Then he cancelled the remainder of the tour and, for security reasons, tediously voyaged to England by way of South Africa with his staff on a neutral, slow-moving steamer.

In London he met Lord Kitchener, now Britain's Secretary of State for War, and once again offered his services, dramatically telling him: 'I will shed my last drop of blood for the British Empire.' This time he was given a direct assignment. Turkey, which still ruled over the dying Ottoman Empire, was allied to Germany and was engaged in an effort to unite Muslims in a Pan-Islamic movement (a jihad, or holy war) against Great Britain and her allies, France, Serbia and Russia. They also called for all Muslims who were fighting with British troops against Germany to desert.

At this time, Turkey was 99 per cent Sunni Muslim and might well have had the power among their religious leaders to influence Muslims worldwide. If they succeeded, Great Britain's lifelines to its Empire would be blocked. What Kitchener asked of the Aga Khan was to enlist all his influential Muslim associates to support an appeal to Muslims everywhere 'not to follow the Turkish call for a jihad'.

The Aga Khan went immediately to work contacting leading Muslims (even inside Turkey) using any means of communication open to him: telephone, cable, personal emissary and – when possible – his own person to convince Muslims that their duty and best interest lay in supporting and sustaining the cause of the Allies. He pointed out that, 'The Turks had every possible chance of fair terms from the Allies, that Great Britain and France were willing to exert all their influence on Russia to safeguard Turkey's interest for the future and most important of all that neutrality would give Turkey that breathing space she needed while Europe was engaged in its grim process of self-destruction.' His efforts were rewarded and a jihad was avoided.

Lord Kitchener now enlisted him to go to Cairo. The British had long been a force in Egypt and were responsible for the neutrality of the Suez Canal. But the current Egyptian Khedive Abbas II was leaning strongly in the direction of Germany. What was needed was some-one to prop up the country's pro-British allegiance. The Aga Khan, playing his one trump card, went directly to Egypt's most powerful Muslim group, the professors of al-Azhar University, the intensely conservative and traditional theological school which is the centre of religious life for the whole of Islam. Education had always been the Aga Khan's call to arms. 'Knowledge', he repeated in many of his speeches, 'is the only talisman by which good can be distinguished from evil.'

He had fought hard for the creation of Muslim universities and had helped to found several. He campaigned for higher standards for students and teachers and almost all the men he had come to influence in Turkey had benefited greatly from his intense interest in education. He stressed to them the autocratic and illiberal attitude of the Germans who would take Muslim youths out of universities to sacrifice them on the battlefield and in return swallow up the independence Muslims now had in Egypt.

It is difficult to assess how much of the battle to keep Egypt from joining the Central Powers (Germany and her allies) the Aga Khan won for Great Britain through his influence, but the pro-German Abbas II was deposed and Egypt was declared a British Protectorate for the duration of the war. However, the Aga Khan's fame as a negotiator for Britain's cause had already reached the man on the street via the press. The *Daily Citizen*, a London afternoon tabloid, even published an anonymous poem in the form of a letter to Kaiser Wilhelm, extolling his success in Turkey:

> Just a question, Uncle Bill; have you heard of Aga Khan?
> He's as proud a prince as you are; he's the boss Mohammedan . . .
> He's a peaceful chap in India, not at all a warlike cuss;
> But he thinks he'd like to take a hand in this colossal fuss;
> And he isn't going to fight for you – he means to fight for us.
> *Aber ja*, Uncle Bill, *aber ja*.
> When the proudest prince of India lays aside his pomp and might,
> Doffs his rank and sheds his titles to join us in the fight,
> You can bet your final twenty marks our cause is pretty right.
> *Gott sei Dank*, Uncle Bill, *Gott sei Dank*.

Riddled though the rhyme was with bald inaccuracy, it did convey the Aga Khan's strong pro-British alliance and made him a hero in the eyes of the average man. This, the Aga Khan realized, placed himself and his family in a dangerous situation, inviting revenge by the Germans. He rented a house in Zurich, reasoning that neutral Switzerland would be a safe haven for his family, but soon learned that German agents were widespread in the country. British Intelligence warned him of a plot by the Germans to assassinate him and told him he must leave. But he had no sooner settled in Zurich when his vision, always poor, suddenly worsened. For a time he thought he was going blind. He was diagnosed as having Graves' disease, an extreme thyroid condition. Reluctant to leave the Swiss doctor who was treating him, he remained.

Two attempts were made on his life in Switzerland. A bomb was thrown in the path of his car, but fortunately did not explode; and poison was placed in his coffee by a German agent employed unknowingly as a waiter by his host at a dinner party (or so the ensuing Swiss police investigation asserted). Fortunately coffee was not permitted him at the time due to the medication he was on. Another guest took only a few sips of the lethal brew and had to be rushed to hospital where he was critically ill but did not die. Several suspects were arrested. The British Government insisted that the Aga Khan heed their advice and immediately leave Switzerland, promising better security for him and his family if he returned to England. Instead, he took Ginetta and Aly back to Maisons-Lafitte. And it was there, a French doctor successfully treating his Graves' disease, that he chose to use as his base without further incident throughout the war.

As a small child Aly Khan was a slender, delicate boy, inclined to nightmares and rather frightened by his father whom he saw infrequently; for the Aga Khan was continually travelling on political and religious missions, visiting Monte Carlo and Aix-les-Bains (where he kept a mistress) or living in hotel suites where he could go his own way. Attracted by the new popularity of Deauville on the Normandy coast and of the racetrack there, as a gift to Ginetta he bought the Villa Popea in the spring of 1914, just before the outbreak of war. (It was later rechristened Villa Gorizia after the town near Trieste which put up a valiant battle for survival during the hostilities.)

The war years were lonely for Aly. Ginetta found little time for him. He spent hours watching Alfredo, the Italian chauffeur, polish his mother's sleek automobiles. His Aunt Emmy taught him to dance, when she was not on the road with a ballet company, and at most times his English governess hovered over him from morning until night. He was a proud child who did not always obey. He spoke French and Italian with his mother and her family, and English with his father, whom he rarely saw and so to the Aga Khan's irritation he was not proficient in the language.

At the war's end the Aga Khan made it a ritual to arrive in Deauville on 25 July, the start of the racing season, remaining three weeks with his own staff of chef, butler and chauffeur. He liked to dress in white flannels and blue blazer in deference to the resort's English influence. Deauville had also been chosen with the hope that the temperate aspect of the seaside resort city would have a therapeutic effect on Aly, who nevertheless had almost died of Spanish influenza in Paris in the autumn of 1918.

The boy's health did finally improve, but life at Deauville seemed to lead to his becoming painfully withdrawn; a situation that was not helped by the fact that, now seven, he took his lessons with a dour English tutor, was tended by a protective English nanny and had no friends his own age.

'One of the nannies, I remember, was an ardent Roman Catholic,' a confidant of Ginetta's recalled. 'One evening the Aga Khan came in and caught nannie saying a Catholic prayer with little Aly, who was naturally supposed to be educated in the Muslim faith. There was a most frightful row . . . and that nannie left the very next day and was replaced by another nurse from England.'

It is difficult to believe that Ginetta did not know something about the Catholic nanny's habits. Without question she honoured her husband's religion. But, with the Aga Khan's frequent absence from their home, Ginetta's family, all dedicated Roman Catholics, spent a great deal of time with her and her conversion had never set well with them. Among her relatives, especially her mother Rosa and her sister Emmy, there was a consensus that Aly should be given some instruction in the religion of his mother's family.

The Aga Khan would not hear of such a thing. Still, with his long absences he had little control and he was not a man who found it easy to be in the company of children. Seeing each other so infrequently, it was not surprising that there was very little genuine intimacy between father and son. Ginetta's brother Mario recalled that the Aga Khan was 'a very grand personage. He had a high sense of authority. And when he saw Aly, it was with the governess, a warm but constrained meeting. More than this could not exist. The Aga Khan kept at a distance from people, even his own son. So there was a restraint and a suspicion. They would never show their feelings [to each other].'

But when his father arrived suddenly there would be armfuls of presents and as he got a bit older, money to spare, a quick 'fuss over him' and then he would be gone.

Early in 1914, almost before any other remodelling work was begun on the villa, Ginetta had had her studio constructed. Now professionally known as Yla (Aly reversed), she had acquired a reputation as a sculptor, had taken on several commissions and was mostly too occupied in the daytime to spend much time with her son. In the evening there was a great deal of entertaining at the sprawling red-brick villa with its wide, private, white sand beach and gaily striped yellow and white beach cabanas.

During the war years, while the Aga Khan spent most of his time shuttling between Paris, London and Aix-les-Bains, continuing what war work he could and seeing to the concerns of his followers, some trapped in war zones, Ginetta pursued her career by day and gave lavish parties in the evening, the villa's private beach and broad terraces brilliantly lighted in summer. With autumn, the venue moved to the luxurious Hotel Normandy, newly completed and almost a next-door neighbour. Its reception rooms were often used by Ginetta for grand affairs at which such ballet stars as Nijinsky, Karsavina and Pavlova (all friends of her sister Emmy, who was now a solo ballerina) danced and the great Irish tenor John McCormack sang.

Deauville during the First World War carried on much as it had during peacetime. The Hotel Royal had been turned into a French military hospital, but the Casino and the Hotel Normandy continued to receive tourists and officers on leave. In summer the beach, edged by cafés and restaurants, remained massed with umbrellas and changing cabins. Deauville also boasted a racetrack, the Hippodrome de Clairefontaine, built in the 1860s. The resort town was 120 miles from Paris and had been originally developed by a half-brother of Napoleon III; Empress Eugénie had been at the official opening. But it was not until 1912 that Eugène Cornuché, the former owner of the chic Paris restaurant Maxim, saw the possibility of Deauville's becoming a watering-place for the rich and famous. He built the Hotel Normandy on the site of a villa owned by the Duc Decazes to accommodate his former clientele, the cream of Paris society, who followed him in the summer months to Deauville. Within a year the Hotel Royal went up, a polo field and clubhouse were constructed, the Casino refurbished and the boardwalk, Les Planches, became northern France's most elegant promenade.

No swimming pool had yet been built but there were numerous Pompeiian bathing boxes with running hot water for ocean fanciers. But unlike the resorts on the Riviera, Deauville had a distinctly masculine, sporting, brandyish air. Great sums of money changed hands every night at the Casino's baccarat tables. But what really mattered at Deauville was the horse – one could not exist without the other. And it was the racing that most attracted the Aga Khan. In Deauville horses were discussed, ridden, sold, betted on, bred and worshipped.

Villas were owned by some of the richest men in France; several Rothschilds, Arpels the jeweller, the Marquis de la Tour du Pin (who had two villas). Famous entertainers like Maurice Chevalier, Mistinguett and the Dolly Sisters visited and appeared at the Casino.

One of Ginetta's close friends was Madame Charlotte Chassigneul who had a gabled, half-timbered, Normandy-style house abutting the Aga Khan's property on the rue Jean-Mermoz. Madame Chassigneul's youngest son was four years older than Aly and she would on occasion bring him with her to Villa Popea. She recalled that the little boy was reserved, 'and ruled with a rod of iron by his mother. We often used to go down to the beach together, Aly, [Ginetta], and my own son, Jacques . . . And sometimes we would motor out into the Normandy countryside and have tea while the boys ran around the fields or climbed trees . . . But I never thought [Aly] a particularly sporting type . . . he did not seem specially fond of games. I never saw him go swimming . . .

'[Ginetta] was very severe with him – much more so than I would ever have cared to be with [Jacques]. If he gave her the slightest bit of trouble she would give him a quick slap across the face to keep him quiet. But, of course, she was full of talent and temperament and was very highly-strung. Otherwise she was an extremely intelligent woman.'

Ginetta was, in fact, unhappy with her private life. Something or *someone* had come between her and the Aga Khan. He had always had mistresses, but when he was with her his attitude had been affectionate. Lately he had been cool, although as generous as always with his gifts;

her jewels were worth several fortunes, her cars were custom-built, her furs opulent. None of this satisfied her. She appeared always on edge. The lovely young ballerina had turned into a hostile, frustrated woman who seemed content only when in her studio hammering, chipping and carving away on the Italian marble she so loved to work with.

She had no talent for, or patience with, motherhood and as Aly matured into boyhood she felt threatened, as if he was the symbol of her own fleeting youth, although she was beautiful, slim, graceful and still in her twenties. Because of the war their money was often tied up or delayed in reaching them. Finances worried her and she became very frugal, carefully watching every household expenditure. Aly was to recall that when a cheque arrived from his father his mother was in the habit of riding her bicycle with it over to Honfleur, a distance of about ten miles, to deposit it in an account there. It seemed an eccentric thing to do when she could have been driven there or dropped it in the post. She was often secretive about such things and Aly was not in her confidence. But on days when she did go into Honfleur she was invariably in a good humour and to his delight returned each time with a special gift – candy, a small toy – for him.

During most of the year Aly led a lonely existence, left much to himself, subject to his mother's moods and his father's sudden appearances. Ginetta kept him away from most other children, fearful of his contracting an illness of some sort. He was educated at home by a series of Swiss tutors. As a young child he had no formal instruction in the history of the Muslim religion (although he was brought up a Muslim), nor was he taught any Eastern language. As he was under his mother's wing at this time, it can only be supposed that Ginetta was responsible for these lapses in what would seem to be mandatory subjects for the Aga Khan's son and heir. His childhood could not have been more unlike the Aga Khan's. He had little identification with Oriental culture and no understanding of his father's or his own position among the Ismaili people. He looked Mediterranean and favoured in colouring his mother, whom he adored and clung to despite her unexpected mood changes and quick temper. It was her approval that mattered to him and he tried as hard as he could to achieve it.

By 1918, Aly was seven years old and the war was moving into its final stage. His father had not been well and came to Deauville only for the racing season, spending most of his time in Paris working on a book. But the child only knew that if he saw his father rarely before, he saw him less often now. He was also too young to recognize the importance of the news on 11 November that peace had come at eleven o'clock that morning. Kaiser Wilhelm, his wife and eldest son had taken refuge in Arnhem, a port on the lower Rhine in the east Nether-lands. The war had come to a bloody end. The British Empire had lost 767,000 men; France 1,383,000; the United States 117,000; Italy 564,000; Germany 1,686,000; and Russia 1,700,000. At least 1,000,000 men were missing in action, and over 12,000,000 had suffered serious injury; many maimed, blinded, or mentally unbalanced.

With his mother, Aly rejoined his father in Paris. But the Aga Khan was now active in working with the peacemakers in the various conferences in and around the city. India had paid a high price in lives and injuries for the Allied cause and the Aga Khan felt strongly that his country's voice should be heard in the peace negotiations. He had begun his book in the winter of 1917, when a kidney condition kept him confined to a hotel suite in Geneva while his family remained in France. The book, entitled *India in Transition* and published in May 1918, was dedicated to his mother and written, he said quoting Tennyson's *Ulysses*, 'For, always roaming with a hungry heart, much have I seen and known.'

India in Transition was an ambitious work meant to give the Western world some insight into the complex Indian problem – the growing desire for self-rule. He covered a full agenda of India's position and attitudes on such varying topics as provincial reorganization, the cen-tral government, the viceroyship, the police, the judiciary, India's claim to East Africa, the status of women, British and Indian social relations and the limits of British trusteeship. His final conviction was that 'a progressive, satisfied, and happy India would be the strongest pillar, next to the United Kingdom, of the British Empire.' In closing he added: 'Britain must remember that for more than 150 years she has been the first Power of Asia, and that the position of her vigorous daughter partners, Australia, New Zealand, and South Africa, would become dangerously weak if the great base of her Eastern authority . . . India . . . were ever to fall into other hands.'

India in Transition was well received in Britain where the Aga Khan's view of India as part of a 'solid yet unchafing union, based on esteem and mutual interest, on the memory of common sacrifice for imperishable principles and the cause of liberty, will unite the foster-child [India] with the grown-up daughters [Australia, New Zealand and South Africa] of the aged and geographically small, but powerful and noble mother country . . . into one beneficent Empire under a beloved sovereign' had strong appeal. In India, where the promise of self-government was not wholly believed and where the hope for total independence was beginning to rise among its people, the dissenters were many.

The abdications of the Kaiser and all the German sovereigns, together with the emperors of Austria and Russia, had an unsettling effect on Great Britain. King George V was not at all anxious to have the Tsar and his family in England and was struggling with a decision on what he should do. Times were difficult and unstable and Britain was not blind to the problems before the country or their diminished power if they lost India. 'It is imperative,' declared Lord Cromer, a former British consul-general in Egypt, 'no stone be left unturned in the endeavour to consolidate the position of the Crown. The Crown is the link of Empire and its fate is inseparable from that of all British possessions.'

There was political agitation and violent demonstrations throughout India in the early months of 1919 following severe crop failures and an epidemic of influenza that killed millions. In Amritsar on 19 April, British troops under General Dyer fired into a crowd and killed 379 people. The massacre happened just when the Aga Khan was trying desperately to get his suggestion of a commonwealth of Asian states in association with Britain adopted by the Paris Peace Conference. Despite his efforts and intense lobbying among Britain's representatives, and his ability to calm incensed members of the Indian delegation, his plan failed.

A new Indian Hindu leader, Mohandas Karamchand Gandhi, had achieved a stature equal to Gokhale and Tilak. Gandhi had actively supported the British in the war in the hope of hastening India's freedom. With the war's end he became an adversary of Great Britain's struggle to keep India under its control and of the Aga Khan's own aspirations to make India a commonwealth country under Great

Britain. Gandhi's campaign was directed toward a free and united India. The cold-blooded use of gunfire by the British at Amritsar had played directly into his hands.

Although he still had warm and paternal feelings toward Ginetta, the Aga Khan's early passion for his wife had long since waned. Towards Aly he felt awkward, remote. Communication was not an easy thing for the boy, either. He hardly knew his father, so seldom had they seen one another during his early childhood, the war and post-war years. Instead of being sent to a boarding school, he was entrusted at the age of nine to the personal care of Charles Willoughby Waddington (Oxford classics scholar, expert horseman and formerly tutor to the sons of an Indian Muslim prince) in Maybury, Surrey, where the Oriental Institute is located.

Aly lived with Waddington and his family, including Thomas, a teenage son, in a comfortable Victorian house beside a watermill. Within a short time, 'he spoke English almost perfectly but with an accent,' Thomas Waddington recalled. 'He was keen on sports – riding and so on . . . and he was tough. We always liked him. We called him Al.'

In nearby Woking, from a priest at the onion-domed Shah Jehan Muslim Mosque (built in 1899), Aly received his first instruction in his religion, which included learning the extent of his father's power as its sacred leader. Whatever yearnings the boy cherished for a normal father–son relationship were permanently sublimated.

Left to herself now, Ginetta suffered bouts of depression. She was addressed in France, not as 'Princess' or 'Begum' (the Aga Khan was referred to as 'Prince', 'Monseigneur', or 'His [or Your] Highness') but as 'Madame Ginetta' by her own and the Aga Khan's staff. Asked once whether the Aga Khan and Ginetta were really married, his valet replied: 'Nobody knows.'

What Ginetta suspected was true. The Aga Khan had become deeply involved with an eighteen-year-old Frenchwoman, Andrée Carron. Her father was the manager of a small hotel in the French Alpine valley of Aix-les-Bains, where the Aga Khan came to take the waters at the popular local thermal spa and where he then decided to build a chalet. The curious part of this grand love affair was the fact that the Aga Khan had first been attracted to one of her three older sisters, Gabriella, who had become his mistress shortly before the war. When he was writing *India in Transition* in Paris (Ginetta having returned to Deauville), he asked Gabriella to leave her home in Aix-les-Bains and join him. She was by then in love with a local young man and refused to do so.

The Aga Khan turned to the dynamic and younger Andrée – a vivacious redhead with great flair and a wish to be a famous designer. He bought her an apartment in Paris and helped her to open a fashion house there with her other two sisters (Gabriella having married her local beau) called Maison Carron-Sœurs. He claimed that he and Ginetta continued to have a great spiritual love during this time. Perhaps that was true; the reality was that he provided lavishly for his wife, but seldom saw her. Andrée might have been his second choice, but once they were lovers he was completely obsessed with her.

Ginetta did not outwardly object. Her career was on the rise and she had been given the commission of several war memorials to execute. This also kept her away from Aly, a family situation much criticized by Lady Ali Shah who strongly believed that her son's followers should feel their Imam had provided them with a worthy successor and that he was living a happy family life. Shahzada had recently died of a lingering illness that appeared to be cancer. This meant that the Aga Khan's marriage to Ginetta could now be legalized. And so in December, 1922, heeding his mother's advice, the Aga Khan took Ginetta and Aly (now twelve) to India for the first time.

Aly stood by his father's side on deck as their ship docked in Bombay, dressed, as his father was, in Indian regalia: astrakhan hat with tassels, golden slippers, princely robes. The youth had never before worn such clothes, nor had he seen his father in anything but European dress. He did not much resemble the Aga Khan: he had Ginetta's large, dark, soulful eyes, widow's peak and handsome Roman features. But in this moment he looked very much like a young prince.

They were greeted by several thousand Ismailis, the dignitaries in golden turbans and crimson, gold-embroidered robes. 'Why have so many magicians come here?' Aly asked his father as they started down the gangplank which was covered with thick Persian carpets.

On this trip he met his grandmother. Initially frightened of Lady Ali Shah, by the end of the visit he seemed more at ease with her. He attended several *jamaat khanas* with his father. These visits proved to be an overwhelming experience, for he had never seen direct evidence of how venerated the Aga Khan was by his followers. He watched with awe as his father lifted his arm to bless them, how they fell down on their knees to him, kissed the hem of his robes.

On 23 January 1923, shortly after their arrival in Bombay, Ginetta and the Aga Khan were married in a small, quiet, legally binding religious ceremony with Aly and Lady Ali Shah present. Ginetta appeared to be extremely happy with her new station. She was addressed as Highness and referred to in the press as Begum Aga Khan. She wore magnificent saris that the Aga Khan had ordered made for her, some trimmed with glittering jewels, and was greeted wherever they went with great respect. Her sister Emmy and her friends in Deauville claimed she returned from the tour of India, where she had visited Ismaili communities in several provinces with the Aga Khan, with a beatific glow to her handsome Mediterranean features.

India, 'beautiful India', had made a great impression upon her. But even more, she had seen at first hand her husband's power over his followers and she stood in greater awe of him and saw herself as a reflection of his influence. She believed that her Eastern marriage was a turning-point in her life and that when she and the Aga returned to Europe things would be different between them. But this was not to be. Ginetta was now more alone than before. Her husband seemed just as devoted to Andrée, and Aly was sent back to England immediately after the Indian tour to intensify his religious studies.

In the Ismaili community in Surrey, Aly was treated with a new reverence difficult for the young boy to adjust to. He was separated from his mother and saw almost nothing of his father. He suffered guilt for his loneliness and for his ever-present need for affection that went either unnoticed or ignored, and which he believed betrayed his weakness of character.

The repercussions of the slaughter at Amritsar were felt not only throughout India but in many countries with large Muslim populations. British officials and residents were on the alert as anti-British sentiments rose. The Aga Khan, who was viewed as a strong supporter of Great Britain and the continuing ties of India to the Empire, was not illogically anxious about his safety and that of his entourage when he travelled in India or to other Eastern countries.

Early in 1923, shortly before he was expected to visit Zanzibar, the Ismaili community sought to equip a number of youths with a uniform and to be allowed to line the streets with them on his arrival and also to utilize them as a bodyguard during his stay. The uniform chosen resembled very closely that of the government police force and they were made to modify it. They were also told that they could not be allowed to usurp any of the duties which appertained to the police or be officially recognized. The visit of the Aga Khan did not materialize but the corps formed was maintained.

On 31 May, the Aga Khan's birthday, a serious disturbance took place in Zanzibar between the Ismaili Volunteer Corps and Shihiri Arabs caused by members of the Volunteers knocking down and trampling on an Arab, whereupon the Shihiri turned out in force and wounded thirty of the Volunteers. Legislation was immediately enacted prohibiting the wearing of dress resembling the uniform of His Majesty's forces. It was quite obvious that the British Government was more concerned about their own position than they were about the Arab–Ismaili dispute, for there was no action to disband the Volunteers.

None the less, Lord Olivier at the India Office was alarmed. A series of heated letters over this issue was exchanged between the Aga Khan and various officials in Zanzibar and at the India Office for more than a year.

In defence of his Volunteer Corps, which the Aga Khan claimed resembled the Salvation Army and had been known for years all over India as well as other parts of East Africa, he wrote to Lord Olivier from Deauville on 11 August 1924:

There are well-known hooligans from the Aden and Somali coast called Washahhari tribesmen who have attacked Ismailis at prayer and wounded about thirty of them and threatened others with death. Instead of deporting the offenders (which is the custom) the Zanzibar police did nothing to protect the Ismailis but actually let them off – every one of them . . . Not unreasonably if a man enjoys the titled rank of a Ruling Prince, he must have, in the East, the obvious and outward symbols of it, or he must give it up . . . And now this institution [his Volunteer Corps] accepted all over India even in the disturbed Frontier for 70 years is being threatened with immediate legislation [to force its dissolution] . . . The whole spirit of British governing bureaucracy in E. Africa and especially Zanzibar is hostile and jealous – despite obvious devotion of Khojas [Ismailis] to Britain . . .

. . . not only I myself since my succession in '85, but my father and grandfather before me since they came to India in 1838 have constantly rendered services to the British Government and Empire and the Sovereign . . . and we have done all we could (often at great risk to our own interests) not only to be loyal and devoted but to actively forward the policy of the British Government. In this my people have played the leading part and . . . have shown on innumerable occasions great loyalty to, and active support of, the British Empire . . . The history of the Northwest Frontier and Afghanistan and British relations with Russia in Central Asia and Persia during the last 60 years contains nothing but one long list of help and support from my people.

In India the support of my people for England has caused them to be looked upon by the disloyal classes [those who were fighting for full independence from Great Britain] with hostility. In Arabia, Syria and Egypt, during the last seventy years, my people have been regarded with suspicion by the French. Before the War in German East Africa, my people were looked at askance by Germans who hated both my followers and myself for wanting the disappearance of the German flag and the extension of British rule.

I appeal to you, Your Lordship, as a matter of justice and fair play to place the facts of this letter before the Colonial Office . . . [maintenance of the Volunteer Corps] has nothing to do with ill-will between settlers and Indians out in East Africa, but is purely between my own followers and the governing classes.

Norman Archer at the India Office, who received the above letter as Lord Olivier happened to be away at the time, attached the following note before directing it on to his superior: 'I may remind you that . . . owing to the action of the Khoja [Ismaili] community, others, such as the Ithnowhari [sic] and Arab societies have commenced forming similar cadet corps and if there is any truth in the rumour that the Zanzibar Government contemplate the abolition of the Khoja corps I should say that these corps have probably shown signs of overstepping the mark and seem likely to become a menace to peace and good order at the times of the various festivals when religious feelings run high.'

The Volunteers, wearing new uniforms, were converted into a Boy Scout Volunteer Corps and the issue resolved. But the matter did bring to the surface the ambivalent feelings the India Office had toward the Aga Khan and created for him 'a bitter strain'. Only a few months earlier he had written a twenty-four-page letter listing and expanding on what he considered to be his contributions to peace and sent it to the India Office for submission to the 1924 Nobel Peace Prize committee. The letter circulated among the top members of the India Office, and their internal memo, reveal surprising hostility.

'[His claims] are greatly exaggerated,' wrote Sir Arthur Hirtzel (India Office, Whitehall, 8 May 1924). 'His [wartime] mission to Egypt (on which he was accompanied by Sir A. A. Baig) was not conspicuously successful. That part of it which was to preach loyalty to Indian Muslim troops was a ludicrous failure – he could only speak to them through an interpreter & they laughed at him [this statement is undocumented; it is unlikely that he needed an interpreter]. His doings on the Continent were entirely private – concerned mostly with his pleasures, & the sale in Switzerland of his German securities. His relations with Indian anarchists and other Oriental riff-raff were not above suspicion . . . I had him closely watched but the result was only to confirm that he was merely an easy-going voluptuary, ready to pay for a quiet life.'

This last statement was a surprising admission. It is doubtful that the Aga Khan knew then, or ever learned, that he was under the surveillance of His Majesty's Government during the war.

Yielding somewhat, Hirtzel continues: 'The Aga Khan [did have] considerable influence . . . in the direction of obtaining easier terms for Turkey in the earlier stages of [peace] negotiation – again pursuing the recovery of his waning prestige in the Indian Muslim world. In the long run peace has resulted from giving the Turks easier terms. To that extent the Aga Khan has worked for peace. His achievements at Lausanne belong to the regime of the late Government and I would strongly urge that before the answer is given to the Norwegian [on the Aga Khan's achievements in helping to secure world peace], Lord Curzon should be consulted. Nobody else can say how much the Aga Khan really did. But however much he did I should still maintain that, not peace, but easier terms for Turkey & the exalting of the horn of Islam was what he sought.'

In the end, the Nobel Committee did not award a peace prize at their 1924 presentations. The Aga Khan was by then in another tangle with the India Office about Ismaili burial grounds in Zanzibar, which had been ceded to him by a nineteenth-century agreement that disallowed the use of the land by Zanzibar for any purpose. A government structure had been built on a park-like section and the Aga Khan wished the British Government to intervene. They refused to do so, leaving the issue to be settled between the two contestants for the land. The Aga Khan eventually won his case and the structure was torn down, but not before he had a final swipe at Lord Olivier and the India Office.

> I can assure you that nothing will hurt British prestige throughout the East more than discourteous methods in East Africa. The enemies of England (who, for that reason alone, are my enemies as well) will turn round everywhere and say: 'Look at the case of the Aga Khan. After seventy

years of devoted services to England the moment he and his followers are of no direct use they are not only thrown but kicked over by the British authorities, and that is all that can be expected when one's utility is gone.'

The glow of the Aga Khan's idyll with Great Britain was dimming, but it would never be completely lost. He remained in awe of the throne and retained his great need to be recognized by the monarch.

THE SPORT
OF KINGS

8

In the late autumn of 1926, not long before her thirty-seventh birthday, Ginetta became desperately ill and was admitted to hospital in Paris. The Aga Khan was in London, where he had bought a 61-carat diamond known as the Golden Dawn for her, although superstition had labelled the giant, flawless gem unlucky. A short time after purchasing the stone, he received word that Ginetta had taken a turn for the worse. When he arrived at the hospital the next evening, she was already dead.

Only then did he learn the truth about Ginetta's sudden illness and death, which were caused by peritonitis from an abortion she had undergone. The father of the child was her chauffeur, a young man to whom she had been drawn during her last lonely months. The Aga Khan was torn between grief and fury (which was later to turn to harsh bitterness – '*That woman*,' he would fume if she was mentioned, 'I don't want to hear her name spoken!').

Ginetta was buried in the cemetery in Monte Carlo next to the child she had lost in infancy. Aly was brought down to Monaco for his mother's funeral. He was fifteen years old and although he and Ginetta had not been close in recent years, it was not by his choice. He was later to tell close friends that he thought she was the most beautiful woman in the world and godlike in her own way; able to make a figure come to life out of stone. He was seen standing straight and apart, trying desperately to control his sobs as her coffin was lowered into the ground.

On 8 December, just ten days later, in what seems a bizarre act, the Aga Khan had his marriage to the dead Shahzada dissolved by legal decree. But it did set straight the record that he was both a divorced man and a widower and free to remarry a European woman if he so wished. For the moment he marked time.

Aly was very much alone during the next few years. His father found little time to spare for him, as his responsibilities as Imam, his tours, his continuing involvement with Indian Muslim affairs, his preoccupation with the beautiful Andrée and his love of horseracing were all-consuming. The young man remained in Surrey under tutorial guidance. In 1929, when he reached the age of eighteen, plans were made for him to go up to Oxford that autumn. He was tremendously good-looking, quite exotic with his mixed Italian and Oriental heritage; and not only had he discovered the opposite sex, women doted on him.

In March of that year, the Aga Khan wrote a letter to Colonel Patterson at the India Office asking to attend one of the Courts with Aly when he was in England that summer 'whether it is held by the Prince of Wales [the future Edward VIII] or by Her Majesty [Queen Mary]. My son Aly,' he explained, 'has now come of the age when, according to Indian custom, he can make his bow once and I would like to take him with me to the Court. He can then start his studies at the University knowing that he has done his humble duty by his Sovereign or his Sovereign's representative.'

This request set up a furore at the India Office. The question was now raised as to whether Aly was to be his father's successor and, if so, whether the government would have to continue the Aga Khan's pension to his heir. 'Headship is hereditary but it is also subject to recognition by the community,' Patterson wrote in a memo. He added that Aly was the son of a mixed marriage and therefore the India Office feared that to present him at Court 'may conceivably introduce complications in future and may imply that he is regarded as heir apparent. Perhaps, we had better consult the Government of India.'

This was considered unnecessary and on Thursday 9 May, Queen Mary received the Aga Khan and Aly at Court. Directly after the ceremony Aly was sent back to Surrey. Since Ginetta's death father and son had grown further estranged. The biographer Leonard Slater dates Aly's revolt 'that was to power his life' from this episode. 'He continued to fear the Aga,' Slater wrote, 'to respect him, often to long for his approval, but there was an undercurrent of defiance which set them at odds.'

On 24 October 1929 the Aga Khan announced his engagement to Andrée. Complications immediately arose out of the fact that Andrée's parents at first insisted upon a marriage in strict accordance with Roman Catholic ritual, which entailed the Aga Khan giving a written undertaking that he would in no way bring any pressure to bear upon his wife to alter her faith after the wedding, and that any children would remain Roman Catholic. Muslim law, however, while it permits marriage with women of other faiths, is definite about the heritage of the father not going to the children unless it has been a Muslim marriage. The law also enjoins upon the faithful the desirability of converting a wife to Islam, although it should not be insisted on against her will.

There were speculations that a great deal would be at stake if Andrée did not convert. Ismailis 'could revolt,' a writer for the *Sunderland Echo* went so far as to suggest, 'and [withhold] the tribute money they pay to receive his blessings. The enormous political influence that he has been exercising for good within the British Empire may also be materially affected.'

There was no need for concern for Andrée Carron became the Begum Aga Khan on 7 December 1929 at the Town Hall in Aix-les-Bains with two Ismaili representatives as witnesses. Andrée's parents did not insist on any guarantee that their daughter would not be required to convert to her husband's faith. On his part, the Aga Khan did not appear to have made any demands upon Andrée that she do so. And Ismailis certainly did not revolt, but generally seemed quite happy that their Imam had found a wife.

It is significant that the wedding dress the bride had specially made for the occasion was in the Aga Khan's racing colours – chocolate brown and emerald green – and that her trousseau contained mostly dresses designed in various shades of the same colours.

The Aga Khan's passion for racing had never been merely idle or transient. He had inherited his love of the sport from his grandfather and his happiest days as a young man were spent building his stables in India. The first English Derby he had attended in 1898 remained one of his most cherished memories and he would often tell the story of how he had placed a small wager of a sovereign on a horse named Jeddah who started at a hundred to one and to everybody's astonishment won the Derby. Edward, Prince of Wales, spotted him in the enclosure and called across to him with a laugh that a horse called Jeddah (the name of the port for Mecca) ought certainly to have belonged to the Aga Khan. From that time he could be seen at most important race meetings in England, on the Continent and in India.

In 1905 he met William Kissam Vanderbilt, the American millionaire, then the leading owner of prize horses in France. Vanderbilt took a liking to the Aga Khan, introduced him to his trainer William Duke (also an American), and extended to him an open invitation to visit the Vanderbilt stables, Harras de Quesnay, near Deauville and observe the training of Vanderbilt's horses whenever he wished.

That was the beginning of his relationship with Deauville, but more importantly his interest in the Vanderbilt stable instilled in him the ambition to win some of the great classic races like the French and English Derbys with a horse bred on his own stud. After his duties as Imam and his involvement in pan-Islamic problems, breeding horses became his main interest and during the pre-war years William Duke was his able teacher in learning what was involved in the making of a good horse. Under Duke's guidance he studied the conformation of thousands of sires and dams, following the history of their offspring, and became quite expert in the science.

The war interrupted his pursuit of his interest in horses and racing. It was not until the first post-war Derby was run at Epsom in 1919 that he picked up the reins of his formerly obsessive pastime. For the following two years he attended almost every important race meeting in England, France, Belgium, Italy, India and Egypt. Then, one spring evening in 1921, he was a guest at a dinner party in London given by the former prime minister Herbert Asquith and his wife Margot. He was seated next to their daughter-in-law, a racing enthusiast, who urged him vigorously to take up breeding bloodstock and racing in England and to contact George Lambton, perhaps the finest judge of racehorses of his day. Lambton, she assured him, was the very man 'to buy a few mares and yearlings' for him.

Not only did the Aga Khan meet Lambton, he gave him a large sum to purchase the finest yearlings to be had. W. K. Vanderbilt had died the previous year, but happily William Duke was still in France and now went to work for the Aga Khan as trainer. Lambton and Duke proved a formidable team. At public thoroughbred auctions in 1921 to 1924, Lambton spent about $400,000 of the Aga Khan's money. But the stakes Duke won for him (the Prix du Jockey Club, or French Derby, in 1924 with Pot au Feu, followed by a succession of top wins), stallion fees that were collected, and the high prices he made at auction with horses they sold more than balanced the budget.

The Aga Khan did not make the mistake of trying to buy Derby winners at the sales of yearlings. Very few colts were purchased, and after the initial success of his fillies, he was lucky enough to have a string of outstanding racehorses produced by them at his newly acquired stud farms at Marly-la-Ville, La Coquenne, and St Créspin. He was now the leading horse owner and breeder in France.

Duke – who had lived for thirty years in Europe – suddenly decided in 1925 to return to the United States. The Aga Khan offered him a huge sum to remain, but failed to induce him to do so. There was a succession of top trainers and breeders after Duke's departure (Richard Dawson and Frank Butters were the finest among them) and he bought an additional five stud farms in Ireland. His influence on the Islamic world remained enormous and his own followers continued to believe in his religious authority. But to the outside world he was becoming better known for his miraculous success as a horse owner than as a religious leader.

'To the Aga Khan,' a racing associate explained, 'racing was not a sport, but a business that had the immense attraction of testing his considerable mental powers to their maximum. The problems of attempting to breed champion racehorses fascinated him. When success was achieved, satisfaction was never tempered by sentiment.' Therefore it was without compunction that the Aga Khan was able to sell a Derby winner at an unprecedented price and purchase a new stud farm with the proceeds.

The new Begum Andrée did not share her husband's passion for horses, but she was wise and acquisitive enough to know that her interest in the sport, however feigned, would greatly please him and that pleasing him was the sure path to the luxuries and independent riches to which her own passions were directed. Hence the green and chocolate wedding ensemble.

When they married he was over fifty and she was not yet thirty. His mistress for more than a decade, she had accumulated a substantial amount of security in jewels (the Golden Dawn diamond ring among them), real estate, investments and hard cash. The Aga Khan has said that it took two years to get her to agree to become his wife. Andrée, however, seems to have accepted his proposal without delay; it was the terms of their contract that took so long to gain her approval. Eventually he settled $800,000 on her, as well as a house in the South of France, an apartment in Paris and various business interests in some of his international enterprises such as textiles, publishing and oil. They then set the date.

Still, despite the bridegroom's generosity, Andrée refused to convert to his faith. This meant they would be married in a civil service and that there would be no Muslim ceremony in Bombay. It was said that he offered Andrée upwards of a million dollars to adopt the Muslim faith and that her dedication to her own, which could not be bought, made him more determined than ever to make her his wife. During this last stand-off (his request for her to convert) the Aga Khan secretly went off to Nice to wait for her decision. He returned a week later to announce that the marriage would take place on 4 December with Henri Clerc, Mayor of Aix-les-Bains, officiating. Andrée countered by changing the date to Saturday, 7 December, a date she considered a luckier omen.

Aix-les-Bains, a fashionable spa in the days of Victoria's reign, nestles into the lower slopes of Mont Revard on the edge of France's largest lake, Lac du Bourget. The Avenue Victoria commemorates the royal visit of the British queen and the Boulevard Pierpont-Morgan pays homage to one of the town's most famous American millionaire guests. During the late nineteenth and early twentieth centuries, the rich, titled and famous came to take the waters. Since the war Aix-les-Bains, which was in the less accessible Haute-Savoie region of France, had lost some of its lustre but none of its natural beauty. On the morning of the wedding snow fell, covering the mountains and chilling the air, and there was something mystical and breath-catching about the panorama.

The Aga Khan and his bride were driven by limousine to the town hall where the ceremony was to be performed at ten AM. Several hundred well-wishers, or the just-plain-curious, raised their umbrellas in a cheer as they stepped out of their car into an icy drizzle – Andrée wrapped in mink, the Aga Khan in a grey overcoat and top hat. Two aides, with black umbrellas poised over the couple's heads, struggled to keep pace with them as they hurried up the stone steps of the Renaissance château that housed the town hall.

Once inside they were ushered into the mayor's sitting-room. A fire in the huge stone hearth warmed the room. Large vases of red roses had been placed on almost every surface. A tricolour and a Union Jack were side by side on a wall flanked by two windows that looked out to the snow-covered mountains. The wedding couple had now removed their outer garments. Andrée wore an emerald green, mink-trimmed dress with an impressive diamond spray pinned to the bodice (the centre stone was over twenty-five carats). A chocolate brown hat framed her artfully made-up face. Her short mink-trimmed boots, gloves and handbag were all in matching brown leather. The Aga Khan wore an English-tailored grey lounge suit with a red carnation in the lapel.

The two Ismaili representatives from Paris, Ali Yvahia Diu and Mohammed Ben Lahsei, added an exotic note to the occasion in their flowing white burnouses and turbans. Andrée's lawyer Maître Durand (who had negotiated her advantageous wedding contract), the Prefect of the Department of Haute-Savoie, M. Borel, Mayor Clerc and an interpreter (part of the proceedings were to be in Arabic) completed the bridal party. There were no friends or family members present. Before the ceremony the Aga Khan gave the mayor $8000 as a donation to the city's poor, and Clerc made him an honorary citizen of Aix-les-Bains. Those formalities dispatched, the mayor married them in a short civil rite and then stepped aside while the two *mukhis* offered prayers to Allah to 'pour the essence of his mercy on the Aga Khan, his representative on earth [this and a wedding address spoken in Arabic and then translated].'

The newlyweds went from the town hall to a wedding breakfast at a chic restaurant where their friends waited for them. An American newsreel crew filmed part of the festivities and then interviewed the

Aga Khan while Andrée sat smiling beside him, a large diamond ring, not visible before the marriage, catching the light of the cameras. It was the first time the Aga Khan had spoken on film. He avowed his happiness, replied when asked that he was confident that his horse Rustom Pasha would win the English Derby. He took Great Britain's side and deplored the violent demonstrations and mass arrests in India resulting from the stand of Mahatma Gandhi and his followers.

The public and press had been told that the bridal couple were going to honeymoon in Italy. Instead they set off in a caravan of three cars, one for themselves, the other two for their staff and luggage, to Cap d'Antibes – a journey of over a hundred miles – where Andrée's new house, La Villa Andrée, awaited her. The grandiose estate was more than she had imagined or hoped for. Their limousine passed through high, ornate gates, wound through a succession of manicured lawns and gardens and drew up to a vast pale pink Mediterranean villa with an imposing façade. The interior of the house, with its marble floors and wrought-iron doors, was equally impressive. The villa had belonged to a rich Turkish merchant and combined Oriental taste with French grandeur. Although not yet complete, several rooms were ready for their arrival and were furnished with museum pieces, fine *objets d'art*, antique Persian silk carpets, opulent draperies and sumptuous fittings.

Six weeks later, Andrée having scoured successfully for antiques to fill the rest of the house (the Aga Khan was heard to complain about the daily invasion of scores of delivery vans), they left for England where they stayed in the Aga Khan's suite at the Ritz Hotel while waiting for Derby Day at Epsom. Rustom Pasha was scheduled to race in the Derby along with Blenheim, another of his horses. For the first time Aly Khan, now nineteen, met his stepmother. They exchanged little more than a cool politeness. Aly, charming, handsome as a film star, and already well known for his eye for feminine beauty, gave no sign of open hostility, but his resentment towards Andrée was quickly discerned by close associates and Andrée herself.

'He was polite, nothing more,' she recalled. 'It was a bit difficult for me but I understood how he felt. I had been through the same thing when I was about twelve; my mother had died and my father remarried.' (Years later she was to add: 'He was always so gay and charming [as a mature man]. Who knows if he was happy or not. He was all mixed up, but I never knew what was bothering him.')

On the long-awaited day of the race, the older and younger Khan sat in the Royal Enclosure not far from King George V and Queen Mary while Andrée remained in London. The new Begum had not yet been given any status at Court and could not enter the Royal Enclosure; a situation that was most difficult for all concerned. Still, the Aga Khan would not have considered missing the meeting.

There was a great deal of excitement as the main race was set to start. To the Aga Khan's unconcealed disappointment his favoured horse Rustom Pasha appeared to fade early and to be out of the running by the time the horses reached the first turn. A horse called Diolite was leading when Blenheim, with the Aga Khan's finest jockey Harry Wragg up, shot from a rear position to challenge the leader. The crowd went wild as Blenheim pulled ahead to pass Diolite and win by a full length at 18–1. Rustom Pasha had been the favourite, and there was some grumbling that the horse might have been pulled back to ensure Blenheim won at better odds and so make his owner a good profit.

Right after the race the Aga Khan was summoned to the Royal Box. 'How much did you have on it?' the King asked with a knowing wink. 'Not a shilling, Your Majesty,' the Aga Khan replied sincerely.

The social position of the Aga Khan and his new wife not only presented a problem for the newlyweds, it was a royal and diplomatic dilemma. Letters flew like confetti back and forth between the Foreign Office, Buckingham Palace, the Lord Chamberlain's Office and the Aga Khan (who wished to have Andrée received at Court and be given the title of Her Highness). The letters, on file in the India Office Library Archives, reveal the tremendous hypocrisy that Great Britain exercised towards the Aga Khan. Neither the Foreign Office nor Buckingham Palace was ever averse to using him at any time that it served their purpose, but they often viewed him with mocking arrogance.

Before leaving for London, the Aga Khan had written to Victor Cavendish-Bentinck, the First Secretary at the British Embassy in Paris, requesting certain courtesies for his new wife and Begum. Bentinck telegraphed Sir Nevile Bland, Britain's Under-Secretary for Foreign Affairs, to help clarify the situation. Bland in turn dispatched a memo to Edmund Curry Gibson at the Foreign Office, dated 19 December

1929: 'Herewith a new horror for you. Could you very kindly tell me how to answer Bentinck?'

This led to some foraging of Foreign Office files and inter-office memos winged their way through its vast corridors. Colonel S. B. Patterson notes in one that the Aga Khan's Italian wife died three years earlier and that he divorced his previous wife, 'a Muhammadan lady whom he married many years ago on the grounds of incompatibility of temper, in other words she bored him.' He says of Ginetta: '[She was] an admirable sculptor. She was very retiring and had no wish to be present at Court or Ceremonies. So far as I know she never came to England.'

The following day Patterson sent another message to Bland adding that Andrée was now 'Her Highness the Begum (or Sultana) Aga Khan. She and her parents are from humble circumstances but as no aspersions to their characters are known, usual courtesies should be accorded. But perhaps we should refer the matter to Buckingham Palace?'

A memo dated the same day replies to a request from the British Ambassador in Paris, Lord Tyrell, as to the treatment accorded socially to the Aga Khan's new wife and whether his wife should return a call made by Andrée. 'If the new marriage of the Aga Khan is monogamous and the lady respectable, Lady Tyrell may return the call' (which seemed to leave the decision up to her).

There was a desperate note from Colonel Patterson stating that he had been to the Lord Chamberlain's Office and learnt that the King was most anxious to know as soon as possible the status and position of the Aga Khan's new wife and her Court designation. The Viceroy of India's opinion was sought. Then there were several memos referring to the anxiety of the Duke of Connaught (a Royal Duke, after all) who was in France and waiting to hear by telegraph how 'he should address the lady' (who had returned to Paris without her husband for several days).

Nothing had been settled by 27 January 1930 when Andrée arrived back in London. 'His Majesty anxious to know how the Aga Khan's wife should be addressed,' the Secretary of State nervously telegraphed the Viceroy.

'Her Highness The Lady Aga Khan would be appropriate and

unobjectionable,' was the Viceroy's reply. Colonel Patterson found this unacceptable. 'It is difficult to understand why a French woman married to a Muhammadan potentate should assume a title normally reserved for the daughters of English Dukes, Marquesses and Earls,' he wrote. Not long afterwards Patterson confides that Their Majesties (King George and Queen Mary) would be relieved not to receive the Begum in audience, something 'they do not look forward to with any great joy', and hoped she would not be 'pushing'. The Earl of Cromer, in the Lord Chamberlain's Office, at last decreed that Andrée must be styled 'Her Highness the Begum Aga Khan' for her presentation at Court, which now seemed inevitable.

It was about this time that the Aga Khan wrote Patterson a letter which he believed would pave the way for Andrée's audience (only the year, 1930, not the month, is now discernible).

As you know . . . I was married to a young European lady at Aix les Bains last December. Now, before I go further I should like to make one or two points clear. I have found that while I have no actual enemies amongst English society . . . legends – absurd and foolish but often injurious . . . get about and are half believed even by people who ought to know better. [It has been rumoured] that I have 'another Mohammedan wife in India'. This is, of course, an absurd lie . . . If I had had another wife in India and I had got married by European law in any European or non-polygamy country, I would and could be run in to prison for bigamy.

Aly's mother died and the other [wife] I divorced many years ago, my divorce being carried out under the most careful and elaborate methods known to Muslim law . . . The divorced lady sometimes continued to use my name and I drew attention legally to it as well and stopped her using it in Government circles in India.

Another legend was the invention that I met and married [my current wife] at a tea shop – not that poverty and want are in themselves in any way *inferior* conditions . . . but I would like the [British] authorities to make most careful searches about her absolute respectability and honesty in

Chambery her native town. She did work with and under her sister, a woman married to a French lawyer in Paris in the dressmaking business . . . but this was after losing all they had at Chambery and to earn her living honestly.

He underlines his '*conviction* that *only those wives* of Princes . . . should be honoured by an audience with their Majesties . . . Both [my wife] and I feel that it is our duty to request for the honour of presentation and in passing like all the other women and making her courtesy before their Majesties. Otherwise all sorts of serious stories might be started. If this is refused it will be a deliberate slur and a most unjust one on her whole past life [which] is an open book at *Chambery* and can be found out at *Chambery*. My concern is that Indians might turn this slur into further lies and legends and create problems . . .'

Finally, in May 1930, Andrée was at last presented at Court to the King and Queen. Such occasions were rigidly formal. For men, white gloves were *de rigueur* (in fact, a man would be sent home either to get them or to remain there before he would be allowed into the Throne Room without them), and they were expected to wear their ceremonial clothes or uniforms. The Aga Khan looked very different from the man who had been summoned to the Royal Box at Epsom. The Iranian attaché Nubar Gulbenkian, who was present, reported: 'There he stood [the Aga Khan] resplendent and majestic in his starspangled silk purple robe with a gold sash, the robe stretching from under his chin down to below his knees; on his head he wore a black hat the size of a lampshade.'

Andrée wore a white gown with the train beaded so that it became a shimmering silver stream as she progressed up the aisle toward the King and Queen, her head held stiffly to support a dazzling emerald tiara, long strands of emeralds around her neck like ropes of green fire in the brightness of the light.

('Andrée may have come from a humble background,' a close friend of hers told this author, 'but she became regal very quickly in her new position. She had innate class, much more than any of the Aga's other wives. When she entered a room or walked down a staircase she commanded attention and she knew exactly how to dress to further her majestic impression. She was, perhaps, too intent on financial matters, but Andrée was a staunch and loyal friend and the only true mother figure in Aly Khan's life. Andrée was especially caring toward him and often fought his cause with the Aga Khan. In the beginning he might have resented her, but Aly grew very fond of his stepmother with the years.')

The more prestigious diplomats dined later with the King and Queen. 'The doors were guarded by the Vice-Marshal of the Diplomatic Corps,' Gulbenkian recalled. 'The atmosphere was one of unqualified grandeur and opulence: gilt chandeliers, gold plate, servants in knee breeches, gorgeous liveries and powdered hair . . . champagne was served but all the labels had been washed off the bottles before the serving, for it was not considered proper that the Royal Family should advertise any particular brand of champagne.'

Having seen one of his horses win the Derby and his Begum presented at Court, the Aga Khan was ready to turn his attention to far more serious matters. India appeared on the verge of revolution; some of her ablest men were in jail, and 'the mood was so ugly,' commented the *Daily Mail*, that 'British financial resources are insufficient to hold rebellious India, and to hold it by force would be foreign to the whole genius of British rule.'

A Round Table Conference on India was scheduled to be held at St James's Palace and King George called upon the Aga Khan to help lead it with the hope that he could ameliorate a difficult situation between some of the hostile factions. When it opened, it did so under a cloud because Gandhi and the Congress Party refused to attend.

A diminutive man, not even five feet tall, Gandhi was spare to the point of looking skeletal: in his dhoti and shawl he seemed like a stick with arms, legs and an oversized head. He was truly ugly; his nose was beaklike, his ears stuck out as though they had been attached to the sides of his bald head with gum. At the age of sixty he was toothless and wore steel-rimmed glasses through which his small eyes were distorted in the magnification. And yet he radiated a kind of impish, almost naïve beauty.

Although he had qualified in London to be admitted as a member of the English bar, he had abandoned Western ways when still a young man and lived abstemiously, in accordance with Hindu ideals of asceticism, including celibacy. Born Mohandas Karamchand Gandhi, he was called Mahatma or 'Great Soul' by his followers and was perhaps the most unlikely revolutionary of the twentieth century.

He was in favour of non-violence and a free united India, yet his presence had brought violent disorder and an India torn by conflicting beliefs. His power was so great that he could exact political concessions from the British by threatening to fast unto death and was able to unify the diverse elements of the organization of the nationalistic movement, the Indian National Congress, throughout the 1920s. He was a formidable figure, already mythic, a true legend in his own time.

In 1930, shortly after the Aga Khan won his first Derby, Gandhi led a 200-mile protest march against the Indian government's salt tax. For this he was arrested and imprisoned. (Ironically, a decade later Gandhi was again arrested and the Aga Khan's Yarovda Palace in Poona was chosen to be his place of incarceration. The Aga Khan approved this plan. He did not believe in Gandhi's movement, but he saw him also as a spiritual leader and respected the man's strong principle. It seemed that Yarovda Palace was a better alternative than to send him to an Indian prison where conditions would be fairly intolerable. Gandhi lived there for nearly a year.)

'God-obsessed India had recognized in his frail silhouette, in the instinctive brilliance of his acts,' Collins and Lapierre wrote in *Freedom at Midnight*, 'the promise of a Mahatma . . . and followed where he led. He was indisputably one of the galvanic figures of the century. To his followers, he was a saint. To the British . . . he was a conniving politician, a bogus messiah whose nonviolent crusades always ended in violence and whose fasts unto death always stopped short of death's door.'

The Round Table Conference on India was conceived by Great Britain to remove Gandhi from power in India and attempt to convince him of England's good intentions. He was, therefore, released from Yerovda. After long deliberation he reluctantly gave in to mounting British pressure (to the great relief of King George and the Congress), and that of the more progressive Indian princes and Indian moderates, and agreed to return to Great Britain after an absence of over thirty years to present the Indian National Congress's case for Indian independence.

Gandhi's trip to London was many months in the planning. On 11 September 1931 he disembarked at dawn in Marseilles (to transfer to the boat-train to London) from the liner *Rajputana*, out of Bombay, and was startled by the several thousand cheering French below on the pier and by the many hundreds of clamouring and shouting European and American reporters and photographers who closed in on him in the ship's lounge as soon as the boat docked.

Finding it impossible to answer questions in the resulting bedlam, he retreated to his second-class cabin where the American correspondent William Shirer found him sprawling on his bunk, a rough homespun shawl over his skinny shoulders, his thin bare legs dangling over the side of his narrow bed. Shirer pressed him to explain what he intended to do in London.

'What he now said almost startled me,' Shirer recorded in his memoir of Gandhi, 'for his stand . . . left little chance, I thought, as I scribbled the words down, for his reaching any understanding, much less any agreement with the British government in London. He would ask the British for three things, he said:

FIRST – Complete independence of India.

SECOND – The status of India within the British Empire to be only on a coequal basis.

THIRD – Safeguards during the transitional stage, if the first two conditions are accepted.'

Explaining his position further to Shirer he added: 'My idea of independence . . . does exclude, absolutely, Dominion status. Two years ago I personally would have accepted Dominion status. Now I believe it is impossible for India.'

'Why?' Shirer asked.

'Because Dominion status, as I understand it, implies a family of nations made up of the same people. Now we are not of the same family as the English. Our race, culture and religion preclude that. We will take on a partnership with the British, but not Dominion status.'

The Conference was held at St James's Palace which was also the home of the Prince of Wales, who called it 'a rambling, antiquated structure, good only for romantic intrigue.' Indeed, Henry VIII had been besotted with love when he built the palace for Anne Boleyn and their initials were boldly entwined in the base of the Clock Tower in Friary Court. Inside, passages led to unexpected steps, which led in turn through asymmetrical hallways and rooms. It seemed an odd, intimidating place for such a delicate conference. Representatives left the building as soon as meetings adjourned and the most important discussions were conducted after the meetings at the palace in the Aga Khan's suite at the Ritz Hotel.

Gandhi did not alter his dress to fit in with Western attire, wearing as always his dhoti and – to ward off the damp, cold, foggy English autumn – a homespun shawl. He looked out of place in the grand luxury of the Aga Khan's suite, but did not seem daunted by it as the two spiritual leaders came face to face for the first time. That day the London papers had carried headlines reporting a strike by the Aga Khan's jockeys, trainers and grooms at his Irish stud farms who believed they were being grossly underpaid. Gandhi asked about this. The Aga Khan explained that he paid his top managers to run the studs and had not been aware of any problem. The Mahatma made no comment. Some of the other Muslim Conference members joined them and discussions began and were to continue on a daily basis over the next three weeks. During this time Gandhi celebrated his sixty-second birthday and observed that, the way things were going at the Round Table Conference, he would have 'to live to be as old as Methuselah'.

It was quite apparent that no agreement would be reached at the Conference's end. The British strategy to avoid any serious commitment to Indian self-rule was to keep the Hindus and the Muslims squabbling among themselves so that Britain could claim that until Indians could agree on what they wanted it was impossible for Great Britain to make any proposals even suggesting independence. Unaware perhaps that he was being used by the government further to confuse the main issue, the Aga Khan attempted to play the role of mediator between Gandhi's followers and militant Muslim groups. Ostensibly he was for future Dominion status for India, but he saw this as being quite a good way up the road. Gandhi wanted immediate independence. Most of the Muslims did not want the British to quit India before their rights were protected and secured. In such a wrangle, the

Aga Khan found himself a man caught in the middle and blocked on both sides, his position intensely frustrating, and his ability to make even the smallest headway hopeless.

There was so little news coming daily from either St James's Palace or the Ritz Hotel that the newspapers had to find side issues to write about. Gandhi's scanty attire became a main topic of conversation. He had appeared in his loincloth at Buckingham Palace to have tea with King George. Asked by an English reporter if he thought this dress was appropriate for such a regal occasion, he replied, 'The King was wearing enough [clothes] for us both.'[1]

The end of the Conference came on Thursday, 8 October. Gandhi had failed to get what he had come for: independence for India. William Shirer puts it succinctly: 'The British were not about to hand over India to the Indians.'

The Aga Khan felt distressed and humiliated over the quarrelling among his fellow Indians. He went off to Deauville to play golf, a game that he found relaxing. Then he joined Andrée in Cannes, where he received disconcerting news from London. Nothing to do with the Anglo-Indian stand-off: it was Aly, who was involved in a relationship with Lady Furness, a married woman and the current amour of the Prince of Wales. The young man's conduct was not becoming for the son of a spiritual leader and his father knew something had to be done right away before his high spirits made him a public scandal.

[1] When the future Queen Elizabeth II was to be married to Prince Philip of Greece in 1948, Gandhi sent a dhoti as a wedding present. Queen Mary (the bride's grandmother) was so incensed that she insisted that it be excluded from the display of gifts at St James's Palace, and so item 1211, *Donor Mahatma Gandhi*, was removed.

9

Lady Ali Shah made her first journey to Europe in 1932, accompanied by several ladies in her court and staying mainly in Deauville and London. Seldom seen in public, she was, however, presented to King George and Queen Mary, who were quite enchanted by her quick intelligence and elegant manner. She returned to London in May 1935, at eighty-four years old, to attend the King's Silver Jubilee. As on her previous visit, she stayed at her grandson Aly's Mayfair house rather than at the Ritz with the Aga Khan. Hotels, she said, were disquieting.

Lady Ali Shah had been insistent on her earlier visit that the Aga Khan spend more time in India and with the Ismaili communities. Now she had come to press him to become a much more important figure in East–West affairs. He was a candidate for Vice President of the League of Nations, which greatly pleased her. But her prime purpose in making her long journey at such an advanced age was her resolve that Aly should succeed his father. Lady Ali Shah had become alarmed at the growing friction between her grandson and his father. Aly's very public affairs with Lady Furness in 1934 and the free-spirited Margaret Whigham (the future Duchess of Argyll) two years earlier, and his extravagant gifts to both women, had been copiously chronicled by a fascinated press. With a grand scale Depression in progress the times were inappropriate to flaunt wealth. Yet the public had clamoured more than ever for stories about the rich, the titled, the famous, and their excesses. Hardly a day passed without an item, often including a photograph, about the youthful Aly and one of the beautiful women in London's fast and free social set appearing in the assiduously read gossip and society columns of the popular press.

Adding fuel to the fire, Aly seemed dedicated to tempting fate with his passion for speed in cars, horses and planes, he was making too public a display of his romantic life and, against the principles his father adhered to, he had affairs with married women. The Aga Khan was decidedly displeased and Lady Ali Shah suspected that her son's new wife might be more than partially responsible for the current discord between Aly and his father.

Andrée had given birth at the American Hospital in Neuilly (a suburb of Paris) to a son, Sadruddin ('Heart of the Faith'), on 17 January 1933. She was far more ambitious than Ginetta, and Lady Ali Shah suspected that she might well be laying the groundwork for her son, rather than Aly, to succeed their father, an acceptable – although not popular – alternative to Ismailis. She was greatly attached to Aly and implored him to live a less flamboyant life and to befriend his stepmother to whom he had been displaying a good deal of hostility. During this trip there were several private meetings between Lady Ali Shah, Aly and the Aga Khan. After this, Aly was more cordial to Andrée (he was later to become genuinely fond of her). The papers were filled at the time with his public wooing of a married woman with a young son, Joan Guinness, and her sensational divorce from her very rich husband. It is a strong possibility that Lady Ali Shah greatly influenced Aly in his final decision to marry the woman to whom he had brought public censure.

Honouring the Aga Khan's wish that Ismaili women discard the veil, Lady Ali Shah put hers aside while in the West but maintained the traditional Persian-style silk trousers and long gowns which she always adopted.

All her life Lady Ali Shah had been an active woman, very hardy. She had thought nothing at all of riding on a mule for hundreds of miles to reach otherwise inaccessible Ismaili communities and four years earlier had travelled overland in such a fashion from Baghdad through Persia. India had been her home since her marriage and she lived to all intents and purposes as an Indian woman. Nevertheless, her heart was in Persia, the land of her birth.

Since the time of her husband's death she had been the linchpin of her son's Imamate. It was Lady Ali Shah who, through her personal staff, kept her son's name constantly before his followers, and it was she who, after the war and until the late twenties, insisted that he pay frequent visits to India to see his people. But for the last few years he had remained in Europe. In 1930 he had sent the nineteen-year-old Aly in his place to visit Syrian Ismailis, his first tour of Ismaili communities. Lady Ali Shah met him in Beirut and acted as his mentor on the tour. Aly was immediately taken by the Syrians, bold, demonstrative people, great horsemen who had adopted the dress and swashbuckling manner of the Bedouin among whom they lived. Adoring throngs turned out to greet him wherever he went, but the Aga Khan's followers still wanted to see their Imam. This was made clear when Aly reached Bombay and revenues were noted to be steeply declining.

Lady Ali Shah refused to criticize the Aga Khan's actions in sending Aly in his place, but she had made up her mind that 'if her son would not come home [to Bombay], then she would have to go and fetch him.'

Her appearance in London, both in 1932 and during the Jubilee weeks of 1935, caused quite a stir. She even gave an interview to a London Sunday newspaper. 'I have never seen a horse-race,' she replied to a question about the Aga Khan's many winners. 'I know nothing about my son's racing, although I do know that he has always been wonderfully lucky. We of the East are fatalists, but I think his particular star must have been in the ascendant when my son was born.' The reporter next inquired about the Aga Khan's marrying a Frenchwoman and whether she had an opinion on this. 'She is my son's choice. If he loves her, then it is enough for me,' she replied tersely.

Lady Ali Shah's visit, and for that matter King George's Jubilee, took place at a time of great chaos in Europe. In February 1935, Adolf Hitler defied the Treaty of Versailles by introducing military conscription, openly creating an air force and increasing the German army to thirty-six divisions. Winston Churchill warned an uneasy Parliament that Britain was 'entering a corridor of deepening and darkening danger along which [she] should be forced to move, perhaps for months, perhaps for years'.

This gloomy outlook was at least temporarily displaced by the increasing excitement over the Jubilee, set for May. King George had been ill and was looking old and bent; he had taken to dining alone in his room because the effort of dressing for dinner was too much. His intimate friends were concerned that he might not be strong enough to endure the strain of the Jubilee. Clearly, he was a man too tired and ill for parades, but the Queen did not back down. To delay or cancel the celebrations at this late stage would instantly give rise to rumours that the King was dying.

Lady Ali Shah watched the procession on Jubilee Day, 6 May 1935, from the balcony of an Ismaili's house which was on the route. The following week she took the train to Paris for Aly's civil wedding to Joan Guinness and then returned to London to be present on 13 June at the Court Ball that was to be the climax of nearly five weeks of festivities.

London court and social circles had been buzzing during this time with rumours about the Prince of Wales and Wallis Simpson. To add to this furore, Edward had given an extraordinary speech advocating friendship with Germany two days earlier and gossip was going around the Court about his 'Nazi leanings' which had much discomfited King George and Queen Mary. Edward attended the ball alone, exchanged a few polite but cold words with his parents, and left. Moments later the King, whose health was rapidly declining (he would die only six months later), also departed.

Queen Mary sat on her throne and glanced around the magnificent brilliantly lighted ballroom at Buckingham Palace. She caught sight of the elderly Lady Ali Shah, wrapped majestically in her Indian robes and leaning on the arm of the Aga Khan. A moving moment occurred at this point, for the Queen sent for the grand old woman and had her escorted to the foot of her throne. Then she smiled, her clear blue eyes lighting up, and motioned Lady Ali Shah to the King's vacated throne beside her. Lady Ali Shah was helped up on to the dais and seated, remaining side by side with Queen Mary, to the great pride of her son, for the remainder of the evening.

But Lady Ali Shah had not travelled all this distance for the glory of being acknowledged by Britain's Queen. Not only had she been concerned about Aly and the Aga Khan's too infrequent visits to Ismaili communities, she remained the prime mover in her son's financial affairs. Age had not diminished her sharp grasp of economics, nor her ability to invest well and to avoid potential disaster. She was a shrewd and clever woman. More importantly, she was a realist and knew that unless something was done soon to tighten the bonds and loosen the purse strings of the Ismailis towards their Imam there would be a continual decline in funds. She was also troubled as to what would happen after her death. The Aga Khan had always left such things in the hands of others, but she had watched over them with a cautious eye. Aly showed no talent (or desire) for business and, after all, the Imamate was a family business.

It is not clear if Lady Ali Shah was the one who came up with the fund-raising idea of celebrating the fiftieth year of her son's Imamate in Bombay with a ceremony in which he would be given his weight in gold. What is certain is that this plan was developed and set in motion during the time of Lady Ali Shah's visit to an England observing with great enthusiasm the King's Silver Jubilee and that she was a moving force in arranging a Golden Jubilee for the Aga Khan.

There was no precedent in the Ismaili faith for a ceremony in which an Imam received his weight in gold. However, remembering old stories told in the last century, Lady Ali Shah and some of the Ismailis' most respected *mukhi* recalled the one most frequently repeated about the Maharajah Shri Bhagvatsinhji, ruler in the nineteenth century of the Indian state of Gondal, who was honoured in such a fashion. This ceremony, *tula-vidhi*, was claimed to be of Indo-Germanic origin and was performed to ensure peace, health, and prosperity to the person weighed.

There were, in fact, other tales told of the ancient years of Hinduism when monarchs were weighed at their coronations against gold from the royal treasury which was immediately dispersed to the poorest of their subjects. On the other hand the Maharajah Shri Bhagvatsinhji had not given the gold from the royal coffers but had received it from the purses of his subjects, 'the poorest vying with the wealthiest in order to provide the precious metal'. And it was from this example that a plan was drawn, the *mukhis* convincing the Aga Khan that a golden anniversary demanded 'tangible recognition, a token of gratitude from every single Ismaili alive'.

Ancient Persian kings, of course, had held open courts where they received gold and gifts from their subjects as alms. And the Aga Khans were all given bounty – food and money – during the *kahada-khuaraki*, the *jamaat khana* and every Friday. But a golden jubilee of the nature that was being planned would not only bring the Aga Khan back to India, it would attract the attention of the world press. To weigh him against gold ingots – at a time when Great Britain could no longer afford to be on the gold standard – was a stroke of sheer publicity genius.

The Aga Khan agreed that preparations should go ahead for a Golden Jubilee to be held six months later in Bombay on 19 January 1936; he subsequently claimed that most of the proceeds were distributed and used for the benefit of his followers.

Lady Ali Shah left London in July 1935, on the long sea voyage home accompanied by a large personal staff including several ladies-in-waiting, maids, a secretary and bodyguards. She was said to be in high spirits and appeared to mind the difficulties of the journey far less than any member of her vast entourage. She was a happy woman now. Her son would come to Bombay the following year. There was a plan that would bring him renewed glory and popularity, and it seemed that there was a rapprochement between the Aga Khan and Aly.

The one thing that Aly and his father had in common was a love of racehorses. Aly took this one step farther. Not only did he breed, buy and sell horses, he also rode them and had recently made a name for himself as an amateur jockey in England and France. The Aga Khan, who tried and failed over the years to interest his son in various sports, such as tennis and golf, was proud of Aly's current achievement and was present whenever possible at the races in which he rode. This brought the two closer together and Aly began to purchase horses for his father as well as himself.

The Aga Khan was in his mid-fifties, but he had not lost his eye for a beautiful woman or a thoroughbred horse. His penchant for young women had not diminished and there was a succession of youthful beauties in his life, a situation Andrée dealt with more complaisantly than had Ginetta. This could well have been because Andrée was able to enjoy all the trappings of being the Begum, rich beyond most women's dreams, and a mother. Far more social than Ginetta had been, she had little time to herself to sulk about her husband's wanderings (which she might, in fact, have welcomed); and also, never one to feed the newspapers with libidinous leads, the Aga Khan managed to handle his affairs in a discreet manner. Careful to select women unknown to the press, he was never seen in public with his mistresses – even those who were with him for long periods. His own ability to keep this side of his life private intensified his disapproval of Aly's high-stepping lifestyle. And he was concerned about the effect Aly's behaviour would have on his followers.

The Aga Khan's weight now topped 250 pounds and frequent travelling to the many Ismaili communities, from whom he collected the *das-sondh* which was responsible for his enormous wealth and for charitable contributions to the poorer members of his sect, presented great difficulty to him. Aly had made two recent trips in his place. The results had been extremely poor, justifying the Aga Khan's fears about the detrimental effect of his son's reported affairs upon Ismaili communities.

That might have been true, but certainly there were other factors including the plight of the world commodities market. The shadow of the Great Depression darkened everything. Banks had collapsed in the United States and Germany. The pound took such a steep drop that on 23 September 1931, England had to abandon the gold standard (which seemed to mark the beginning of the end of the British Empire to many historians).[1] The country recovered to some degree from the crisis by drawing out gold from India and Egypt, which were both under its control; but this in turn seriously deflated their economies. Ismailis in India, Egypt, Zanzibar and Turkey were all hurting in their pocket books.

There was still another deep-seated reason for his followers not digging deeper. There could be no doubting the Aga Khan's dedication to Muslim causes or his followers' religious devotion to him, but his life was in Europe and his allegiance seemed to be to Great Britain.

---

[1] In the gold standard countries the value of the national currency was fixed in terms of gold, and anyone could demand payment in gold. The currencies were therefore practically fixed and interchangeable. Once Britain, or any country, went off the gold standard their currencies became unstable.

His revered position as Imam could overcome such grumbling, but with Aly it was quite another matter. No outer robes could conceal his Western ties. Despite his religious schooling he had been raised as a European. In an England besotted with the glamour of the Prince of Wales and his current social set, he had become known as 'the black prince'. Ismailis took that as an insult. (In fact, the Foreign Office rejected the suggestion that he be granted the title of Prince.)[1]

The women in his life and in his bed were among the most beautiful and well known in Europe and America. He claimed he was on a small annual allowance of £600 from his father – which was true. But he had inherited his mother's wealth: her homes, and the considerable financial interests that the Aga Khan had given Ginetta during their marriage. At her death, Ginetta had left an estate of several million dollars to her only son.[2]

Not only was Aly substantially richer since his mother's death, he was 'a very handsome, very dashing young man, with great charm – the kind of charm that makes women feel important,' Thelma, Lady Furness claimed. In 1933, Thelma was the acknowledged mistress of Edward, Prince of Wales. She had been at several parties that Aly had also attended and her allure had not been lost on him. As it happened they were both in New York in late January 1934, Thelma to be with her twin sister Gloria Vanderbilt (who was involved in a complicated

[1] The British Government and the India Office were aware that Aly Khan was referred to in the press as 'Prince', although he had never used the title in any official context. In the issue of the *Ismaili* (the Ismaili community magazine) of Sunday 12 December 1937, the caption of a photograph of the Aga Khan and his son included the description: 'His Serene Highness Vali-ahed [heir to the throne] Prince Ali S. Khan'. The India Office immediately informed the Indian Government that should Aly Khan or the Aga Khan try to use the title in an official capacity, steps would be taken to 'set them right'.
[2] A great proportion of Ginetta's fabulous collection of jewellery 'disappeared' at the time of her death, much of it appropriated by her sister Emmy. Emmy Magliano's husband, the former American dancer Terence Kennedy, recalled her wearing these jewels in spite of his protests. 'One night she appeared in the wings of the theatre in Paris [where they were appearing together] with diamonds a go-go, bracelets up one entire arm. She went out on stage with them. I was furious, but that was Emmy. Nothing could be done. She still had all those diamonds after we were divorced. But I understand the Germans took them from her during the war.' Terence Kennedy later married Mathilde Marks, heiress to the Marks & Spencer fortune, and became involved with a number of philanthropic foundations which he and his wife either fostered or set up.

and scandalous custody suit[1]), Aly having been to Florida to look over some horses with an eye to adding them to his father's or his own stables. As fate would have it, Thelma and Aly were seated next to each other at a small dinner party. They saw each other again for dinner, went dancing and by the time Thelma embarked for England to be reunited with the Prince of Wales, Aly was on board ship with her.

'All this [attention],' Thelma wrote in her autobiography, 'was very gay, very flattering, particularly when it comes from a man as debonair, as decisive and as imaginative as Aly. Aly had . . . a way with women; this comes from his combination of good looks, self-assurance and sensitivity to subtleties . . . He follows in the tradition of men who sat on peacock thrones and constructed Taj Mahals for the women they loved.'

On shipboard, Thelma dined every evening with Aly. 'I hear Aly Khan has been very attentive to you,' the Prince of Wales said when they were reunited.

'Are you jealous, darling?' she asked. Edward had overcome this emotion if he ever was jealous, for Thelma was to learn that while she was away and conducting an indiscreet affair with Aly, the Prince of Wales had fallen in love with another woman, Wallis Simpson. The rest is history.

These might have been called 'the dancing years' in England. Former social barriers had been gradually broken down since the war, and that once all-exclusive body known as 'Society' had merged 'steadily if imperceptibly into that less highly-esteemed . . . association of international celebrities known as "café society".' This was the decade which saw the rise of Wallis Simpson and the fall of King Edward VIII, the golden years of film, night clubs, and the irreverent lyrics of Cole Porter and Noël Coward – private lives were becoming increasingly public.

Aly Khan fitted into these years as if they were designed especially for him. He bought a house in Aldford Street in London's fashionable

---

[1] Mrs Vanderbilt was accused by her husband's aunt, Gertrude Whitney, who was seeking custody of the child, 'Little Gloria', of 'improper conduct' between herself and Lady Milford Haven.

Mayfair and furnished it in a highly eclectic manner: serving tables in the dining room were illuminated by motorcar headlights set in the walls, antiques were placed side by side with sleek, modern pieces and the master bedroom resembled a luxury suite on an ocean liner. Slim and graceful, he was an expert dancer and seemed to require little sleep, for he pursued with enormous energy his outdoor pleasures during the day and his amorous adventures at night.

With his new coterie of friends drawn from the worlds of the social register, café society, theatre and the sports arena, and his constantly growing legend as a spirited (and conquering) Lothario, he had shed most of the outward shyness which had characterized him as a boy. Whatever he decided to do he did with tremendous enthusiasm and preparation. To become a better rider, he picked out the jockeys who were rated the best, watched them closely, cultivated their friendship and took their advice. When he entered racing as an amateur jockey he rode winners from the start. He took a house in Warwickshire, hunting country, bought one of the best horses in the sport, Clansman, and rode with the Master of the Hounds, jumping gates and hedges at the top of the hunt.

In 1931 he registered his own racing colours in England: green and red, the colours of the Ismaili flag that the Aga Khan used abroad but earlier had not been able to claim in Great Britain. A year later Aly was racing cars and learning to fly. Speed had become a way of life. He was in a car crash in January 1932 which landed him in hospital for a week. It was after he had recuperated from his injuries that he and the Aga Khan, finally responding to his mother's pleas, set out together for a tour of Ismaili communities.

Both father and son wore Indian dress on this journey, which – though it looked right and natural on the Aga Khan – had something of the appearance of a stage costume on Aly. They encountered serious problems en route and faced grave danger. There was at the time an opposition sect in India, known as the Khoja Reformers' Society, who were highly critical of the pro-British tone of the Aga Khan's speeches. Attempts were made to break up Khoja meetings at which the Aga Khan appeared and there were letters threatening assassination. On the next tour, a few months later, Aly went alone and although the trip was not shadowed by threats, it was not successful as a fund-raiser.

His father decided Aly should read for the bar (for what reason was not altogether clear, as he had had no educational preparation) and so upon his return he spent a short time in legal studies, soon realizing the profession was not for him. The difficulty he faced was not only his own lack of direction but with the view others had of him. No one took seriously any of his attempts to succeed at something – as a jockey, aviator, racing-car driver or law student. Because of his good looks, wealth and exotic background, the press had cast him in the role of romantic, carefree playboy who seemed to be in a race to see how fast he could go and how many beautiful, desirable women he could seduce on his way. After a time, Aly began to believe what he read about himself. This was, perhaps, a better alternative than dealing with the shaky uncertainty of the truth.

He had been born of parents who came from two cultures – East and West; two religions – Muslim and Catholic. His youth had been spent in isolation from other young people. At the age of fifteen he lost his mother and was inducted into the religious belief of his father's Muslim sect that the Aga Khan was a sacred religious leader; that he, himself, was a direct descendant of Mohammed and would be viewed with the same awe by his followers when he succeeded his father, an eventuality he had trouble accepting. Had he been raised in India or in any other Oriental society, he would have been better able to deal with such an exceptional situation. After all, as a child and a young man, his father had been surrounded by disciples, a mother who guided him in the direction his life had to take, and a culture that was accepting. Aly had none of these supports. He could not envision what his future was meant to be.

He was also in a religious quandary. How does one equate a father who is regarded as a saint by the tenets of your faith with a father who is a man with all man's lusts and weaknesses in the reality of everyday life? The Aga Khan had only one wife. But he also had a mistress in Paris (there would always be a succession of women who occupied that place in his life), and other women when he so desired (which was more often than one would have thought for a man of his age).

Like his father, Aly was never attracted to an Oriental woman. He was twenty-three when he fell in love deeply for the first time. She was a tall, slim English beauty, three years his senior, fair and slightly haughty and she was married. Her name was Mrs Loel Guinness, *née* Joan Barbara Yarde-Buller, daughter of Lord Churston, who was descended from King Edward III. She had been married to the Guinness heir when she was 19 and he only 20, and their wedding was the society highlight of 1927.[1]

The Yarde-Bullers were wealthy in their own right, but with her marriage Joan was now the hostess of her husband's town mansion, 11 and 12 Carlton House Terrace overlooking St James's Park, and spent summers at his parents' spectacular estate in Mougins, near Cannes in the South of France (where an airstrip had been laid down so that Loel's private plane could land), and at Deauville where they also owned a villa.

It was at a dinner party in Deauville, in the late summer of 1933, that Aly met Joan; Loel was abroad. There is a story that Aly was so taken with his first sight of her that he leaned across the table and asked: 'Darling, will you marry me?' She laughed and informed him that she was already married and the mother of a young son. That did not stop Aly. He wooed her with flowers and private, romantic messages until finally she agreed to meet him secretly. Soon they had embarked upon a very serious and all-consuming affair that culminated eighteen months later in a sensational divorce trial that made the front pages of newspapers worldwide.

Loel Guinness testified that his wife had gone off to South America at one point with Aly and that she told him she had 'formed an attachment' to him and wanted a divorce. Evidence was produced showing that Joan and Aly had occupied a suite together at a Paris hotel. The divorce was granted, custody of Joan's young son Patrick was won by Loel and Aly Khan was made to pay all court costs. The scandal was such a headline affair that Aly and Joan went off to the Bahamas to escape reporters, determined to remain sequestered on a well-guarded private estate until the final decree was handed down.

On 18 May 1936, Joan and Aly were married quietly in Paris with

[1] Thomas Loel Guinness was the only son of Benjamin Seymour Guinness, who increased the family's considerable English holdings by moving to New York in the 1890s and building a formidable empire of corporation directorships by the time of the First World War. Loel returned to his father's home in England as a young man.

the Aga Khan, Andrée, and Lady Ali Shah present and looking elegant in her jewelled sari. The bride, stylishly slim, wore a simple black silk ensemble trimmed in white, and a broad-brimmed black straw hat with a white bow that framed her narrow, piquant face. Aly was in a conservative dark double-breasted suit with a white carnation in his buttonhole. In photographs the eye is caught by the Aga Khan, rotund and smiling, his white jacket and metal-framed glasses glittering in the bright spring sun. However he might have felt about the public nature of his son's romance and winning of a bride, there is little doubt that he had great hopes that marriage and fatherhood would give Aly a sense of maturity and of his responsibilities.

Following the civil marriage, the bridal party was chauffeured across Paris to the Muslim Mosque for a religious ceremony. Persian carpets had been laid on the floor in the splendour of the Hall of Prayers where, according to Ismaili custom, the wedding couple sat on the floor. There were no guests or members of the press. Joan was given the name Tajudowlah ('Crown of the State'), not a Muslim religious name but based on Qajar royal titles; at this time she had not yet converted to the Muslim faith. They posed for photographs outside the mosque and then motored to Antibes for a honeymoon at Andrée's secluded and luxurious villa. The new Joan Khan (her title was to be a source of much contention to the British Foreign Office and not settled for a number of years) was two months pregnant and suffering from morning sickness.

As autumn approached Aly installed Joan in a rented villa, Le Soleil, in Geneva to await the December birth of their child. That month was to be a tense period for almost every British subject. King Edward VIII, besotted with Wallis Simpson, was contemplating abdication. Lady Diana Cooper, a close friend of both the King and the Aga Khan, suggested that Wallis call the Imam and ask him to speak to Edward. Lady Diana seemed convinced that he could influence the King to follow reason, not his heart. The Aga Khan was in Antibes, close to where Wallis was sequestered during those historic days. Calls were exchanged and the Aga Khan did speak to Edward, but obviously not with any success. From a disappointing attempt to dissuade the King from taking so drastic a step, discussions moved on to the possibility of Edward's going to the Aga Khan's private estate in Geneva after the dark deed of abdication was done. In the end, the ex-King decided to stay at Enzersdorf, a castle near Vienna owned by the Austrian Rothschilds.

The Aga Khan was still in Antibes but left for Geneva a few days later to welcome his first grandson, Karim, born on 13 December 1936 in a private clinic in Geneva. There was a good deal of discussion having to do with Joan's adamant choice of the child's name, which is one of the ninety-nine Muslim names for God. The Aga Khan did not like the name. 'I thought it sounded beautiful in any language, in Persian, in Arabic, in English,' Joan said in defence of her obdurate stand. Aly took her side and the Aga Khan relented.

It did not seem in any way a defeat to him, because with Karim's birth, the continuation of his line was now assured should anything happen to both Aly and Sadruddin.

10

American-born Sir Henry Channon, better known as 'Chips', was a Tory Member of Parliament, married to a Guinness and 'close enough to important events and important people' (his own words) to give his famous diaries, written over a period of thirty years, considerable social and political importance. On 8 June 1938, he wrote:

> At the Opera (Rigoletto – amazingly old fashioned and funny) I had a long talk with the Aga Khan, who told me that he thought there were only three men in Europe who wanted war: Goering, Winston Churchill, and President Benes.[1] We talked of charm, and turning to the French wife [Andrée], who is beautiful, and chic, asked her who was the most attractive man she had ever met. 'Heetlaire,' she surprisingly retorted. Evidently the dictator turned his persuasive powers on her, and obviously succeeded completely in demolishing her French prejudices.

'Chips' was assuming that, being French, Andrée would automatically dislike and distrust the Germans. However, having been raised in a tourist town like Aix-les-Bains, and by parents who ran a small hotel and were dependent upon English and German guests for their security, this was not the case. Nor did 'Chips' consider the Aga Khan's influence on his wife, for he had been won over by Hitler several years before this incident, when he had visited Germany in 1934 on behalf of Muslims of German citizenship and was assured that their interests would be safeguarded.

That would not turn out to be the case, but it must be remembered

[1] Eduard Beneš, President of Czechoslovakia, 1935–8, 1946–8.

that few Europeans actually knew what was going on inside Germany. Also, it was fashionable for politicians and well-known people to go to meet Hitler in the mid-thirties, just as it was to visit Mao Tse-tung thirty years later. Curiosity about the Führer was intense and many famous people accepted Nazi Party invitations to be their guests, as did Andrée and the Aga Khan in April 1938. They had lunch with Hitler at Berchtesgaden where, the Aga Khan reported, they talked about horses. He claimed that Hitler asked how much one of his stallions was worth.

'Thirty thousand pounds,' he replied.

The Führer then seriously enquired if he would take forty German Mercedes cars in exchange.

'What would I do with forty Mercedes?' the Aga Khan answered, further suggesting that he was not a motor salesman.

Politics, he later wrote, were not discussed. Yet he did meet Propaganda Minister Dr Joseph Goebbels, Hitler's Minister of Finance Hermann Goering and several other Nazi officials in Berlin. An effort on the part of the Nazis to charm their guests succeeded. The Aga Khan came away with an impression that they were reasonable men, that Hitler was interested only in achieving a better life for Germans, and that, unlike Kaiser Wilhelm, he was not militant.

William Shirer, by then posted in Germany as an American correspondent, believed the Aga Khan was 'extremely naive, ill-informed and easily seduced'. On his return to Great Britain, the Aga Khan 'suddenly voiced support [on the radio] for Hitler's demand that Austria and Nazi Germany should be united'. So well had the Nazis convinced him of their good intentions that it did not occur to him that the so-called *Anschluss* (the annexation of Austria to Germany) was Hitler's first step in his determination to control all of Europe by one means or another.

With monumental misjudgement the Aga Khan followed his speech on the BBC with an article in *The Times* not long before Hitler's invasion of Czechoslovakia in which he wrote, 'What Hitler has achieved required outstanding qualities. Why not take him at his word?' There were others in England who shared his view, but for anyone to have believed that Hitler was not militant as late as 1938 seems much more than naïve. Only a few short months after Hitler was made Chancellor on 30 January 1933, Nazi stormtroopers were let loose all over Germany and began a reign of violence and terror, viciously savage and brutal. From this time 'all forms of democracy were openly scorned. Germany was a kind of federation; this too was ended and all power was concentrated in Berlin. Everywhere dictators were appointed, who were responsible only to the dictator next above them. Hitler was, of course, the dictator-in-chief,' wrote the Aga Khan's countryman, Nehru, as early as 1934.

The philosophy of a dictatorship had attracted the Aga Khan's interest during the economic disaster Great Britain had suffered when the country went off the gold standard in 1931. His concept of a dictator was a leader who had the first and final word on the economic life of his followers; a solid, well-meaning businessman, of good moral character and godly leanings who, because of the power granted him (or taken by him), could shepherd his flock without interference through bad times. There was a vast and irreconcilable difference between his concept of a dictatorship and Hitler's philosophy of barbarism, suppression, brutality and disregard for human life.

Shortly after the Round Table Conference had ended in 1931, the Aga Khan was asked by the British Broadcasting Corporation to give a radio address about the benefits or impediments attached to dictatorships. The issue was then being hotly debated in Europe as Hitler's popularity rose in Germany. The Aga Khan was chosen as a speaker on the radio (there were several others giving both pro and anti opinions) because he was, by the definition of the national broadcasting company, 'a Dictator *de facto* – one whose word is bond to millions of Muslims and one whose paramount power not one of these would desire or dare to question'.

'One advantage the Dictator has is that things could not be very much worse than they are now,' he said in the first section of his speech.

> Politically we find the centre of modern civilization, Europe, not only a house divided against itself, but, if we compare it with the disastrous conditions that prevailed in the last years of the nineteenth and the early years of this century, it is actually worse.

Now there is general anarchy; no one knows what are the commitments of each State towards another, how far they are allied, and how far they are enemies. Every country's hand seems to be against its neighbour, and the clear-cut policies of the pre-War groups are unknown . . . Central Europe, and especially Germany, has been turned into a vast factory where the people are under-fed and under-paid in order to throw on the world market (in the form of reparations) goods which compete with the purely economic produce of other nations.

I should deem it my first duty as Dictator to make as nearly as can be *im*possible the overwhelming calamity of another world war, and to rectify the acknowledged errors of the peace concluded twelve years ago. To this end the demilitarization of the world by the abolition of national armies and navies would be a first essential . . . the force I would provide would be internationally owned . . . Ordinary voluntary forces could be established for aiding the police on occasions of sudden necessity.

My Dictatorship would uphold, rather than break down, national autonomy within a super-national world . . . . I would make of Germany and Austria one nation, restoring to them such truly Germanic territory as has been acquired by others.

He continues for approximately forty-five minutes to draw a picture of a godhead dictator, one man who has the world in his palm and can therefore heal all inequities; education would have a wider meaning, 'every European child being taught an Eastern language, and every Asiatic child a European language'. There would be a system to teach health, 'the laws of sex and parenthood, and on art and the life of the soul . . . and above all, direct communication with the Unseen'.

He would, he said, limit his dictatorship to twenty years, at which point, 'I should hope and believe the better world for which I had prepared would not so easily fall back into the state of spiritual, intellectual, social, political, and economic anarchy which has been the fate of mankind today.'

A great ingenuousness pervaded his words but there was also an undercurrent of sincerity. He believed strongly that people needed not only to be led, but to be told what they must do for the betterment of all. He thought Hitler and the Nazi Party could bring Germany up from the ashes of a lost war and the brink of bankruptcy and so ensure the economic balance in Europe; that it was time to forget past grievances and suspicions. His views were not popular with many in England. The horror of war with Germany was only thirteen years in the past. Still, there were certainly those who, if not pro-German, were sympathetic to the German cause. But very few would have agreed that a dictatorship – *any* dictatorship – was for the good of the people in *any* country and most would have added that a totalitarian country posed a serious threat to its neighbours.

An extensive correspondence between the Aga Khan and the India Office had begun in November 1933, over the Aga Khan's wish to be given a sizeable piece of land over which he would have jurisdiction and control (perhaps to further his vision of a dictatorship for his followers). For, although he was the indisputable leader of the vast Ismaili sect, his people had no territory of their own. The controversy continued and in October 1935 he wrote to Thomas, Earl of Willingdon, Viceroy and Governor-General of India, that he should be given a territory 'in order to give my heirs and successor a permanent influential status in India consistent with the prestige and dignity of my ancient lineage and with my family tradition of loyal and devoted service to the British Crown'. He added that his grandfather, Aga Khan I, should have been made a ruling prince for his services in Sind.

There was concern in the India Office that there would be large migrations of Ismailis to any territory the Aga Khan might be awarded. But it seems unlikely that he ever really considered the idea of transporting members of his sect from their present homes to a new land. Such a concept would have contradicted his earlier views that his followers in foreign lands should integrate in language and customs while retaining their religious beliefs. His first petition to the British Government was for territory in Sind.[1] He met Sir Samuel Hoare,

---

[1] Sind, then a part of Bombay Province, was 48,136 square miles in size (very near the area of North Carolina, the 28th largest state in the USA, larger than Scotland and Northern Ireland and 80 per cent of the area of England and Wales), with a population

Secretary of State for India, on two occasions late in 1933, to discuss the matter. Without the Aga Khan's knowledge, the India Office then researched and wrote a long account of the history of his forebears as seen by that office,[1] concluding that it seemed 'anomalous that in India the Aga Khan should desire the *status* of a ruling Prince having regard to the religious history of the Shiahs'. They were also not proposing to hand him Sind, or it would seem any other land.

A private letter from Lord Willingdon to Hoare, dated 13 February 1934, considers the social advantages of the Aga Khan's being a ruling Prince while remaining under law an ordinary Indian citizen. 'When this is conveyed to the Aga Khan, he will have nothing of it,' the Viceroy wrote; adding that he foresaw 'danger from politicians and their autonomous legislatures' if such a plan were put forth.

This communiqué appeared to stir up the entire India Office. 'I see two objections to the Aga Khan's wishes,' R. A. Butler wrote in a memo. '[i] He will be of no use to us if not a British subject; [ii] the Aly Khan does not seem worthy of this special treatment.'

Lord Willingdon dispatched a letter to the India Office on 11 March which stated that 'to make the Aga Khan a ruling prince would detract from his usefulness to Britain; to make his title hereditary would bring his son – who, I confess, is not a very desirable person [into power]. I should think it is almost certain that His Majesty [George V] would thoroughly disapprove of such a suggestion.'

---

of about 4.5 million. In 1937 it became autonomous and at the time of Partition in 1947 became part of Pakistan.

[1] The report states: 'The Aga Khan claims to be the lineal descendant of Ali through the Fatimite Caliphs . . . Ismailia doctrine, obviously developed in Alexandria from Gnostic sources, was that God was not the Allah of Islam but a transcendental being only revealed by the agency of his creature, Universal Reason (Logos). Logos begat Universal Soul (Psyche) which begat Time, Space and Matter. From the latter there came Man. Man aspired to reunite with Logos through ascending his ancestry. To assist him in doing so the divinity derived principles of Reason and Soul became incarnate in the form of the Imams, descendants of Ali and Fatima.

'The Imamate appears still to be hereditary and has been so treated by the British Government. In Sind some years ago an unsuccessful attempt was made in the Court to challenge the sole right of the Aga Khan to the offerings of the faithful, it being asserted that these were alms to be held in trust for the whole community [see ch.6]. Political officers in Western India say that the enthusiasm of the Aga Khan's followers for himself and his predecessors has not yet been evoked on behalf of his son [Aly Khan], who visited Western India last year to collect alms, but had a disappointing reception.'

Three days later another memo circulated the Political Department. 'It is my considered opinion that the Aga Khan's spiritual and religious influence is on the wane and it is unlikely his son will have any influence at all. Promotion to ruling prince would remove him from the sphere where he can be of use to us to a sphere in which he would be of no use at all. Such a promotion also involves the creation of a sham state. We have too many ridiculous states already . . . The reason he gives for making this request seems somewhat at variance with the line he has taken at the R[ound] T[able] C[onference] – the widest extension of provincial autonomy.'

On 23 March a draft letter (apparently never sent) in the archival files inquires: 'Is there any information – in light of the Aga Khan's request for territory – of his becoming King of Syria? . . . It seems to be a not very delicate form of political blackmail.'[1]

This apparently ended the Aga Khan's petition for a territory of his own. He turned his energy and his interests back to the business affairs of his Imamate, his personal finances, his stables and his family.

By the mid-thirties he had built a worldwide financial empire with main offices in Bombay, Paris, London and Geneva. He worked almost entirely at home whether he was in France, Switzerland or England, relying on assistants he trusted and who had been hired because of their business acumen (the majority were European, not Ismailis). His wealth (despite his mother's concern) was no longer dependent upon the money given to him by his followers. In Asia he controlled ten manufacturing enterprises, including jute mills and a marble factory, and there were investment trusts in Kenya, Uganda and Tanzania. He controlled newspapers and printing companies in Kenya, Uganda and Tanzania. In Ireland and France he had eight stables and stud farms and 350 horses. There were his private holdings in oil and real estate, and his numerous residences, antiques and art. These were balanced against the community institutions in Asia and Africa that he had financed and that were under his sole authority; schools, hospitals, social centres, sports grounds, housing projects and *jamaat khanas*.

---

[1] The letter backs Abdul Majid, supported by the French Government, as a more likely candidate for the throne of Syria.

Representing India's Muslim population, in 1935 the Aga Khan became actively involved in the League of Nations, which had been established at the end of World War I, its purpose the promotion of international peace and security. This was during the time of Italy's successful attack on Ethiopia, in defiance of the League's economic sanctions. He strongly believed there was no valid excuse for Italy's aggression, for there was no large Italian minority in Ethiopia deprived of their independence or civic and economic rights. But he was against sanctions, arguing that the remedy was simply to shut the Suez Canal and thereby cripple Italy's shipping industry. At a session in the League's Geneva headquarters he was voted down, but this defeat only spurred him on to work even harder to get some of his other views across.

A week before Italy's invasion of Ethiopia he had made an impassioned speech on behalf of his own native country.

'India is troubled by the League's lack of universality and by the great preponderance of energy which the League devotes to Europe and European causes,' he said. 'India is troubled by these dramatic failures [and its] criticism of the League is directed to its shortcomings and not its ideals.'

This was the same year, 1936, as his return to India for his Golden Jubilee and the year the Government of India Act, which offered the Indian provinces some local autonomy, came into being – the last major piece of Indian legislation enacted by the British Parliament until the dramatic statute in 1947 that would end the British raj in India.

He was unanimously elected President of the League in 1937 and was asked to carry on until the opening of the 1938 session in Geneva which would have meant calling and presiding over a special session, had one been found necessary (it was not).

At the end of 1937 he made an emergency flight to Bombay (which took three and a half days at the time), when Lady Ali Shah suffered a stroke shortly after her weekly ritual of a Turkish bath, Turkish and Persian massage, manicure, pedicure, and (in the Eastern fashion) a henna dye on her hair. To his great sadness her mental faculties had been badly impaired but she did recognize him. He returned in February. She died at the age of 88, half an hour before he arrived at her bedside. She had literally lived her life for him and although she had not approved of his European wives or his decision to reside abroad, she never allowed these differences to come between them. She was a strong-minded woman, mystical in her beliefs, dogged in her efforts to help her son with his Imamate and in his financial affairs which during the last years of her life had been transferred and spread between several advisers with offices in Paris and London. To her death, she remained the one person he completely trusted, however austere and demanding she had been. With Lady Ali Shah gone, there was little to draw him back to India now. In a matter of months, world conditions were to isolate him from his homeland for five years.

He stood strongly behind Chamberlain's decision in the matter of Germany's demands to control Czechoslovakia, believing with the prime minister that Great Britain would not 'be justified in going to war to prevent the Germans of Czechoslovakia from declaring their choice by plebiscite, and in consequence to compel them to remain under Czech rule.' He said he saw an almost incredibly exact analogy with the Muslim–Hindu issue in India. With hindsight he had this to say: 'I stand before history . . . as a strong, avowed supporter of Munich [and say] without hesitation that I thank God that we did not go to war in 1938 . . . In the perspective of history Britain would be seen to have gone to war, not on a clear-cut honourable, and utterly unavoidable issue, but in order . . . to prevent a plebiscite by which a regional racial majority might seek to be united with their brothers by blood, language and culture.'

Like Chamberlain, he truly believed that there would be 'peace in our time'. But a year later, on 3 September 1939, following Hitler's invasion of Poland, Great Britain and France declared war on Germany. Hitler proclaimed, 'Germany today; tomorrow the world.' Edward VIII's younger brother, now George VI, wrote in his diary that day that Hitler had gone to war 'with the knowledge that the whole might of the British Empire would be against him'. Great Britain's three self-governing Dominions, Canada, Australia, and New Zealand, indeed, rapidly joined forces. 'Once again defence of the rights of a weak State, outraged and invaded by unprovoked aggression, forced us to draw the sword,' Winston Churchill, newly-appointed First Lord of the Admiralty, declared. 'Once again we must fight for life and honour against all the might and fury of the valiant, disciplined, and ruthless German race. Once again! So be it.'

The Aga Khan listened to Neville Chamberlain making the solemn proclamation of war from London over his wireless set in the villa in Antibes. Behind Chamberlain's slow, deliberate announcement, sirens wailed their first air-raid warning. An unrelenting sun shone with much splendour on the South of France that day, and for the next ten days, and the crowds on the beaches in their gaily coloured bathing costumes were unconscious of the monstrous catastrophe that would soon engulf them.

For the moment the war seemed unreal. Nine months later a sense of shock prevailed at the Nazis' technical brilliance. By 9 June 1940, Denmark and Norway had fallen. Britain looked to France, believing the French were strong enough to stand up to Hitler's dazzling blitz-krieg tactics of heavy aerial bombardment. Three million French soldiers stood ready along the Maginot Line. The Aga Khan, Andrée, young Sadruddin and members of their domestic staff packed only the essential things that could be taken with them, and made their way to neutral Switzerland just in time. For on 22 June the Maginot Line was outflanked by German forces, the Netherlands and Belgium invaded and Luxembourg overrun. Within two weeks Allied forces were evacuated from Dunkirk and the Germans were marching into France.

At the very outbreak of hostilities in September 1939, Aly Khan, with no previous military experience, joined the French Foreign Legion because of its international nature and was sent to the Legion's desert headquarters at Sidi Bel Abbès in Algeria. A little less than a year later he was transferred out of the Legion to serve under General Maxime Weygand, Supreme Allied Commander in Syria, where his Muslim connections would be put to use. Within a few weeks Syria capitulated and Aly Khan fled over the frontier to Palestine and joined the British forces in Jerusalem. A series of telegrams on file in the India Office archives records the difficulties the British were having in finding a suitable post for Aly. 'For your [HM Consul] personal infor-mation we are finding it very difficult to place him,' one telegram complains. But on 13 November 1940 he was given a commission in HM

Land Forces as second lieutenant, to be promoted to acting major when he took up his commission. That was set in motion when, two weeks later, he was put to work in intelligence and special propaganda, speaking often to the Muslim world by radio from Beirut.

'Help Britain with everything in your power,' was his oft-repeated message. 'Eastern countries under British influence do not sufficiently appreciate the independence they enjoy. Such independence would be fictitious without Britain's armed protection . . . Speaking as a Mohammedan, I feel that whatever differences you have had with the British democracy you should remember that religious freedom and all its essential qualities have received what appears to be a death sentence in those countries which have fallen under totalitarian influences. Religious freedom and all it implies exists untrammelled in all Mohammedan countries where there is British influence.' He also made special appeals to Ismailis of the French Indian territories[1] to rally to the cause of General de Gaulle, who had escaped to London where he headed the Free French forces after the defeat of France.

Joan and Aly now had a second son, Amyn, born a year after Karim in December 1937. The two boys, only three and four years old at the time, travelled with their mother as Joan followed Aly to Beirut, Palestine and Cairo. Finally it was decided that Joan should take the children to Nairobi; they would be safe with the Aga Khan's loyal followers in Kenya. Joan stayed with them for a month and then left them there in the care of their English governess, Doris Lyon, and rejoined her husband who was now a lieutenant-colonel with the British army in Cairo.[2] The boys, meanwhile, lived a lonely but fundamentally pleasant life in a comfortable house, called Aga Khan Bungalow, with vast rolling lawns and the sound of war at a great distance.

There were not many European children in Nairobi, but as it happened Princess Elisabeth, daughter of the exiled Prince Paul of

---

[1] French possessions in India consisted of Pondicherry and Karikal in Tamil Nadu state, Yanam in Andhra Pradesh, Mahé on the Malabar coast of Kerala, and Chandannagar, an island town near Calcutta, all remnants of France's imperial ambitions in India in the 17th and 18th centuries. Not until August 1962 were these enclaves formally transferred to India.

[2] For his wartime services Aly Khan received the US Army Bronze Star and from the French both the Legion of Honour and the Croix de Guerre with palms.

Yugoslavia, was also living there and so the three children played together. The household at Aga Khan Bungalow also contained an English housekeeper, Mrs Bishop, and an Ismaili tutor, Kaderali, who taught the boys their Islamic prayers, the history of Islam and Arabic nursery rhymes.

Aly Khan managed to see his sons on rare occasions when he had a few days' leave and could find transport to Nairobi. 'It was in uniform that I first remember seeing my father,' Karim was to recall. 'I am still conscious of how impressive he was – his dynamism, his life force.'

Aly was, in fact, running away from demons within. He was a handsome man, but his skin was tinged with the pale reminder of his Persian heritage. In mixed company this had always created a problem for him and he felt quite certain that Joan's family and English friends held him in small esteem because of this. Like his father he had an eye for beautiful women and was not of a monogamous nature.

His immediate superior officer in Cairo was Colonel A. D. Wintle, and the two became great friends. 'I was told by General Wavell that the only risk I ran in having him on my team was that he was irresistible to women, could not leave them alone. And that the Germans knew it . . . I once asked him why he chose to pose as the great lover when he could have been remembered for so many better things.

'"They call me a bloody nigger," was his reply, "so I pay them out by winning all their desirable women."'

At the time Aly joined Wintle's highly-trained intelligence team they were briefed to find out if and when the Germans might send an army to reinforce the beaten Italians in the Western Desert.

> I had always been able to read the German mind and its intentions [Wintle explained], even to the point of knowing that they loved to start offensives on particular dates related to humiliating set-backs they had suffered in the Kaiser's War. I looked up my old diaries but nothing clicked . . . Very late one night I was in my caravan, sifting through great heaps of these souvenirs looking for a clue, when Aly breezed in.
>
> 'You know A.D.,' were his opening words, 'I feel in my bones that the Germans are already here.'

We sat down together and re-examined every scrap of enemy material our patrols had picked up that day, searching anxiously for the vital clue that would confirm our joint intuition.

'Look, A.D.,' he shouted. 'These have the code letter "K" on them.'

This turned out to be what they were hoping to find. There is no 'K' in Italian (the language of the confiscated papers). The K stood for Kaiser and the date after it related to the day the Germans expected to land in the Western Desert.

An assignment was then given Aly in Syria.

I got together with Aly [Wintle continued] and persuaded him that he could be a second Lawrence of Arabia – a Prince Aly Khan of Syria. He shrugged with great good humour and said that my parallel was rather unkind because he was not interested in little Arab boys . . . [Another time] we were in the Mess at GHQ . . . having a jolly game of pontoon, when three Syrian Ismailis burst in and prostrated themselves at Prince Aly's feet. At that moment I saw a different man . . . his handsome face, normally masked by a sort of cynical bonhomie, took on a gentle, pontifical, beneficent air I had not seen before . . . Aly was two people and one of them – the one the world seldom saw – was godlike in the truest sense.

Aly was not English. In fact he was a bit of a Zulu. But he was also an original, which is the highest compliment I ever pay to a foreigner.

Aly would not have been pleased with Wintle's patronizing remark. He loathed the idea of being a foreigner in any land. He thought of himself as a citizen of the world but a British patriot. He was, after all, born in Italy, brought up in France, educated in England; his father, though born in India, was a British subject and the leader of people from dozens of countries – a position he expected one day to inherit. Unlike his father, he had no sympathy towards the Germans and this created a further strain on their always difficult relationship.

He was putting his life on the line as an officer in the British army. He held British citizenship and had carried a British passport for years. Why then would Wintle consider him a foreigner?

While his son was engaged in the Allied struggle, the Aga Khan, Andrée and Sadruddin were living at the Palace Hotel in St Moritz, an elegant establishment in the spectacular setting of the Swiss Alps, mountains towering majestically in the distance. The Palace was seething with intrigue; secret agents moved in and out suspected by all but the truly blind. The hotel was home to some of Europe's richest émigrés. But many, like the Aga Khan, had been cut off from their major sources of income. Jewels were bartered and fortunes were made and lost as overseas real estate exchanged hands for ready cash.

For the first time in his life the Aga Khan was feeling the pinch.

The Germans had taken over a hundred of his finest horses when they occupied Deauville. None the less, before the occupation he had been able to transport some of his horses to his stables in India. He sold several of them for £6000 each, but the British Government froze the funds and he wrote to India's Secretary of State begging to be allowed to bring the money to Switzerland as he had his wife, young son, tutor and Indian staff to support. When permission was granted, he quickly engineered the sale of two of his most famous horses to the United States. In July 1936 the Aga Khan had sold Blenheim, winner of the 1930 Derby, to an American owner. Now he sold Blenheim's son Mahmoud, who had won the 1940 Derby only a few weeks previously, and Bahram, who had won the Derby for him in 1935, for the tremendous sum of £60,000 and asked to be allowed to bring that money to England. He claimed that the transactions were forced upon him, as his assets were frozen because of the war, but the financial straits of a multi-millionaire elicited no sympathy from British breeders, who were furious at being denied the services of two high-class stallions.

His request was placed on hold and in desperation he turned to the

Shah of Persia. In perhaps the most shocking decision of his life, he asked to be given Persian nationality (to circumvent the freeze on transfer of funds of British subjects). The Foreign Office was adamant in its attempt to dissuade him from doing such a thing (and seemingly quite certain the Shah would not be prepared to comply 'save on the basis of a resigned Iranian' – in other words, a native Iranian who wanted the return of his citizenship).

His situation grew more difficult. He had a problem with his tear ducts that further impaired his vision and had to go to Zurich for an operation, which though successful was expensive and left his eyes with a painful sensitivity. There was now a daily flurry of telegrams between the Aga Khan and Camadia Cassamalli, who represented his racing interests in India, attempting to work out a way to dispose of the stud farm in India to fund the purchase of quantities of pearls and emeralds which could be more easily exported than money.

It was at this point that the British bank worked out a method by which he could bring in the money he had made in the United States by selling the two horses. Instead of transferring cash, he was allowed to invest it in British companies and his bankers were in turn able to advance him the funds he needed. The telegrams appear to have stopped about this time and his life in Switzerland showed signs of becoming more extravagant. The Aga Khan made several trips to Cairo to see his grandchildren and to visit the Khedive, who also returned the courtesy and travelled to St Moritz.

Many interesting people passing through stayed at the Palace Hotel, so life was never dull. There were many wealthy Germans ('up to no good and without revealing how they obtained permission to leave the well-guarded confines of the Reich . . .'), among them Prince Max Hohenlohe, who sent numerous secret reports on the Aga Khan to Ribbentrop, Hitler's foreign minister. The Germans were considering the possibility of winning the Aga Khan over to their side to pass on information that might be of value to their cause.

'The Khedive of Egypt,' Hohenlohe wrote in one of his frequent letters to Ribbentrop, 'had agreed with [the Aga Khan] that on the day the Führer put up for the night in Windsor they would drink a bottle of champagne together . . . If Germany or Italy were thinking of taking over India, he would place himself at our disposal to help organize the country. He was counting for that on his well-known following and on several young maharajahs.'

The Hohenlohe letters go on to claim: 'Although the Aga Khan is not always reliable, his judgement has not been bad by any means. It should be further noted that, although he does not have his funds in England, he has placed them in such a way that he is now in Switzerland hard up for money to such an extent that he asked me whether I could afford to help him out with some cash for a while.'

At the end of this correspondence, which covers roughly two weeks, Hohenlohe concludes that because the Aga Khan had such close financial ties to Great Britain, he could not be considered trustworthy. There is strong reason to believe that Hohenlohe was manufacturing a complicated fiction involving the Aga Khan in order to guarantee his own well-being out of Germany. He was being paid to recruit partisans who could help the German cause by supplying information. No likely recruits, no pay; and more pertinent, he would be called back to Germany where life was extremely bleak and could in no way compare with the comfort and luxury of the Palace Hotel in St Moritz.

In fact, early in the war the Aga Khan maintained sympathies with Germany and felt quite confident that the Nazis would come out of the conflict the victors. He was known to advise friends to invest money in Germany and not in Great Britain or France (this was before the fall of Paris). Ginetta's old friend from Monte Carlo, Lawrence Moschietto, who had recently renewed her acquaintanceship with the Aga Khan, was living in Switzerland at the time and recalls that he tried his best to convince her of Germany's potential to win the war. Born in Monte Carlo, and since then a French citizen, she never backed down in her solid belief in the Allies and their cause.

A report reached the India Office from the Foreign Office on 14 June 1941, that the Aga Khan had travelled from Switzerland to German-occupied Paris at the invitation of Hitler. The India Office replied the following day: 'We do not believe that he [the Aga Khan] would accept an invitation from the Germans to return to Paris. But it is possible his wife may have influenced him.'

The Aga Khan had not left Switzerland, but his house in Paris had become the meeting-place for Nazis (who were occupying it). Sumptuous dinner parties were attended by German officials as well as celebrities with pro-German sympathies (Maurice Chevalier, Sacha Guitry and Danielle Darrieux were all frequent guests), but the name of the host was unknown to the India Office.

Considering the Aga Khan's lifelong pro-British views, this period of his life seems an aberration. He had been misled, or duped, or charmed by Hitler's attention to him before Britain and Germany were at war and at a time when he felt he was being treated with very little respect by the British Government. His inability to bring funds out of Britain intensified this dissatisfaction. Not until the fall of Paris on 14 June 1940 did he begin to move back to his former allegiance to Britain. From that time he became well aware, through Aly as well as his many other contacts, of the ruthless brutality of the Nazis and felt great fear for the safety of his Muslim followers in German-occupied countries, who were not the Nazis' chosen Aryans.

By 1942 there were upwards of a million Indian troops and volunteers were coming in at the monthly rate of fifty thousand. Although India escaped the horror and destruction of war, her men fought heroically in the Middle East, defended Egypt, liberated Abyssinia, played a strong role in Italy and, side by side with their British comrades, expelled the Japanese from Burma. 'The loyalty of the Indian Army to the King-Emperor, the proud fidelity to their treaties of the Indian Princes, the unsurpassed bravery of Indian soldiers and officers, both Muslim and Hindu,' Winston Churchill wrote, '. . . makes a glorious final page in the story of our Indian Empire.' Meanwhile, the two great Indian political parties, the Congress and the Muslim League, were 'either actively hostile or gave no help'. Gandhi fervently believed that Indian troops should not be fighting, that India should remain passive in the world conflict. It was towards the end of August 1942 that the Congress Party committed itself to an aggressive policy. Railways were sabotaged. Riots spread over large areas of the countryside. Britain feared that the whole war effort in India was being jeopardized at a time when they faced the possibility of a Japanese invasion.

A unanimous vote was taken in the Viceroy's Council (Lord Linlithgow was then the Viceroy) to arrest and intern Gandhi, Nehru, and the principal members of the Congress Party. The British War Cabinet quickly endorsed this policy. When the Aga Khan heard of Gandhi's arrest he got a message through to the Foreign Office offering Yarovda Palace in Poona, the scene of his first marriage, as 'alternative accommodation'. Yarovda, virtually deserted for years, was in a state of disrepair and with high windows and stone walls, a gloomy, foreboding structure. Gandhi referred to it always as 'Detention Centre, Poona' in his writings.

The moment the palace doors closed behind Gandhi (who had been allowed to keep his wife and staff with him), mob violence was set in action. Firebombs ignited police stations and government buildings, telegraph lines were destroyed and railway tracks pulled up.

For Gandhi, his stay at the Aga Khan's 'palace' was an unrelieved tragedy. His inability to stop the widespread violence, even after a long and nearly lethal fast, was a terrible blow. Then, in late December 1943, he suffered a great personal sorrow. Kasturbai, his wife of sixty-two years, called by everyone Ba or Mother, became seriously ill with chronic bronchitis. Upon learning this, the Aga Khan arranged to have penicillin and other medication sent to Yarovda. The government gave permission for her sons and grandsons to visit her. She managed to hold on precariously for nearly seven weeks while Gandhi sat by her bed day and night. Finally, as her condition grew worse, he ordered all medication and food except honey and water to be withheld.

'If God wills it,' he said, 'she will pull through, else I would let her go, but I won't drug her any longer.' She died the following day, 23 February 1944, her head resting on Gandhi's lap. She was cremated and her ashes buried inside the palace grounds, on the Aga Khan's property. Ten weeks later, on 6 May, Gandhi was released from Yarovda.

The Aga Khan was to refer to the years of World War II as the unhappiest of his life. There is little reason to doubt him. Cut off by the exigencies of war from the majority of his followers, tens of thousands of whom faced death and injury on the battlefield, he was a spiritual leader separated from his flock and the British no longer required his services. He had never before known a time when he could not have access to whatever funds he needed. His family was scattered, his son Aly in jeopardy. His health was poor; his French stables plundered; his Irish stud farms closed for the duration.

His marriage had run into problems shortly before the war and their move to Switzerland. Andrée had neither the spirituality nor the reasonableness he was perhaps looking for in a wife. She was a materialistic woman, ambitious and greatly possessive. She had accepted with a certain grace the Aga Khan's penchant for beautiful younger women and the knowledge that, despite his advancing years, he almost always had a mistress – sometimes two. But she bitterly resented any of her husband's wealth being spent on other women and she was highly incensed by the inequity of their positions; he could do as he wanted, but she had to conduct a circumspect life and silently accept his infidelity. (Although there were always rumours, quite possibly true, that Andrée was seldom left to pine alone when the Aga Khan was away from home.)

By 1943, Andrée, now in her forties, was aware that the Aga Khan was besotted with a woman nearly forty years his junior (and over a decade younger than herself) who had been his mistress for six years, and that the end of her marriage was close at hand. The Aga Khan had never found it easy to remain a lover to his wives once they had a child. Andrée was wise enough to understand that quirk in his character. But they had always had great confidence in each other's counsel and advice. Andrée had been disenchanted with the Germans much sooner than the Aga Khan – which, perhaps, had caused a schism. (He never liked his wives or mistresses to take an opposite position to his own.) However, it is much more likely that Andrée had never encountered the powerful competition and dogged determination that her husband's current mistress possessed.

The other woman was the vivacious, statuesque, beautiful Yvette Labrousse, Miss France of 1930. Born near Marseilles, the daughter of a railway porter, Yvette (and her mother, who was ambitious for her daughter to an extreme) had been determined to raise her position in life since childhood. (She once told a good friend, 'My father had no ambition; he could have been a station master.') Entered by her mother in several regional beauty pageants when she was a young girl, after winning the title of Miss France at the age of nineteen, she was seen with some of the richest men on the Riviera. The Aga Khan was one of her admirers and they had enjoyed each other's company as early as 1933. They met again in Cairo in 1937. Yvette was living there at the time as the mistress of a rich Egyptian; the Aga Khan had come to Cairo to see his Egyptian followers and to visit the Khedive. When he returned to France, Yvette followed.

Yvette actually left Cairo because she was in love with a young man she had known for years and whom she had decided she must marry. Her mother was not in the least happy about this situation and Yvette was obviously confused as to what she should do. The Aga Khan was fully apprised of the circumstances. Completely caught up in his attraction to the young woman, he arranged a meeting where they could be alone.

The story goes that he arrived at their rendezvous with an expensive leather suitcase, obviously bought for the occasion. At a propitious moment in their discussion, he opened the valise. It contained clean, new notes amounting to one million francs. There were no strings. She could walk out of the room with the suitcase that very moment. The money would still be hers, an engagement present, he told her, if she decided to marry her young man. And it would be hers with much more to come, if she decided to stay with him. How long it took Yvette to make up her mind is not known. But a short time later, in August of that year, the Aga Khan bought a property at Le Cannet overlooking Cannes, and Yvette, in whose name the property was registered, worked with architects and designers to supervise the building and decoration of a house they planned to occupy (part-time for him) together.

Apparently he had no plans to divorce Andrée at the time. Sadruddin was only five years old and his younger son's well-being was of the utmost importance to the Aga Khan. The child was, after all, a possible future heir to the Imamate. In a divorce (according to a premarital contract) his custody would remain with the Aga Khan, but at present he was still too young to be separated from his mother and Andrée could not be faulted in her maternal ability.

With the threat of the Nazi occupation of France, Yvette left their newly completed house and stayed in a hotel suite in Geneva while the Aga Khan and Andrée resided in St Moritz. The two Swiss cities were separated by a circuitous train journey which, none the less, the Aga Khan made frequently. Certainly, one of his financial pressures during his war years in Switzerland was supporting himself, his younger son, his wife and his mistress in reduced but still luxurious circumstances, when most of his funds were blocked. It was also difficult for him to adjust psychologically to such a tightly budgeted existence when he was actually one of the six richest men in Europe (he was also probably the only one of this group who, as the head of a religious sect, paid no income tax – anywhere).

As the war progressed and the end of their exile looked to be much farther off than anyone had hoped, Yvette, with her mother behind her, pressed for a more permanent arrangement while Andrée – well aware of the burgeoning power of his current mistress – grew increasingly hostile. By September 1943, the war not yet having taken a final turn towards victory, with France still occupied and fierce fighting continuing in Italy, the Aga Khan divorced Andrée on the grounds of 'mutual dislike and diversity of characters'. He claimed he still held her in high regard, but the timing of the divorce gave evidence that their relationship had reached an impossible impasse. Andrée received a generous settlement (to be paid when the Aga Khan was once again in control of his finances), remained in possession of the houses in Antibes and in Aix-les-Bains, as well as an apartment in Paris, and took a large chalet in Gstaad.

The Aga Khan had dealt with all of his wives according to the Quran, which declares, 'Woman is to be treated with equal kindness and generosity, whether she is a sharer in a man's weal or woe as wife, or one from whom he has been compelled to part company.'

During his years of exile in Switzerland, he spent many hours every day studying the Quran along with other books of Muslim theology. His attitude towards marriage and divorce was not entirely coloured by his faith, which did not recognize *muta* marriages but allowed a man to take up to four wives. Technically, he could also have concubines, but of course none of this would have been legal in the countries in which he chose to live. The mere statement that he no longer loved his wife would have been all that was necessary to secure an Islamic divorce if he swore that he had not had sexual relations with her in the preceding three months (this does not work in reverse should the Muslim wife want to divorce her husband).

Of all the Muslim sects his was among the most tolerant. It espoused the philosophy that personal serenity and happiness were the main objects of life. This apparently justified his marriages to European women, even in the case of Andrée, who although married by two high Muslim priests had never given up her Roman Catholicism. The irony was that in Andrée's faith she remained married to the Aga Khan under the laws of her religion which did not recognize divorce (she was indeed never to remarry).

In the early months of 1944, while the Aga Khan waited out his last months of exile, air warfare turned overwhelmingly in favour of the Allies, who wrought unprecedented destruction on many German cities. This powerful offensive led the way for the Allied landings in Normandy on 6 June. In August, Paris was liberated and the Germans routed from southern France. Andrée returned to Antibes to find her home in good order, for although the other houses had been occupied by the enemy it had been under the protection of Kitty Briand, a close friend of hers who was a trusted confidante of the Germans. (Her house in Aix-les-Bains also escaped harm as it had been protected by the mayor, who was to achieve notoriety and public disgrace as a collaborator.)

The way was cleared for true and late-blooming love to conquer. On 9 October the Aga Khan, for the fourth time and three weeks preceding his 68th birthday, and Yvette Blanche Labrousse, for the first time and shortly after her 35th *anniversaire*, were married in the simple parlour of the Mayor of Vevey, a town near Geneva on Lac Léman. The civil ceremony was followed by a Muslim wedding and the new Begum became Om Habibah, which had also been the name of one of Mohammed's wives. The Aga Khan preferred to call her *Yaky*, compounded from the initials of their names; the house he had built for her in France was called *Yakymour* – the last four letters from the French word for love, *amour*. They each called the other 'Yaky' in private or if in the company of family or close friends. Formally, Yvette referred to her husband as 'the Prince', and he addressed her as 'the Begum' (a title that Andrée was also allowed to use). By her staff she was called 'Highness', by friends Yaky.

The bride, willowy and six inches taller than the Aga Khan, with waving chestnut hair and glowing complexion, was a woman of great style. She possessed a quick wit and seemed able to make her husband laugh no matter what mood he was in. She had enormous zest, was a passionate skier and to everyone's amazement, even his own, the Aga Khan had a go at the sport (his enthusiasm waned in the first season when he fell, although he was not seriously harmed). The early months of 1945 were happy ones for him. And as the war news brought hope of victory before the summer he turned his thoughts to re-establishing his stables, the old horse fever rising again.

Allied victory in Europe was won on 7 May 1945, when Germany signed an unconditional surrender in Rheims. This was a period Churchill called the 'grand euphoria' of 1945. At that moment Great Britain seemed, the future prime minister Harold Macmillan wrote, 'masters of the world and heirs of the future'.

'Not only was the whole of their empire restored to them,' James Morris added, 'not only did they share with their allies the governance of Germany, Austria and Italy, but to an unprecedented degree the Mediterranean was a British lake. It was an imperialist's dream . . . With imperial armies deployed across the world, with a Royal Navy of 3500 fighting ships and a Royal Air Force of unparalleled prestige, in theory the British Empire was a Power of unparalleled prestige.'

And in a speech shortly after the German surrender, Churchill exuberantly told a London audience, 'The British Commonwealth and Empire stands more united and more effectively powerful than at any time in its long romantic history.'

That section of the Empire known as the jewel in the crown, India, thought otherwise. The unilateral declaration of war by the British Viceroy in 1939 had been bitterly resented by Indians. 'There was something rotten,' Nehru commented, 'when one man, a foreigner and a representative of a hated system, could plunge 400 million human beings into war without a slightest reference to them.'

With the end of the war in Asia on 2 September 1945, India was now set on its way to freedom. 'As long as we rule India,' Lord Curzon had said, 'we are the greatest power in the world. If we lose it we shall drop straight away to a third rate power.'

There was now to be both a historic and a difficult time in India as its people fought for independence, not all interpreting it to mean the same thing. The Aga Khan in a meeting with the British Consul in Zurich maintained the view that 'the idea of a united and independent India is as hopeless of realization as a United Europe [the various states did not share language, food, customs or religious beliefs, he claimed]. According to him, the cause of discontent in India is due to the intellectual proletariat ... His general attitude is, of course, conservative, capitalistic and a little cynical,' the Consul reported to the India Office.

The final chapter in the long story of British rule in India began on the sun-bright morning of 24 March 1947, when Lord Louis Mountbatten, great-grandson of Queen Victoria, second cousin to Edward VIII and George VI, war hero and astute admiral, destined to be India's last Viceroy, was installed upon his scarlet-and-gold throne in the ceremonial Durbar Hall of Viceroy House in New Delhi. Mountbatten firmly believed 'that it was impossible to be viceroy without putting up a great, brilliant show'. This he arranged with perhaps more pomp and panoply than even Curzon could have mustered, all designed to display an aura of power and dazzlement that would give him the upper hand in his negotiations with the Indians. Within a week he was faced with the hard truth. He had no time to lose to effect the transfer of power. 'The scene here is one of unrelieved gloom,' he wrote in his first report to Britain's new prime minister Clement Attlee on 2 April 1947. 'The only conclusion I have been able to come to is that unless I act quickly, I will find the beginnings of a civil war on my hands.'

The match that could ignite such a potential hell-fire was held in the hand of an improbable leader of India's Muslim masses, Mohammed Ali Jinnah, who would one day be called the Father of Pakistan. The Aga Khan had known him since he had come to Bombay as a young man to set up a legal practice there; they had worked together on the All-India Muslim League and the various Round Table discussions in London in the late twenties and early thirties. He admired Jinnah for his indomitable strength of character, his persistence in his cause, which was to liberate India from British colonial and imperialist domination and to obtain for Muslims a homeland of their own and separate from Hindus – although he did not agree with him on either count.

He often compared Jinnah with Mussolini, 'He would admit no superior to himself in intellect, authority or moral stature. He knew no limitations of theory or doctrine . . . In the view of both Mussolini and Jinnah, opposition was not an opinion to be conciliated by compromise or negotiation.'

Mountbatten quickly found this to be the case. He had employed a revolutionary scheme to bring his negotiations with India's leader to a speedy agreement that would spare India a bloody civil war. Talks would be initiated between himself and the four leading Indians – Gandhi, Nehru, Vallabhbhai Patel (a rabid anti-Communist) and Jinnah. He was confident at the start that the outcome would be as he believed most Englishmen wished it to be, a self-governing united India. He was determined to overcome Jinnah's desire to partition the country to create a Muslim homeland.

After winning over the three other Indian leaders, Mountbatten would later admit that in ten hours of one-to-one discussions: '[I] tried every trick I could play, used every appeal I could imagine to shake Jinnah's determination to have partition: Nothing would. Nothing . . . could move him from his consuming determination to realize the impossible dream of Pakistan.'

Mountbatten did not realize that he held the trump card. Jinnah was dying of tuberculosis, a secret he guarded fastidiously. He only had months to live. Ironically, if Mountbatten had not been in such a rush, the history of India and Pakistan might have been quite different. As it was, just three weeks after he had arrived on his mission he had his staff draw up a plan for the partition of India.[1]

The sun had gone down on Britain's Indian Empire. On the date that Pakistan's own flag flew over Karachi, India's in Delhi, Queen Victoria's great-grandson King George VI presided over a small ceremony at her beloved Balmoral Castle. Lord Listowell, the last Secretary of State for India, delivered up his seal of office to India's last emperor. From 15 August 1947, the King was no longer entitled to sign his name George RI, *Rex et Imperator*. A few days later he wrote to his mother, Queen Mary. She noted: 'The first time Bertie wrote me a letter with the I for Emperor of India left out, very sad.'

The King suffered a coronary thrombosis the night of 5 February 1952. His death was not known until his butler brought his tea early

[1] Mohammed Ali Jinnah became Governor General of Pakistan but died in 1948.

the next morning. His elder daughter, a young woman of twenty-five, was now Queen Elizabeth II, but she would never be Empress of India. The Aga Khan was no longer to be called into duty by the British or by the Indian Muslims. His political days had ended with the war, and perhaps even before then. In truth, he was no longer of particular interest or use to Great Britain once India had ceased to be under their rule. This was a hard blow to the Aga Khan, for he considered many members of the aristocracy to be his true friends and they saw very little of him from this point.

But his power within his own sect, despite his three European wives and his many years on the Continent, was not on the wane. In fact, it was about to rise again.

With the war's end came the release of the funds in the Aga Khan's financial empire. Yvette greatly pleased him and he was in high spirits, feeling well enough to make a tour to Ismaili communities in East Africa. He was given tumultuous welcomes at all the *jamaat khanas*, but he was much aware that his 'power over Muslim India had gone by default'. With the war and his long absence from India and involvement in politics, the Muslim world had grown away from him.

'In some quarters,' one observer commented, 'he was shrugged away as an old family retainer of British imperialism. Others dismissed him as a rich man from the West. The youths who had blossomed to manhood in the shadow of [the Indian National] Congress or the Muslim League thought of him vaguely, but respectfully, as an Elder Statesman who had flourished in the heyday of the British Raj and had achieved some success as a breeder of fine horses. There was no resentment against him, even among the Congress extremists. He was a prince, but without territory, and his subjects, bound to him by a voluntary spiritual allegiance, still revered him to a degree denied the more earthly maharajahs.'

The need to help unite his followers spawned the idea for a Diamond Jubilee to celebrate his sixty years as Imam. He flew from Marseilles to Cairo, where he would remain for several months to prepare for the tour, with Yvette, his long-time English secretary Freda Blane Meyer (now married), and his Ismaili assistants, a Mr Vaziea Eboo and a Mr Ismaili Abdulla. Each filled out excess baggage customs forms that added up to over a hundred pieces (although listed as '. . . probably a small amount of excess baggage').

This time, in an even more glittering ceremony than his Golden Jubilee, he would be presented with his weight in diamonds on 10 March 1946 in Bombay's Brabourne Stadium which could accommodate 100,000 people. The Diamond Jubilee committee now went a step farther. There would be a second celebration and weighing to be held on 18 August in Dar es Salaam. Such a grand double event was certain to receive world coverage and give the Aga Khan's name fresh lustre. It would also bring Ismaili Muslims together in both Asia and Africa, raise funds for their benefit, and help his people to put the great sacrifices of the war behind them.

Partition was more than a year in the future. There were endless bloody clashes between Muslims and Hindus, but the Aga Khan felt himself and his people immune from such horror and continued with his arrangements. For eight weeks before the Diamond Jubilee was scheduled he and the Jubilee Committee worked diligently. The new Begum, Aly Khan (now out of the service and living in France) and Sadruddin were all to join him on this unprecedented celebratory trip. No other religious leader was known to have sponsored such an event. There was, of course, Queen Victoria's Diamond Jubilee (which remained a vivid memory of the Aga Khan's for he often recalled it to associates). But brilliant occasion that it was, there had been nothing as exotic as the proposed weighing in diamonds of the Aga Khan.

For days before the Aga Khan's arrival in Bombay, crowds had been gathering under an unyielding sun in Brabourne Stadium. Vast camps outside sheltered 60,000 people from all over India. On the designated day, thousands more plodded barefoot or glided in limousines to join them. They had already waited eight hours past the appointed time in almost unbearable heat. Food vendors made the most of the delay and the scarlet-turbaned servants of the rich and titled ran back and forth to find appropriate fare to serve to their masters. The ceremony was held up by a serious hitch. The crowds were ready. The Aga Khan and his family were dressed and set to leave Malabar when told to do so. But the diamonds had not arrived.

Lent for the occasion by the Diamond Control Committee of the

British Board of Trade, and packed and sealed in eighteen steel boxes, they had left on schedule from England aboard HMS *Derbyshire*. But the ship had been diverted to Karachi in the early hours of the morning, before its expected arrival in Bombay, to await government clearance. The delay would have meant a postponement of the ceremony. Aly Khan got on the telephone and arranged for a plane carrying armed guards to be dispatched to Karachi to collect the diamonds.

Meanwhile, inside Brabourne Stadium, the assembled spectators (in seats that cost from £1000 for those near the dais to small change for those at the top of the grandstands) sat beneath brightly-coloured umbrellas to ward off the heat. Women were dressed in highly decorated saris. The exotic costumes and uniforms worn by the male delegations from the Aga Khan's disciples in Syria, Lebanon, South Africa, Madagascar, Iraq, Persia, Central Asia, Burma and Zanzibar were reminiscent of the troops and deputations that attended Victoria's Golden and Diamond Jubilees and the many brilliant Indian Durbars held earlier in the century. The air screamed and jangled with the wailing half-tones of Oriental music played through shattering amplifiers by a band dressed in colourful native costumes. Over all shone the grilling sun.

The ringside seats held what seemed to be the entire, glorious contingent of the representatives of the Indian royal heritage; fourteen ruling princes, including the Maharajah of Kashmir, the Maharajah of Baroda, the Nawab of Cambay, the Samsaheb of Nawanagar, the Maharajah of Porbander, the Nawab of Chatari, the Tikasaheb of Karpurthala and their wives and children, adorned in exquisite gilded fabrics and wearing fortunes in jewels.

It was nearly six PM when the Aga Khan arrived seated in an open vehicle with the Begum Yvette beside him; Aly Khan and Sadruddin, both in white robes and black astrakhan hats, in a second open car directly behind them. A great cheer rose and echoed in the stadium and the band, hitherto playing their polyphonic mysteries, switched to a piece by Elgar (not easily recognizable in their curious arrangement).

The Aga Khan wore a dazzling blue turban and silk coat and sat beneath a massive green umbrella. The car, a sleek, black, open-topped Rolls-Royce especially imported from England, churned up the dust as it made its way up the gravel path, surrounded by functionaries and preceded by the Karachi Ismaili Bagpipe Band, tartan shawls over their dust-speckled white robes and playing on their cumbersome instruments a screeching Scottish dance. They were an unusual sight, to be sure, but it was to Yvette that all eyes were drawn. She was wearing a white silk sari sewn with 1500 diamonds. To display them to their best advantage, the umbrella that shielded her from the harsh rays of the sun was lowered every few seconds so that the stones would catch and refract the light. It was an incredible spectacle. Perhaps no other woman had ever worn so beautiful or expensive a gown. It left the crowds gaping with wonder and doubly anticipatory of what had been promised to follow.

The Imam and his family were helped on to the flower-bedecked platform where an enormous weighing machine, altered somewhat from the one used a decade earlier to celebrate the Aga Khan's golden anniversary, was set up on one side and two gilt sofas and two chairs (to accommodate the Aga Khan, the Begum, and Aly and Sadruddin) on the other. There were radio newscasters from London, Paris, Chicago and New York surrounding the dais with their microphones. This time the microphone system worked well and the crowds sat restlessly but respectfully for over two hours as passages were read from the Holy Quran and speeches were made to honour the Aga Khan. Then came the moment everyone was waiting for.

The Aga Khan was assisted on to the swivel seat of the weighing machine by the office bearers of the Aga Khan Legion, dressed in red robes. The crowd *ooohed* and *aaahed* as one by one, eighty smallish, transparent plastic bullet-proof jewel caskets, each filled with sparkling diamonds, were laid on the scale, while in jarring juxtaposition newsreel cameramen photographed the scene in a whirr of sound and the Aga Khan's assistants on the dais touched their heads to the floor in prayer.

The Aga Khan tipped the scale at 243½ pounds, to 'ear-cracking applause'. This was equal to about $3 million-worth of diamonds, the majority of which were polished gems, including one rare stone valued at over $150,000.

The diamonds were to be returned to a syndicate in London and re-loaned for the ceremony in August in Dar es Salaam, and the Aga Khan would be given the equivalent cash amount of their worth, raised by his disciples, which was to be placed in a special trust fund devoted to the economic and educational welfare of the Ismaili community.

The Aga Khan and his party, about forty guests, close friends and family brought by private plane from Europe (one recalled to this author the Begum constantly whispering to those near to her as greetings were being extended, 'Wash your hands before you touch your face') drove back to Malabar Hill through the streets of Bombay, cheering crowds lining his way. The trip had been an exhausting one and he returned in early May to Le Cannet to relax. Three months later the Aga Khan, the Begum, Aly and Sadruddin were on their way to Dar es Salaam, the capital of Tanganyika (now Tanzania), where many political exiles had gone during the war. The Diamond Jubilee weighing ceremony was performed once again, this time before 70,000 people including the governors of Tanganyika, Kenya and Uganda, at the sports arena of the Aga Khan Club. He wore a heavy robe of white and silver brocade, studded with five-pointed stars, and a turban of green and gold silk. The Begum was dressed in the same jewelled sari she had worn in Bombay.

The Aga Khan tipped the scales two pounds heavier than in Bombay (perhaps because of his robe) and announced that 'the money subscribed to the value of the diamonds will be used for clinics and schools.' Schools were built and opened for girls in Ismaili communities, a project that was begun with proceeds from the Golden Jubilee. Classrooms were separated by sex, according to custom, and previously facilities for girls were rare.

There was scathing criticism in India of the Aga Khan's display of riches and its seemliness was questioned in view of current conditions. 'At such a time and hour in the country's history,' a Bombay newspaper editorial protested, 'the Arabian Nights picture in which diamonds fill the air and a man becomes a god is something beyond human conscience. One feels surprised, hurt and indignant beyond words at the Government permitting fifty thousand individuals to come to the city, and providing them with facilities for travelling, feeding and housing, when the city's temper is none too sweet and when famine threatens our beloved province.'

But the Jubilee Committee had been right in its conviction that the sight of such a cache of diamonds, the Arabian Nights ambiance and the uniqueness of the weighing would grab headlines around the world. Most people assumed the Aga Khan kept all the jewels. And they were ready to believe that he was most certainly one of the richest men in the world. Only a very few press reports mentioned the charitable distribution of the funds or gave more than brief accounts of the Aga Khan's religious position, the Ismailis, or their Imam's good works. American, English and French newspapers and magazines printed front page or cover photographs of the Aga Khan seated on the giant scales, his weight balanced by all those transparent boxes of gleaming diamonds. The accompanying articles reminded the reader that he had been weighed in gold only a decade earlier. Great masses of people thought of him as a rich potentate who sat on a throne of gold. He was Indian wasn't he? Perhaps a maharajah. But they did not equate that with his being a religious leader. Therefore, as public relations the dual Jubilee events were a mixed success. The Aga Khan's name was once again well-known, but perhaps not for the most positive reasons.[1]

The Aga Khan became a septuagenarian in 1947. His grey hair had thinned considerably. There were dark circles beneath his eyes and the thick magnifying glasses he wore could not mask or replace his failing sight. After his return from Dar es Salaam he had one medical problem after the other that required surgery; prostate, colon, cataracts. He felt death might not be far away and his affairs were not in good order. He was concerned about Aly, whose marriage to Joan was about to come apart and whose sexual escapades were almost daily reported in the press. His love for speed in cars, planes, or when riding a horse had become an obsession. He seemed to be courting disaster on a daily basis and he took little interest in the financial empire the Aga Khan had built or in the charitable side of the Imamate in his pursuit of pleasure.

Whatever his son's marital problems might be, the Aga Khan was extremely fond of Joan and although he saw his two grandsons Karim

---

[1] Various Diamond Jubilee Trusts were formed (see Appendix II), but it appears that at least part of the money raised by the two events found its way into the Aga Khan's private holdings.

and Amyn infrequently, was pleased with the reports of their good demeanour. With the passage of time, Yvette had revealed a steely side to her nature. She pampered him shamelessly. He gave her costly jewels while he recuperated from his various illnesses at Yakymour, but he confided to one friend that Yvette was 'the only woman who can make me cry'.

He had fallen into the routine of spending a few hours a day at the Villa Jane-Andrée in Antibes (a thirty-minute drive from Yakymour). The ex-Begum had mellowed considerably and she now got on particularly well with Aly and had become an intermediary between father and son. Rumours spread that the Aga Khan was drawn once again to her charms.

Unlike Andrée's villa in Antibes, Yakymour was not as spacious or elegant, although it did not lack in luxuriousness. A guest recalls dining alone with the Aga Khan at a long refectory table, the two men facing each other at one end. Along the centre of the table were tall gold vases filled with long-stemmed red roses. The menu was written on a small plastic memo pad placed on the right-hand side of the Aga Khan's plate. They were served by an Indian in native dress and a French maid in a frilly white lace cap and apron, short black skirt and black silk stockings that revealed a pair of extremely shapely legs.

As each course was presented, the Aga Khan would lean over and say something like, 'Perhaps you don't like squab. Would you prefer fish or veal?' No matter that the guest replied that the dish being served was just fine, a few moments later another tray would arrive with an alternative. And whatever else was served for dessert there was always a chilled silver bowl of ice cream. He was quite passionate about ice cream and could eat several quarts of it, made in his own kitchen of the thickest cream and freshest fruit, every day.

He was not always so generous when he took guests out for dinner in a restaurant. Seldom would there be less than a dozen at his table. He would assiduously study the wine list and order four bottles of the best vintage. The sommelier would offer a sample of each for him to taste. When he had decided which was the best bottle, he would declare, 'This is for me,' and order the other three to be distributed among his guests.

Although Yvette did not cook, she supervised everything that came out of the kitchen to make sure it would pass muster with her husband's prodigious and extremely cultivated palate. And when he had guests he would rise from his seat at the dining table to see that what was being served to them was a suitable specimen. When the well-known American writer John Gunther dined at Le Cannet one evening, the Aga Khan reached over his shoulder as he was about to remove a halved cold lobster from a serving tray on to his plate. 'Excuse me,' the Aga Khan said, 'don't take that one, take this one,' and made the exchange himself.

He was at this time writing, with the aid of the British author John Cornell, his autobiography *World Enough and Time*. For exercise, attended by his favourite nineteen-year-old caddy, he played golf; for amusement he went to the Casino at Monte Carlo. He also had a new house in Paris, in the rue Scheffer, off the Avenue Henri Martin, but he was seldom there more than three months a year, during which time he gave and attended spectacular parties and costume balls. He enjoyed eating and would frequent any restaurant, no matter how humble, if he heard the food was extraordinary.

He was dispirited in the summer of 1948 over the wretchedness caused by the partition and the tragic news that Gandhi had been killed by an assassin's bullet that past January as he made his way to a Sunday prayer meeting. Yvette decided that he might be distracted by the beauty of a camera safari to Africa. The Aga Khan accepted the idea immediately and plans were put into action. Sadruddin, on holiday from Harvard University, flew to Le Cannet from Boston to join his father on the expedition, which included a few friends of the Begum's, the Aga Khan's personal physician, a nurse, fourteen trucks of food, four white servants, five white African hunters and sixty native servants including six cooks and six laundrymen. Yvette brought Paris dresses to wear in the evenings. And campsites were fitted with electric light and porcelain baths with running hot and cold water that were put into working order before the Aga Khan's party arrived at each stop.

The meals that were prepared were quite incredible. Fresh bread, fish, butter and eggs were flown in daily from the nearest supply centre and the party had brought smoked salmon, caviar, foie gras, tins of asparagus (the Aga Khan's favourite vegetable) and dozens of cases of champagne, the finest wines and aged brandy.

Despite the grandeur of the trip and the glory of the wildlife and scenery they were exposed to, the Aga Khan cut the safari short. It seemed to him that if he could wander about in the jungle this way and not feel ill, it was time he returned and got down to the business that was closest to his heart – his widespread enterprises as a racehorse owner and dealer. This was the one interest that he and Aly shared; and in which to his constant delight, his elder son had proved to be an expert.

'If only Aly could choose his women as well as he chooses his horses,' he once said. And Yvette had evaded a reporter's question on whether one of the Aga Khan's Derby winners was to be sold for stud with, 'Who can tell? We have so many problems of mating in this family.'

12

Aly Khan maintained a frenzied pace and had done for years. His energy was so excessive as to seem abnormal. He seldom went to sleep earlier than four in the morning and habitually rose again at eight-thirty. Aides and servants trailed breathlessly behind him as he dictated letters in French and English and walked around his homes and offices while speaking on the telephone. As a young man he had seemed solemnly determined to prove that he could do everything anyone else could do – only faster. He was always at the top of the hunt when he rode to hounds. He raced his horses with reckless abandon. In the thirties, before his marriage to Joan, he had driven in all the famous Grand Prix races in France, Monaco and Italy.

To Aly it was all 'fabulously fun', which is how he described a 10,000-mile round-trip flight – the longest civil flight ever – from Bombay to Singapore in 1932, flying over treacherous jungles in a single-engined plane with no radio. He had a lot of experience at big-game hunting, shooting 'everything considered worth shooting except an elephant,' he claimed, 'and I don't intend to kill an elephant.' However, he had bagged three lions, seven tigers and some twenty or more leopards and panthers while on foot, not from the safety of the elevated platform called a *machan* (following, it would seem, the practice of his grandfather Aga Khan II).

Aly became co-proprietor of his father's racing interests in 1946. By that time the Aga Khan had chalked up winnings of well over £900,000 in Britain alone. The Khan family together now owned five stud farms totalling some 3000 acres in Ireland and about 250 horses, whose value was estimated at £3,000,000. The Aga Khan was an extremely good judge of horses; Aly was an unsurpassed horse-trader. Between them they made an almost unbeatable pair.

Racing was one of the only things on which Aly had displayed a continuing concentration and exhibited more than a dilettante or temporary passion. The Sport of Kings became very big business in the hands of the Khans, father and son. Aly's horse-dealing coups had astonished the experts for years. Back in 1938, when he was twenty-seven, he bought Bois Roussel which, only three months later, won the Derby. In 1947, one year after he and his father joined forces, he acquired Avenger just three weeks before the colt won the prestigious Paris Grand Prix at odds of 33–1. This coup was followed by his winning the Derby with My Love at odds of 100–9 three days after he took possession of the horse. He claimed he liked to play hunches, but his steady record of winners indicates more than luck. He would complete a horse deal, the documents signed by him and delivered to his father's suite at the London Ritz Hotel, down the corridor from his own, within twenty-four hours of the start of negotiations.

'People don't realize how seriously my father and I take our horse-breeding business – or what great quantities of dollars we have earned for Britain,' Aly told the journalist and author Gordon Young.

The 'Good Old Aga', as he was rather patronizingly being called in Britain, was spending most of his time at Yakymour since the war's end, enjoying the company of the lively Yvette or playing golf in nearby Mougins. It was claimed that he often gambled at the Casino in Monte Carlo in the afternoons, cashing a cheque for two million francs at Lloyds Bank, and with the banknotes wrapped in newspaper 'waddled off to punt against the Greek Syndicate', who, headed by Aristotle Onassis, controlled the tables.

Aly's interest in speed, sports and bloodstock did not fill his entire life. He too was often seen in Monte Carlo and in the chic clubs and casinos on the Riviera, where dress codes were vigilantly observed. 'I was therefore amazed,' the Riviera chronicler Stanley Jackson wrote, 'when Aly Khan walked in [to the restaurant of the Cannes Casino] dressed in corduroy trousers, a creased linen jacket

1. The child Imam, Aga Khan III, aged eight, at his installation in Bombay as spiritual leader of the Ismaili sect of Shia Muslims.

2. *Below left*: In his ceremonial clothes. The sword was especially fashioned for his diminutive size.

3. *Below right*: Aga Khan III as a child, with his mother.

4. Theresa Magliano, or Ginetta as she was familiarly known. A ballet dancer who later became a sculptor, she was the Aga Khan's second wife and mother of Aly Khan. Their marriage was not legally recognized until shortly before her premature death.

5. Aly Khan aged 16, in oriental attire. He had toured Ismaili communities on behalf of his father.

6. The Aga Khan and the Begum Theresa at the races in Ostend in 1926, the year before her death.

7. Andrée Carron and the Aga Khan at their wedding in Aix-les-Bains, December 1929. She had been his mistress for over a decade, replacing her older sister in his affections. At first Aly Khan hated his father's new wife; later he became fond of her.

8. *Above left*: Aly Khan at the Calcutta race course in 1933.

9. *Above*: A wide smile as the Aga Khan leads in his horse Blenheim, winner of the 1930 English Derby.

10. *Left*: The Aga Khan and Begum Andrée.

11. Begum Andrée in a sari embroidered with diamonds, a giant stone at the closure of the neck.

12. Begum Andrée and her son, Sadruddin, second in line of succession, on the beach at Deauville, 1935.

13. Following much scandal, Joan divorced her husband Loel Guinness and married Aly Khan in a civil ceremony in Paris in 1936: (*left to right*) Aga Khan III, the groom, Prince Sadruddin, the bride.

14. The Aga Khan at the Ritz Hotel with Mahatma Gandhi and Sarojini Naido during the All London Round Table Conference on India in 1931. Let out of prison to attend, Gandhi was later to be incarcerated at Aga Hall, the Imam's palace in Bombay.

15. In the shadow of his father. Aly Khan talks to the jockey as the Aga Khan leads in Bahram after his win at the 1935 Epsom Derby.

16. Before the Second World War the Aga Khan was an admirer of Hitler. On a visit to Berlin in October 1937, he is seen talking to Obergrüppenführer Lorenz at a dinner given by von Ribbentrop.

17. At his Diamond Jubilee in Bombay in 1946, the Aga Khan was weighed in diamonds.

18. Aly Khan with his two sons Karim (*left*) and Amin in 1946. The boys were attending Le Rosey in Switzerland, often called the School of Kings.

and silk muffler . . . He was smaller than I had expected [he was five feet six inches tall], quite roly poly [having gained weight and now weighing about 160 pounds] and going bald [this was in 1947]. He was soon chatting merrily away about Maxine Elliott's luxurious villa, the Château de l'Horizon, which he had just bought for £35,000. I gathered that Aly would preserve the water chute down which guests could slide straight into the sea [he did], if they preferred that to the huge swimming pool, but he had no intention of switching on her imitation moon for dark nights.[1]

'Suddenly he jumped to his feet and shot off to greet a very pretty brunette . . . they were soon dancing cheek-to-cheek, locked in trancelike mutual admiration,' Jackson continued. 'It was said that he dipped his fingertips in rosewater to prolong his lovemaking and boasted cynically that he never shot until he saw the whites of their eyes.' One of Aly's lovers claimed that he was able to hold an erection for hours.

The ancient Arabic art of *Imsák* was said to be responsible for Aly's extraordinary sexual prowess. As a young man he had gone (as the Aga Khan had before him) to a doctor in Cairo with whom he had spent six weeks studying the control of his muscles so that he did not reach a climax. 'He liked the effect it had on women,' one friend claimed. 'He liked to get them out of control while he remained in control – the master of the situation.'

Aly's romantic adventures brought him international fame; the press stepping lively to keep up with the 'most recent No. 1 equestrienne of his romantic merry-go-round'. Attractive women had a startling effect on Aly. A beautiful young society matron sitting across from him at dinner at this time recalled that, 'suddenly he began staring at me, very intently, not moving his eyes. Then his nostrils began to flare; I swear they did, just like Rudolph

[1] The American actress Maxine Elliott, known as 'the Venus de Milo with arms', was the most sensationally beautiful woman on Broadway at the turn of the century, and so successful that in 1908 she opened her own theatre on West 39th Street, Manhattan. In the 1920s she retired to the South of France with her actor husband Nat Goodwin and became well-known for the wild and extravagant parties she gave at their lavish home, the Château de l'Horizon, where her guests included Scott and Zelda Fitzgerald, W. Somerset Maugham, Isadora Duncan and many royal personages and potentates.

Valentino's in the silent movies. I was at a complete loss. What do you do when a man flares his nostrils at you across the table? Flare your nostrils back and treat it as a joke? Or do you just sit there and feel uncomfortable? I'm afraid that is what I did. All through dinner, every time I raised my eyes, he was staring at me and flaring his nostrils.'

'The trouble with Aly,' an intimate of his ventured, 'is that he is grossly over-sexed. If he would stop chasing women he probably would be all right. But the man must have three or four of them at a time. He doesn't chase tarts. He runs after lots of decent respectable women. And he has made many enemies doing it.'

One of Aly's favourite diversions when not pursuing women or one of his demanding sporting activities, was viewing movies. He had added a projector and screen to the many other luxuries at Château de l'Horizon. In the early days of the summer of 1948, the most popular film in Europe was *Gilda* starring Rita Hayworth,[1] a role that earned her the name of 'Hollwood's Love Goddess'. Aly had the film run several times, fascinated by Rita as she sang (her voice was dubbed by the singer Anita Ellis, but he only learned that later) 'Put the Blame on Mame, Boys', oozing sex in a form-fitting gown while dancing and peeling off a pair of elbow-length black gloves.

Aly had just ended a short affair with Pamela Churchill, the red-haired, free-spirited daughter-in-law of Winston Churchill, a particular hero of his. In fact one of the largest of the ten bedrooms at the Château was called the Winston Churchill Room from the days when he had been the former owner's guest. Pamela left Château de l'Horizon by sea with one of Aly's closest friends, the Fiat heir Gianni Agnelli. Aly did not seem too disturbed by this, especially when he learned that Rita was on the Riviera.

He had voiced his desire to meet Rita to Elsa Maxwell, gossip columnist, friend (and occasional enemy) of the rich and famous, grossly overweight, celibate (she said), and famous for her parties (always paid for by other people). Lady Luck was in his corner.

---

[1] *Gilda* was released in 1946 in the United States two years later in Europe.

Rita Hayworth was arriving in Europe at any moment. And it so happened that Elsa was helping to arrange a party on 3 July at the elegant Palm Beach Casino. She would, she promised Aly Khan, make sure he was invited and seated next to Rita.

'The Love Goddess' was married to the actor-director Orson Welles, but the marriage had fallen apart and Welles was living with an Italian woman. Not that Rita needed to be lonely. She was being wooed at the time by Aristotle Onassis and the Shah of Iran, but chose to ignore the telephone calls, flowers and gifts from both these two powerful men. The failure of her marriage had been a great disappointment. She greatly admired Welles and they had a small daughter, Rebecca. She was in a depressed state and considering returning to the States sooner than originally planned. Maxwell urged her to attend the party where Aly Khan was also to be a guest.

Rita initially declined the invitation. Finally, not a woman to give up easily, Maxwell insisted she must not languish in self-pity.

'I have nothing to wear,' Rita lamely protested.

Maxwell told her to go and buy a new dress in the boutique of the Hôtel du Cap where Rita was staying. 'Come in late. Make an entrance,' she prodded.

It was nearly midnight when supper was to be served. Everyone had arrived an hour or so earlier. The room was glittering, the doors thrown open to the soft breezes of the Mediterranean night. Rita stood on a landing, a winding staircase before her, dressed in a stark white, Grecian gown that hugged her sun-bronzed shapely body; her red hair was loose around her bare shoulders and around her neck was a shimmering emerald and diamond necklace. She looked spectacular and heads turned towards her as she started to descend, slowly and majestically, head up, never looking at her feet.

Aly was at her side when she reached the bottom step and never more than an arm's length away from her for the rest of the evening. He was a smooth and expert dancer; his expertise at seduction equally adept. At about 3 AM they left the party and drove up to where the steep road on the precipitous Grand Corniche overlooked the Mediterranean coastline, miles below, a ribbon of lights charting its path.

Rita's secretary and travelling companion, Shifra Haran, said, 'The Prince was immediately *smitten*, but Miss Hayworth definitely was *not*.'

If not *smitten*, Rita was certainly charmed, because she went back to the Château de l'Horizon with him and did not return to her hotel until later that next morning. Aly was to have flown that day in his private plane *Avenger* to Ireland where Attu, one of his newest acquisitions, was to race, but he cancelled his trip. Rita had agreed to return to his grand Mediterranean villa in the afternoon. When she arrived, three hours late for their appointment, she was dressed in white shorts, her hair loose and her face free of make-up. Aly was stunned by her natural beauty. They danced cheek to cheek in the sumptuous ballroom of the spectacular house, just the two of them, a record player spinning Gershwin, Porter and Berlin.

When he left for Ireland the next morning, Rita had promised she would remain in the South of France until his scheduled return, five days later. While he cheered Attu to victory, Rita was deluged with huge, daily bouquets of red roses. The day before his arrival, a Gypsy woman (who spoke Italian and was accompanied by a translator), appeared at Rita's hotel, insisting on seeing her. Intrigued, Rita asked her up to her suite. The woman predicted that she was 'about to embark on the greatest romance of her life. He was someone she already knew . . . Rita [she insisted] must relent and give in to him totally. Only if she did that would she find happiness at long last.'

Aly's hand in this prediction seems likely, but Rita was strangely convinced by the fortune teller's words. She extended her trip so that she and Aly would have more time together. She all but moved into l'Horizon for the ten days before she had to return to Hollywood where she was committed to start a new film. The impressive white, green-shuttered, three-storey Château with its dozens of sun-filled rooms, paintings by the great Impressionists (whom Aly collected), the magnificent sea views from the immense terrace that almost encircled the gracefully sprawling building, where Aly liked to lunch stripped to the waist to enjoy the sun, the Olympic-sized swimming pool, the safe in his bedroom that contained thousands of dollars in many different currencies so that he could fly off in *Avenger* to any exotic place he wished on a whim, and the quality of pampering she received from Aly's exotic Indian staff and servants all contrived to fuel her romantic nature. Aly's great charm completed the seduction. Rita believed herself to be deeply in love with him.

'Hollywood's Love Goddess' she might well have become, but Rita Hayworth's roots were rough and humble. Born Margarita Cansino in Brooklyn, New York, she was the daughter of Eduardo Cansino, a professional Spanish dancer, who took her out of school at the age of twelve to dance as his partner (made up to look older) in Tijuana across the border from southern California, and who (according to her own tortured confession) had abused her sexually since she was ten. They were known as the Dancing Cansinos and Eduardo passed her off as his wife in the 'raucous, off-shore gambling ships' and Mexican gin mills and casinos in which they performed. Her mother, the exotically named Volga Hayworth, was an American showgirl who became an alcoholic (as did Cansino, later in his life), and seemed to have more than she could handle with Rita's three younger brothers, all of whom were less than a year apart in their ages.

At the age of seventeen, shapely, a dark-eyed, raven-haired beauty, she was signed by Twentieth Century-Fox only to be dropped, to her father's great disappointment, a few months later. He turned to a promoter named Edward Judson, twenty-two years Margarita's senior, to help her get another contract. Judson took over the girl's life, creating a new young woman by subjecting her to painful electrolysis to raise her hairline, dying her hair red, dressing her in more glamorous and form-fitting clothes, and renaming her Rita Hayworth. He made every effort to remove the tell-tale traces of her Latin background, which in Hollywood at that time was passé: Mexican spitfires were now out of vogue. Judson did get her a seven-year contract with Columbia, but first he married her. Then he pressed her to have sex with studio executives to further her career.

She was the mistress of Harry Cohn (head of Columbia Pictures) and then the rich and powerful Howard Hughes, neither of them known for his respect for women. She did not emerge as a star in major films until 1941, ironically portraying a Latin woman in *Blood and Sand*. She was 23 and becoming more secure about herself. Judson threatened to disfigure her if she left him, but she got up her courage and walked out on him with the help of strong-man-actor Victor Mature, who was then her lover. It was never known what threats were made or if force was used, but Judson let her go without a public fight. A few months later, to everyone's surprise, Rita married Orson Welles. However Welles, whose realistic radio adaptation of H. G. Wells's *The War of the Worlds* had terrified a nation into believing men from Mars had landed in New Jersey, was well-suited for the role of Rita Hayworth's husband and mentor. He immediately took control of his wife's appearance, career – and education. A brilliant man, he attempted to make Rita into his vision of what she should be – a beautiful, gracious woman with brains enough to star in films of a higher intellectual calibre than those she had been making. He seemed to be following the sort of scenario he had helped create for the domineering, possessed tycoon in *Citizen Kane*, but it did not work any better in real life than it had on film.

The break-up of their marriage left Rita shaken and it was at this time that Aly entered her life.

Hollywood and film stars had never been a part of Aly Khan's world. Rita was his introduction into an unexplored sphere of glamour. He knew little about her personal history and it is doubtful that it would have made any difference to him if he had. He was captivated by her extraordinary beauty. Only a few female stars (Vivien Leigh, Virginia Bruce and Elizabeth Taylor, perhaps) could claim to be more beautiful off-screen than on. Beauty on screen can be greatly enhanced by a star's photogenic qualities, skin that has a third dimension on film, eyes that glow, bone structure that draws the light. Rita photographed extremely well and had a marvellous way of moving, walking, dancing or merely tossing her head back that made the viewer take note. But off-camera she was truly ravishing with her olive skin, large dark eyes, framed by that startling mass of red hair, and a body that seemed to be pure perfection.

After little more than a week, Aly could not resist showing the world his newest conquest. He organized parties at the Château. This was a fatal error, because Rita suddenly found herself in a hostile environment. Aly's social friends were inclined to put her down. Mostly they conversed in French, which she did not speak. She had never had to be a hostess to the rich and social – only the rich and famous, which was an entirely different matter. According to Shifra Haran, 'It was too overwhelming for her.'

Aly appeared to understand what had happened. Fearing she might return to Hollywood he arranged a motoring trip to Spain, which he believed he had managed in great secrecy. Somehow the press got wind of their 'elopement' and when they arrived in Madrid they were harassed by reporters and photographers. They moved on to Seville, her father's birthplace, where her elderly grandfather Padre Cansino happened to be visiting his relatives, rather simple, poor people. Rita invited them all to a family gathering at a local restaurant and Aly joined them and watched fascinated as Rita danced the flamenco with her grandfather.

'She danced like a real Spaniard,' one bystander recalled. 'Her white arms flashed above her head as she clicked her fingers. Her skirt had wings as she spun round and long, loose red hair floated above her shoulders.'

Aly proposed marriage to her, promising he would apply for an immediate divorce. To his shock, fearing their social and cultural differences, she refused him and shortly after left for Hollywood to be reunited with her young daughter, Rebecca Welles, and to begin *The Loves of Carmen* for Columbia. Aly followed in hot pursuit. He took a Mediterranean-style house across the street from her movie-star mansion in Brentwood and plied her with gifts of jewellery and a small poodle puppy. Before long they were spending almost every evening alone together, usually at Aly's so that Rebecca would not be aware of the depth of the affair, and to avoid the press. Shifra Haran claims that it was an intensely passionate time for them both. 'I never saw the prince as a sex maniac,' she later said. 'It was *Miss Hayworth* who was insatiable.'

Of course, Miss Haran could not have been a witness to their love-making. She is reporting her instincts and reactions in seeing them together just before, just after or when planning their assignations. From the time she was a child, Rita had been used and abused sexually. Her father and Judson had trained her well in how to arouse and satisfy a man, and she knew how to win men of power like Harry Cohn and Howard Hughes. But Welles had wanted much more of her and her failure to hold him had wounded her deeply. In a sense Aly was helping her heal those wounds. He wanted nothing more of her than her love and possession of her body. On her part, she was determined to make sure he never became bored.

To their chagrin, the press began to hound them once again. They took a trip to Mexico which turned out to be a horror, members of the press everywhere they turned. Once back in Hollywood, she had contract troubles with Harry Cohn who wanted her to start a film that she did not want to make. In the end she was suspended. Free now from the studio, her divorce to Welles final, she left New York where she had been staying, on 15 December 1948, a bitterly cold, snowy morning, and boarded the *Britannic* for Southampton with Aly. Four-year-old Rebecca and the child's governess were with them, but would continue on to Paris where Orson Welles was waiting for a Christmas reunion with his daughter. Aly and Rita were to spend the holidays at his stud farm in County Kildare. Rita was much looking forward to a lovers' honeymoon.

But in Ireland she seldom saw Aly. Once back in his world of horses and racing he became totally preoccupied. Let it be said that by this time in his life (he had recently celebrated his fortieth birthday), Aly was considered one of the most important figures worldwide in thoroughbred breeding, racing and selling. Although he accepted what he believed to be the inevitability of it, he gave little thought to the idea of his future as Imam. His faith in his religion was strong, but he was far less interested in the problems of his father's followers than in his own private life. Nor could he see himself dedicated to the financial responsibilities of Imam, continually having to raise money through and for them. And as his father had not been well recently, he feared that he might have only a few short years before being called upon to fulfil his destiny. Meanwhile, he was determined to cram as much living as possible into the time left to him.

Finally, realizing he was neglecting Rita at the stud farm, on 31 December he flew her to Paris to collect Rebecca and then continued on to Gstaad, where they would join his two sons, Karim, 12, and Amyn, 11, to celebrate the New Year, 1949, at the ski resort's renowned Palace Hotel. Aly was still married to Joan, who made a quick exit from Gstaad before her husband arrived with his glamorous new mistress. The situation was one that created a press circus and scathing headlines sharply criticizing a mother (Rita) who would drag her daughter around Europe while she engaged in an illicit affair, and a father (Aly) who would subject his blameless wife and young boys to such heathen behaviour.

The London newspaper the *People* blazoned the headline: THIS AFFAIR IS AN INSULT TO ALL DECENT WOMEN. In the castigating article that followed, Aly was called, in a denigratory manner, a 'coloured prince'. The *Sunday Pictorial* added further insult by publishing a photograph of Rita and Aly side by side with one of Joan and her two sons under the headline A VERY SORDID BUSINESS, adding gratuitously words of dialogue Rita had spoken in *Gilda*: 'If I had been a ranch, they would have called me the Bar Nothing.'

The Aga Khan and the Begum were at Yakymour during this time. He was not well and unable to walk without a cane and someone at his side to help him. His unhappiness over his son's notorious affair was not helping his general malaise. He spent most of his evenings with his wife listening to Mozart and Verdi recordings. Recently he had made the statement that his life was going 'to cease being like a Hollywood film. I shall now leave the Casinos to others. As for Aly, his life is his own affair.'

He did not truly subscribe to this last assertion, for he began to put pressure on Aly to end the affair with Rita or stop seeing her until a divorce from Joan (whom he very much liked) was arranged. It was not that he did not understand how Aly could become enamoured of such a beautiful woman. He was the last one to cast stones. But he had always dealt with the women in his life in a discreet fashion. There had never been press coverage that would compromise the honour of a man who represented a religious sect. Aly had thrown caution to the wind when he fell in love with Joan, and here he was repeating the same outlandish behaviour. It did no good for Aly to explain to him that Rita was a famous film star whose every move alerted the press. The Begum tried to pacify her husband, to no avail. Finally, plans were set in motion for Rita and Aly to come to Yakymour to talk to the Aga Khan. What he did not know at the time was that his son's mistress was pregnant.

Rita was dressed in a conservative, caped suit, her abundant red hair brushed back smoothly from her lightly rouged face, when she arrived with Aly at the Aga Khan's villa. It is difficult to know what her decision might have been had she not been pregnant. She had suffered a near-death experience during an abortion the year after Rebecca's birth. It is unlikely she would have chosen to repeat the experience. But these were not the days when a public figure could have a child out of wedlock without serious repercussions. And also, Aly was madly in love with her, and desperate for them to marry.

The Aga Khan finally agreed and gave his approval, but not until he was assured Joan would be well provided for. Joan did what had to be done with great dignity and speed and, with the Aga Khan's help, secured a divorce in Paris by early May. (Asked why the marriage had not worked, Aly replied, 'Joan always knew more than I did. She came to speak to me about some things and I grew an inferiority complex. So, of course, I was miserable.') There was the matter of a marriage settlement for Rita. Perhaps to prove the depth of her emotions for Aly, or to savour her integrity in the matter, she rejected any arrangement to receive money from Aly if the marriage should fail. In appreciation he presented her with a magnificent diamond necklace valued at $150,000, the date of the wedding, to be held at his Château de l'Horizon, was set for 27 May at 1.15 PM, and a small number of invitations were sent out. Once this was done, he learned that French law did not recognize a marriage performed at a private home.

Aly applied to the French Minister of Justice for permission (as the Duke and Duchess of Windsor had done successfully twelve years earlier), but it was denied. The date and time were adhered to, but the ceremony was to be held at the Vallauris town hall with a luncheon for sixty guests to follow at a restaurant nearby. As the day drew closer, Rita began to panic. She was aware of the Aga Khan's disapproval and warned by several friends that Aly would never be faithful. Then there were some Ismailis from Paris who had come down several days before the wedding to help her understand the new religion she was pledged to take on (she was a Catholic).

Suddenly Rita was aware of the effect her marriage could have on young Rebecca's life and – possibly more immediately – her own career. Orson Welles, who she was always to say was her greatest love, was in Rome at the time. She telegraphed him just three days before the wedding was to take place telling him she had to see him, that it was a terrible emergency. 'I couldn't get any plane,' he told the biographer Barbara Leaming, 'so I went, stood up in a cargo plane to Antibes . . . [When I arrived at her hotel there] were candles and champagne ready – and Rita in a marvelous négligée. And the door closed, and she said, "Here I am. Marry me."'

He did not make little of this request. Rita was in a painful situation and he was sensitive to her dilemma. She was terrified that she was taking a wrong, perhaps fatal, step in marrying Aly. At the same time she was two months pregnant and unwilling to have an abortion. Whatever she felt for Aly, Welles had a strong hold on her emotions. He reasoned with her as he always had done and she listened. She was in a state of extreme anxiety and he managed to calm her, to explain that he couldn't remarry her because he was otherwise involved; nor would she find it a happy solution if he could. Against his better judgement he had to advise her to go through with it and assure her that time would take care of some of her other concerns. No law could stop her from divorcing Aly if it didn't work out.

'She was marrying the most promiscuous man in Europe,' Welles said, 'just the worst marriage that ever could have happened. And she *knew* it! It was a *fatal* marriage, the worst thing that could have happened to her. He was charming, attractive, a nice man . . . but the *wrong* husband for her.'

The ceremony at the town hall became a media event with reporters and photographers from all over crushed together to photograph and speak to the newlyweds. The next day they went through a Muslim ceremony. This was followed at l'Horizon by one of the biggest, gaudiest wedding receptions ever held on the Riviera. Rita seemed to have invited the world, for more than 500 guests (among them representatives from almost every major American and European newspaper) consumed 600 bottles of champagne, fifty pounds of caviar and mounds of other gourmet treats. Rita, in a cream lace Dior dress and hat, cut the wedding cake with a glass sword she and Aly had found in an antique shop in Paris, wielding the awkward weapon in toreador fashion. Then, while the band struck a chord, a corps of servants marched to the swimming pool which had been scented with two hundred gallons of eau de cologne and threw in two massive floral pieces; one shaped like an M (for Margarita), the other like an A for her new husband. Later, Yves Montand sang, the guests danced and Rita sat in a chair surrounded by Ismailis who knelt beside her, a guest recalled, 'and kissed her foot. Extraordinary! And each one had something to give her, pearls, a little gold object. It was extraordinary! . . . all those people whom she had never seen before, all different types with women dressed in native [Indian] costume . . . going down on their knees to her.'

In his memoirs, written five years later, the Aga Khan recorded, 'This was a fantastic semi-royal, semi-Hollywood affair; my wife and I played our part in the ceremony, much as we disapproved of the atmosphere with which it was surrounded.'

For the next few months the newlyweds seemed to be travelling endlessly, all the time in the public spotlight, at racing events, night clubs, galas and charity affairs. Aly was bent on displaying his movie star wife to the world. In August, after fainting twice at crowded exhibitions, Rita no longer accompanied Aly on many of his rounds of festivities. To her humiliation he was photographed with other women — always young beauties.

The Aga Khan put on a happy face for the public. Privately he was much disturbed. His successor mattered greatly to him. He had developed a one-man welfare state. Eighteen per cent of the 2.5 million inhabitants of Bombay were totally illiterate, but the figure, thanks to his emphasis on education, was less than half that in his sect. The same was true of poverty and disease among his followers. He had lived a full life, there had been many women, high spending, but he had also expended a tremendous amount of energy on helping the poorer members of his sect, building schools, hospitals and roads for their communities as well as working on engineering plans to bring in water and electricity to areas that had none. This could not have been done without the large receipts of money he managed to raise from his loyal and more prosperous disciples.

But the sum could shrink visibly after his demise if things stood as they now did with Aly, of whom his followers knew little except for the sensational headlines they read in the newspapers.

On 28 December 1949, Rita gave birth in Switzerland to a daughter whom they named Yasmin. Aly, Rita, the new baby and Rebecca settled into a chalet in Gstaad, where the winter campus of the elegant boarding school attended by Aly's two sons, Karim and Amyn, was located.

Le Rosey, where Aly Khan's two sons were being educated, was called 'the school of kings' because so many future monarchs had been members of the student body, including Prince Rainier of Monaco and the then-current Shah of Iran, Mohammed Reza Pahlavi. (The entire dynasty to which the Aga Khan had been related through his mother and great-great-grandmother had been deposed in 1925 and replaced by the Pahlavis.) During Karim and Amyn's tenure their schoolmates included the Duke of Kent, the Marquess of Dufferin and Ava, and the son of Victor Emmanuel III, the deposed King of Italy. There was also a plethora of society scions, heirs to vast fortunes and lesser aristocrats. Still, there was a general head-turning on Sundays in spring and summer when the school was occupying its primary campus, a huge château at Rolle, a small village on Lac Léman between Geneva and Lausanne. For it was then that the Aga Khan made a regular weekly visit to his grandsons.

'At noon precisely,' Michael Korda, also a student there, wrote in his family memoir *Charmed Lives*, 'the huge car . . . a Rolls-Royce, with blacked out windows and discreet French *corps diplomatique* licence plates . . . would draw to a halt in the gravelled courtyard, under the medieval clock tower. The two boys would walk over and fall to their knees, a black window would descend with a low, electric hum, and a pudgy hand would be extended from within the car. Each boy would kiss it in turn, and the hand would then distribute to each of them a single new Swiss five-franc piece; the window would be raised, and the car would silently move forward, circle around the fountain and vanish down the driveway.'

The ominous aura in Korda's description could be attributed to the vivid youthful imagination of the viewer. However, the Aga Khan's vast, custom-built black car did have a hearse-like appearance and his grandsons, like the subjects of most monarchs, were expected to do obeisance to him. More traumatic to the brothers was the public exposure to their peers and the business of having to wait in the courtyard of the school for this ritual, when they would have much preferred a private meeting.

The Aga Khan and Yvette spent time during the summer months near Geneva at the house he had given her before they were married and which was only a short distance from Le Rosey. Pictures exist of the Aga Khan with Amyn and Karim, their father and the school's headmaster M. Johannot taken in the grounds of Le Rosey, so they did see more of him than a hand proffered through a car window. It was true, however, that their grandfather was not comfortable with children, perhaps because he had never been a child himself. But there was something about Karim, the elder of the two, with his sober, adult manner that reminded him, he remarked to Freda Blane Meyer, his personal secretary of twenty years, of his own youth.

Karim was nine and Amyn seven when they entered Le Rosey in 1945. They spent the better part of the next nine years under its influence. (Korda's anecdote would have taken place in 1950 or 1951.) Karim had a fine physique, a mop of dark hair, soulful eyes, and a somewhat sly, mischievous smile. There was only the slightest hint of his Eastern antecedents. Amyn was slimmer, wore glasses and was the more studious of the two. They were called rather unceremoniously 'K' and 'A' by their schoolmates, and after a while by members of their family as well.

Whatever close family life the brothers had was with their mother, their half-brother Patrick Guinness, and members of Joan's family in England and Scotland. The Aga Khan was not inclined to family gatherings. Between school terms at Harvard, Sadruddin lived in Antibes and Aly moved about between l'Horizon, his houses in London and Paris, and his stud farms (he seldom went to Deauville any more). The Aga Khan frequently spoke to family members on the telephone. When he had something to discuss, he would ask them to come to Yakymour (a request that was always treated as a command, not to be disobeyed without dire consequences – a tightening of the purse strings, lectures, and a frigidity that would take long to melt). His sons were not included in his social or home life. The same might be said about his relationship with his grandsons. He was the patriarch, he kept in constant touch with his heirs and they came to him when he obliged them to do so. But there were no happy family gatherings at Yakymour for holidays, birthdays or other festive occasions.

The Aga Khan briefly saw his granddaughter Yasmin, in the spring of 1950 when she was three months old. He came away with an uneasy feeling about Aly's present wife and speculated that their marriage was inevitably headed for collapse. He had taken his daughter-in-law Joan to his heart and still had great affection for her, which might have coloured his views. It was clear to him that Rita 'looked upon her marriage as a haven of peace and rest from the emotional strain of her work in the theatre and on the screen.' In other words, that her career took precedence over a marriage that was mainly a means of relaxing and being entertained between engagements. This would never do for the wife of a future Imam.

The Aga Khan was not blind to Aly's shortcomings as a husband – his blatant philandering, gambling and tendency to leave his wife alone for short or long periods while he pursued his own pleasures. And, of course, he expected Aly's wife to be forbearing in all these foibles, a good companion, a fine hostess, and the kind of mother who would take full responsibility for the raising of her children so that he would not have to concern himself with them. Aly had treated Joan in the same cavalier manner. The Aga Khan was also keenly aware of Aly's spendthrift ways that were making him run short of money, even with his great inherited wealth (which was protected so that he could not get immediate access to the capital).

Father and son had some unpleasant conversations about Aly's extravagant spending habits. The Aga Khan was fearful that after his death, Aly would use up the sect's resources in his profligate activities. Both Aly and Rita needed to be made more aware of their position and the responsibilities attached to it. He ordered Aly to embark on a three-month tour of Ismaili communities in Africa and insisted that his wife accompany him. During this time the Aga Khan and the Begum would visit India and Pakistan.

Rebecca and Yasmin were left in the care of a governess and nanny at l'Horizon and Aly and Rita departed for an extensive tour of Africa a few days before Christmas and Yasmin's first birthday.

The trip was a ghastly experience for both of them. They quarrelled violently. Rita was left to herself as Aly attended *jamaat khanas* and met his father's followers, and she had no idea how to fill her time in places like Zanzibar and Nairobi. Aly carried off his assignment as emissary for the Aga Khan with enthusiasm. The problem was that he also managed to find time for numerous liaisons with women. Late one night, Aly came back to their hotel in Nairobi from one of these assignations to find Rita gone and a letter informing him that she was returning to the States for two months. He correctly suspected that she planned to end the marriage. He had no way of contacting her as she had not left a forwarding address, nor an explanation of what he was to do about the two children, Orson Welles's daughter and his own, who were at l'Horizon in Cannes.

In fact Rita had flown from Nairobi to Nice by chartered plane, taken a taxi to l'Horizon, packed up the girls and was off to Paris en route to New York within twelve hours of her arrival in France.

'Miss Hayworth somehow got it into her head that either Aly or I myself might try to take her daughter away from her, kidnap the child indeed. Therefore, when she ran away from my son she took the child with her,' the Aga Khan wrote.

'The moment I got back to Cannes [from his eastern travels] – that very night – Miss Hayworth, without having let me even see the baby, took her and ran away . . . She could surely have delayed her departure . . . and have let me see the baby,' he complained.

He became obsessed with Rita's implied accusation that either he or Aly would have considered acting illegally to keep Yasmin in Europe and devoted several pages in his memoirs to refuting the notion that this would ever have even been considered.

Had Miss Hayworth made more inquiries, she could have found out what in fact are the Ismaili religious laws and the code which governs all my followers and my family in these matters. Under this code the custody of young children of either sex rests absolutely with their mother, no matter what the circumstances of the divorce. Unless we were criminals, therefore, we could not have contemplated taking the baby, Yasmin, from her mother. When they are seven, boys pass into their father's custody, girls remain in their mother's until puberty when they are free to choose.

Rita initiated divorce proceedings almost immediately after she reached California where she entered into negotiations for a new film contract. She also instituted legal action to ensure that Yasmin would be given a million-dollar trust fund. (Her pre-marriage contract nullified any claims she personally might have made. But Rita did have a small fortune in jewels given to her by Aly.) The Aga Khan was highly indignant: '. . . there is no way under Islamic law by which a child can possibly be disinherited by his or her father.' If Aly were to die, he explained, he would not be allowed to will away from his legal heirs more than one-third of his property; two-thirds would go to his heirs (in this case Karim, Amyn and Yasmin, to be divided equally). 'Yasmin is bound to get her proper share of any estate which he leaves,' he continued, and then added the plea (this was in 1953 and he had seen the child but once in her life): 'I can only hope that when next Miss Hayworth comes to Europe she will bring her small daughter with her, so that her father's family can see her and have the pleasure of making her acquaintance.'

Karim and Amyn learned of their father's marital problems from the other boys at Le Rosey (many of them avid readers of the popular press and the scores of American film and gossip magazines obtained by Roséans at Cadineau's international book store in Gstaad and a similar establishment in Geneva). Their schoolmates were thoroughly devastated that two fellow Roséans had lost a glamorous movie-star stepmother, dashing their hopes of meeting the voluptuous Rita and others in her circle. The brothers appeared to be less affected. They remained close to their mother and in awe of their father, whom they firmly believed was more sporty and debonair (important qualities for a man by the standards of the school) than any actor on the screen.

They were greatly attached to each other. Karim was the protective brother, and yet Amyn (younger and almost the same height) was mature for his age. Islam was not taught at Le Rosey, but the brothers had a private tutor from Lucknow, India, who moved to Geneva in order to instruct them in the history, culture and tenets of their faith in whatever time they had free from lessons.

Their youth and education were far less restrictive than their father's had been. As school boarders they saw their parents only at holiday breaks. The end of summer was usually spent with Aly at l'Horizon, the rest of their free time with their mother in England or her sister in Scotland. The arrangement seemed quite normal to them, for they were living in a society of youngsters who all shared separation from their families and accepted it as the proper way for a gentleman to be raised.

'Being a gentleman was not that easy to define, except to [the Duke of] Kent, who explained that it meant being an Englishman,' Korda recalled of Roséan discussions on the matter. 'As an Englishman myself, I was inclined to agree with him,' he added.

The brothers also considered themselves Englishmen. After all, their mother was from a distinguished English family and their father had been educated in England. They were not friends of Korda, Kent and their circle, as they were younger and so in different classes.

It was equally important for a Roséan to be good at sports, which were compulsory and occupied three hours of each day. When the school was in Gstaad for the three-month winter season the students lived in the chalets (about fifteen in each, with a teacher) that dotted the snowy slopes of the surrounding Alps and skied down to the main building for breakfast in the icy dawn ('in ski trousers and sweaters . . . a silk scarf round our necks to give just the right kind of sporting look, made even more effective by a pair of Ray-Ban aviator's goggles looped over the neck of our sweaters,' Korda recalled). Competition to ascend from *Le Groupe D* in skiing to *Le Groupe A* was keen, and the top skiers were held in high regard. Karim and Amyn, who had been coming to Gstaad since they were small children and had been on skis at an early age, both made *Le Groupe A* in their second year as Roséans.

The rest of the school year they engaged in sports as varied as rowing on Lac Léman, rugby, tennis, swimming and mountain climbing. Karim was especially drawn to boats and water sports (which he enjoyed when he was at l'Horizon). He was more withdrawn than his younger brother and perhaps more introspective. The school had a fine academic side. French was the required medium of communication, the boys spoke English in private and, although it was not spoken at home, they also had a background in Arabic. Latin and German were taught, European history, geography, the arts, science and mathematics. Oriental history was only lightly touched upon and India's culture cursorily dismissed.

Le Rosey was one of the most expensive schools in Europe and Roséans were well looked after in a general atmosphere of luxury. In the evening they dressed for dinner – shirts and ties – and were served by pleasant Swiss waitresses. Their rooms were cleaned by maids, who also polished their shoes and took care of their laundry.

Rooms were allocated by age group and so the brothers did not share the same quarters. There were communal showers, but with plenty of hot water, not like the icy sprays endured by boys at English boarding schools. There was a girls' school nearby and dances were held in the autumn. Also, because it was an international school with students of many nationalities, there was much tolerance for a boy's background no matter how exotic it might be.

While his sons were safely shielded from the world in the Swiss Alps, Aly Khan was struggling to extricate himself from his second marriage. He had fallen in love again with a film star – this time Gene Tierney, who had made quite a sensation in the title role of the screen adaptation of Vera Caspary's *Laura* in 1944. They had met in the Argentine where Aly had flown on racehorse business and Gene was making *Way of a Gaucho*. Gene possessed an exotic green-eyed beauty, great style and panache. She had had a youthful wartime affair with John F. Kennedy and had recently been divorced from the designer Oleg Cassini (who was then courting Grace Kelly).

Gene had a fragile side to her nature, a vulnerability that neither Joan nor Rita had exhibited. She had suffered severe trauma when her daughter by Cassini was born retarded after she contracted measles during her pregnancy. She was desperately attracted to Aly, his high spirits, charm and exciting lifestyle. She travelled with him all over Europe and to the States for about a year. Anyone could see how deeply in love with him she was. Twice she told reporters that they were engaged and would soon be married in France. But no announcement was forthcoming from Aly.

Unsure of herself and on the edge of a breakdown (which Aly did not observe), Gene pressed him to seek permission from his father to marry her (a requirement in Aly's position). He went to see his father at Yakymour and they talked for several hours to no avail. The Aga Khan was adamant that his son should not, and would not, marry another movie star and that if he did he would risk any chance of becoming Imam upon his death.[1] Aly reported this to Gene and suggested that she remain his mistress, an idea that did not displease him. But she could not accept this arrangement. Tearful, hysterical scenes ensued and when they were in Paris together Aly, unable to cope with them any longer, walked out on her.

She suffered a severe nervous breakdown and was flown back to the States where she was admitted to a sanatorium in Hartford, Connecticut, remaining there for eighteen months, and then a short time later entered another institution for eight months. She was off the screen for seven years, never regaining her status as an important Hollywood star. During the length of his affair with Gene Tierney, Aly was having problems gaining access rights to see Yasmin. Rita was still fighting to obtain a large trust fund for their daughter, and it did not help that she was piqued over his public wooing of Tierney (despite the fact that Rita was at this time planning to marry the actor-singer, Dick Haymes).

Aly's private life was being reported almost daily with banner headlines in the popular press both in Europe and the United States. In the late summer of 1953 there were letters threatening Yasmin's life and Rita's lawyer, Bartley Crum, asked the Aga Khan, 'as the spiritual director of the Muslim world', to guarantee the safety of Rita and the child. This appeal made its way into the press, seeming to imply that members of his sect were responsible. Fortunately nothing ever came of the threats, but in fact the Aga Khan did hire private bodyguards for Yasmin for a time without informing Rita that this had been done.

Shortly after this trying episode, Rita left Rebecca and Yasmin in the care of a Mrs Dorothy Chambers in White Plains, New York,

---

[1] In such a case the Imamate would have to go to a direct lineal descendant. There were at this time three: Sadruddin, Karim and Amyn. But it would be a precedent, for there had been no such event in fourteen centuries of the Imamate.

while she and Haymes remained at a luxurious Manhattan hotel. It was never disclosed who tipped him off, but a reporter gained entry to Mrs Chambers's house by claiming to want to rent it. Photographs of Yasmin were worth a good price to magazines and he had come, he later claimed, simply wanting a photograph of the child. What he found shocked him and he took a number of pictures, without interference apparently from Mrs Chambers, who he said was proud to point out of the window and identify the girls. The house and yard were a filthy shambles. Yasmin was playing in a 'trash-littered' yard; Rebecca Welles was sitting on a back porch 'heaped with trash'; unwashed dishes, pots and pans overflowed the kitchen sink and counters, paint was peeling from the walls. These photographs appeared in *Confidential* magazine and then found their way into other periodicals. Articles and editorials sharply criticizing both parents were printed in the States and abroad.

The children were placed under the protective custody of the Children's Court. Neglect charges were filed against Rita. Aly happened to be looking at horses in California at the time and flew to New York. Although the Aga Khan had always tried to stand back from Aly's problems, this time the words 'Muslim' and 'Ismaili' were being used by the tabloids in a pejorative manner. He knew something had to be done immediately. What followed was crafted through his lawyers, whose strategy was to help Rita have the charges dismissed as quickly and neatly as possible and to force her finally to sign a reasonable financial settlement which would give Aly liberal access rights and provide for Yasmin to have instruction in the Ismaili faith.

Aly was reunited with his daughter, whom he had not seen for a year, in New York. Although still under the court's jurisdiction, both Yasmin and Rebecca were returned to their mother with the consent of Aly and Welles. It was several months before child neglect charges were dropped by the court which now found Rita to be a fit mother. Rita signed an agreement with Aly stipulating that Yasmin spend eleven weeks each summer with him and, when she was older and attending boarding school, four weeks during vacation and all school holidays or breaks of one week or less. He, in turn, was to put up as a bond $100,000 before Yasmin's arrival to ensure her return (a condition that infuriated the Aga Khan). Rita was to be paid $8000 a month child support. It was also part of the agreement that Yasmin was to have two hours' weekly instruction in her father's faith from the age of seven.

Aly's troubles were creating great problems for the Aga Khan. There had been a subversive campaign among members of the sect calling for his and Aly's abdication from their spiritual leadership. While the Aga Khan was visiting East Africa in 1953, things reached such a pitch that a special council was called to meet in his hotel suite to discuss what should be done. The end result was a decision that all members of the East African communities be requested to sign a declaration of loyalty to the Aga Khan, and be excommunicated if they refused. Statements were issued to the press that attempts to damage the Aga Khan's name were the work of a few agitators. There followed in Europe and Africa a series of laudatory newspaper articles stressing the loyalty of the Aga Khan's followers.

The Aga Khan was seventy-six and his health was failing. Something, he believed, had to be done to secure his family's hold on the Imamate. It appears to have been his idea several years earlier to mark his seventy years as Imam with a Platinum Jubilee to be celebrated in Karachi where he had been born. He decided that although August 1955 would be the correct date, his Platinum Jubilee should be held as soon as possible and 5 February 1954 was chosen. A tremendous effort was made to prepare so huge an event in time; seating had to be constructed for 50,000 people, arrangements made for the platinum to be sent to Karachi, celebrations planned. The press was fed releases about how the money that would be raised would be used for uplifting the Ismaili community – so that, the Aga Khan declared, 'by 1960 every Ismaili in Pakistan should have a profession or business of his own.'

Aly and the Begum accompanied the ageing Imam to Karachi by plane. He arrived at midnight on 31 January with a heavy cold and the early festivities had to be cancelled. Two days later he met members of his sect from all over Europe and the East and on the given day he arrived at the scene of his weighing dressed in splendid robes. There was a general toning down of the grandeur of the first two jubilees. The Begum wore a beautiful sari but was not arrayed in the fortune of jewels she had displayed at the Diamond Jubilee. And there was a good deal less than the wild enthusiasm that had been exhibited then and at his Golden Jubilee. Still, the Aga Khan was loudly cheered as he was helped on to the ivory scales. He weighed just over 210 pounds (the slimmest he had been in many decades thanks to a diet his doctors had ordered). Unlike his previous Jubilee, this one was a symbolic ceremony, an ounce of platinum used to balance every 14 pounds that he weighed.

The Aga Khan returned home to Yakymour afterwards feeling much weakened by the journey. His health was steadily declining. He was nearly blind, his heart was impaired, his liver diseased. Though he hated it, he was forced to use a wheelchair. The press had not let up on their unflattering coverage of Aly, who seemed always to be photographed with a beautiful woman on his arm.

To the Aga Khan's further distress, there were billboards all over London advertising a brand of coffee 'rich and dark like the Aga Khan'. Was all the respect he had won for himself and for Muslims to be lost? He called a family conference. A campaign was put under way to counteract the bad press and to present the Imam and his family in a more spiritual light. While he remained at Yakymour recuperating from prostate surgery, the Begum endured the scorching July heat of the desert and made a pilgrimage to Mecca. Clad in the long white rough cotton robe (the *ihram*) which all pilgrims wear so that rich and poor cannot be distinguished, her head covered, her feet bare, she walked over dirt and blistering rock, smoothed by the millions of pilgrims who had passed before her, to the black stone (a meteorite) and kissed it as they had also done. In deference to her European sensitivities, she carried a white parasol against the sun and wore dark sunglasses.

While the Begum was in Mecca, Karim and Amyn went on a tour of Ismaili communities in East Africa. In Nairobi, Karim, now seventeen, stood up before a large gathering of his grandfather's followers bringing a greeting from their Imam and conveying his wish that as many students as possible should become teachers as there was a lack of members of that profession in their faith. Education of children of their sect, he stressed (sounding very much like his grandfather), to be really effective must be in the hands of Ismaili teachers.

'There is a false notion among some persons,' he told them, 'that

as Ismailis are a business community they need not have much education. The British people are also a business community, but they
pay great attention to the development of sound all-round education
of the people. In fact no branch of human society needs so much
education as industry and commerce.' Karim's success on this trip was
duly reported to the Aga Khan and it gave him great pleasure. He had
grown especially fond of his older grandson. Karim was an intelligent
young man with a responsible character. He showed no signs of having
inherited his father's wild streak. Karim was extremely well-disciplined,
took (if somewhat shyly at first) to public speaking and inspired generous donations from Ismailis, the members of the Aga Khan's staff who
had accompanied Karim on the tour reported back to him. He had
seemed tireless under harsh conditions, extreme heat and long, uncomfortable journeys. And although he was exceptionally mature for his
age, he exuded youth and enthusiasm. The Aga Khan could not help
but think about the young queen now on the throne of Great Britain
and the renewed hope and energy she had brought to her subjects
after a difficult post-war adjustment.

Knowing he might have little time left, he began to plan for the
future of the Imamate after his death.

14

Aly recklessly continued to play fast and loose. He was forty-two, slim again though balding, and he had the energy of a much younger man. One of his visitors to l'Horizon in 1953 describes how he wore nothing but a brief white bikini, 'which spectacularly emphasized his dark sun-bronzed body . . . He came bounding down the steps to the swimming pool and sat beside me at its edge . . . His brown eyes sparkled . . . his white teeth gleamed . . . as he flashed a smile at me.' He held a book in his hand: Alfred Charles Kinsey's newly-published, controversial *Sexual Behavior in the Human Female*.

His disastrous relationships with Rita and Gene had not diminished his interest in beautiful film stars. There had been recent affairs with Merle Oberon, Joan Fontaine, Yvonne de Carlo, Greece's Irene Papas, Italy's Lia Amanda, and France's Lise Bourdin and Danièle Delorme. He lived life at a fast pace. Rita had called him a speed maniac. Three times while skiing he had broken a leg – twice during their short marriage. As a gentleman jockey he 'whipped home' more than a hundred winners. While flying, motor-racing and simply driving the treacherous mountain roads of the Riviera he several times came dangerously close to accidents in which he could have been maimed or killed. He had endured and survived intact forced air landings, near speedway collisions and irate husbands. All of these incidents were reported by the press so that the public conception of him was as Europe's quintessential derring-do playboy.

Aly was a more complicated man than the press reported. He was in the thankless position shared by all heirs to a throne. He lived his life in the glare of publicity with no set job and no knowledge of how long he might have to wait in the wings. But he seemed confident that once he took centre stage he could carry off the starring role. He had a strong spiritual side to his character and his knowledge of his religion and the history of his people was encyclopedic, both developed during the years he spent in England studying his faith under his diligent tutor and with no friends his own age. From the time of his mother's death, school holidays were spent in tours to Ismaili communities and now when called upon he could perform well as he had as his father's emissary on tours to the Ismaili communities and on the recent trip with Karim to Africa. However, he was far happier when he was, as he liked to call it, 'horse-trading' and had made tremendous profits for himself and his father with their stud farms and race winnings. Unfortunately, he was also a compulsive gambler and at present was almost a million dollars in debt to the casinos in the South of France.

His foibles drew down the wrath of a father who had done much the same things (even at this time of his life, the ageing, sick Aga Khan had a mistress in Paris), but who had greater funds to draw upon and had managed to escape criticism and public censure; a father whom his faith demanded he looked to for spiritual guidance – as would, he believed, his own son when his turn came. He seemed undisturbed when the question arose in interviews given to his biographer Gordon Young at the time. From early childhood he had been treated with reverence by Ismailis. His future was ordained and he accepted the eventuality of becoming Imam as pragmatically as an heir to a throne would accept his or her future powers and the obeisance of their subjects.

The trip to Africa with Karim had brought Aly closer to his son. They were able to view each other up close, often under trying circumstances, difficult flights, intense heat, public appearances and long hours of discussions with Ismaili leaders. Aly now had greater respect for Karim's intelligence and his ability to cope with complicated issues. Their childhoods had been quite different. Karim's had been far more normal, with an attentive mother and the relative freedom of attending school with boys of his own age and from various walks of life.

Karim was to say not long after this time that he actually knew his grandfather much better than his father. During the war they had seen very little of each other. Then after the war he had gone straight to Le Rosey and spent nine years there, seeing his father rarely. From there he had gone to Harvard. 'With my grandfather, the relationship was completely different. He called members of the family to him. It didn't matter where you were or what you were doing. When he said, "I want to see you," you turned out. And after an hour with you he knew everything that he could learn from you. He had a remarkably inquisitive mind. So, whereas I knew my grandfather as head of the family, I knew Daddy less well, and more in the form of an older brother.'

Yet, he called Aly 'Daddy', and would always refer to him in that familiar and small-boy manner.

They spent more time together at l'Horizon, playing tennis (Karim was almost up to professional standard), swimming in the pool and the sea, taking long walks along the shore where they would discuss spiritual and secular matters. Karim did not have Aly's love of horse- or motor-racing, but he enjoyed most other sports, soccer and skiing especially. Aly visited him more frequently during 1953, his last term at Le Rosey. Karim was a good draughtsman and excellent at mathematics. His mother favoured the idea of his going to the Massachusetts Institute of Technology. The Aga Khan preferred that he attend Harvard as Sadruddin, three years older than Karim, was already there studying Middle Eastern history and had founded the Harvard Islamic Association.

'I was too young to ask his reasons,' Karim told an interviewer. 'I did not dare to ask him then, and never did.'

Aly believed the Aga Khan's motivation was twofold: an ocean would separate Aly from his son, limiting his influence, and Karim would be placed under the eye of Sadruddin who was much more inclined to follow the Aga Khan's directives.

Karim took the entrance examination for Harvard's Department of Engineering, passed it, and was admitted for the autumn term of 1953. Before he left for Massachusetts to begin his university life, his grandfather sent for him and they talked at great length. The Aga Khan stressed the mission he expected his heirs to carry out after his death – to continue to build a better life for his followers through education. He also related to his grandson his views on the deeper meaning of their faith. Karim recalls his grandfather testing his knowledge of their religion. 'He could extract more from a human being in a short conversation than anybody else in a lifetime,' he mused.

Harvard in the 1950s was geared to the sons of upper-middle-class or wealthy families. The atmosphere at that time was not too different from Le Rosey in that the students were pretty much of the same élite backgrounds and were well looked after. All the accommodation included a sitting room, bedroom and private bathroom which were looked after by daily maid service. Freshmen shared these rooms and often four young men occupied a suite consisting of two bedrooms and a sitting room. Unless the thermometer reached 86 degrees, jackets and ties were required at all meals. Women were not allowed in the rooms except on Saturday evenings after seven-thirty, and then for only three hours (the student body called this the twilight seduction time).

Karim shared a suite of rooms in Wigglesworth Hall with three other freshmen. One of them, John Fell Stevenson, the son of Adlai Stevenson, the Democratic ex-governor of Illinois (who had lost the 1952 presidential election to General Dwight Eisenhower), became his closest friend.[1]

Stevenson recalled that when he first met his roommate Karim 'was dressed casually in a plain brown leather jacket, open white shirt, creaseless baggy trousers, and shoes which I believe had never been shined. This attire [except for mealtimes] changed only slightly for the better in the following years.'

'There was nothing formal or stand-offish about K,' another friend told this author. 'His pre-university education had been at a school [Le Rosey] that I understand had many foreign princes. At Harvard he was unique. Had he been stiffer about himself, he would have created a somewhat hostile attitude from his peers. But he was low-key. He dressed down and had few airs. He was tremendously self-disciplined both about his studies (he seemed always to be at the top of his class) and on the athletic field. There was an overwhelming amount of media coverage about "a prince at Harvard". K tossed it off. He was somewhat shy and I recall seeing him walking around the campus on his own in the first few weeks that he was at Harvard. But he quickly became just one of the guys.'

[1] Karim's other roommates at Harvard were John S. Ames III, Charles Stephen Heard and, from Geneva, Eric Franck.

Karim asked to be called K, as he had at Le Rosey, and that form of address was always used by his classmates and professors. He did not make friends easily, but once he did his natural wit and charm submerged his initial shyness. It helped that Sadruddin was by this time well-established at Harvard. Sadruddin's influence over the younger man was strong. After a term, Karim switched from engineering to Islamic studies under Harvard's exceptional Oriental scholars Sir Hamilton Gibb, Professor Philip K. Hitti, and Professor R. N. Frye. He did extremely well, his name appearing frequently on the Dean's List for his good grades.

He had a passion at the time for playing the bongo drums and practised 'drumming on anything available,' young Stevenson commented, 'waste baskets, automobile fenders, desk tops. If there wasn't anything to hit, he'd snap his fingers . . . This mood struck at odd times. He would be walking to class when suddenly his dexterous finger-snapping and resonant whistling would invade the academic calm. You could hear him a block away! . . . Many a time the quiet [in their shared rooms] was shattered by his beating out the time on the shower wall [while he was showering]!'

He excelled in his studies but he managed to find time for sports. He was an excellent all-rounder: soccer, hockey, skiing, tennis, running and rowing. Harvard allowed athletes to play only one competitive sport in a season. In his freshman year he chose his favourite, rowing, and worked hard on the Charles River but met with great disappointment when he did not make the crew, despite his perseverance. 'He was lean but too stocky for the light crew and too short for the heavy crew,' Stevenson recalled (although Karim was just under six feet tall).

In the winter, when he had time at weekends, he ski'd at Stowe, Vermont. In his moments of relaxation he liked to listen to music (particularly of the mamba variety) and read (history and classic novels) and he often played records while studying. For a college student his private library was formidable; his pride was an autographed set of Winston Churchill's works. He seldom went out with his mates or dated, generally preferring to spend his time reading. He did not drink and adhered faithfully to the customs and religious practices of his faith, praying three times daily. (None the less, his first question of

Stevenson when they met had been, 'Where is Radcliffe [the nearest all-woman school]?')

He did enjoy a skiing weekend with Stevenson from time to time. 'His ski clothes were a sight to behold,' his friend laughed. 'Turquoise elastic ski pants, a multi-coloured tennis sweater, and a black "beanie" hat. Any doubts one might have had upon first seeing this apparition were quickly dispelled as K took to the slopes. He was a top-notch skier.'

Stevenson also joined him for several trips to New York. 'K put on one of his two suits, dark grey or dark blue and one of his twelve ties, of which six [were] dark blue and six dark brown,' Stevenson remembered. 'Since he had only one pair of shoes, dirty black, there was no problem there. [In New York] K usually had a date. He had quite a large selection to choose from, however, and I never saw him get really serious over any particular girl, though he may have had a favourite from time to time ... Karim impressed me ... because he had a purpose – he wanted to help people. It wasn't adolescent sentimentality or showing off; he meant it.'

Stevenson (who was not driving) was involved in a terrible car crash while on a trip to Indiana with two of their other close friends, both of whom died. Karim flew to his side and remained with him at the hospital until it was certain that he was out of danger. They were to remain lifelong friends.

Despite his family's enormous wealth, Karim had no car of his own. Mostly he walked. Sometimes he borrowed Stevenson's car if he did have a date, which at Harvard consisted of a movie (either foreign films or Westerns, his favourites) and a steak house for dinner. 'They say his grandfather had a tremendous appetite,' Jane O'Reilly, whom he dated for a time, remembered. 'I guess he inherited it. [He also ordered a] shrimp cocktail with Russian dressing for his first course. He was very fussy about that Russian dressing.'

Amyn joined him in his third year at Harvard. Karim was once again the older protective brother. He did not have the flamboyant reputation of his Uncle Sadruddin (Sadri as he was known at Harvard), who got into continual scrapes with the Cambridge police for driving an improperly registered Daimler car, was a frequent party-goer and seemed to know how to pick the most beautiful young women for companions. Karim dated girls who were 'suitable', not on the wild side and whose parents were socially prominent. He kept up a lengthy and frequent correspondence with Sylvia Casablanca, the attractive sister of a fellow Roséan, whom he had dated during his last term at Le Rosey and who lived in Geneva. When he returned to Europe between terms, it was Sylvia whom he saw almost exclusively, leading to hints in the press of a possible engagement.

He was good-looking and possessed the best features of his exotic, mixed heritage, an English mother and a father who was half-Italian and half-Indian. He had dark hair and eyes, a fair complexion, a winning smile and a lithe body. He was the kind of young man who looked good in tennis clothes, ski outfits, or standing on the deck of a ship with his dark hair blowing in the sea breeze. (One of his professors claimed he bore 'an extremely remarkable resemblance to Marlon Brando'.) At first meeting he seemed shy, but his ability and inclination to take over situations immediately dispelled that image. He did not have his father's Oxford accent. His was more mid-Atlantic, with a dash of Continental phrasing tossed in. He mainly conversed in English, but he was just as fluent in French. According to his closest friends he expected his father to succeed the Aga Khan, thus giving him many years for youthful pursuits and intellectual growth.

Articles appeared in the press from time to time casting doubt upon Aly's succession, with speculation that the Aga Khan could name Sadruddin or Karim as Imam to succeed him. 'Why should there be any doubt?' Aly angrily replied to a reporter from the London *Daily Express* who told him there had been rumours he would never be Imam.

None of the Aga Khan's possible successors seems to have been taken into his confidence, although in May 1955 he had already made up his mind whom he would name as his heir. The secret was concealed in his last will and testament drawn up at that time with the aid of his lawyers and his Swiss adviser, Maître Ardoin, and locked away in the vaults of Lloyds Bank in London with instructions that it should not be opened until after his death.

Not only the Imamate, but many millions of dollars were at stake. Whoever became Imam would inherit the bulk, although no one doubted that the Aga Khan would provide for the rest of his family

19. The Aga Khan divorced Andrée in 1942 and married his mistress of four years, a former Miss France, the statuesque Yvette Labrousse, forty years his junior. They are seen here in Tehran's marble palace for the wedding of the Shah of Persia to Princess Soraya in 1951.

20. *Left*: Rita
Hayworth as
Gilda. Aly fell in
love with her at
first sight. She
was not so sure
about him until
they spent the
night together
at his home, the
fabulous Château
de l'Horizon.

21. *Above*: They
were marred in
Vallauris, France.
Thousands
crowded the
street to catch a
glimpse of them.

22. *Right*:
Arriving in Capri
on Aly's yacht,
the *Zaca*. They
were followed
wherever they
went.

23. *Left*: Princess Yasmin, daughter of Aly Khan and Rita Hayworth, was a pawn in her parents' divorce. Rita finally allowed the child to see her grandfather. They hit it off exceptionally well, and Yasmin was to become especially fond of the Begum.

24. *Below*: At home in Yakymour the Aga Khan and the Begum play backgammon, *c.* 1955. The house was decorated with sea murals and shell wall fixtures.

25. On the terrace of Yakymour. The Aga Khan was seriously ill. His will was made, but his successor remained a well-kept secret.

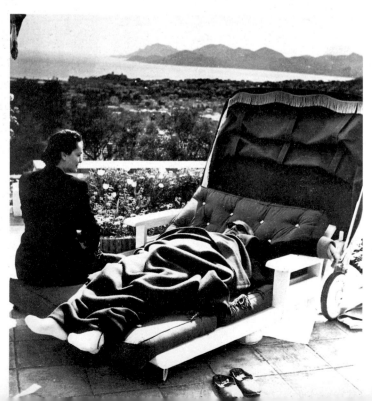

26. The failing Aga Khan visits Paris for the last time. The woman on his right, an old friend, helps with the transfer from train to limousine.

27. Princess Yasmin leaves Switzerland after the death of her grandfather in 1957. Aly Khan had been passed by in the succession.

28. The funeral of Aga Khan III in Aswan. In defiance of established custom the Begum walked with the male mourners.

29. In 1957, Sadruddin married Nina Dyer, a London model and former wife of a German steel baron. Nina collected wild animals and expensive jewels. The marriage later ended in divorce and Nina eventually took her own life.

30. Aly Khan rode his famous horses as well as breeding and training them. He was never to get over his exclusion from the succession, although he always supported his son, Karim Aga Khan IV.

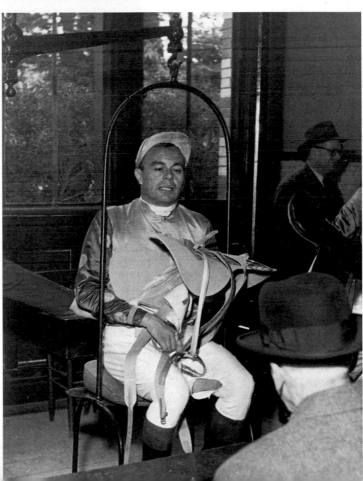

31. *Above left*: As a young boy Karim loved to ski. He later took part in the Olympics, without placing.

32. *Above right*: Karim relaxes after stroking the school crew to victory at a regatta in Switzerland.

33. *Below*: Karim with one of his early girlfriends, Sylvia Casablancas (in white gown and bando on her hair).

(and perhaps a mistress or two – or three). But there was the prospect that if Aly was passed over for either his much younger brother or his son, he would have to answer to them as he did to his father and go to them if he needed more money because of a cash flow crisis (which was his constant problem). The Aga Khan's health became even more precarious in the summer of 1956. The Begum had recently completed the decoration of a new house, a villa in Versoix, on Lac Léman near Evian, where the Aga Khan liked to take the waters. The house was renamed Villa Barakat (meaning 'blessings') and arrangements were made for the healthful waters of Evian to be delivered to the villa every day for the Aga Khan's use. His declining physical condition brought out a new sense of family in his sons. Both Aly and Sadruddin bought homes close to Villa Barakat although Aly was in Switzerland less often than his half-brother. There were the stud farms and horses to oversee. He still rode whenever he could and brought a good percentage of his mounts into the winners' enclosure. He also liked the social life of London and Paris and was seldom seen anywhere without the company of a beautiful woman.

Rita Hayworth's marriage to Dick Haymes was in serious trouble. Unable to cope with marital and career problems along with the care of her daughters, she asked Aly to take five-year-old Yasmin for six months. He happily obliged and made arrangements for her and her governess to occupy a wing of l'Horizon. The first weekend after her arrival in Europe, Yasmin took the train to Versoix to visit her grandfather.

Yasmin appears to be the only small child with whom the Aga Khan ever found it easy to communicate, perhaps because she was the first and only girl born in his family. When he moved back to Yakymour at the end of the summer and she was at nearby l'Horizon, he saw her frequently. They would take drives along the Croisette, the chic avenue that curved with the Mediterranean through Cannes, and he would point out all the famous Riviera landmarks. He told her about Queen Victoria and his first visit to the South of France and to Windsor Castle. In December, he helped her celebrate her sixth birthday at Yakymour. When he asked her what she wanted for a present, she turned her excited gaze on the glittering crystal chandelier that hung overhead in the front vestibule where they were standing.

'That!' she cried exuberantly.

The chandelier was taken down and brought into a room where there was enough space for her to examine it. 'I think you should put it back up,' she decided solemnly after a long and careful examination, circling the massive piece.

'You don't like it now?' he asked.

'The sunshine disappeared,' she replied soberly.

At this time Aly became seriously involved with a gamine fashion model for the couturiers Jacques Fath and Givenchy, whose real name was Simone Bodin, but who called herself Bettina. Aly was in love with her as perhaps he had never been with another woman, for he claimed, and appeared to have become, fairly monogamous. He asked her to give up her work (which she did) and move in with him in his Paris house on the Boulevard Maurice-Barrès and had a bedroom completely redecorated in her favourite shade of golden yellow as a surprise. And he gave her carte blanche to do what she wanted with the decor of l'Horizon. 'This is your home, Zinette,' he told her, using one of his pet names for her; the other being 'Zine'.

Bettina brought a woman's touch and immediate order to l'Horizon and to Aly's lifestyle. She was an exquisite creature, porcelain skin, with glowing red hair that cast off an aura when caught by the light, lively green eyes, a well-defined facial structure and freckles that defied make-up. Born in Brittany, in the north-west region of France, and raised in Normandy, she had never lost her enchanting country-girl charm despite the world of glamour and sophistication that she conquered when coming to Paris as a young woman. Most people who knew Bettina in those early days, recall most her 'feline grace'. She moved with extraordinary style. 'I think it was Bettina who brought the word "cat-walk" [where models parade designers' clothes] into the language,' one of her contemporaries said.

Yasmin – Yassy, as her family called her – took to Bettina straight away and a strong bond grew between them. Karim and Amyn spent August 1956 at l'Horizon as well, giving Aly's three children a chance to become better acquainted. Bettina seldom left Aly's side. She was there at l'Horizon or in Paris to be a hostess to his friends, however late or unexpectedly he showed up with guests. She was with him cheering for his horses at the races, waiting for him whatever the hour at the casinos in which he liked to gamble; when he travelled without her, she was there to greet him on his return. The American actress Kim Novak was photographed smiling intimately up at him on one of these trips and there were gossipy hints that perhaps Aly was tiring of Bettina. When he showed up with Novak at l'Horizon, Bettina was the same charming hostess, no scene was made and Novak appeared to turn her interest quickly in another direction.

The Aga Khan grew fond of Bettina. She and Aly talked about marriage, but decided to wait, a decision that seemed to be mutual but was more likely a display of Bettina's selflessness and wish to do what she thought would please Aly in their relationship.

Romance was in the air among the Khan clan. Sadruddin, twenty-three in the winter of 1956, had fallen in love with the exotically beautiful, rather eccentric Nina Dyer, three years his senior, born in Ceylon and the daughter of an English tea planter. She had glorious titian hair and a stunning figure. At twenty she had left Ceylon and, after an unsuccessful attempt to be an actress, moved to Paris where she became better known for her affairs (Nicolas Franco, brother of the Spanish dictator, was one of her conquests) than for her new career as a fashion model. She was only twenty-two when she met the thirty-two-year-old millionaire German industrialist Baron Heinrich von Thyssen. Two years later they were married. The bridegroom's gifts to his bride were an island in the West Indies (reportedly populated by white elephants), a 22-carat diamond ring, a string of black pearls and other jewellery worth over half a million dollars, a baby leopard and a fully-grown black panther. Ten months later they were divorced and Nina (claiming adultery on von Thyssen's part), received all of her wedding gifts as well as a fifteen-room villa in Versailles which she shared with 'two hundred parrots, eight Pekinese, two borzois, a leopard and a panther' (according to press coverage). She had also negotiated a $3 million financial settlement.

The Aga Khan was not initially pleased with the idea of Nina as a wife for Sadruddin, but eventually gave them permission to be married and 15 July 1957 was set as the date of the wedding. That spring the Aga Khan showed visible signs of failing. His weight went from 225 to 170 pounds in only a few months. He said it was nothing, that he had simply lost his appetite. He decided it would do him a world of good if he and the Begum went to Chantilly (twenty-one miles north of Paris), the Newmarket of France, where racing has been at the heart of the community since 1836. At Chantilly the Aga Khan could watch the racing from his car, drawn up beside the track, which would at least make things easier for him.

Shortly after his arrival, a searing heat wave gripped Chantilly. 'He should never have come here!' the Begum told Aly. He insisted on remaining. A day later his condition turned from serious to critical. With the Begum, Sadruddin, Nina Dyer, a local heart specialist and two nurses the Aga Khan was placed aboard a chartered aircraft to be taken to Geneva. He refused to go to hospital. He wanted to be taken to his new home, Villa Barakat.

An ambulance waited for him at the Geneva airport and his request was honoured. He was carried up to his bedroom on a stretcher and lifted on to the enormous bed. Several doctors gathered downstairs to talk to the Begum as the nurses tried to make him comfortable. The Begum was informed that there was no hope. The Aga Khan's heart was failing and cancer had spread throughout his body. It was a matter of time.

How much time? the Begum wanted to know. She was told a week at best. Aly called Karim at Harvard to return immediately. Amyn had vital tests to do and would follow in a few days. Yasmin, who had returned to California to live with Rita again, was, as it happened, on her way by ship for her summer stay with Aly. Bettina was to meet her when she disembarked and bring her to the Villa Barakat. When the child arrived at her grandfather's estate on 9 July, the grounds and reception rooms were filled with *mukhis* and Ismaili leaders. Bettina and Aly each held one of Yasmin's hands tightly as they led her through the lines of the Aga Khan's followers who had come to pay their last respects to their Imam.

The Aga Khan smiled gently when he saw the little girl draw up shyly as near to his bed as his four doctors would allow. 'Yassy,' one of the doctors claimed the Aga Khan said, although he did not understand the words that followed, 'you keep looking for the sunshine.'

In the early morning of 11 July, Aly, Sadruddin, Karim and the Begum began their vigil by the dying man's bedside. Bettina and Nina waited in a connecting room. Yasmin was being kept occupied in another part of the house. The Aga Khan was unconscious. At 12.45 PM he died. The Begum moved to the windows and drew the curtains; she was sobbing softly. The reign of Aga Khan III had ended. In his dying days he had made no mention or sign of who was to succeed him. It would, by the natural course of things, be one of the three men present and, following historical precedent, his elder son Aly. Despite his many disagreements with his father, Aly seemed at that moment confident that this was the case.

He immediately took charge of the situation. The answer to the succession would be in the will, which would be read by the Aga Khan's lawyer in the villa's ground-floor sitting room the next morning. The crowd that was gathered in the grounds of the villa, religious followers and members of the press, had to be informed of the Aga Khan III's death and the fact that he had not named his successor on his deathbed.

Aly said his last goodbye to his father and then led the rest of the family down the villa's curving staircase and out on to the terrace. It was over 90 degrees in the sun and Aly, his face drawn, showed signs of grief and exhaustion, his open-necked shirt revealing beads of sweat. He made the announcement. Ismailis dropped to their knees.

He greeted reporters and told them there would be a press conference soon and the new Aga Khan would address them. Then he disappeared back inside. Early the next morning Maître Ardoin, an official from Lloyds Bank (Foreign) Ltd, of 10 Moorgate, London, and Dr Otto Giesen, one of the lawyers who had drawn up the will, arrived. Aly hurried with the rest of the family (Amyn having just arrived, too late to see his grandfather alive) to the luxurious sitting room with its Oriental decor. Even Yasmin was brought in to hear the reading of the will. The curtains were drawn so that those inside could not be seen by the hundred or so Ismailis standing in the garden near the windows waiting to pay homage to their new Imam as soon as the announcement was made.

Maître Ardoin stood between Aly and Sadruddin, the rest were seated. Giesen in a clear, unemotional voice, with a slight but noticeable German accent, began to read. There were several pages that contained the Aga Khan's marital history (from Shahzadi to the present Begum) and the provisions made for each of his wives. (The distribution of the Aga Khan's great wealth would follow in a codicil to the will.) As Giesen ended this section he glanced up from the document and looked around the room. If he wanted everyone's attention he had it. This was obviously the moment they had been waiting for. He lowered his eyes to the paper in his hand as he read the Aga Khan's final wishes.

'Ever since the time of my ancestor Ali, the first Imam, that is to say over a period of some thirteen hundred years,' he intoned, 'it has always been the tradition of our family that each Imam chooses his successor at his absolute and unfettered discretion from amongst any of his descendants whether they be sons or other male issue.'

Aly paled. These words left no doubt in his, or any one else's mind in that room, that Aly Khan was to be passed over.

Giesen continued.

'And in these circumstances and in view of the fundamentally altered conditions in the world in very recent years due to the great changes which have taken place including the discoveries of atomic science I am convinced that it is in the best interests of the Shia [Muslim] Ismailian Community that I should be succeeded by a young man who has been brought up and developed during recent years and in the midst of the new age and who brings a new outlook on life to his office as Imam.'

Eyes shifted from Sadruddin to Karim and back.

'For these reasons and although he is not now one of my heirs, I APPOINT my grandson KARIM, the son of my son ALY SALOMONE KHAN, to succeed to the title of AGA KHAN and to be the Imam and Pir of all my Shia Ismailian followers, and should my said grandson KARIM predecease me then I APPOINT his brother AMYN MAHOMED, the second son of my son ALY SALOMONE KHAN, as my successor to the Imamate. I DESIRE that my successor shall during the first seven years of his Imamate be guided on questions of general Imamate policy by my said wife YVETTE . . . BLANCHE LABROUSSE, the Begum Aga Khan, who has been familiar for many years with the problems facing my followers and in whose wise judgement I place the greatest confidence.'

However much Aly might have suspected his father could have passed him by, he was unprepared when the Aga Khan's final wishes were read out. Bettina recalled that his 'father's preference for [Karim] was a kind of public humiliation. He was never quite the same from that day on.'

But Aly pulled himself together and crossed the room to Karim. 'The Imam is dead, long live the Imam,' he said and kissed his son's hand before backing humbly away.

KARIM AGA KHAN IV AND QUEEN ELIZABETH II

A masterly document, the Aga Khan III's will revealed little concerning his great personal wealth. Whether this was done to avoid death duties or simply to keep his full financial worth hidden from his heirs is difficult to know. His private dealings were closely interwoven with the business affairs of the sect, which were always kept fairly secretive, and most countries in which it had communities exempted religious organizations from taxation which meant there were no public records. But his investments ranged from his multi-million-dollar horseracing empire to personal and investment property throughout the world, mining interests, textile mills and publishing. His will and codicil simply made sure that certain bequests were set out. What remained of the Aga Khan's estate after these disbursements appears to have been funnelled through the Imamate with his successor as inheritor.

In the will, the Begum was left Yakymour, Barakat, the house in Paris and all their contents, which included some priceless antiques, masses of exquisite silver and a library of rare books. She also had a king's ransom in jewels given to her by her late husband, numerous prize thoroughbred racehorses and multi-million-dollar personal holdings in real estate, oil, stock and other investments.

Aly and Sadruddin were to share their father's jewellery, which consisted of a huge cache of large diamond, ruby and star sapphire rings, cufflinks, tie clasps, stick pins and walking sticks (one had a carved tiger's head with ten-carat diamonds for its eyes and a ruby-studded collar round its neck). Aly was to be allowed to purchase any horse in which he and his father had been co-owners; the Aga Khan's other horses were to be sold by public auction (as were his cars and the contents of his hotel suite at the Ritz in London), the proceeds to go into his estate, which would go to his widow (one-eighth), Aly and Sadruddin (seven-eighths to be divided between them after legacies and duties). Eventually, under the provisions of this clause, the three heirs would receive approximately the same amount in cash, about $3 million each. As the Begum's share was without encumbrances, she would receive hers first.

The Aga Khan's three grandchildren had pre-existing private trusts, set up when they were younger (they were rumoured to have been half a million dollars for Yasmin and several times that amount for Karim and Amyn). His staff at the time of his death and now redundant were given tax-free wages and pensions for eighteen months. His private nurse during the last years of his life received $30,000 and several other former employees received similar legacies. Any arrangements with his mistresses were left discreetly out of the will: he had provided for them separately, as, of course, he had also done in his divorce settlement with Andrée (although he left instructions in his will that the members of his family treat the ex-Begum with continuing respect and kindness).

No mention was made in the document of the huge sums he had invested in corporations, oil shares, banks, trusts and newspapers. Karim appeared to be in shock when he came out of a private meeting with his grandfather's solicitors. He was enormously rich. He was to control his grandfather's vast international business empire and the income generated from his followers' gifts and donations, the amount he would retain for his own purposes having been left to his discretion. As with his predecessor, these figures are not available. It is claimed that Karim Aga Khan takes a smaller percentage than his grandfather, but what that is, or how much it involves, remains a private matter between Karim Aga Khan and his financial assistants (although the figure of 8 per cent has been rumoured).

He had also inherited great responsibilities and emotional demands. At twenty, he was now the spiritual leader of the entire Ismaili people. His mother claimed that he did not regard it as a burden. 'He had a strong sense of mission, an instinctive thing that works automatically,' she said. Probably that was true, but the young Imam seemed to be under tremendous strain as he went out to greet the press on the rolling lawns of Barakat the morning after his grandfather's death and read them the provisions of the will relating to the Imamate. Aly stood silently beside his son, his face impassive. The press were watching closely for any sign of animosity between the two, or evidence of depression or disappointment on Aly's face, but he maintained perfect composure.

A short time later mourners and the press were allowed to view the Aga Khan's body, clothed in a white satin shroud, his frame shrunken by his long illness, surrounded by red roses and resting in a triple-sized oak coffin placed on a raised dais in the large central hallway of Barakat. A giant bouquet of white flowers was at the foot of the coffin. No one was prepared for the crush that ensued as followers, press and the plain curious, brandishing cameras, filed past the bier and then pushed forward to see other rooms in the house. In less than an hour the doors were closed to the public.

The following morning a chair — the old Aga Khan's dining chair, chosen by the Begum for this purpose — was taken out to the magnificent rose garden at the rear of the house to be used for Karim's enthronement ceremony. The sun blazed down on the dark uncovered head of the young man — not attired in Oriental splendour as the old Aga Khan had been at his *gadi*, but in a sober blue suit, white shirt and conservative striped tie — as he walked between two rows of Ismaili leaders and seated himself in the gold brocade upholstered chair. By dressing in European fashion, he had made a silent statement. He would, like his grandfather, be his own man and chose to dress as it pleased him.

The ceremony was brief, prayers said, a passage from the Quran read, and then the men whose holy leader he now was, one by one approached him to pledge their loyalty and then backed reverently away. (Amyn, Sadruddin and Aly were not present.) After this homage, Karim sat patiently for photographs before making the following statement to the press:

'My grandfather dedicated his life to the Imamate and Islam, both of which for him always came first, and above all other considerations. While I was prepared that one day I might be designated the Aga Khan, I did not expect it to be so soon. I follow a great man in a great responsibility and he could have given me no more appreciated honour than to bequeath me this spiritual leadership. My life, as his, will be dedicated to the service of my followers.' He had written the short statement himself and read it with genuine feeling.

At nine the next morning a funeral cortège of twenty-seven sleek black limousines, led by a hearse carrying the oversized coffin, was escorted by motorcycle police from Barakat through the centre of Geneva to the airport and directly on to the runway where a chartered DC6 aircraft was waiting to transport the body to Egypt. The Begum had been given authority to direct the burial plans and had been left $150,000 for this purpose; Aswan had been chosen for the site of the Aga Khan's entombment. He had requested that he be buried in a dry place, where his body would be preserved like those of the pharaohs for centuries, and they had recently built a sprawling white-domed villa, Noor el Salaam, nearby on the River Nile.[1] She planned to build an airtight mausoleum with a raised crypt on a hill near the villa. The Aga Khan would be laid temporarily to rest in a vault in an inner courtyard of the house, and moved to his final resting place when it was completed.

Karim and the Begum stepped out of the leading car in the cortège; Amyn, Sadruddin and Aly (all the men were wearing black silk suits) from the second vehicle. The five close family members (it had been decided that Yasmin should remain in Switzerland) accompanied the body to Cairo. For the 600-mile air journey to Aswan's airport, which had not been in use for several months, they transferred to two smaller aircraft, Amyn and Sadruddin taking a slightly later flight than the one with the coffin and the rest of the family. The remaining mourners took scheduled flights to Cairo, transferring to smaller aircraft to travel on to Aswan.

This area of Egypt had suffered a recent drought and the temperature remained in the high nineties. Under a blistering sun, bare-backed men swept the mounds of sand from the runway with palm-leaf brooms so that the first plane could land. The Governor of Aswan, local officials (holding a massive wreath from President Nasser), Sir Edward Twining, Governor of Tanganyika (Queen Elizabeth's representative),[2] and

[1] The house at Aswan was the property of the Imamate, but provision had been made for the Begum and the new Aga Khan to enjoy it during their lifetimes and that Karim could pass it on to his heir.

[2] The following letter was sent to Karim, Aga Khan IV, by the Private Secretary to the Queen:

'On this sad occasion of the death of his Highness the Aga Khan I am commanded to convey to you the deep sympathy of the Queen in the grief which you and the Ismaili people in many lands share in the passing of your Holy Imam.

'His Highness will be remembered by all for the wise guidance and selfless leadership

a handful of reporters and photographers, cameras ready, stood on the edge of the airfield flanked by troops from the Egyptian armed services.

The plane landed with a grinding sound in a thick cloud of dust. A red fire-truck, its warning bells clanking, tore out of a wooden shed and sped towards the grounded aircraft. There were a few moments of concern and then the aircraft's doors were swung open and the Begum, shrouded in black, was helped out by two attendants. For a moment she seemed stunned by the intensity of the sun and paused at the bottom of the gangplank unsure of her next move. Karim Aga Khan disembarked directly after her and took her arm. Aly followed. The Governor and the rest of the waiting group had moved across the field and stood at a respectful distance as uniformed Egyptian soldiers unloaded the coffin 'like a packing case. No funeral march, no flags at half-mast, no guard of honour,' a German newspaper reported.

From the runway the heavy coffin was half-dragged, half-carried, a good distance to the banks of the nearby Nile where a team of men laboriously managed to lift it on to an imposing barge, almost allowing it to slip into the water at one point. By this time the river was crowded with modest boats filled with mourners, press and the inquisitive. Immediately upon their arrival at the airport, Karim, the Begum and Aly had been driven by limousine to the Cataract Hotel in Aswan, which appeared to be an error for then they were rushed without pause to Noor el Salaam to await the arrival of the coffin.

When they reached their destination, joined now by Amyn and Sadruddin who had come from the airport in a second car, they found to their distress that the barge carrying the coffin was having trouble in mooring at the villa's small landing stage, a problem exacerbated by the low waters of the Nile. Sadruddin, soaked in perspiration, strode on to the docking platform to give instructions to the soldiers accompanying the barge. Karim stood back, still holding the Begum's arm, Aly and Amyn behind them.

which he has freely given during his many happy and eventful years. His energetic and devoted work for the League of Nations in a life dedicated to the service of his followers and to the welfare of mankind will long be remembered.

'In the arduous responsibilities which you will be called on to bear as leader of your people, her Majesty extends to you her sincere greetings and prayers that you may long fulfil your role as counsellor to the Ismaili community who owe to you their allegiance.'

Finally the coffin was transferred safely on to the wooden landing platform and carried by the soldiers to the imposing villa, looking like a gleaming white mirage in the dazzling sunlight, followed by a stream of mourners and sightseers who had managed to get out of their boats along the nearby banks and scramble on to the shore. The coffin was placed in a rotunda in the entry of Noor el Salaam. As the family and mourners gathered around it, several passages from the Quran were read. The family returned to the hotel immediately after while the crowds were dispersed by the soldiers left to guard the body.

As soon as Sadruddin was back in the hotel, he telegraphed his fiancée Nina Dyer (who had gone directly from Geneva to Paris), 'Aswan glowing heat – complete chaos – impatient to return to you.' With the death of the old Aga Khan, their wedding had been post-poned until the end of the forty-day mourning period, an old Muslim practice, and Nina was busily occupied reorganizing their plans.

That evening, dressed in a fresh black silk suit, Karim Aga Khan, looking pale and exhausted, his brother and uncle in attendance, his father mysteriously absent, met the local Ismaili community leaders, dignitaries and the press in a private room at the hotel. It seemed there were problems in Syria where the Ismaili community favoured Aly over Karim as the new Imam. A rally of 50,000 Syrian Ismailis had decided on the day the announcement was made to acclaim Aly Khan as their leader. In fact, while Karim was meeting the Ismailis and the press, Aly was making plans to fly to Syria in support of his son. The incident could have proved divisive, but, however disappointed Aly might have been over his father's will, he was dedicated to the support of Karim as Imam.

A devotional service was held in Aswan's Abu-Shok mosque the following morning. To honour the universality of their faith, Aly (looking haggard, but he had been on the telephone almost the entire night with Ismaili leaders in Syria) wore a Pakistani Persian lamb hat, Sadruddin a Burmese skullcap, Amyn and Karim fezzes. Karim led the congregation in prayer. Aly later confessed to Bettina that he had been tremendously moved and impressed with the way Karim fell so naturally into his role as Imam. He presented a much different image to his predecessor. Despite his clothing, he looked European, his skin fair, his features strongly marked by his mother's ancestry. Slim, handsome enough to be mistaken for a film star, he spoke with a Harvard twang that edged his upper-class English accent. Yet Aly was right, according to the others who were present. Karim had suddenly acquired the aura of the office he now held, much as the young Queen Elizabeth had so quickly taken on an air of majesty. His bearing was regal, his voice rang with sincerity, and he accepted, without any perceptible uneasiness, the obeisance of his subjects (including all members of his family), extending his hand to be kissed, standing erect as his followers touched their foreheads to the ground in prayer.

In the afternoon, the mourners returned to Noor el Salaam. The old Aga Khan's heavy oak coffin was carried on their shoulders by his four closest male survivors (with additional help from the Egyptian Army) through the inner court of the villa to the vault where it was lowered to the ground. In one more disastrous miscalculation, the door to the vault was too narrow and, as everyone stood waiting in the broiling sun, workmen were sent for to widen it with chisels and hammers.

It was late afternoon before the coffin was placed in the vault and the door sealed. Karim led the mourners out of the inner court where their cars were waiting. This was not to be the old Aga Khan's final funeral service. There would be another when he was reinterred in the mausoleum being built on a nearby hillock. But the bleakness of the ceremony was somewhat less of a tribute than one might expect for a man whose life encompassed almost a century of historic events and who was an active participant in many of them.

He had taken part in the fall of the British Empire and independence of India, an honoured mourner at the funerals of Queen Victoria, Edward VII and George V. He had adorned himself in full Indian regalia for the Indian Durbars at Lord Curzon's request and tried his best to help Britain keep India in the Empire. He had been a legend since his youth, and was one of the few surviving representatives of the Victorian age.

Where then was the glittering cavalcade of princes, resplendent in scarlet and gold, the exalted panoply he so much admired? His faith demanded simpler homage, but the old Aga Khan, with his passion for pageantry and his admiration for the British monarchy, might well have hoped for something more spectacular to mark his leaving his earthly kingdom, even knowing as well he did, that his was a wanderers' domain, with no true home.

It had perhaps been a miscalculation on the part of Lady Ali Shah and the Aga Khan III's early advisers to revive an old Oriental custom and weigh him against gold, diamonds and platinum to mark the respective anniversaries of his long reign. The grandeur and sheer uniqueness of these ceremonies could easily obliterate the serious things he had accomplished – his work as President of the League of Nations where, as he said in a speech before that assembly, he was pledged to the lessening of military burdens in all peace-loving countries, 'for a decrease in the financial load which those burdens impose, for the security of civil populations against indiscriminate methods of warfare and, above all, for security against the very idea of war'.

He was a member of the Disarmament Conference for seven years. ('Why did it fail?' he had asked in a speech at his Diamond Jubilee in 1946. 'Ultimately because of hate. And yet why did people hate each other? It was because of fear. Where there is fear there is no love.') For more than half a century he had carried out delicate and difficult missions for the British in the Middle East and Asia.

Only his own people seemed to be aware of his financial genius (admittedly helped greatly by Lady Ali Shah and a host of advisers, bankers and accountants, most of whom were not Ismaili), the way in which he had invested Ismaili community funds with such shrewdness had made his sect the best-fed, best-housed and best-educated group of Muslims in the world.

The Begum had been adamant about burying her husband in Aswan. No one seems to have dissented. Husband and wife had obviously spoken about this eventuality, for the mausoleum design had been drawn in the last year of the Aga Khan's life. Still, it appears a curious choice for the Aga Khan to have made. The sacred burial grounds in India where his parents were interred would have seemed more likely; or Karachi, scene of his birth and of his Platinum Jubilee. His widow's hand is evident in his entombment in the Land of the Pharaohs. It was where they first fell in love, where they were married, and where she planned to live for at least part of the time each year. This presence could not help but keep her central to the Imamate as Ismailis would come to Noor el Salaam to pay homage to their dead leader, who had been Imam longer than any other in the history of their religion.

In his will, the old Aga Khan had also designated his widow to be Karim's closest adviser on 'general Imamate policy' for a period of seven years. He was perhaps thinking about his relationship with Lady Ali Shah and how wise she had been on his behalf where money was concerned. Or perhaps he wanted to maintain a close tie for his widow to the current Imam. He had come to trust Yvette's judgement. And there was no doubt that she was a bright woman and knew a great deal about the affairs of the Imamate, having been his right hand during the last years of his life. But the arrangement was not an easy one for Karim, who had long ago broken his mother's maternal hold (something the old Aga Khan had never done) and who was of a strongly independent nature.

For Karim, 'the shadow of the Begum' loomed large. If Aly was surprised to see how naturally he wore the cloak of power, so were all the others who had thought they were close to him – Amyn, Sadruddin, the elders of the sect, even women friends and school contemporaries. No one, except his grandfather and his mother, had perceived the strength of character that was concealed beneath his seemingly gentle, ingratiating exterior. Suddenly they were exposed to what one close associate called 'Karim's iron will behind a deceptive small boy's winning smile'.

'Karim Aga Khan felt a genuine fondness for the Begum,' one of these associates said. 'But he clearly resented the restriction that had been placed on him for it was evident from the very beginning of his becoming Imam that she was not going to take a back seat or allow herself to be charmed by him out of her position of power. And she was protected by some of the old Aga Khan's staff and religious followers who wanted to make sure his wishes were honoured.

'In the first months after the Aga Khan's death, most major decisions were referred to her for counsel – and the Begum did not always agree with Karim Aga Khan. He wanted to take the Imamate into the twentieth century and some of his methods seemed [to the Begum] too modern – or at least too much of a jump from old world to new world in too short a time.'

Karim was conscious of the need for his immediate acceptance for the productive continuity of the Ismaili communities. He recalled the success he had in winning over community leaders when he had toured East Africa with his father in 1955. And so he instigated a head-spinning tour of Ismaili communities that included civic and religious functions and were bound to be heavily covered by the press just two weeks after his grandfather was buried: 4 August, Karachi; 9 August, Bombay; 12 August, Nairobi; then a week's tour of East African communities including Zanzibar. The Begum appeared to think he was moving too fast, that time should be given to allow Ismailis to mourn their dead Imam with due respect. Her advice was to wait, but he went ahead anyway, well supported by most of the Ismaili leaders, who expected to follow their Imam's decisions, however young he was. The date of his grandfather's death, 11 July, became a day to be celebrated by his millions of followers as the Day of the Imamate. He next dispatched his father to Syria (perhaps to distance him from the limelight and controversy still raging in the press over Aly Khan's being passed over in the accession). Ismailis there had now rescinded their first proposal to break away and look to Aly as their Imam. But Aly's task was to convince them that Karim was well qualified to carry on for his father, who had, after all and as was his right, named him as his successor.

A herculean task awaiting the new Imam would be to preserve the rigid discipline which was such a remarkable feature of the widespread Ismaili communities during his grandfather's rule, and which had survived the disrupting influences of two world wars. Attempts had been made in 1954 in some communities in East Africa to call for the Aga Khan's abdication. These influences had quickly and peacefully been put down by the much larger numbers of his supporters. Now the question arose how far this allegiance was based on personal loyalty to the late Aga Khan and on his natural gift for leadership.

His grandfather had kept the far-distant Ismaili communities together by his investment policies and by reorganizing the finances of communities and individuals, setting up an investment trust for receiving and lending money at low interest rates to Ismaili traders and to those buying or building houses (he had promised not long before his death that every Ismaili would eventually own his own home). His educational, social and economic influence in these communities had increased in the last years, perhaps for one strong reason – education, which had always been his watchword. There were now well over a hundred Aga Khan schools in East Africa and it would be up to Karim to convince his followers that education and all the causes instituted by his grandfather would go forward and prosper under his leadership. It would be no easy task for a man of such young years and without previous training in the job that faced him.

He had gone directly to London and his mother's home in Eaton Square to rest after his grandfather's interment before leaving by plane for his scheduled tour. He had one more year at Harvard before receiving his degree. His mother would have liked him to return, but that would not be possible in the near future. While in England, he was shocked by the daily tabloid accounts of his supposedly private life as a Lothario out to replace his father as an international lover. Most of the newspapers were already speculating on who his future bride would be. Sylvia Casablanca was high on the list, but beautiful girls were named from Hungary, Egypt, France, and even Hollywood – some he had never even met, others who were his father's lady friends. He was good-looking, extremely photogenic, and there was always the old adage: like father, like son. Readers were inclined to believe these highly imaginative stories.

His formal installations as Imam in East Africa, Uganda and Pakistan were scheduled for the end of the year. Before then, on 5 August, Queen Elizabeth II conferred on him the 'dignity' of Highness, which Queen Victoria had bestowed on his grandfather.

The new Aga Khan was English through his mother and carried a British passport. He was, therefore, a subject of the youthful Queen, who had ascended the throne in 1952 at the age of 25 and was only a decade older than Karim. To her he was the head of a large Muslim sect and to be respected as such. But he had no power or connection that would be of any use to Great Britain, no country to do commerce with, no political allies that could be helpful, no vast oil wells or munitions factories to bolster resources.

'The old Aga Khan was a legend, exotic, part of the history of the British Empire and its occupation of India – beautiful, mysterious India,' a member of the Queen's staff said.

He brought up images of Curzon, Gandhi, great durbars and Indian princes loyal to the Crown. But, of course, all that was over, done with. The Queen saw this new, young Aga Khan as just another businessman, terribly rich, mind you, but not someone she would like to include in her inner circle, not even remotely, I would think. She was never comfortable in the presence – however formal – of fast-living men like the Aga Khan's father, Aly Khan, and I suspect she imagined [especially after all the press coverage to this effect] this young man would be cut from the same cloth.

The Queen was having a spot of difficulty in her marriage in the late fifties. I don't think Philip was often in her bed – or his own, for that matter. She appeared to be very much in love with him. But things were not easy and I suspect she was – well, after all, even Queens get randy. There were moments when she could be caught off-guard when a dashing man paid her a compliment – even a simple one. She had a way of blushing – very girl-like. Rather endearing. I think the name Khan was a red flag and he wasn't on any of the Palace lists. Although I don't believe he was in England too often – except to see his mother or for the races when his father had a horse entered.

Karim returned to London from his whirlwind tour of Ismaili communities convinced that he needed an able staff, quickly put in place. Michael Curtis, who had recently left his job as director of the London-based *News Chronicle*, a liberal newspaper, was engaged as his personal aide to help with future tours, press relations, drafting speeches and just about anything that might require careful handling. Curtis then set about gathering a supporting staff. His first major assignment was to oversee Karim Aga Khan's three installation ceremonies in Tanganyika, Kenya and Uganda. A decision was made that both Aly and Princess Joan (as his former wife was now known) would accompany their son to present a united front.

They arrived by chartered plane at Dar es Salaam's international airport on 16 October 1957 and were greeted by a large crowd that included Tanganyika officials, Ismailis and a guard of honour formed by a troop of Aga Khan Boy Scouts and Girl Guides. There was a procession of limousines escorted by uniformed motorcycle police officers through the large city to Government House where Karim was to be an official guest.

Dar es Salaam (Arabic for 'House of Peace') was the capital of Tanganyika,[1] a large metropolis of over a million people on the Indian Ocean. For many years it had been the capital of German East Africa. During World War II it had grown and become a haven for political exiles and the city was host to an exotic mix of cultures. It was an important port for oceangoing vessels, although native lateen-rigged dhows still carried goods bound for coastal Africa and south-west Asia. German, Swahili, Arabic and English were all spoken. This multi-cultural atmosphere was a perfect setting for the installation of an Ismaili Imam.

The press was in full force and photographs circled the globe of the elaborate ceremonies held on 19 October; a flag march of Ismailis to the Upanga, the scene of the enthronement ceremony, marching bands and a procession of decorated floats. Dressed in a traditional robe and astrakhan hat, the Imam, accompanied by his parents and the Begum, entered the ceremonial area in an open car, to the cheers of a crowd of about ten thousand people. The Imam mounted the steps to the dais decorated with flowers and flags, where he was to be enthroned, and gave a short address in English in which he vowed to devote his life to his people, once again stressed education and brought in the subject of atomic energy as a means for industrial progress.

He was then seated on the enthronement chair. Ismaili dignitaries, wearing scarlet robes and gold turbans, invested him. A gold-embroidered robe was placed over his shoulders, a sword, chain and ring were presented to him. A rather lengthy religious service followed during which nine hundred Ismailis came on to the dais, one by one kissed his hand and pledged their loyalty to him. He looked strikingly

---

[1] It remained the capital of Tanzania, the republic formed from independent Tanganyika and Zanzibar.

handsome and fit. Never once did it seem that he was tired or uncomfortable sitting in the unrelenting glare of the sun. He had recovered from his initial shock at being thrust into so high a position at so young an age. He seemed vitalized by the ancient ritual, the obeisance of his followers, the ringing cheers of the crowds as he rose, left the ceremonial area and returned to the open car, which once out of the centre of the city sped directly to the airport. There, with his mother and Michael Curtis, he flew to Nairobi for his second enthronement, a repetition of the Dar es Salaam ceremony on a slightly smaller scale.

Things did not run so smoothly at his third and final enthronement in Uganda, where the ceremonies had to be switched at the last moment from the Nakivubo Stadium to the Aga Khan Mosque as King Mutesa II did not take well to the idea of any one other than himself being enthroned in Uganda. To add to this problem, the Imam and his party arrived in a thunderous downpour and all Michael Curtis's arrangements for a tumultuous welcome had to be cut short as Karim, sheltered by a large black umbrella, made his way to his waiting car.

The sun came out for the ceremony the next day, a duplication of the one at Dar es Salaam, which went exceedingly well. There was an enthusiastic response of 'Zindabad!' ('Long live the Aga Khan!') from his followers after he had given a heart-warming speech urging the Ismaili community 'to work hand in hand with all other citizens'.

'Listening to him making his speeches with knowledge, grace, and calm,' his mother said, 'not once were my palms moist. He has a great faculty for acquiring facts, can learn anything, is mad to learn.'

It appeared his grandfather had made the right decision. Karim was up to the task before him – to energize the sect with youth, exuberance, an able mind and a past without scandal. Aly, it seemed, was a sacrifice the old Aga Khan believed had to be made. He was there with Karim during the entire length of the tour, smiling at dignitaries, proud of his son's ability to adapt so well to his new position. But at the same time there was a great sadness about him. 'He had the look of a once very rich man who had lost his fortune and knew time had run out,' one of his colleagues said.

16

Aly had spent his entire life waiting for a job that he would never be given. Horses, fast cars, gambling and glamorous women had filled his time. But he was devoted to his faith and had always been ready to serve his father and his followers when called upon to do so. From childhood it had been drilled into him that one day he would be the spiritual leader of his sect. On his father's death, he believed he was ready and would have performed well. After all, he had had years of watching the old Aga Khan on the many tours of Ismaili communities they had taken together. And he could not see where the events in his personal life had been any more sensational than his father's three divorces and his many attractive mistresses.

He cast blame for his having been denied the Imamate on everyone and everything other than himself and his lifestyle. He confided to colleagues his belief that the Begum was responsible. She was the one woman he had never been able to charm and during the last months of his father's life she had seen to it that they were never alone; it was at this time that her influence over the Aga Khan had grown the strongest. 'The Begum thought if Aly was Imam she would have nothing more to do with the Ismailis, but Karim, being so young, would let her give him advice for many years,' Halldis Poppe, the Aga Khan's nurse and employee for over twenty-five years, acknowledged. Baron Guy de Rothschild was to comment: 'Do you think, after all, that the Aga was so wrong? Aly was not meant to be Imam.'

But Aly felt the problem was not with him but with the media which seemed to find him far more worthy of salacious coverage than his father had ever been, and for simple reasons. Aly, even when in his forties, was handsome, dashing and enough on the wild side to make intriguing reading. Photographs of him were infinitely more interesting to the women who read the social columns and tabloid press than those of the bespectacled, rotund old Aga Khan. And many of the women Aly had squired were film stars like Rita Hayworth, Gene Tierney and Joan Fontaine, society women like Lady Furness, famous models like Bettina, and daughters of titled fathers like his wife Joan. They were often married already, and Lady Furness was a mistress of the Prince of Wales as well. His father chose women generally unknown to the public and although he was a married man for most of his life, he made sure his mistresses and future wives were single women who had lived fairly private lives. The Begum had been a beauty contest contender, but the media had not taken much interest in her until she married the Aga Khan.

Seldom did a reporter write about the serious work Aly did for his sect – the long, arduous tours he had taken on behalf of his father and his efforts to help further the Aga Khan's aims – or the grand business success he had made out of the stables that he and the Aga Khan co-owned. He was regarded by the press, and so the public, as a womanizer, speed-demon and playboy – and the old Aga Khan had allowed the media coverage Aly received to influence his decision to cut his elder son out of the succession, fearing (perhaps correctly) that Aly's public reputation would cause a loss of respect and revenues to the Imamate. The Begum might well have pressed the point to keep Aly at a distance from his father, but the Aga Khan's will naming Karim was drawn up long before his final ordeal.

There was no questioning Aly's loyalty to Karim. But his son's succession as Aga Khan IV had been a great humiliation as well as bringing him to a point in his life when he suddenly felt useless, unwanted, unneeded. Not only had he been rejected as his father's successor, Amyn had been designated second in line and the Begum had been named his son's adviser. If the future of the crown of Great Britain could be designated by a dying monarch, a comparison might have been Victoria passing by Edward after all his years of waiting for the throne and naming his older son, the Duke of Clarence, with the reversion to the Duke of York. (In fact, the Duke of Clarence died young and the Duke of York did eventually succeed as George V.)[1]

[1] Recent controversy over the present Prince of Wales and his suitability to reign has given rise to a similar suggestion that the crown might pass on the death of the Queen

Aly was now further from the seat of power than his half-brother Sadruddin and his stepmother the Begum, and in the position of often having to ask his son for money.

The terms of his father's will also forced him to expend a large amount of his inheritance on buying the Aga Khan's share of their stables. The Begum refused to accept less than an expertly appraised market price for each thoroughbred. Considering that it had been Aly's acumen that brought so many horses wearing their colours into the winners' ring, raising their value with each win, it seemed unjust, but it did demonstrate the Begum's hard head for business.

Aly was forty-seven at the time of his father's death, a man still very much in his prime. Bettina remained his constant companion. Untrue rumours circulated that they were secretly married. It was generally assumed that they were living together (which they were), and Aly had never before been seen so frequently in one woman's company – even during the years of his two marriages.

Sadruddin had married Nina Dyer (who was renamed Princess Shirin, 'Sweet' in Persian) on 27 August 1957 at his home in Geneva, Château Bellerive, with his nephew, Karim Aga Khan, officiating in a traditional Muslim ceremony which followed the obligatory civil procedure at the local town hall. A young British photographer, Tony Armstrong-Jones (later created Earl of Snowdon on his marriage to Princess Margaret), took the picture of the newlyweds – Sadruddin carrying his bride across the threshold of his home – that appeared on the front page of the London *Daily Express* and from there around the globe. But it was not long before those close to Nina and Sadruddin could see there was trouble ahead.

Nina was restless and appeared unhappy from the start of the marriage. She knew the old Aga Khan had never approved of her and confessed to close intimates a lurking suspicion that Sadruddin would have been named in Karim's place had that not been the case. Sadruddin had also become more serious, deeper into his religion since the

---

to his elder son William. An article in the *Sunday Times*, 5 December 1993, pointed to the parallel of Karim Aga Khan's succession to his grandfather: 'Perhaps like Aly Khan, Prince Charles would then feel free to adopt the role of roving ambassador and diplomat prince to which he might be suited.'

death of his father. He was not the same light-hearted, fun-loving young man to whom Nina had first been drawn.

The great difference in their ages made it difficult for Aly to have a man-to-man relationship with Sadruddin, whom he always regarded more as a stepson than a half-brother. The family members had never been clannish. In Sadruddin's case, he remained closer to his mother than his father, the Aga Khan, after his parents' divorce. Sadruddin, Amyn and Karim were good friends at Harvard, but Karim's lofty rise to Imam shifted the association on to a new and unfamiliar plateau.

In August, shortly after the old Aga Khan's death, Karim visited his father at Château de l'Horizon for several days. Bettina was there but she tried to stay in the background to allow them more time alone – the first since Karim became Imam. The situation was awkward. Aly, who bore no resentment toward his son (all his anger was directed at his dead father and the Begum), was still unsure of how he should respond to this young man who was now his Imam. Bettina noted that there was an effort on Karim's part for them to fall back into the roles of father and son. However, this had never been the basis of the relationship between Aly and Karim. When they were together they became comrades, Aly taking the position of older member and so to be deferred to when required. They swam, played tennis ('[Karim] was a better player than his father and had Aly running all over the court,' Bettina recalled), and talked late into the night about the tours Karim planned to make, and his hopes of returning to Harvard one day. Aly confided to Bettina that Karim did not seek his advice in spiritual matters or on Ismaili concerns.

The new Imam was not arrogant. He was filled with the self-assurance of youth and his belief in the wisdom of the old Aga Khan – if he, Karim, was chosen to succeed him, his grandfather must have known that he was also endowed with the innate wisdom of an Imam. Aly tried hard during the time they had together to recapture some of their past camaraderie, to overcome the new obstacles, but he was not his usual vital self. The sadness that would remain with him had already begun to show. It was obvious that the relationship they once had could not continue under the present circumstances. Their roles had been reversed (although Karim always referred to Aly as 'Daddy') and once this visit ended they could no longer even pretend that things were the same.

From his time with his father at l'Horizon until almost a year after his enthronement tour, Karim travelled from one Ismaili community to another. For the most part, his followers were middle-class merchants. Yet there were great contrasts. One large Ismaili community was in the ancient kingdom of Hunza, now in Pakistan, at the peak of the precarious Karakoram Highway (the most treacherous stretch of Marco Polo's old silk route), where 70 per cent of the mountain tribesmen, reputed to live longer than most people (in fact there were many Hunza tribesmen over the age of a hundred), were Ismailis. His sect was also numerous across the border in western China, central Asia, Afghanistan, Iran, Syria, East Africa, and, of course, in Pakistan and India.

His visits to these communities were often stressful. Generally, Ismailis were more prosperous than most of the other followers of Islam. They were, and remain, a business brotherhood, never forgetting, as a member of Karim's staff recently told this author, that they are a 'minority within a minority'. There are an estimated 935 million Muslims worldwide, over 800 million of whom are Sunni and approximately 130 million Shiite. Ismailis are numbered among Shiites but only represent about twelve per cent of that number. Their minority status has made them stand back from major religious issues within the world of Islam, avoiding alignment with any one group of their Muslim brethren, and concentrate their attention on better living conditions, education, health matters and business enterprise within their communities. As a group they are therefore more affluent, educated and liberal in their attitude towards women than Sunnis and other Shiites, a situation that if not handled with extreme care could cause resentment and present great difficulties for them.

Karim not only had the problems of distance (he had chosen an American education and a home in Europe, whereas his followers were mainly in Asia and Africa), culture and outside forces to bridge, he was determined to overcome the playboy image of his father which many of his followers feared he might have inherited. They were able to dismiss the old Aga Khan's flamboyance and many wives because he was largely responsible for their current well-being. It was the Aga

Khan III who had united the far-flung communities with his great business acumen and his struggle on their behalf for better education than any of their neighbours.

In his year 'on the road' Karim collected nearly $100 million in contributions, topping his grandfather's figures for any one year. He then made what the world considered a surprising decision, to return to Harvard and resume his studies so that he could get his degree in economics. Amyn was still attending classes there and, to Nina's great irritation, Sadruddin decided to do likewise. (Nina was not cut out for university life and spent most of her time in Europe.) Before he had been called to Switzerland to the bedside of his dying grandfather, Karim had been planning education and research as a life occupation. He had received straight As throughout his three years at Harvard and was considering going on to the Sorbonne in Paris for post-graduate study. Now he felt he could not take that much time away from his duties as Imam.

He registered at Harvard for summer school so that he could catch up with his class after missing the end of the previous school year and continue his studies in economics and Oriental history. It was a bizarre situation. While Karim studied until late at night and brought Harvard a soccer victory by scoring two goals against Yale, the only player on either side to do so, he had a full-time secretary, Mme Beguel, a Frenchwoman who had previously helped him on his tour, to assist with his voluminous correspondence ('People all over send me regular reports. But I must make the final decision,' he told one interviewer), Michael Curtis (living for the time in Boston) to deal with the press, and he was putting together plans to set up an independent Ismaili newspaper.

He clearly loved Harvard. Something was always going on, he explained, 'the way the light hits the trees in the fall, the sound of doors slamming in the early morning, the look of a professor moving in a world where he wrestles with a problem'. His involvement in sports continued. 'I can't imagine myself without athletics. We push, shove, laugh, cry out for a goal and everyone knows a sense of life. We are there to win. After all that you think better,' he told an interviewer. (He maintained a rigid silence where his personal and spiritual life was concerned.)

He divided his time between offices he rented in a local hotel, the campus, and his new accommodation on campus in Leverett House with a view overlooking the Charles River. His bedroom was simply furnished with a single bed, chest, chair, blinds and no curtains at the windows, the walls decorated with inexpensive copies of paintings by the French Impressionists (the school of art much beloved by his father), and bookshelves for his growing collection of volumes on Oriental and English literature. His sitting-room was no more luxurious. He seldom went out at night, studying until midnight, when he took a coffee break and went back to his room 'to hit the books till 2 or 3'.

Life profiled him in a cover article entitled 'Senior at Harvard: The Aga Khan', eight weeks after he returned to college. He smiled boyishly in the glossy cover photograph, books in hand, wearing a Harvard tie and crested blazer. His classmates called him 'K' as they had at Le Rosey; his professors, 'Mr Khan'; and the press, 'Prince Karim, Aga Khan IV'. He had managed to do what he wanted and still retain his hold on his followers, as Princess Joan was confident he would be able to do. He even became a member of the Harvard Soccer Varsity Team (# 11) and played in the big game of the season (21 November 1958) against their arch-rival Yale.

The *Boston Globe*, reporting Harvard's 1–0 victory, wrote: 'Many of the soccer spectators were more interested in Karim, Aga Khan IV, than in soccer. It probably was the last chance in a lifetime to watch the spiritual leader of 15 to 20 million Muslims trying to kick a soccer ball into a net. For "Kay," [*sic*] as his teammates call him, it was a debacle. The senior failed in two tries, one considered an excellent chance . . . On the field, the Aga Khan was a soccer player every minute . . . And a gum chewer, too. A hard, earnest gum chewer who bites down as though intent on destroying his [gum].'

When a cameraman approached Karim, he withdrew into centre ranks and his teammates shielded him from the lens. It was the end of a difficult afternoon when people had chased after him with cameras trying to get a picture for their personal collection.

During Karim's first months back at Harvard, he and his father were separated by an ocean. When Aly and Bettina were not at l'Horizon, they could be found at Aly's elegant Paris house in the Boulevard Maurice-Barrès in the Bois de Boulogne. For the time being Aly had lost interest in his horses and studs. The social whirl no longer held much excitement for him and Karim had no need at present for his services. There was a huge void in his life. Bettina was concerned for his mental health as he slipped frequently into sombre moods of depression.

Fate played a kind hand when President Iskander Mirza of Pakistan came to Paris for a meeting with President Coty of France. The previous year a new constitution had been adopted and Pakistan became a republic within the British Commonwealth. Mirza was its first elected president and was besieged by a great many problems in holding his economically impoverished country together – famine, Pakistan's conflict with India over Kashmir which bordered India and Pakistan (in 1956, Kashmir would incorporate as an Indian state), and corruption within his government. Aly offered him the house on the Boulevard Maurice-Barrès with its great salon, grand staircase and enough bedrooms to accommodate Mirza's huge entourage while he and Bettina moved temporarily into a friend's vacant flat. Before he left Paris, Mirza offered to appoint Aly as head of the Pakistan delegation to the United Nations. Aly accepted.

A flurry of derisive newspaper articles in Pakistan, France, England and the United States followed, questioning Aly's credentials for such an important diplomatic assignment. Aly ignored them and flew to Karachi for a briefing with Pakistan government officials and then continued on to New York where he took an elegant apartment and offices on 65th Street, off Fifth Avenue. Bettina remained in France, but they spoke daily and arrangements were made for her to join him as soon as possible. He sounded a happy man. He had found a purpose and, ironically, his entire family – Karim, Yasmin, Amyn and Sadrud-din – were all in the United States.

He appeared confident the day he presented his credentials to Secretary-General Dag Hammarskjöld at the United Nations. New York was in the grip of a July heat wave. A broiling sun seared the grounds of the United Nations Plaza, more than a hundred brilliantly-hued flags hardly moving in the still of the steaming air. Aly emerged from his chauffeur-driven car looking fresh and cool in a dark blue suit and walked briskly into the building as press cameras clicked and people gawked.

34. *Above*: Life would never be the same for the 20-year-old Karim Aga Khan IV, seen here shortly after the proclamation ceremony at his late grandfather's villa in Switzerland. Aly made sure he was not in the photograph.

35. *Right*: The installation ceremony in Nairobi, part of a triple enthronement. An Ismaili official presents him with the Sword of Justice.

36. *Below*: Karim's enthronement at Dar-es-Salaam as the 49th Imam of the Ismailis.

37. Handsome, fabulously rich and charming, the Aga Khan IV resembled a film star more than a religious leader, but he was dedicated to his new position.

38. At his estate in the Malabar Hills, Bombay. He chose, as had his grandfather, to live in Europe and had homes in Switzerland and France.

39. Aly turned his attention to world politics and became a representative to the United Nations (as is Sadruddin). He never lost his love for horses and beautiful women. With Elizabeth Taylor at an art and jewel auction in 1957.

40. Aly and Group-Captain Peter Townsend after a race in which both were entered. Townsend won the bronze horse which Aly is pretending to feed.

41. Love and contentment entered Aly's life when he met the Paris model Bettina. They made plans to marry, but a tragic car crash took Aly Khan's life beforehand.

42. At Dauphine Station, Paris, where Aly Khan's body was taken by special train for burial. *From left*: ex-Begum Andrée, Bettina, and the Begum, widow of Aga Khan III.

43. The divorced Lady James Crichton-Stuart was a model before her marriage to Karim. This picture appeared on the cover of *Queen* magazine.

44. Called 'the wedding of the year', it took place in Paris in 1969. Sarah was now Princess Salima, the Begum Khan.

45. A family wedding portrait in the library of Karim Aga Khan's 11th-century house in Paris where a fabulous reception was held. *Foreground*: Princess Joan Aly Khan, Karim Aga Khan, Princess Salima, and the late Aga Khan's widow. *Rear*: ex-Begum Andrée, Prince Sadruddin, Prince Amin, and Princess Yasmin.

46. Princess Yasmin bears a marked resemblance to her mother Rita Hayworth.

47. The dowager Begum in the gardens of Yakymour, her home in the South of France. For seven years she and Karim Aga Khan were at loggerheads. His marriage ended the impasse.

48. La Villa Merimont in Geneva where Princess Salima gave birth to their first child, Princess Zahra. Two sons, Hussain and Rahim, soon followed.

49. Initially Karim had little interest in the fabulous stables he inherited. When he realized how profitable they were, he became one of the world's leading horse breeders.

50. Karim looks over his temporal domain, the strip of Sardinian coast that would become the famous resort area known as the Costa Smeralda.

51. A rift developed between Karim Aga Khan and the Begum in the early 1980s that would finally end the fairytale marriage.

'He smelled of lemon and talc,' one of the United Nations secretaries commented. 'And he had a smile that dazzled.'

He had three weeks to write his maiden speech to the Assembly, conferring daily with Bettina over transatlantic telephone. 'He had to prove himself to the world,' she told the author Willi Frischauer. 'Immediately after making the speech [to the Third Emergency Special Session of the General Assembly] he called me,' she added. 'He was pleased with the reaction [strong applause].'

The stability of the Pakistan government was greatly threatened at this time. Aly's friend and mentor President Mirza had abrogated the Constitution and granted power to the army under General Muhammed Ayub Khan.[1] Aly's position was difficult. The General Assembly were concerned that Ayub would become a dangerous force in that part of the world. Aly turned his maiden speech into a plea for understanding of the problems of new, small, struggling nations like Pakistan. 'All of them, in relation to the Great Powers, are weak – geographically, politically, and economically,' he told the Assembly in vibrant upper-class English tones touched by the remnants of the French accent acquired during his childhood. 'But there is one way in which they are not weak . . . They are strong in their determination to survive and succeed.'

He was so well received by the members of the Assembly that the following month he was elected Vice President of the General Assembly. He was tremendously energized. Perhaps there was a *modus vivendi* for him, after all. He recognized his unique qualifications for the work he was doing. 'He was European and Oriental at the same time, a Muslim, yet steeped in Western culture, one of the few men capable of truly understanding both sides,' one historian wrote of him.

Bettina joined him in New York. Although Yasmin was living on the West Coast, he arranged to see her quite often. Rita, married yet again, this time to the Hollywood producer James Hill, had made some legal moves and withheld access rights to ensure that Yasmin received her proper inheritance from the Aga Khan's estate. Off the screen for three years, she had finally returned to play ageing ladies

---

[1] In 1960, Ayub assumed presidential powers, abolished the office of prime minister, and ruled by decree.

in both *Pal Joey* and *Separate Tables*. She had recently severed her long-standing association with her attorney Bartley Crum (who had acted for her in all her legal suits against Aly) and now encouraged the relationship between Aly and their daughter. Things became so amicable between Rita and Aly that on one trip to see Yasmin in California, he and Rita danced together at a party given by their mutual friend, and his one-time lover, Merle Oberon.

Some of this was façade, or perhaps even desperation. Rita was drinking heavily and her fifth marriage was on the brink of divorce. Aly might have appeared to be a safe haven for her to berth her troubled life. And Aly knew that with the worsening of the situation in Pakistan, his position at the United Nations could well have a limited run.

But his relationship with Bettina was solid and Rita's attraction for him had faded long before.

The Begum worked for over a year supervising the completion of her husband's mausoleum and making the extremely complicated arrangements for his burial. Five hundred honoured guests had been invited from around the world and adequate accommodation had to be found for them. She had leased the 300-room Cataract Hotel for the exclusive use of her guests, but there were still not enough rooms. A smaller establishment, the new 50-room Grand Hotel was also engaged. The problem was that the Grand was not yet finished; in order to make it ready for occupation, furniture and fittings had to be brought from Cairo and installed before the Begum's guests arrived for the entombment, which was scheduled for mid-February 1959 – and it was now the second week in January.

Also, Aswan was not equipped to handle the influx of perhaps thousands of Ismailis who would make the journey to pay a last homage to their dead Imam. A tent city was raised on the outskirts of Aswan and an emergency bridge constructed to span the Nile at the remote point of Noor el Salaam to avoid the previous problem of a flotilla of boats being unable to dock nearby. (Aswan was across the river from Noor el Salaam.) Three thousand pilgrims made their way to Aswan.

Aly was in the States, still working at the United Nations, and would be absent from the proceedings. Certainly, an exception could have been made for him to take leave from the Assembly to attend his father's burial. Not to do so was his choice, made to avoid any conflict or provoke a situation such as had occurred in Syria after his father's death. Karim Aga Khan, Amyn and Sadruddin arrived in Aswan the day before the funeral and went directly to Noor el Salaam where the old Aga Khan's coffin, covered in white silk, was lying in state in the inner court.

Karim, who had stopped en route for a meeting with Egypt's President Nasser, met the Begum to discuss the arrangements for the entombment ceremony. Technically, Muslim law dictated that women did not attend the final rites. A tent had been erected in the grounds for the women to wait with the Begum as she sat in a gilded chair while the men carried the coffin past her and continued on to the mausoleum. The Begum adamantly demanded to be a part of the procession. Karim refused to back down. This was not a matter of a widow's rights being ignored or women being discriminated against. This was an ancient Ismaili custom and part of the ceremonial rite. The Begum would not give in. 'As Imam I insist you follow my orders,' he told her. The Begum was silent. He left Noor el Salaam for a suite that had been reserved for him at the Cataract, looking greatly irritated but confident that she would bow to his judgement.

The funeral procession formed at three the following afternoon. Karim, Amyn, Sadruddin and the old Aga's former valet, Solomon Bandely, all dressed in white robes, lifted the heavy casket on to their shoulders with several other Ismaili leaders and made their way up the hill overlooking the Nile to the elaborate fortress-like stone mausoleum (which in the end had cost a great deal more than the original sum left to build it). As planned, the procession went by the women's tent, but as it passed, the Begum, her secretary and her maid, all wearing hooded white chadors, emerged and joined the procession.

Karim said nothing during the short ceremony or on his return to the house, but he left immediately without a word to the Begum. Her open defiance of him and of the practices of their faith infuriated him.

He left with Amyn and Sadruddin the next day without speaking to her.

Shortly after her husband was laid to his final rest and Karim had left, the Begum led a large procession of women in hooded white chadors back to his mausoleum, making sure the press were there to take photographs. 'Prince Karim did not want me to follow the procession on the grounds of Ismaili rites,' she told reporters, adding some acerbic comments about the family and excusing her action by claiming she had been 'tired and did not want to wait for hours in the gilded armchair in which I was to sit.' Then, with a sudden spurt of anger she said, 'I know that Prince Karim does not have the slightest intention of following his grandfather's wishes so far as I'm concerned!'

She was absolutely right, for Karim did not speak to her again until the seven-year period his grandfather had designated for him to be under the Begum's guidance had expired.

Aly had distanced himself from these family hostilities. He was regaining his *joie de vivre*, taking a renewed interest in his horses and in 1959 had one of his best seasons in years, winning both the One Thousand and Two Thousand Guineas races at Newmarket with Petite Etoile and Taboun – a rare double win. He had found a career in which he was happy, the diplomatic service, and became Vice Chairman of the Peace Observation Commission at the United Nations. Best of all, he was in love as he had never been before. He and Bettina planned to be married in August 1960. Having just been named Pakistan's ambassador to Argentina, where he was to report for his assignment in Buenos Aires in September, he wanted to take Bettina there as his wife. He had yet to ask Karim for permission to marry, but he felt certain this would not be denied.

He was in high spirits on the rainy evening of 12 May, when he and Bettina set out in a Lancia which Aly had on approval for possible purchase, to attend a dinner at the house of their friends the Gerard Bonnets. A small group of his closest friends had been invited: Baron Elie de Rothschild, Baron and Baroness Guy de Rothschild and Stavros Niarchos, the Greek shipping tycoon, and his wife. Aly had spent the afternnon at Longchamps, a disappointment because his horses had not performed well, but he seemed undaunted. Long ago he had given up cigarettes and alcohol and seldom saw the inside of a casino. But he liked to play bridge and after the races he had joined friends at the staid Travellers' Club for a few rounds. (Not that he was a member – he would joke that he didn't care much for men's clubs but he wouldn't turn down an offer to join a women's club.) He returned home and by the time he had answered some calls and dressed for dinner it was nearly nine PM, the time they were due at the Bonnets' house in Ville d'Avray on the outskirts of Paris, a thirty-minute drive. He asked Lucien, the chauffeur, to sit in the back seat so that he could try the Lancia for himself, and perhaps because he knew he would drive the car at greater speed.

The night was penetratingly damp. Bettina wore a deep green Balenciaga tweed wool coat over a matching suit and long gloves, but as she was shivering in the seat beside him, he placed his arm around her shoulders. He turned the corner on to the Boulevard Henri-Sellier, which forms the boundary between the districts of St Cloud and Suresnes (near the St Cloud racecourse). There was a small Renault going slowly directly in front of the Lancia and Aly decided to pass. His foot hit the accelerator pedal. Suddenly, he was blinded by the headlights of a car coming straight at them in the same lane. Bettina screamed. The cars crashed head on. Moments later Bettina and Lucien stood in shock by the side of the battered Lancia. There was blood on Bettina's face and right leg from cuts, but she felt fairly sound. Neither Lucien nor the driver of the other car and his two passengers appeared injured. But as she stared down she could see Aly, blood running down his face, his body crushed and motionless between his seat and the steering wheel.

'Aly! Aly!' she shouted while Lucien tried to open the door on the driver's side, but it was jammed.

The police came. An ambulance arrived and Aly was extricated from the twisted metal of the grey Lancia and placed on a stretcher. Bettina went with him to the hospital. He had a fractured skull, and both his legs and possibly his neck were broken. He died, not having regained consciousness, at a few minutes before midnight in a lift on the way to the emergency operating theatre.

Bettina was in shock. She remained in hospital that night and was taken home by ambulance the following day and carried upstairs on a stretcher to the bedroom she had shared with Aly for several years.

Immediately the gold brocade blinds fringed with ivory tassels were pulled down over every window to obscure the view from the eyes of the reporters who lined the pavement outside, cameras poised to get a shot of someone peering through a glass pane, in hopes that it might be Bettina.

'He died,' one of his bridge companions at the Travellers' Club commented, 'before his luck ran out.' Aly Khan might not have agreed with that. In his opinion his luck had only just begun.

17

Aly's fatal accident was front page news all over the world. Graphic images of the twisted, battered Lancia, the bloodied head of Aly seen through the shattered windscreen, Bettina standing stunned, blood on her forehead and leg, as the ambulance men removed him from the death vehicle, followed by clips of Rita, Gene, and other glamorous women who had fallen for his charm, were flashed on television screens around the world.

Twenty-four hours after Aly's death, Karim, Amyn and Sadruddin flew to Bettina's side. (Nina had broken her leg in a skiing accident in Switzerland and remained at her home in Geneva.) Aly's body was brought from the hospital mortuary to the house on the Boulevard Maurice-Barrès, where it was embalmed. Ismailis arrived from the Paris mosque and Karim conducted prayers for the many mourners, friends, associates and Ismailis, who had gathered at the house. The ex-Begum Andrée, who had maintained a close friendship with Aly, was there (looking trim and chic in a couturier black ensemble), along with the Baron de Rothschild and many of the top society names in Paris who had been intimates of Aly's. Bettina was kept under sedation in her bedroom for the first day, a loyal friend from her modelling days by her side. By the second morning, learning that Karim Aga Khan was to arrive immediately, she pulled herself together and came downstairs.

Aly's death had been so sudden that there was a sense of disbelief. Speed and cars had always had him under their spell. 'Some day Aly will kill himself if he doesn't slow down,' was an often-repeated fear among his family and friends. But no one expected it to happen on a city thoroughfare in Paris. Aly had been unique. For thousands of Western women he conjured up sensual images of the exotic — and the erotic. He was the glamorous dark prince, fearless of speed, winner of the hearts of the world's most beautiful women, he was mysterious, sexy – and of course, fabulously rich. For an equal number of Eastern women he represented the dazzling Muslim prince who had won the hearts of some of the west's most beautiful women. There was something titillating about that.

Bettina was beside herself with grief. Aly had been her life. Her dreams for her future were completely tied to him and she had been counting the days until they were married. Karim spent much time comforting her, taking over the burden of planning the funeral. Aly's will made two special requests – that his horses be withdrawn from racing for ten days after his death and that he be buried in a newly-constructed mausoleum on the Ismaili sacred burial grounds in Syria. This final request was to create a complex problem for over a decade. The ritual of the reading of the will was done by Maître Ardoin in the library of the house the afternoon that Karim arrived. No one who sat in the dark-panelled, book-lined and memorabilia-filled room had any idea what the contents of the document might reveal. (There had always been rumours in the press about illegitimate children.) Tremendous secrecy surrounded the entire affair. The blinds were drawn to ensure privacy from photographers with telescopic lenses.

There were two surprises: Aly had made significant bequests to a woman and her teenage son only slightly known to the family, and the estate far exceeded what any of his heirs expected. Aly had done a turnabout since his father's death, gambling very little, spending on a much smaller scale, and investing his money not just wisely, but with great success. To add to these improvements, the previous year his horses and stud farms had become some of the most valuable in the world.

A generous spirit filled the numerous pages of his will, drawn up earlier in the year. Bettina was well provided for with a lifetime income, and the house on the Boulevard Maurice-Barrès. Aly remembered all close friends, staff and associates with small legacies. Karim received the major portion of the real property – Ginetta's legacy to Aly, her houses in Deauville, Paris and Cannes; Aly's estates, l'Horizon, Daranoor in Gstaad, several more in India (including Yarovda Palace in Poona, where Gandhi had been imprisoned and which Aly had inherited from his father), the bungalow in Nairobi occupied briefly by Aly, Princess Joan and their sons during the war; another house in Chantilly, land in Pakistan and shares in American oil companies. Aly also left Karim his stud farms and stables (estimated to be worth over $9 million at the time).

'What am I going to do with the horses?' Karim asked Ardoin.

'You may not be interested now . . . but one day, who knows?' the lawyer replied.

Yasmin and Amyn shared the rest of Aly's estate (still considerable) with Karim. With Yasmin's legacies from her grandfather as well, Rita no longer had any cause to be concerned about her daughter's financial well-being. Rita was now divorced from James Hill. (When asked by her lawyer the year in which they had married, Rita could not remember it. 'You don't remember?' he asked with surprise. 'I don't remember what year it was. I do remember it was Groundhog Day.') Unable ever to be alone, Rita was deeply involved with Gary Merrill, ex-husband of Bette Davis who had divorced him on grounds of being 'drunk and disorderly . . . incapable of behaving properly in front of his family'. Rita and Merrill were both drinking heavily and photographed brawling in public, not with each other but with the press and fans who intruded on their privacy.

Public opinion once again swung against Rita. There were ugly articles in the press about her rowdy behaviour and her poor performance as a mother. It was said that she was carrying the torch for the dead Aly Khan. Rita was a confirmed alcoholic. To complicate matters she was suffering from some yet undiagnosed problem that was causing irrational behaviour and memory loss that Aly's family feared might place Yasmin's well-being in jeopardy. Rita appeared to be in the early stages of dementia. Eleven-year-old Yasmin's situation was discussed by her father's family although no decisions were made. She attended a Swiss boarding school for a good part of the year and so she was far removed from Rita and the serious problems she was enduring.

Aly had chosen Syria for his final resting place because of the great love shown for him by the Ismaili community there which he had visited more frequently during the years than his father. But there were fears that if he were buried there his grave could become a martyr's shrine, for there remained a group of Syrian Ismailis who still believed Aly was the rightful Imam. To add to this concern, Syria was a troubled country at this time, with increasing opposition to Egypt's domination of the United Arab Republic.[1]

It was agreed by Karim and Bettina that Aly should be interred temporarily at l'Horizon until his wishes could be carried out. (It is unclear whose decision it was, but Yasmin was not brought to France for her father's interment.) Accompanied by Bettina, ex-Begum Andrée, Karim, Amyn, Sadruddin, and Ismaili leaders from the Paris mosque, the coffin, covered with the red and green Ismaili flag (also Aly's racing colours), was taken by special train from Paris to Cannes, a twelve-hour journey because scheduled trains took precedence. The exhausted group of mourners arrived at their destination after midnight. A large group of Ismailis was waiting. The night was cool and clear, the sky star-filled, the moon strong enough almost to turn night to day.

As the train stopped a short way from the grounds of l'Horizon, the coffin was carried the remaining distance, past an open grave that had been dug just outside Aly's study windows and into the central hallway, where next morning the public were allowed to pay their last respects to him. The crowds that had gathered during the night far outnumbered the mourners who were expected. The vast grounds of l'Horizon were bordered on one side by railway tracks, where a police guard did its best to hold back the swarm of people so that a passing train would not create a tragedy. As the train reached the edge of the property, a police officer was pushed into its path and killed. There was both order and greater grief on the part of the crowds from that terrible moment.

The Begum joined the rest of the family (Nina was still nursing her ski injuries in Geneva) for a simple service conducted at the graveside by Karim. He looked exhausted and his eyes were rimmed with red, but he was in complete control, spoke eloquently and movingly, and lifted the mourners' spirits with his prayers. Bettina and her modelling

[1] Egypt and Syria had become the United Arab Republic in 1958, with Gamal Abdul Nasser as president and Cairo as its capital. Separate Egyptian and Syrian nationality were abolished, the citizens being termed 'Arabs' and the new nation 'Arab territory'. The Arab homeland was designated as the entire area between the Persian Gulf and the Atlantic coast. A few months later Yemen was brought in to form the United Arab States. Syria withdrew from the union after a military coup and Yemen soon followed, thus ending the attempt at union.

friend remained at l'Horizon for a few days before returning to Paris. The rest of the mourners dispersed shortly after the service. Karim flew back to Massachusetts to receive his degree but returned to Europe within a fortnight.[1]

On 20 June a memorial service was held at the Islamic Cultural Centre and London Mosque near Regent's Park. Bettina was not present. Karim, Amyn and Princess Joan sat in the front pew surrounded by men and women bearing titles of great families, legend and power. The old Aga Khan would have revelled in the glory of such a splendid showing. There sat the bejewelled and portly Maharajahs of Jaipur and Cooch Behar (their titles now honorary), the Duke of Bedford, the Marquess of Tavistock, the Marchionesses of Bristol and Winchester, the Earls of Carnarvon and Rosslyn, the former president of Pakistan, Aly's old friend Major-General Iskander Mirza, Viscount Astor, Major the Hon. John Jacob Astor, Mr Evelyn de Rothschild, the Turkish ambassador, the High Commissioner of Pakistan, the Netherlands ambassador, Countess Fitzwilliam, Lord Twining and enough additional society, racing and literary names to entrance the crowds waiting outside to catch sight of these famous people.

The Queen did not send a representative, but she did write Karim Aga Khan a personal message of condolence.

Like his father and grandfather before him, Karim held a British passport. Technically he was the Queen's subject. But he was more of a citizen of the world than Aly and the old Aga Khan. He was not torn between two cultures – Oriental and European – as his grandfather had been. His ties to India and Pakistan were through his Imamate and his business interests. He knew only what he read or was told about the days of the raj, the glory of the British Empire, India's struggle for independence, and the partition of India and Pakistan. And in the schools he attended and in his limited social life, he had not encountered the ethnic slurs that (however veiled) Aly had experienced. In fact there was nothing either distinctly or vaguely Oriental about Karim.

---

[1] The body of Aly Khan remained interred at l'Horizon for more than twelve years until, on 10 July 1972, the coffin was exhumed and flown to Damascus for reburial in a specially built mausoleum at Salamieh.

What Karim learned from the example of his father and grandfather was to diminish public interest in his private life and emphasize the work he was doing for the Imamate, and to carry out all his ceremonial duties with meticulous regard and preparation. He had a much more hands-on approach to Imamship than his grandfather, going to his followers' homes, engaging dozens of people in conversation at each public outing (although not a gregarious person by nature) and adding, whenever possible, a personal touch in his replies to the hundreds of letters he received and answered each week. This was not an easy task, for his followers were in number equal to more than one-third of the Queen's subjects in all of Great Britain, and his personal staff something like one-thirtieth the size (he was still forced to maintain a domestic staff of hundreds to care for the many homes he had inherited).

Shortly after the memorial service in London, he left for an intense thirty-day tour of Ismaili East African communities with Michael Curtis, Mme Beguel and two other secretaries. He met Ismaili leaders, inspected Boy Scout troops, schools and housing developments, went to see people in their homes, however humble. It was July and August and the heat was suffocating, but Karim always looked cool in the white summer suits he wore. When the tour was over, he retired for a few weeks to Aly Khan's former house at Gstaad (now his), but he got little rest.

His interest in his father's horses and stud farms had been greatly increased when he studied the ledgers of Aly Khan's recent successful seasons and went to see his newly-inherited three stud farms in France – Marly-la-Ville, Lassy, and St Créspin (which had a delightful Norman-style cottage on the property which he thought he might use from time to time). All three were doing exceptionally well, as were the seven Irish stud farms that were now also his. While on his tour of East Africa, he had decided to carry on the racing tradition of his family. He gathered at Gstaad the managers of his French stud farms and Maître Ardoin to tell them of his decision, to learn from them what he could, and to plan the coming season.

'Prince Aly knew every horse in the stable and its history. He had a great instinct for the game,' Robert Muller, the manager of Lassy, revealed. 'His Highness, Prince Karim, started from scratch, but it did not take him very long to catch up.'

In his first season of involvement one of his horses, Charlottesville, won the French Derby, the Prix du Jockey Club, the Grand Prix de Paris, and the Prix du Prince d'Orange, collecting more than $200,000 in prize money.

Karim was showing a prodigious talent for business, and he had discovered that he not only had a head for it, he very much enjoyed the challenge. His next undertaking was introduced to him by his half-brother Patrick Guinness (Princess Joan's son by her first husband, Loel Guinness), a British banker who had just returned from a trip to the islands in the Mediterranean and was enthusiastic about the potential of Sardinia, a virtually untouched Italian island which he believed could – with proper development – become a sanctuary for the very rich who desired privacy and a calm port for their yachts.

Patrick Guinness had been alerted to the commercial prospects of Sardinia by John Duncan Miller, a Briton who was in charge of European operations for the World Bank which financed numerous ecological projects including a successful one to eliminate mosquitoes on the Sardinian coast. He was so taken by the extraordinary beauty of the land that he bought acreage at a very low price leading down to a pristine white beach. When Guinness saw the property he too purchased land there. A few weeks later, Karim followed suit. He saw 'an opportunity for demonstrating that landscape can be tamed without being spoiled'. The Consorzio Costa Smeralda, with Karim, Guinness, Maître Ardoin and a small group of other investors and associates was formed and more than 3500 acres with close to 38 miles of uninterrupted coastline was acquired. Plans were drawn up to develop the most desirable part of the island, creating a yacht harbour and building luxury villas.

He suspended his business ventures in September 1960 to embark on a stiff forty-day tour, concentrating almost the whole of it on Pakistan in the same way he had done in East Africa a few months earlier. His intention was to give his followers close access to their Imam and for him to study first hand and in depth the problems suffered by this community.

General Muhammed Ayub Khan had just assumed presidential powers and Pakistan was a dictatorship, with Ayub ruling by decree. Things had shifted quickly. The hope for peace within the country and between Sunni and Shiite Muslims under Mirza appeared to be a lost dream. The new city of Islamabad, a presidential palace and other government buildings then currently under construction, became the interim national capital, and Dhaka the legislative capital for a federal Islamic republic with two provinces (East and West Pakistan) and two official languages (Bengali and Urdu). Women were denied the vote (they were enfranchised in 1965 and six seats were reserved in the legislature for women).

Communal strife in Pakistan was constant. Eight weeks after Karim left, several thousand Shiite Muslims were massacred by Sunnis in Madhya Pradesh state in India and there were heavy reprisals in Pakistan. For years there would be border clashes between India and Pakistan and the latter and Afghanistan. There were now several million Ismailis living in Pakistan (population 110 million) and their well-being was uppermost in Karim's mind.

In such treacherous times, it was important for his followers to feel protected. Karim advised them to remain aloof from political debate, an attitude that in the past had always preserved the safety of Ismaili communities. He worked night and day, meeting with provincial governors and community leaders. As Ismailis were generally fairly middle-class, he was shocked by the conditions in which some of his followers lived and approved plans for Karimabad, an Ismaili housing project designed to provide comfortable two-room apartments with indoor plumbing for 800 families who had previously been living in mud huts or on the streets. The apartments would cost the occupants only thirty-five rupees a month (less than a tenth of their average income), and they would own their homes after twenty-five years.

Before Karim left Pakistan he also helped to found an orphanage and contributed $600,000 of his own money to set up an industry to help his followers. Pakistan was desperately short of foreign exchange and the funds made it possible for an Ismaili group to import machinery for use in two textile factories and equipment for a canvas factory, the profits to be used to support the orphanage. He continued his spending spree by giving money towards the building of a technical high school and to establish a Prince Aly Khan Library at Karachi University. In a very short time, he had divested himself of over a million dollars of his personal fortune which at the time was estimated to be worth about $56 million.

He was surrounded by followers wherever he went. His speeches were well-received, and the *jamaat khanas* he opened were consistently successful. He told his followers that his aim was for every Ismaili family to own their own house and every Ismaili child to receive a good education. He rode over rocky, undeveloped land by jeep, even on mule-back, to reach Ismaili communities never before visited by an Imam. He was the first Imam in the 1400-year history of his sect to have visited the Hunza tribesmen.

He was driven, possessed. He saved little of each day for relaxation or sleep. Every night he studied his notes and made his decisions on what he must do to help his people. Most of them, admittedly, were better off than the majority of Muslims; but the Ismailis in Pakistan were the poorest of the sect's communities. Karim was determined to end poverty among them. He enlisted the help of Pakistan's Ismaili leaders and encouraged the professional and business people, invariably affluent, of city communities like Karachi to help the struggling village and farm groups and to form a financial and social self-help network, providing loans to Ismaili businessmen who were short of cash. 'The advantage of being an Ismaili,' one member of the faith explains, '[is that] as a community it gives us status and protection and in turn we must serve it.'

Following the Ismailis' age-old custom, Karim avoided taking a political position. He carried on his grandfather's dictum that his 'followers' first loyalty is to their country, while their spiritual loyalty is to himself.' The Ismailis in Pakistan were more liberal among themselves than most of the country's rigid Muslim society, but they did not attempt to impose their beliefs outside their communities. Karim Aga Khan was as adamant against women wearing the veil as the old Aga Khan had been, but he still advised Ismaili women in Pakistan to wear headscarves if it was the custom in their area.

The number of members of his sect remained about the same as it had been at the turn of the century, although Ismaili communities in the Soviet Union and China, known to exist before the First World War, seemed to have disappeared. The days of looking for converts, as had been the case in the nineteenth century, had long since passed. What was paramount was to take care of all those who practised the faith.

Karim went back to Gstaad at the end of his Pakistan tour to rest and to hold meetings with Michael Curtis about the progress of the newspaper, the *Sunday Nation*, that they were planning to publish in Nairobi just after the new year. His name was often linked in gossip columns with beautiful women whom he escorted to society and charity balls in London or Paris, but there seemed to be no great love affair. Speculation was often feverish on who among his companions might make him a good wife and carry off the role of Princess and Begum. In a rare admission in 1961 he told an interviewer: 'There is little likelihood of my marrying an Ismaili. It would create a privileged position for her family, and that would be contrary to Ismaili law.'

His routine was spartan, even at Chalet Daranoor in Gstaad. It seemed incredible that only a short time before Karim had been a student at Harvard. On 17 December 1961 he celebrated his twenty-fifth birthday. He had lost touch with his youth. Although he might attend specific galas and dinner parties, his life was mainly his work, and his work was to minister to the well-being of his followers. When not travelling, he was at his desk at 7.30 every morning. He prayed three times a day. In Gstaad, he worked until 10.30 AM, ski'd for three hours, ate a simple lunch, and returned to his desk until 7.30 in the evening. Three secretaries were employed to help him with his reports and letters to his followers, his financial and business affairs and social correspondence. He often went down to one of the local hotel restaurants for dinner and would return, much as he had done at Harvard 'to hit the books again'; this time doing private research on his various projects, or making notes for a meeting he was to have the next day.

In the summer of 1961 he flew to Washington DC at the invitation of President John F. Kennedy where they met in the Lincoln Room of the White House and discussed conditions in the African and Pakistani communities with which Karim was so familiar. Amyn had graduated from Harvard and frequently joined his brother in Gstaad. He also had a handsome four-level, three-bedroom house in New York where he now worked in the United Nations Department of Economic and Social Affairs. Sadruddin (legally separated from Nina), was High Commissioner for Refugees at the United Nations. The three men held a short family reunion in Manhattan before Karim returned to Europe.

He was determined to steer clear of the tabloid press that had so exploited his father's life. There were no film stars linked to his name, no wild exploits at racetracks or car rallies. His life was filled with the utmost luxury, he had the money to do whatever he cared to. He still enjoyed skiing and was by now seriously involved with the business of breeding and racing his horses. *The* woman had not yet entered his life, and although he was flattered by the attention the female sex paid him, he was reluctant to play the role of Lothario. He took his calling most seriously. 'You know what thrills me, what really *thrills* me?' he asked a reporter from London's *Daily Mail*. 'Well, I believe the community's secondary schools in Dar es Salaam and Kampala have the highest pass rate in school certificates of any Asian school in East Africa.'

In 1964 he went into serious training and was a member of the British Alpine skiing team at the Winter Olympics held at Innsbruck, and came in fifth. Austria won the title. He had inherited Aly's yacht, which he docked in the South of France and had become such a good yachtsman that he had recently replaced it with a larger, more powerful model. He had kept up his tennis game and remained highly competitive at it. He was trim, taut, handsome, one of the richest bachelors in the world. Even his closest friends, family and advisers wondered when he was going to find a young woman he wished to marry.

'The Aga Khan is a perfectionist,' Nina Dyer said. 'I don't think there are many women who can measure up to his standards. She has to have beauty, brains and dedication. And not mind being the last in line behind [millions of] Ismailis seeking his attention.'

The second largest island in the Mediterranean after Sicily, Sardinia, where Karim Aga Khan was planning his real estate venture, had a long and ancient history. An early trade centre, it was mentioned in Egyptian sources in the 13th century B C. Settled by the Phoenicians and Carthaginians before Rome conquered the island in 238 B C, it passed to the Vandals after the fall of Rome and then to the Byzantines. Battles were fought for possession of the island by Pisa and Genoa. It wound up in the fifteenth century belonging to Spain, which ceded it in the eighteenth century to Austria, which then awarded it to Victor Amadeus II of Savoy, self-styled king of Sardinia (1718–30).

After the 1861 annexation of the two Sicilies, Victor Emmanuel II of Sardinia (1849–61) was proclaimed the first King of united Italy. The region received some autonomy with the abdication of Victor Emmanuel III, the last king of Italy (1900–46), and the Italian constitution adopted in 1947, the following year.

Self-government, however, did not bring the islanders prosperity. Sardinia (located just south of Corsica) was an economically deprived region with little industry and high unemployment. Rebel tribes of bandits roamed the craggy mountains that constituted the greater part of the country. There were numberless fishing villages along its coastline and seafood of varied and exotic variety was plentiful, but there were no fish hatcheries or commercial means to package and ship the fresh-caught fish. Because of the forbidding mountainous terrain farmers raised sheep and goats, and small amounts of wheat, barley, grapes and tobacco.

At the southern end of the island was Sardinia's one large city, the capital Cagliari, which had a university. The small section of Sardinia that Karim Aga Khan had named Costa Smeralda (Emerald Coast), for the sparkling green of the waters that rimmed it, was in the extreme north-east corner of the island on the Tyrrhenian Sea, that part of the Mediterranean that separates Sardinia from Italy.

Sardinia was an island of great contrasts; rugged slopes and a magnificent, encircling coastline that looked out on to a sea of great beauty and bounty. The natural wonders of the coastal region – the promontories, headlands, bays and miraculously clear striated waters – drew tourists who were the island's main source of revenue. As there had been no modern development, however, no great hotels or tourist attractions, this resource was limited. The majority of Sardinia's population were poor. The newly-named Costa Smeralda, which was only a small area of the island, had been sparsely populated but not immune to raids by the bandits. They hid in the caves of the wild Sopramonte mountains and swept down from the hills to rustle sheep, prey on travellers and small village merchants, and on occasion cut off the ear of a hostage being held for ransom. The danger this posed initially concerned Karim Aga Khan and the consortium, but the attacks stopped along the Costa Smeralda almost as soon as work was begun in the spring of 1965, for it was recognized that the developers were bringing jobs and a measure of prosperity to the formerly poverty-stricken region. (Fifteen years later, however, the son of a rich Ismaili would be kidnapped and a ransom paid for his safe return.)

The land for the project (finally comprising the 38 miles of coastline, with white sand beaches and soft rock sculpted by centuries of winter winds and waves, and some 32,000 acres of rocky land) was owned by peasants. It was bought up cheaply bit by bit by the Consorzio, of which Karim Aga Khan was president. An environmental protection service was established to fight pollution and protect endangered species. A rare breed of wild horses, a third the size of the average equine, ran in the hills above it. The tremendous task of turning this desolate area lacking power lines, fresh water and a harbour, into a luxurious holiday haven for millionaires lay before the Consorzio.

A vast infrastructure of roads along the coast and through the boulder-strewn hills was begun. Then came drainage and power supplies. A harbour was created and named Porto Cervo. A private airline, Alisarda, was established and several passenger planes purchased to make two flights a day from Italy to Porto Cervo where an airfield had been built at Olbia, a few miles inland from the harbour (those fortunate enough to own yachts could, of course, arrive by sea). Plans were drawn by several internationally prominent architects for hotels and a colony of elegant villas, the majority glimmering in soft pastels and white in the island's sunshine, their red-tiled roofs dotting the landscape. Each villa was set on a minimum site of one acre and the building code allowed a density of only five people per acre. This meant that if a prospective owner wanted living-in servants and rooms for guests, a plot of three acres or more would be required.

'We are tough about our standards,' Karim said at the time. He described these as a 'modern interpretation of traditional Sardinian architecture,' but it might better be called 'instant ancient'. The consortium began with five hotels in soft, faded pastel pinks and browns that would give a weathered look (while inside bartenders mixed martinis and French chefs prepared *haute cuisine*).

An army of landscape artists was brought in and exotic flora planted and nurtured along with myrtle and plane trees to blend in with the native frangipani and other shrubs and trees. Entire small villages dotting the curving coastline were designed with modern shopping plazas, atmospheric cafés, and stylish discothèques, all adhering to the strict code of the exteriors. Porto Cervo, where the harbour was, became the hub of social activities. Karim had grown obsessed with his dream, which quickly, and with a huge investment of eighty to ninety million dollars by the consortium (Karim's personal investment was one-tenth of that), became reality. He had created his own special place on earth (which the press was fond of calling 'Agaland'). And yet, except when his family joined him, there were few Ismailis on the Costa Smeralda, nor was an Ismaili community to come into being at any time in the near future.

For himself, Karim built an enormous, rambling white villa on a cliff that overlooked the emerald sea (which at differing times of day and weather could vary from turquoise to deep azure blue). The view was spectacular, the house equipped with every conceivable modern comfort, indoor and outdoor pools, tennis courts, and luxurious, self-contained guest quarters. The interiors of the complex were a combination of Oriental and Mediterranean influences, colourful tiles, bamboo and exotic fabrics. He acquired a new, commodious yacht,

Amaloun, a Mystère Falcon jet and a helicopter to ferry him back and forth to a Corsican airfield until the landing strip and equipment on the one he was building at Olbia was enlarged to accommodate jets.

The occupants of the first completed villas, only two years after the start of the project, set the tone for the colony that would follow: there were two Rockefellers, a Rothschild and several of the English nobility (Princess Margaret became a frequent visitor). Princess Joan and Bettina both had villas and Yasmin came during school breaks (which certainly proved that a unique harmony existed among the important women in Aly Khan's life).

The calm seasonal waters of Porto Cervo's harbour quickly filled with some of the handsomest and largest yachts that sailed the Mediterranean. New residents and guests arrived, servants carrying their Gucci and Vuitton suitcases packed with the season's most stylish resort clothes. One writer sniped, 'The Costa Smeralda smells like money.' Another compared Karim Aga Khan's Costa Smeralda with what Monte Carlo had recently been to Aristotle Onassis, 'except that he has never been beset by troubles with the ruling prince'. In this case, he was in essence the ruling prince because Sardinian officials, pleased at the Costa Smeralda's financial advantages to the island's economy, let him have his way in most things.

There were other differences between Karim's and Onassis's terrains. Monte Carlo, Monaco's main city, had been founded and built by Prince Rainier of Monaco's ancestors. Onassis had acquired financial power there, but his personality was not a part of the character of the region. The Costa Smeralda was Karim Aga Khan's dream, conceived as a resort for largely villa-owning residents, a select few who could afford the prices charged by the consortium for their luxury accommodation. The first clientele were mainly summer sports-loving people – yachtsmen, tennis players, sun-followers – who valued their privacy. Monte Carlo was greatly dependent upon tourism and the financial benefits of the money made at its famous Casino. And unlike Sardinia, Monaco's economy (especially since the wedding in 1956 of Prince Rainier to the film star Grace Kelly) was riding high. There was almost no unemployment, some of the world's most famous stores crowded its elegant thoroughfares. Not only was the cost of living astronomical, the cost of building was almost out of sight, which did not prevent

Monte Carlo from resembling a city in progress with new villas constantly going up, up, up. They seemed to be rising one on top of the other as there was no other way to expand, the small principality of Monaco being about one-tenth the size of the Costa Smeralda (although Prince Rainier was working on a successful plan to reclaim land from the sea to enlarge his territory about 15 per cent).

In 'Agaland' construction workers were plentiful and inexpensive. Building costs were low because labour was cheap and easily available (in Monte Carlo, most labourers had to be brought in from elsewhere). There was no shortage of fresh fish and seafood at modest prices (to the merchants – prices at the hotels were from the outset extremely high). Anything that was needed could be shipped the relatively short distance from Naples or Rome, but the consortium built a supermarket to equal the modern ones recently completed in the South of France so that everyday essentials along with gourmet items were right at hand.

Karim was living the life of a financial tycoon. He flew everywhere in his Mystère executive jet, which had six seats and a sofa for three and was equipped as an office large enough for two conferences to be held simultaneously. He also had a pressurized turbo-prop four-seater which had made 82 landings in just over two months on his last tour of East Africa. He maintained a permanent crew of two pilots and two co-pilots, four full-time and three part-time secretaries, and Dr Hengel, his industrial adviser, who had his own staff of ten. He travelled with his French butler Joseph and his chauffeur Lucien, who had been with his father in the Lancia when it crashed.

He carried a mountain of files with him whenever he flew or drove anywhere. 'I used to drive a lot after Grandpa died,' he told a reporter in 1968, 'but now I find . . . I prefer to study my papers. But I still drive sometimes.'

In Paris he kept a two-seater Maserati, a four-door Maserati and a Mini-Cooper S; in Sardinia and Switzerland, Volkswagens. He owned many more houses, but the ones he actually occupied were a château on the Ile de la Cité in Paris (together with an adjoining house which he converted into offices), the legendary L'Horizon, the house in Geneva that Aly Khan had bought near the old Aga Khan's Swiss residence when his father was dying, which Dr Hengel used for his offices (Karim also had a suite of rooms for his personal use), the chalet in Gstaad, Green Lodge, a bungalow on the racing property at Chantilly, another, St Créspin, on the Normandy stud farm, and the villa in Sardinia.

Karim did not neglect his racing stables and stud farms for his Sardinian paradise, and his winnings were constant. 'I didn't realize racing would take so much time,' he explained to a *Life* interviewer. 'During the peak season it means half a day five days a week. Then I have to make more time, so I must study files in the car. I have to know precisely where my time goes . . . the French say there's *une philosophie du cheval* and it's true. Horseracing is a world of its own. Relationships in it go very deep. It was an area of Daddy's life I didn't understand when he was alive. He was an expert. He analysed form every single day and himself decided what races the horses should be entered for.'

The youngest owner of a large stable in France, he was greatly respected for his accomplishments. 'Don't make any mistake,' he often said when one of his horses lost. 'You race horses to win.' And he won consistently. Privately, he claimed he had never bet on a race.

He was equally successful with his business enterprises for Ismaili communities as he was in his private undertakings. Management consultants were brought in to advise local businessmen and to keep them abreast of technological progress in the West. Karim invested about $5 million of his own money (obtaining matching funds by the communities) to launch three major companies in East Africa that had under their aegis textile mills, pottery works and real estate. (Several years later the companies were floated on the stock market and a large profit was made.) In Kenya workers were trained in the making of high quality leather, their finished product outselling by 300 per cent other local tanners.

The youthful Aga Khan was fast becoming a billionaire and his followers were enjoying a financial boom such as they had never before known. With financial security had come better housing, health care and educational facilities for the members of his sect. There is no way of knowing if Aly Khan would have been able to succeed as his son had done, whether the fact of being Imam would have directed him along the same path to prosperity. He had shown a great talent for

investment, especially in the last few years of his life when he led a
more stable day-to-day existence. But Karim was a wise choice. His
youth and energy, his unsullied past, his charismatic personality and
his modern approach to their ancient culture, which was leading them
to a better, more self-sufficient life, had found immediate acceptance
by his followers.

Both Aly and the old Aga Khan had needed a woman's love; seemed
unable, in fact, to succeed without it (the old Aga Khan had been
married – albeit to four successive wives – from the time he was
nineteen years of age). Karim was still a bachelor in 1965 when he
celebrated his twenty-ninth birthday at a special Durbar held in Karachi
at the Aga Khan Gymkhana grounds amidst delegations of Ismaili
communities from all over the world. He had been Imam for eight
years. He travelled tirelessly to Ismaili communities: at least one
extended tour was embarked upon each year. He had the love and
respect of his followers.

His main aims were to serve the poor by helping them to help
themselves, to encourage means to bring water to the dry regions
where Ismaili communities were situated, to continue to build upon
the considerable progress his grandfather had made in the education
of his followers, both male and female, to establish business enterprises
suited to the resources of the diverse Ismaili communities (desert,
mountain, sea and city) so that the people could earn a higher living
wage, experience economic independence and enjoy a better life.
Increasing medical facilities and the accessibility of good health care
was also high on his list of priorities. The scale of his activities in
achieving these goals had increased dramatically in the last few years
of his Imamship.

What he had done was to encourage his followers to organize central
committees in their communities which would meet weekly to discuss
their problems and institute a plan of action to diminish them. But
Karim Aga Khan was doing more than helping his own followers.
He believed strongly in doing what he could to improve health and
education conditions in the countries where his people lived as well
as in their own communities. There were crippling diseases, major
health needs and few trained nurses in Pakistan. By the mid-sixties the
Aga Khan Foundation had grown into a sophisticated, well-financed

(by Karim Aga Khan himself and donations), non-profit-making organization capable of making an immediate impact on such problems as the health care crisis in Pakistan where several million Ismailis lived.

The Aga Khan Foundation instituted a nursing school, increasing its facilities to keep up with the large yearly rise in enrolment by adding new equipment, more staff teachers and additional space. Qualified doctors and nurses were encouraged to go out into the slums of cities where they were badly needed, for the very poor had no money to go to hospitals and often feared them.

The Imam's followers were grateful for all the good things he had done for them, but their feelings went a great deal deeper than gratitude. 'Karim Aga Khan has an aura that is almost visible,' an Ismaili told this writer. 'It echoes in his voice and shines in his eyes. He has a wisdom that can only come from godliness.'

But when asked if he had ever had a mystical experience, Karim replied, 'Anyone who prays regularly will have once or twice perhaps a special sense of elevation. It is true in A[myn]'s case and in mine . . . to ascribe it to a mystical experience would be presumptuous. But it is uncommon, perhaps.'

In Karachi, a few days before the Durbar, he visited Honeymoon Lodge, the birthplace of his grandfather. The old house was perched on top of a towering hill. Over a hundred steps led to it. As he approached the bottom of this daunting climb with a group of his followers, he turned to them and requested they remain where they were and let him mount the steps alone. The men did as he asked and watched as he went up slowly, his pace even, his eyes on the top step of the precipitous climb. When he reached his destination, he stood silently, meditating for about ten minutes, the sun directly over his shoulder, the air still, the men below just as motionless.

'I want to build a house here,' he told the Ismailis when he joined them again. 'It reminds me of the past.'

As, indeed, the Durbar might well have done, for it had all the Oriental pageantry of the great celebrations given in honour of his grandfather. Karim was dressed in brilliant robes and thousands of his followers prostrated themselves before him. As a gift from them he was asked to accept a bungalow to be constructed on the crest of the hill near Honeymoon Lodge. He accepted gracefully and work was begun shortly after his departure.

Like Queen Elizabeth, whose life followed a certain pattern of migration from one stately home to another, Karim Aga Khan's life was now set into a routine: Gstaad for skiing in December, January and February; Paris and the French races in the spring; London (to meet staff at the Ismaili Centre and for the Derby, the Oaks and Newmarket sales) the South of France and Sardinia in the summer; Asia and East Africa in the autumn for his annual visit to Ismaili communities, also flights to New York for business and social reasons, to Ireland to check on his stud farms, and for special meetings in other countries on business or personal pleasure whenever they could be fitted in.

The year that followed the Karachi Durbar was particularly trying. In the spring Nina Dyer, six years after her divorce from Sadruddin, committed suicide by swallowing a bottle of sleeping pills in her luxurious apartment in the Paris suburb of Garches. Now thirty-five years old, she had been living a fairly reclusive existence and was known to have been drinking heavily. Stories circulated that she was sorry she had ever divorced her first husband, Baron Heinrich von Thyssen, with whom she had dined a week earlier. He attended her burial (without religious ceremony), as did Sadruddin. Overshadowing her grave was a seven-foot-high wreath of 1000 roses which leaned against the wall of the cemetery a few feet away. On it were inscribed the words, '*De Heini à Nina*' – from von Thyssen.

Nina's death seemed almost as astonishing as her life. She had not lost her good looks or her sizeable fortune when she decided to take her own life. But she had few friends. She left no personal bequests. Her will asked for the sale of all her possessions, the proceeds of which were to go for the protection of animals (several animal agencies were named as benefactors). Her jewellery went at auction for nearly $2 million. There was also her apartment in Paris, the house in Switzerland, a good art collection and many valuable antiques.

Sadruddin was greatly disturbed by her death. He had not married again, although there were constant rumours of serious attachments (the widowed Jacqueline Kennedy among them) which the press hinted might lead to marriage.

On 6 October 1966, just three months after Nina Dyer's suicide, Karim Aga Khan's half-brother, 34-year-old Patrick Guinness, was killed when the Italian sports car he was driving hit a tree head-on as he swerved to avoid a bus on a main road in the Swiss Rhône Valley leading to the Simplon Pass. He left a wife, the former Dolores von Fürstenberg, and three small children. Princess Joan was understandably distraught and Karim was dutifully protective of his mother that summer in Sardinia. He was particularly fond of Patrick, and the two of them had worked closely in the development of Costa Smeralda. His death was a shock and brought back harsh memories of his own father's fatal car crash.

That autumn riots swept Pakistan and Ayub was forced to step down in favour of a military government headed by General Muhammed Yahya Khan. There was political unrest in Kenya and the state had taken over control of the economy in Tanzania. Karim stayed as far back from these governmental plights as possible. But he had to make sure Ismaili communities in those countries were safeguarded and that their (and his) business investments were secure. He maintained good relations with the new governments while avoiding any direct involvement in political matters.

For the next two years he was led a frantic pace by the pressures of his Imamate, his extensive travel agenda and his hands-on involvement with the Costa Smeralda, working with architects and environmentalists. There had been a series of short affairs, but real love appeared to have eluded him. When he arrived in Gstaad early in December 1968 close observers noted that he seemed lonely, tired and somewhat restless. He was talking about possibly selling the chalet, although previously the Alpine resort had always held fond memories for him. It was here that he had spent his winters while attending Le Rosey and where his parents' marriage (before Aly Khan's affair with Rita Hayworth) had seemed its happiest and his home life the least complicated.

December in this mountain resort is a time of particular gaiety. The main street of the village bustles with activity, the snow-covered slopes are alive with the whoosh of skiers, the dozen or so restaurants crowded at every meal, and the Palace, that *grande dame* of glamorous Alpine hotels, its thousands of night-lights a glittering display that could be seen for miles, booked solid by the famous and socially prominent.

There was a constant parade of festive parties both in the places where the public gathered, the hotels and night clubs, and in the extraordinary chalet-style homes occupied by film stars (Richard Burton and Elizabeth Taylor, Julie Andrews and Blake Edwards, and Sean Connery among them), famous writers (the town having had a literary heritage since Ernest Hemingway, forty years earlier, had written *A Farewell to Arms*, at a table in the front tavern-bar of the Rössli Hotel), musicians (the great violinist Yehudi Menuhin lived in Gstaad, and brought together some of the world's greatest chamber music instrumentalists for concerts in a nearby ancient church), and a galaxy of the rich and the titled. It was difficult to remain dispirited long in such a stimulating society.

Gstaad also drew the pick of the international singles crowd, American heiresses looking for love European style (often finding it with ski instructors), rich divorcées and widows hoping to even better their circumstances the second time round, beautiful actresses and models searching for a wealthy Prince Charming.

One of the loveliest young women in Gstaad that season was the twenty-nine-year-old Lady James Crichton-Stuart, recently divorced after nine years of marriage. Her maiden name had been Sarah Croker-Poole, daughter of Lieutenant-Colonel Arthur Croker-Poole, a former English officer in the Indian Army. Sally, as she was called, was born in New Delhi and educated in England where she had met her husband, the younger twin brother of the current Marquess of Bute, John Crichton-Stuart. Only minutes at birth had denied James the hereditary title and the ancestral home and wealth that went with it. He was no luckier in his marriage. There were no children and there were problems between the couple almost from the start. They had separated several times and reunited before the divorce.

Tall, willowy, with thick chestnut hair that she streaked blonde, large, velvet-brown eyes and elegant facial bone structure, she had worked in recent years as a fashion model. This was the time of swinging London in miniskirts, and the top model of the day was a skinny blonde teenager named Twiggy. Sally did not fit that mould but she was so exquisitely photogenic that she was in high demand, especially for hair, jewellery or make-up assignments. She possessed one of those long, graceful necks that seemed to have been designed for heavily jewelled necklaces and she carried her head in a thoroughly regal manner.

Lady James, as was her proper title, and Karim met fittingly earlier that year at Buckingham Palace at a dinner party given by the Queen. Karim was mesmerized by Sally's beauty, her charm, her ability to speak Urdu (he had never met another European woman who could), and her naturally majestic bearing. By New Year's Eve he was certain he was in love with her and wanted to make her his wife. She appeared to have little resistance to this plan and displayed a growing interest in his faith.

Lord and Lady James Crichton-Stuart were Catholics and, although Sally had a civil divorce decree, in the eyes of the Catholic Church she was still married. As she planned to convert to Islam and be married in an Ismaili ceremony this proved not to be a problem for Karim and Sally,[1] but they did not rush into setting a date. For the next six months they saw each other frequently in London, Paris, the South of France and Sardinia, where Sally spent the summer. At the end of this time she had converted to Islam and 28 October was set as the wedding date.

They would be married privately first in Paris in a civil ceremony, then seven days later in a small Ismaili ritual followed the next night by a grand wedding reception at Karim's thirteenth-century château (once a monastery) on the Ile de la Cité near Notre-Dame. They tried to keep their plans secret, not wanting the press to make a circus of their wedding. (Karim could hardly forget his father's wedding to Rita Hayworth.) But the guest list for the reception, which was to grow to 800, included Princess Margaret and her husband Lord Snowdon (the former Anthony Armstrong-Jones who had covered the wedding of Sadruddin and Nina Dyer as a photographer for a London newspaper). They would be flown to the ceremony in Karim's private jet.

October turned out to be a glorious Indian summer, the trees and shrubs in and about Paris slow to colour. Then, just three days before the wedding, the temperature dropped dramatically and Paris was a most magnificent blaze of autumnal reds. By then, Karim and Sally

---

[1] Lord James Crichton-Stuart petitioned the Church for an annulment, but this was not granted until 1970, a year after his former wife had married Karim Aga Khan.

had exchanged vows in complete secrecy in the civil ceremony, performed on 22 October in the ornate parlour at the town hall of the
Paris Fourth District by the local mayor, M. Georges Teolière, wearing
his red, white and blue sash of office. No banns were posted on the
town hall noticeboard and the couple were accompanied by only four
witnesses: Sadruddin, Amyn, Lt-Colonel Croker-Poole, and the bride's
brother Anthony.

The bride's neat, short brown dress had a matching Eton jacket and
a miniskirt that showed off her long, shapely legs. In contrast, Karim
wore a conservative blue suit. The two exchanged formal vows with
a brief 'Oui', the mayor wished them well and twenty minutes after
they had entered his office they were man and wife in the view of
French law. That evening Karim entertained about fifty people, including Princess Joan, the old Begum looking chic, the bride's mother and
some close friends at his Ile de la Cité home, half a mile from the town
hall, driving back across the Seine through rush-hour traffic.

At eleven AM, one week later, the couple were married for the
second time at the residence in an Ismaili Muslim ceremony attended
by leaders of Ismaili communities in twenty-three countries. The bride,
who took the Muslim name Salimah, wore a dramatic white silk sari,
Karim a white tunic and pants and a black astrakhan cap. Ismaili
women guests were dressed in brightly coloured saris, the men in
outfits similar to the groom's. They brought with them symbolic gifts
of gold, silver and pearls. In sharp contrast to the extravagant champagne that would be served the next evening for their gala wedding
reception, marriage toasts were raised with crystal glasses of orange
juice, Coca-Cola and the sour milk drink known as *lassi* in accordance
with the Muslim law against alcohol. The ancient château was filled
with huge bowls of magnificent flowers and the sun streamed through
the leaded windows on this crisp, clear October morning, giving a
gleam and polish to wood surfaces and the amazing amount of silver
and gold on show. Beyond the windows the great buildings of the Ile
de la Cité were framed by a deep blue sky.

The earliest inhabited section of Paris, the Ile de la Cité is encompassed by the two arms of the Seine and set like a ship, Notre-Dame
as its stern, the Pointe as its prow, and moored to either bank by a
series of historic bridges, the Pont-Neuf the oldest (1607). Once ancient

Lutetia, the cradle of Paris, it is an island within a city. But when the foundation stone of Notre-Dame was laid in 1163 it was not selected as a site by mere chance. Notre-Dame was constructed as a sanctuary where boatmen on the Seine could worship their gods. As time passed it became the royal, legal and ecclesiastical centre of France and so it is easy to understand the appeal of the Ile de la Cité to Karim. It was here that, at the age of ten, Henry VI of England was crowned king of France and where Napoleon I and Josephine were crowned Emperor and Empress of France. History and antiquity cocoon the area which at night seems an enchantment with the illuminated Notre-Dame framed against a dark filigree of trees and the swirling reflections of lights on the surrounding waters of the Seine.

Of course, the château had gone through many major alterations since the thirteenth century but the ancient architecture had been preserved. Handsome vaulted rooms, huge stone fireplaces and spiral staircases remained. Most of the old stone floors were covered with thick Persian rugs, tapestries were hung on the foot-thick stone walls and many of Aly Khan's prized antique pieces were displayed throughout the vast interior. Despite its size and pedigree, the château possessed a great welcoming warmth, especially with fires blazing and the hundreds of burning candles casting flickering fingers of flame. There were magnificent electrified antique chandeliers in all the reception rooms, but Karim preferred the old-world atmosphere of candlelight and would often have as many as two hundred candles lit for a modest-sized dinner party.

The night of what the press referred to as 'a diamond-encrusted wedding reception', 28 October, the exterior of the stone château was floodlit and the front door was covered by a giant marquee where most of the bejewelled and elegantly dressed guests were greeted by Princess Joan and Amyn. Huge crowds had gathered on the street outside and stood behind wooden barriers guarded by caped gendarmes. There was the feeling of a Hollywood premiere with camera flashes exploding and cheers rising as dark, sleek limousines drew up and the prominent guests were helped out and up the path to the entrance. A more private approach was arranged for Princess Margaret, Lord Snowdon and their party which included the British Ambassador to France Christopher Soames and his wife Mary, the Earl of Lichfield and Mr Jocelyn Stevens, who were driven to the home of Karim's neighbour, the Comtesse de la Motte, and escorted through her court-yard (which entered his back garden by an iron gate, opened especially for the royal entourage). The Queen's sister was the most eminent but not the only royal guest. Prince Alexander of Yugoslavia and Prince Victor Emmanuel of Savoy were also present. The French Rothschild family attended in force and Hollywood was represented by Charles Chaplin (a good friend of the old Aga Khan), his wife, the former Oona O'Neill, Danny and Sylvia Kaye and David Niven. The new Begum, Karim wearing a white oriental-style silk tunic and black trousers and beaming beside her as they greeted their guests, seemed to be born to her current position. She stood tall and radiant, groomed impeccably, her hair smoothed into an upswept hairdo that added inches more to her height, her gold embroidered sari just the right touch of ostentatiousness, her smile and graciousness displaying charm enough to convince the world of her right to be both Begum and Princess.

Champagne of the finest vintage was served amid the white stone pillars of the reception rooms. The glorious array of food that followed was grand enough to have pleased the groom's late grandfather, the old Aga Khan, whose widow – elegantly gowned and lavishly bedecked with jewels and wearing spike heels which added to her stature – towered above both the bride and groom.

The following day the newlyweds were the honoured guests at an intimate lunch given by the President of France and Mme Pompidou. That evening they travelled on Karim's private jet to Lyford Cay, Nassau, where they remained for a week under assumed names in the largest suite of the most luxurious hotel for a 'secret honeymoon'. Reporters did get wind of where they were, but not until they were about to return to Paris. This would be the last time for quite some while that they would enjoy anonymity and privacy. Shortly after New Year's Day 1970, just ten weeks following their marriage, they left on an extended tour of Pakistan where the Begum would be introduced to large groups of her husband's followers and be subjected for the first time to the responsibilities of her new position. She was already being prepared for what lay before her.

Every day before their departure she went through briefings on the scores of places they were to visit, the people they were to meet, and was given instructions in the protocol required in meeting officials, their wives, local governors, military authorities and university chancellors. The public relations for the tour were being handled by Karim's old colleague Michael Curtis and the schedule, although smoothly organized, was back-breaking.

Princess Salimah would be meeting thousands of people whose eyes would be fixed on how she conducted herself. She had no training other than the days of work with Curtis, and although Karim would be with her, he would have too much on his own agenda – speeches, meetings, negotiations – to concern himself with his wife's problems as Begum, should she find them difficult to cope with. It was not an easy way for a marriage to begin.

19

In his day, the old Aga Khan's name and bulky likeness was featured in news stories as an icon of sorts, a man who conjured up images of Great Britain as an Empire, the time of the raj, and as a reminder and relic of a mysterious and ancient past. During Aly Khan's lifetime, his exotic good looks and audacious behaviour made whatever he did the lead story in the tabloid press and gossip columns. With Karim Aga Khan it was a different matter. Once the Costa Smeralda had gained momentum and his stables were known to bring in more revenue than those of his father and grandfather, articles and photographs of him were more likely to be found in publications like the *Financial Times*, *The Wall Street Journal*, and *The Economist* than in the popular press. As his grandfather had predicted, Karim had ushered in a new age to the Ismaili sect – an Imam as financial guru.

He had advisers, his most relied upon being the two dependable members of his staff, Dr Hengel (an economist and investment consultant), and his attorney Maître Ardoin. But he always made the final decisions on his private investments like the Costa Smeralda enterprise, his racing empire, newspaper acquisitions (the one in Kenya now run by Gerard Wilkinson, a perspicacious Irishman who would later become a key figure on Karim Aga Khan's personal staff), along with those for the sect, which he would advise on modern methods of manufacture, sales, promotion and expansion as well as helping to arrange financing for these purposes.

A telephone to connect him with his business interests in Europe, Asia and Africa was never far from his hand or ear. His jet plane remained ready at all times for take-off to any suddenly called foreign meeting. He had difficulty separating business from pleasure, and one of the reasons why he had decided he should sell the chalet in Gstaad was that he no longer found it feasible to spend more than thirty minutes a day on the slopes.

There was always the feeling when he was in a room with his staff, no matter how high their position, that he was the boss (not the Imam, for he had few Ismailis on his personal business staff and those that were did not hold key positions). It could be seen less in his attitude, which was cool, collected and always thoughtful, than in theirs. His assistants seemed able to speak freely and frankly to him, laugh when the situation called for it, but they were always restrained, highly respectful and deferred to him. A sense of camaraderie simply did not exist. Out of his hearing, he was referred to as 'the boss' or as 'HH' (His Highness); in his presence that line of intimacy was never crossed. His staff addressed him as 'Your Highness' or 'Sir'.

He could relax for short periods on skis, or while on his yacht (although he generally brought secretaries, files and assistants aboard). With the exception of his short honeymoon in Jamaica he took no vacation that was not shared with his business interests. The tour of Pakistan, which he viewed as an extended honeymoon, lacked private time for the newlyweds. He had chosen to take his bride on a lengthy trip to a place where his role as Imam and hers as Begum took first priority.

Complicating the situation further was the shortage of time the newly-named Princess Salimah had been given to prepare for what was before her and the lack of any previous experience with the protocol and expectations of the role that had been so suddenly cast upon her. But as a model, and as the wife of the younger son in a titled English family, she had led a life that called for her to look good and be able to accept her position with grace. These two attributes would be of great help to her.

The Begum's schedule was to include many solo appearances, official visits that either Karim Aga Khan could not attend because of his heavy schedule or were to child care organizations and women's groups which fell more into a begum's province. There would also be frequent occasions while they were on tour of Ismaili communities when she would accompany him to Ismaili or government events; which required an understanding of both religious and political protocol. A recent convert to her husband's faith and never before having been involved in political matters, this was no simple task. But she was given expert guidance by members of her staff, chosen because of their expertise in such things.

To complicate matters even more, this was a time of upheaval in Pakistan. There had been disastrous riots in late 1968 and early 1969. Martial law had been declared, the former president Ayub Khan resigned and the government had been taken over by the head of the army, General Yahya Khan. In the early months of 1970, when Karim Aga Khan and the new Begum were on tour in Pakistan, secret meetings were being held by the various and opposing political factions. Zulfikar Ali Bhutto was the leader of one such group, the People's Party.

Bhutto was a charismatic and contradictory man. Raised in an affluent family in India during the time of the Empire, he had attended university in California and at Oxford and had climbed to power in Pakistan with amazing swiftness rising from being a member of the Central Cabinet, to Foreign Minister, to the founding of his own People's Party.

At the time of Karim Aga Khan and the new Begum's tour, Bhutto was beginning his climb to power. He had just been released from jail (for having incited the masses) and had delivered a stirring speech to the court that finally liberated him.

'Our people . . . feel the pain of privation and yearn for the happiness of their children,' he said in a moving voice, 'Their poverty is unimaginable but yet they hope for a better future . . . Starvation has dried the milk in the mother's breast . . . It is not the law of God that our people must live eternally in despair and that their children should die of disease and want.'

Uprisings occurred along the route that Karim Aga Khan and the Begum travelled. Roads were often lined with heavily armed police. Occasionally shots could be heard in the near distance. Despite reports of massacres in East Pakistan, Karim Aga Khan kept to the tour agenda. Large communities of Ismailis lived in East Pakistan, usually in their own sections of cities (Dhaka with over 4 million population being the centre) and villages where they could pray together. Most Ismailis were getting by despite the difficulties East Pakistan had suffered. Although travel was dangerous at present, Karim Aga Khan was determined to visit each and every one of these communities no matter what the obstacles, knowing that by doing so he would bring his followers great comfort.

Happily, there were no serious incidents while they travelled by land through that thickly populated area (nearly 2000 people per acre), down the Ganges past miles of rice paddies and tea plantations, flying in a small two-engined plane over tropical jungles and swamps. East Pakistan (which would eventually become Bangladesh) was one of the poorest regions of the world, totally dependent on imports for survival, and unable to feed its own people from the vastly over-populated, humid, low-lying, alluvial land. The region also had a tropical monsoon climate difficult for visitors to endure. Karim Aga Khan had chosen January for the tour as it was ordinarily the dry season, but this year the rain and the humidity were relentless.

Dhaka was midway on their journey. They had arrived three weeks earlier in Karachi in West Pakistan to a well-publicized and tumultuous greeting by thousands of Ismailis who pressed against the crush barriers at the airport for their first glimpse of the new Begum. The sun was blinding and the reflection on the silver wings of the jet plane made it difficult to see the Imam and his wife as they came down the metal staircase, Karim Aga Khan in a white tunic suit leading, directly followed by several male members of his staff wearing conservative business suits; the Begum (dressed in a white sari, gleaming in the brilliance of the lighting) several paces behind, accompanied by two of her husband's female secretaries in European dress.

Princess Salimah stood with imperial bearing, smiling while being presented to government officials and Ismaili leaders, a large umbrella held over her carefully coiffed golden hair by a servant to ward off any possible chance of sunstroke although the temperature was at a safe, if humid, eighty degrees. Photographs were taken. Then the entourage was led to a line of black limousines, where Karim Aga Khan and the Begum were helped into the leading car. They were followed to the newly-constructed Honeymoon Lodge by several floats decorated with flowers, two Aga Khan Bands and files of marching uniformed Aga Khan Boy Scouts and Girl Guides (the groups formed early in Aga Khan III's time as a means to give young Ismailis a special sense of purpose). The festive atmosphere recalled the welcoming ceremonies for the old Aga Khan at the time of his Platinum Jubilee.

They would travel to Hyderabad (India), Dhaka, Rawalpindi (north-east Pakistan), Lahore (east central Pakistan), Peshawar (north-west Pakistan, near the famous Khyber Pass) and the capital city of Islamabad, as well as to dozens of small villages and towns between these main centres. Karim gave speeches in most of them, and in late January in Rawalpindi, an important industrial and commercial centre which at that time was the capital of Pakistan, hosted a dinner, with Princess Salimah at his side, in honour of the country's dictator, the new President of Pakistan General Yahya Khan and his entire cabinet.

On 14 February, while Karim Aga Khan and the Begum made their way through the troubled country, Bhutto announced that he and several other People's Party stalwarts would 'fast until death' to effect the lifting of the draconian martial laws General Yahya Khan had imposed. Only a few months later Pakistan was embroiled in bitter elections.[1] Karim carefully avoided taking a political stand, although his silence as to the General's dictatorial leadership and his gracious treatment of him were seen as a form of endorsement, despite his possible reluctance to believe that was the case.

Pakistan's economy was in a terrible shambles, with income per capita down to a shocking low of $156 a year ($126 in East Pakistan); 76 per cent of the population (97 per cent of the Muslim faith) were illiterate. Only a little more than 100,000 Pakistanis received anything beyond a secondary education.[2] These figures were almost entirely

[1] The opposition were campaigning for a new constitution and the restoration of democratic government. The first direct universal voting in Pakistan since independence took place in December 1970 (ten months after the visit of Karim Aga Khan) and the moderate socialist Awami League under Mujibur Rahman, who were in favour of full independence for East Pakistan, won an overwhelming majority. General Yahya Khan cancelled the election results, banned the Awami League, and imprisoned Mujibur Rahman on charges of treason. East Pakistan declared its independence as Bangladesh on 26 March 1971, but was placed under martial law and occupied by the Pakistani army, which was made up entirely of troops from West Pakistan. In the ensuing civil war, which lasted a year, 10 million refugees fled to India and hundreds of thousands of civilians were killed.

[2] About half of Pakistan's population in 1970 lived in East Pakistan, one of the most densely populated areas in the world, where the life expectancy was 43 and infant mortality 20 per cent.

reversed among the four million Pakistani Ismailis who enjoyed a per capita income several times the national average, with a small percentage of illiteracy and a large percentage of students who continued on to higher education. Such positive statistics did not stop Karim Aga Khan in his speeches from stressing education as he always had done. He also made it absolutely clear that Ismailis were loyal subjects of the land in which they lived (and held passports) and would abide by the laws of their country's ruling party, which in essence meant he was telling them that they must not rebel against whatever form of government was imposed upon them.

For the Begum, this first tour to Pakistan was a draining experience which she handled, however, with great skill. The travel was arduous, the official engagements often trying. She was expected to look cool, collected and beautiful – and she did. The effort was not easy given the humid climate and the long hours of public appearances required of her. English was the official government language, which was a relief. She spoke Urdu when required (spoken by 7.5 per cent of the population), and there was a member of her small staff who could translate the many regional languages when necessary.

She also had to adapt herself to the more restrained and often subservient position of women in Pakistan, both within and outside the Ismaili sect. Her natural character was outgoing. She enjoyed a good conversation, had strong opinions and a sense of humour. Her admiration of her husband's liberal views towards women and their place in society was keen. Seeing women still in purdah disturbed her, but she kept her disapproval to herself lest she offend someone's beliefs. Like his grandfather, Karim preached independence and education for men and women alike, and few women within the sect still clung to the veil. Ismaili women had a pride of bearing, a self-confidence that was evident. Although they attended single-sex schools and did not sit with the men to pray, their opinions on community matters were freely given and carefully considered and they were encouraged by their parents to continue their education to university level.

When the new Begum had lived in India as a young girl, it had been as the daughter of a high-ranking British officer, mostly set apart from the people and the poverty of India during the late forties and early fifties. Pakistan was a poor, struggling nation, which although fairly new, was obsolete and retrogressive in everything from medicine (there was only one physician for every 4500 people and the equipment in hospitals was terribly out of date), to communications (only 225,000 telephones, the majority used by the government and the small élite class) and transport (railways were antiquated, roads poor and there were fewer than 175,000 passenger cars in the entire country).

But great beauty was also to be found in a land that was bordered on one side by the Arabian Sea and stretched for a thousand miles to the mountain wall of the Hindu Kush and the towering peaks of the Himalayas where the great Indus River rises and flows through the fertile Indus plains. This was contrasted with the harsh land of the Eastern Plains and the Thar Desert and the desperate condition of the people of East Pakistan.

Here and there were echoes of the pomp and luxury of the lost land of the raj, the panoply of imperial power once wielded by the British Empire. The great palaces and government buildings of that era remained, but they often seemed like a luminous mirage that disappeared into crumbling disarray upon close inspection. Perhaps it was because of the pervading decadence that so many non-Ismailis came out to see the Aga Khan and his Begum whenever they were known to be arriving in a public place. In his immaculate white tunic suits, standing unruffled and smiling, his wife regally at his side, strikingly beautiful, her elegant silk saris clinging to a slim figure of supple curves, Karim looked like a film star stepped out of a scene with his leading lady on his arm. But when he spoke, it was immediately evident how dedicated he was to the position he held. This was not a role he was playing. It was real life – *his* real life and also that of his wife, who by the end of the tour realized she would soon become the mother of his first child.

Yasmin, recently graduated from Bennington College, was now a delightful young woman who greatly resembled her mother during her own youth. She celebrated her twenty-first birthday in December 1971. The press called her Princess Jasmin (sometimes referring to her incorrectly as Princess Aga Khan), which in the United States gave her a glamorous aura. She had come into a large part of her inheritance and was independently rich. She bought an apartment in New York overlooking Central Park and supervised the decoration, a marriage of Hollywood glamour and Oriental chic. Her good friends were Christina Onassis and Margaret Trudeau, the young wife of the Canadian prime minister Pierre Trudeau. She was seen about town with rich and titled suitors and was a favourite of the society gossip columnists. Without being sure, or entirely committed, she thought she wanted to have a career as an operatic soprano. Marriage was pushed from her thoughts as she concentrated on singing lessons.

Her faith was extremely important to her. She was close to Karim and turned to him often for advice and for the sense of family she missed from Rita, who lived on the West Coast and was going through a sad, disturbing time in her career and private life. Within a year she was to appear in her last film. Besieged by financial difficulties, the unfaithfulness of her men friends and a puzzling struggle to remember things that had recently occurred, she was a lonely woman and adrift. Her older daughter, Rebecca Welles, lived in the state of Washington, also on the West Coast but at a distance of a thousand miles, and they seldom saw one another; and Yasmin was three thousand miles away on the East Coast.

'I don't see Yassy much,' Rita told Jim Watters, the entertainment editor of *Life*. 'I can't afford to fly back there [to New York] all the time. Yasmin can afford it, but she only visits once or twice a year. She calls me on the telephone sometimes . . . She'd like to be an opera singer, but her voice isn't developed yet. She'd better be more than beautiful-looking if she's going to make it. But she doesn't have to worry. She has money . . . I've told her if she wants to be an opera singer she shouldn't smoke, but she does. She's a happy girl and very nice, but she has to work if she really wants to make it.'

Yasmin had a good voice but was not truly gifted. Before long she came to realize she would not have a career of any consequence in opera. Actually, she was grasping for something more meaningful in terms of an occupation that could help others. She was torn between two cultures and by the physical distance from her father's family, to whom she felt closely aligned. Summers were partially spent in the South of France with her grandfather's widow. She greatly admired the middle-aged Begum and considered her a kind of mentor, or substitute mother. Perhaps, more importantly, she was able to discuss her various problems with her which she was unable to do with Rita in her confused state.

Her father occupied a special place in her heart. For the last few years of his life, when she was a child and at her most vulnerable, they had had an extremely close relationship. She had adored him. He had brought excitement and warmth into her life, which had been lonely at that point. His sudden death when she was only eleven years old had been a stunning blow from which she still had not recovered. The first thing anyone saw upon entering the front hallway of her apartment was a giant photograph of Aly Khan in a silver frame that sat on an antique oriental gilt chest. What security she had came from being a Khan.

It was not until the late seventies that Rita and Yasmin, then nearing thirty and still unmarried, established a close relationship. Rita was in the early stages of Alzheimer's disease, but fading fast. Yasmin became more than her mother's protector, their roles were reversed. Rita was unable to make decisions for herself and Yasmin stepped in and took control. She brought Rita to New York and bought her a $600,000 condominium near her own apartment and hired a full-time nurse-companion for her mother. Rita was slipping away almost daily and Yasmin fought to keep her lucid. It became her crusade. Rita's memory span grew shorter. She could no longer remember what was said to her five minutes earlier and could not care for herself or handle her financial affairs.

Yasmin was now Rita's contact with the real world. She petitioned the court to become the conservator of her mother's financial and physical well-being and was immediately appointed as such. Rita's encroaching early senility meant that Yasmin had to engage nurses to care for her mother around the clock. In 1982 Yasmin became a board member of the Alzheimer's Disease and Related Disorders Association and initiated a worldwide campaign to raise money for research and to publicize the devastation of the disease and the growing number of people who suffered its effects. She quickly became a force in the fight for funds for research to help those afflicted.

Yasmin had found her purpose in life. Karim Aga Khan, who had always been fond of his much younger half-sister, backed her in her new role as fund-raiser. One of the main tenets of the Ismaili faith was to help others with whatever excess resources you had – education, intelligence, drive, money. Her grandmother, the Begum Sultan Shah as Yvette was now called, added the advice that a balance had to be struck between helping others and living a full life oneself. That meant marriage and possibly, if Allah granted it, children. But for now, while Rita lived in her childlike state, Yasmin's private life was placed on hold.

Horseracing had always been the sport of kings. Now it was the sport of queens as well, for Queen Elizabeth was inextricably connected with the sport. At her father's death she had been compelled to take over the royal racing stables. But horses had been her greatest passion since childhood. 'If I am ever Queen,' she had told her governess, Marian ['Crawfie'] Crawford, at the age of seven, 'I shall make a law that there must be no riding on Sundays. Horses should have a rest, too. And I shan't let anyone dock their pony's tail.' (Once she was Queen, no more was said of such a decree being proposed to Parliament.) At the age of ten her favorite outdoor game was to harness Crawfie with a pair of red reins that had bells on them and off they would go.

'Sometimes,' her governess remembered, 'she would whisper to me, "Crawfie, you must pretend to be impatient. Paw the ground a bit." So I would paw. Frosty mornings were wonderful for then my breath came in clouds, "just like a proper horse," said [Elizabeth] contentedly. Or she herself would be a horse, prancing around, nosing in my pockets for sugar, making convincing little whinnying noises.'

After being allowed to stroke her father's great, undefeated race-horse Big Game, she confessed that she did not wash her hands for several hours afterwards, since she felt 'it was such an honour to touch so brilliant an animal.'

By the age of sixteen she had already taken a concentrated interest in the care and management of the royal stable and during the war, when she and her sister Princess Margaret lived at Windsor Castle, had looked after her own horses. But the first racehorse she owned, Astrakhan, a thoroughbred filly foal, was given to her in 1947 as a wedding present by the Aga Khan III. A competitive racehorse owner since that time (one of the most powerful and successful in Great Britain), the Queen's horses have often come up against those of Karim Aga Khan, their winnings falling about equal.

But the Queen's feeling for horses was of a far more personal nature than Karim Aga Khan's. She rode four or five times a week – tough, firm riding with a tight saddle and absolute command of the horse. She was a horsewoman of international class, strong, determined and quite without fear. Very much like the old Aga Khan, the Queen, to this day, keeps books of racing pedigrees beside her desk, and like Karim's father, Aly Khan, has a keen eye for a well-bred line. This is one area of her life where it is impossible to say her success has been due to her position.

Karim Aga Khan, on the other hand, valued horseracing strictly for the excitement of the sport and the business aspects. He had become prodigious in his knowledge of bloodlines, of odds, of training and riding techniques. The Queen appreciated this and their rapport grew because of it. They met at race meetings and occasionally he and the Begum were invited to dine at the Palace or at Claridges as they did in the mid-seventies on one of the Queen's infrequent visits to a public restaurant.

His red and green colours had flashed home winners enough to gain the ear and the respect of all serious horse breeders. Karim Aga Khan was by now one of the top three or four stable owners in the world (stables in the United States and South America sharing top honours with him) and the most influential owner-breeder in Europe. He was quick to say that in the beginning he had known nothing about horses and 'had no interest in them . . . I asked incredibly stupid questions – and I still do.' But what had started as a hobby was now a business that had become a major occupation and the questions he asked were of the best experts in the field. The economics of the business fascinated him, presenting a challenge. He did extensive research and talked to experts in depth with each new venture and though he might not have been aware of the extent of his knowledge, built by his avid curiosity and thirst for information, by the 1970s it was encyclopedic.

In the late 1960s he had formed a syndicate for his prize horse Silver Shark and sold a million dollars' worth of shares. More recently he had turned down an offer of nearly £3 million from a similar syndicate for Charlottesville, the magnificent progenitor which his father bred and which he kept at stud in Ireland. His horses were consistent winners at the Irish Derby, the English and French Oaks, and the French Grand Prix. Directly following the Grand Prix each year he would host the traditional Grand Prix Aga Khan party at the Pré Catalan restaurant in the Bois de Boulogne, a ritual begun by his grandfather and continued by his father. It would start at 9.30 PM and end about 3.15 AM, and there would be some 300 guests. It was an event he much enjoyed and often he would linger even after it was over, talking to a few of his remaining guests.

But of all Karim Aga Khan's business interests – his stables, Sardinia and his venture into the highly competitive and treacherous newspaper world – the last presented him with the most personal challenge. It was back in 1958, while still at Harvard, that he had empowered Michael Curtis to go to Nairobi and buy the financially troubled, right-wing *Sunday Post*, which appeared to be looking for offers. His motivation was to establish a free press in Africa where immigrant communities, including the Ismailis, were being asked to choose between Kenyan and British nationality. Karim was advocating that his followers take Kenyan nationality and he believed a free press would bolster their confidence in a democratic Africa.

(Later, when he was asked why he had decided to found a media empire in East Africa, he replied: 'Oh, you know, it seemed to me important that there should be one or two media establishments in that part of the world which could report *hopefully* competently, *hopefully* responsibly, *hopefully* seriously on the constitutional moves, on the political structures, on the economic evolution, on the social evolution, on the objectives that were on the minds of African leaders at the time for their countries.')

The chairman of the *Sunday Post*, an Englishman with a broad Yorkshire accent, glared across the table at the Aga Khan's emissary. 'Well, Mr Curtis,' he growled, 'we've considered your proposal very carefully. But [we] have come to the conclusion that *nothing on earth* would induce us to sell out to an *Asian*.'

Undaunted when Curtis reported this to him, Karim Aga Khan bought a small, poorly equipped Swahili paper, *The Nation (Taifia)*, which was distributed at the time mostly in the native bazaar. Curtis was then dispatched to locate the most modern state-of-the-art printing machinery available. Within two years Nairobi and the United States were the only places in the world to have the new, revolutionary, printing technology that made print and photographs far clearer and cleaner than before.

At breakfast every morning, wherever he was, Karim liked to have the *International Herald Tribune* and the *New York Times* waiting for him, which sometimes meant the newspapers had to be sent by special courier and on numerous connecting flights to reach him. The first thing he did, one of his staff recalled, was 'to rub his finger across the front page to see if it smudges. His second reaction is to hold the paper close to his face, to study the density of micro-dots on the photographs.' He was diligent in his task of seeing that *The Nation* used the best photo-reproduction possible. To achieve the perfection he demanded he put together a consortium of well-established newspaper proprietors – the Canadian Lord Thomson of the *Sunday Times* and three others. Of the four, Thomson was the only one to become personally involved in the actual publishing of *The Nation*, even to finding appropriate columnists.

Kenya's politicians were up in arms, suspecting a religious leader like Karim Aga Khan to have a devious, ulterior motive in publishing an independent newspaper in Africa. Jomo Kenyatta, an African Nationalist and the first President of Kenya (1964–78), had outlawed opposition parties and established in 1969 a one-party state. He was greatly feared in liberal circles, for he was infamous for his intolerance of dissent in any form. Karim Aga Khan's free press did not escape his wrath.

Gerard Wilkinson, whom Karim Aga Khan had brought in to help run the newspaper, recalled an incident in 1974 when Kenyatta was particularly enraged by some articles that had been printed in *The Nation* stressing the unfairness of a one-party government (although the Aga Khan removed himself from personal political comment, he did not restrict the newspaper from putting forth a particular viewpoint with which he might agree).

'It was the official opening of the Nairobi Serena Hotel, which the boss [the Aga Khan] partly owns,' Wilkinson remembered, 'and when the boss went into the cloakroom to spend a penny Kenyatta followed him inside. Two boys were with him, both from his own tribe . . . "I'd like to talk about this boy [he pointed to one] becoming chairman of *The Nation*." The Aga Khan replied that he found the idea surprising, since the boy [about eighteen] had no knowledge of newspapers. "Think about it," said Kenyatta, menacingly.'

The Aga Khan refused to give Kenyatta control. When Kenyatta called for a dilution of foreign ownership in 1973 he floated 40 per cent of the company, which still left him the majority of shares. But he now appointed Hilary Ngweno as the first African editor-in-chief, a move that appeared to strengthen his position and cause Kenyatta to back off. Despite the tremendous outside pressure, *The Nation* became an established and successful newspaper and Karim Aga Khan began to add other papers under his proprietorship, 'a singularly improbable' newspaper tycoon, wrote Nicholas Coleridge in his book *Paper Tigers*: 'instinctively secretive, prepared to go to the utmost lengths to try and protect [his family's] privacy.'

This was, and remains, true. 'There are certain things I will fight for . . . the right to privacy is an important issue which is going to become *more* important rather than less,' he has said. 'Technology is so sophisticated now that, in effect, there is no privacy left . . . Technology enables you to do anything you want. If you don't do it from the ground you do it from space.'

But he added, 'African and Western society are very different . . . You cannot titillate African curiosity with the same things. They're not interested. Their tribes live differently; their families live differently; their dress habits are different. So that form of journalism doesn't have any relationship to African society whatsoever.'

He also claimed that he was a newspaper owner by accident, but that hardly seems the case as the idea had been one he had aggressively sought since his year as a Harvard senior. His reasons were perhaps dissimilar from other newspaper tycoons like William Randolph Hearst and Lord Beaverbrook, and more recently Robert Maxwell and Rupert Murdoch. The need for a free press in Africa to assure his followers of the stability and democratic policies of the country in which they had chosen to live had, he said, propelled him to become a newspaper owner. Still, he was engaged in building a private newspaper empire that would become one of the world's ten greatest, with his flagships, *The Daily Nation*, *The Sunday Nation* and the Swahili *Taifa Leo* speaking for an Africa that had never known a free press before his ownership.

While he gave a lot of time to his growing press investments, he remained as dedicated to the continuing development of Sardinia and the constant high performance of his horses, all of which required a tremendous amount of travel (he was on the road, so to speak, at least six months a year). Although Princess Salimah would eventually travel with him – by his own estimate 90 per cent of the time – after the tour to Pakistan in 1970 she remained for the most part of the next two years in a new home, a seventeenth-century stone château called Aiglemont in Chantilly, forty-five minutes north of Paris.

The house – 'a mixture of a timeless royal château, a UN-style business centre and a 100-stall racehorse stable – on two hundred wooded acres with its own lake,' was to become the official Ismaili world headquarters with a modern office building constructed on land just a five-minute walk from the main residence. (Previously he had conducted his Imamate and business from the offices next door to his home in Paris.) But it was also to be, from this time, his family home. Construction began on a new wing almost as soon as the Aga Khan and the Begum returned from Pakistan. A prayer room was built along with a nursery.

For in the autumn of 1970, Princess Zahra was born, and the following year Prince Rahim. There were great celebrations among Ismailis. The Imam now had an heir. As past history indicated, however, this did not necessarily mean that young Rahim had his future as the fiftieth Imam in the bag. Three years later, in 1975, the Begum gave birth to their third and last child, Prince Hussain.

MOVING INTO
THE TWENTY-FIRST
CENTURY

20

The 1970s gave birth to the social phenomenon known as the 'jet set' and Karim Aga Khan was swept along with it. He and the Begum would fly in their custom designed jet from their home in Chantilly to England or the South of France to attend a party given by friends, remain until about one AM, and return home directly afterwards where he would be ready for a meeting at eight that same morning (sometimes earlier if he wanted to see a particular horse being trained). They gave frequent formal parties – usually in Paris – where the guest list was official and at which there would be many people neither he nor the Begum had previously met. Members of a large social circle, they also gave regular dinners and cocktail parties in honour of friends – the Guy de Rothschilds (who had also been close family friends of Aly Khan), the French prime minister (Georges Pompidou until 1974, and then his successor Valéry Giscard d'Estaing, 1974–81, both of whom were good friends), or Princess Grace and Prince Rainier of Monaco, among others. Sadruddin and Amyn (who had not married) were his closest confidants along with the Begum who travelled as often as she could with him. Unlike his grandfather and father, Karim appeared to have found lasting love and companionship with his first wife.

He still ski'd when he could, though not competitively, and when at Chantilly got his exercise by running in the woods as regularly as his work allowed. He wore contact lenses 'because spectacles are difficult to ski in'. He played a major role in the lives and education of his three children. Despite the pressures of his position and his unremitting travel schedule, he was very much a family man and priority time was always reserved so that he and the Begum could be with their children. A prayer room was built in their home in France and he supervised prayers and instructions. When they were old enough to do so, the children sailed and ski'd with him and Zahra became as good at sports as her brothers. He remained devoted to his mother, and attentive to Yasmin. Karim Aga Khan was not only the head of the Ismaili sect, he was the patriarch of his family and they would come to him with their problems or to relay their present news or to ask his advice on important decisions.

Yasmin was in constant touch with her half-brother. Rita's condition was deteriorating and Karim Aga Khan was supportive in Yasmin's determination not to place her in an institution. For seven years after Nina Dyer's death, Sadruddin had been romantically linked to numerous women that the press hinted might lead to marriage. He was married for the second time in 1972, to the attractive and social Catherine Aleya Sursock whom he met in New York where he was actively involved in work for the United Nations. Sadruddin had been consultant to the Secretary-General of the United Nations and worked on special Afro-Asian projects in the early sixties. From 1965 to 1977 he was the United Nations High Commissioner for Refugees. The following year he was presented with the United Nations Human Rights Award.[1] He had an apartment in New York but used as his main residence Château de Bellerive in Geneva, the estate that he had once shared with Nina Dyer. He ski'd, sailed, and had a prodigious collection of Islamic art and of kites, which he much enjoyed flying – indeed, he was a master at the sport.

Amyn had homes in Paris and Geneva and assisted Karim in work for the Aga Khan Foundation, which by the mid-seventies had branches in Bangladesh, Canada, India, Kenya, Pakistan, Portugal, Great Britain and the United States. The Foundation played a major part in Karim Aga Khan's life. Much of his time was spent on its behalf. Because of it he travelled more than he had previously, seeing that its work was carried out – schools built, classroom equipment and books brought up to modern standards, medical staffs increased, pipelines completed that brought water to arid areas. He worked hard and he played hard.

---

[1] Prince Sadruddin was also awarded the Hammarskjöld Medal (German UN Association), 1979; Olympia Prize (Greece), 1982; Grand Cross, Order of St Silvestro (papal), 1963; Order of Homayous (Iran), 1967; Order of the Royal Star of Great Comoro (Comoro Islands), 1970; Order of the Two Niles (Sudan), 1973; Commander's Cross with Star (Poland), 1977; Commandeur de la Légion d'Honneur (France), 1979.

He remained the major force behind the development of the Costa Smeralda, which by the early 1970s had become one of the most prestigious and luxurious resorts of *le beau monde* in the world. He was a founding member of the Mediterranean Yachting Association and still thoroughly enjoyed his yacht in whatever time he could spare when in Sardinia. Like his father he had a passion for fast, expensive cars – Maseratis and Lamborghini two-seaters. Unlike his father and grandfather, he seemed uninterested in tossing his hat into the international political arena. However, the presence in Third World countries of the Aga Khan Foundation and the changes it made to the welfare of many millions of people, although not politically motivated, would bring a fair number of better educated people to the voting boxes.

His frequent tours to Ismaili communities continued. He saw his role somewhat differently than had his grandfather. He avoided pomp and pageantry. He had more of a hands-on approach with his followers. He went to see things for himself – housing and hospital conditions, classroom methods, the farms and factories and business establishments in which Ismailis laboured.

But then times had greatly changed. The Aga Khan III had been caught up along with his followers in the disintegration of the British Empire, the independence of India and the Partition. By political design, the Aga Khan III had blended the 'unblendable' East with the West. He died a statesman without a state, but he can be credited, perhaps even more than anyone else, with the establishment of the All-India Muslim League which (although that was not his intention) led to the creation of the predominantly Muslim nation of Pakistan. The welfare of his Ismaili subjects was always of first importance to him. It was he who first handed them the torch of education and who first won success (however small in the beginning as women clung to their old ways) in attempting to lift the veil from the faces of Ismaili women. But he was not an enterprising businessman like his chosen successor. Nor did he have Karim's energy, even as a young man.

Aga Khan III had taken the enormous pool of wealth that came from the practice of tithing in his sect and transformed it (albeit with a great deal of help from Lady Ali Shah) into a thriving financial empire for his people. It was, after all, Aga Khan III who had set up the Golden, Diamond and Platinum Jubilee Trusts which had financed business, education and charity enterprises in Ismaili communities. Karim Aga Khan was dedicated to the same principles as his grandfather and had applied all his considerable talents to bringing a better standard of living to his followers.

'Being Ismaili,' Karim Aga Khan once explained, 'is more than a religion. It is a way of life.' To Westerners it remained a curious way of life, hard to understand when there was no central seat for the Ismaili faith, and prayer leaders who were ordinary businessmen with no religious power over the members of their mosques; that power being invested solely in the Aga Khan. Exercising this power he issued *farmans* (edicts) deeply affecting the lives of his subjects.

In the early part of the century, several hundred thousand of his community had migrated from India and Pakistan to East Africa, where they held on to their old citizenship. Recognizing the potential problems created by minorities in a country where they were not citizens, Karim gave a *farman* that these followers change their passports and their allegiance. It proved a wise move for they were better able to find work and to secure their positions.

His next *farman* was to order that Ismailis in countries where a strict colour bar existed should go elsewhere. Only South Africa fell into this category and 3000 Ismailis left for Kenya where they soon became a progressive and self-supporting community with the help of the Aga Khan Foundation.

Nothing drew his wrath more than when the Western press questioned how he could function as a religious leader of a primarily Eastern sect when he spent so much time in Europe, where relatively few of his followers lived. 'I see my people more than the Pope and other less mobile religious leaders do,' he has said privately. 'And I can reach my people almost overnight if they need me.'

This, of course, was true. He spent many months of each year in his black-and-gold jet plane flying to Ismaili communities in Egypt, Syria, Iran, Kenya, Zanzibar, Tanzania, Comoros, and, of course, India, Pakistan, England, France, Canada and the United States. He received, even in the most remote villages of the Third World, great welcomes in which almost the entire Ismaili community turned out. In Geneva he had set up a holding company, called Industrial Promotion

Services, to do market research in the areas where Ismaili communities were located. Several experts in market development were then dispersed from these organizations to determine the industries that best fitted the resources in these individual communities. By the late seventies hundreds of thousands of his followers were working in businesses (such as leather, jute, fabrics, pottery, farming and agricultural products) organized by Karim Aga Khan. The profits were ploughed back into a growing educational network – nursery schools, medical schools and a series of modern hospitals, low-cost medical insurance and low-interest building loans.

Ismailis believed Karim Aga Khan had created a miracle. One Western journalist referred to his efforts to make the Ismailis 'the yeast of Islam'. However, his contribution to Islam and its culture was broader than that, extending to Muslims in other sects as well as his own. His extensive travelling in Muslim countries had given him a new and consuming interest, Islamic architecture. When visiting a city, he would take time out from his schedule to study ancient and new buildings, a professional photographer at his side to take pictures. In 1977 he began to award prizes both for restoring old Islamic buildings and for designing new ones. But a new purpose, to start a programme for the study of Islamic architecture at an American university, added more scope to his original idea to make Muslims interested in their own architecture.

As a young man, Karim Aga Khan had wanted to take a science degree. He had, in fact, applied to the Massachusetts Institute of Technology before enrolling at Harvard and MIT had accepted him on the basis of his grades. But his grandfather, he claimed 'put the kibosh' (one of the American phrases with which he often peppered his speech) on his plans. MIT and the university he did attend, Harvard, were close by each other. Islamic architecture was not previously a subject that was given much academic space in America. But MIT and Harvard were two of the most prestigious universities and if a centre for Islamic architecture could be inaugurated on one of those campuses it would bring it to the attention of the West.

In 1979, after several months of negotiation with the science boards of both establishments and with an initial gift of $11.6 million, he established the Aga Khan Program for Islamic Architecture at MIT and Harvard (the programme director's office being located at MIT), which he defined as 'a major cultural effort to preserve and restore the values and practice of architecture that reflects the Islamic spirit.' The joint programme embraced both research and teaching in Islamic architecture and linked both MIT and Harvard with universities in the Muslim world in exchange programmes for students. A photographic archive, the Roach Visual Library in Islamic Architecture, also heavily endowed by Karim Aga Khan, was established on the MIT campus.

He was a doggedly serious man, yet always vital, interesting. He liked to talk, although seldom about inconsequential matters, and one could see the excitement building within him as his articulate sentences whipped out one after the other with alarming speed.

By the 1980s he was not only a bridge between East and West as his grandfather had been before him, but between tradition and modernity. Some 95 per cent of his followers lived in nations that had high rates of illiteracy, disease, population growth and unstable governments. But Ismailis remained the most economically active and progressive element in the Muslim communities, shopkeepers, manufacturers, professional people. There was no need for Karim to receive his weight in precious metals or stones. The more financially able his followers became, the more money flowed into his coffers in their tithing contributions and donations, and a substantial part of that cache was returned to Ismailis in the continuing betterment of his health, housing and education programmes for them. So successful was he in his business endeavours on behalf of his sect, that he poured millions of dollars from the Foundation into regional programmes that helped the population at large ($30 million a year was disbursed for health care programmes alone).

The line he had to walk was narrow, for many Ismaili communities were entrenched in countries ruled by dictators – Saddam Hussein in Iraq and Assad in Syria,[1] which had become a breeding ground for international terrorists and where there were hardline policies against

---

[1] General Hafez al-Assad and his pragmatic Nationalist Party, dedicated to the defeat of Israel, the improvement of relations with other Arab states, and the reduction of Syria's dependence on the Soviet Union, took over the government in November 1970.

political opposition. Despite the precarious climate in the country, Aly Khan had been reburied in Syria, as his will had instructed, shortly before Assad took power. This gave Karim even more reason to walk gently and, at the same time, reap the benefits of his father's former close alliance with the Syrians. After years of having to deal with strict right-wing governments like Kenya, Uganda,[1] Iraq and South Africa, Karim Aga Khan had become a deft diplomat, able to juggle the needs of his people with the pressures of politics. Getting his followers out of a country where they were either unwanted or in danger was no more difficult than smoothing the way for their resettlement elsewhere. The fact that the Foundation became responsible for the welfare of Ismailis forced to relocate made for easier acceptance in their host country.

Asked in 1979, yet again, why he lived in the West when the majority of his followers lived in the Third World, he replied, 'The reason is simple. My grandfather believed that the Third World, and more particularly the Islamic world, would make far more rapid progress if they were able to learn the lessons of the industrialized nations. Hence, many of the development strategies, such as co-operative banking and housing, which he introduced to the Ismaili community were based on Western models.'

This was only the partial truth. The old Aga Khan was a staunch admirer of Western women as well as Western progressiveness and he had once possessed a great loyalty and attachment to Great Britain and a continuing attraction to the European style of living. In Karim's case, he *was* European, born and educated for the most part of the first eighteen years of his life in Switzerland. He had homes in England, Ireland, France and Sardinia. His mother was English, his father half-Italian, and Karim was married to an Englishwoman. He was bound to his followers by their faith, not the countries of their citizenship or the continent of their birth.

He liked to compare an 'enabling' to a 'disabling' environment. Enabling meant a country in which private enterprise flourished. 'By

[1] In August 1972, Major General Idi Amin took power in Uganda and soon ordered all Asians out of the country. Within three months all 60,000 had left, most of them for Britain. Close to 10,000 Ismailis resettled in London and nearby towns and in time became British subjects.

a disabling environment,' he explained to a reporter from *Forbes*, 'I mean a political and social situation in which legal restrictions or prejudice shackle enterprise, in which land or buildings are summarily expropriated, expatriate work permits denied, or the remittance of expatriate salaries refused, trade preferences rescinded, dividends withheld.

'Nationalization of private educational and health facilities as well as of commercial enterprises,' he continued, 'has led to the near collapse of whole sectors of some countries' economies, to low pay, corruption and decline in the performance levels of key professions.'

He still nearly always refused to give interviews about his personal and family life, although he did allow *Life* to come to Aiglemont in 1981 to take pictures of the children, the Begum and himself for a photographic essay and an interview. In answer to questions about his father and grandfather he revealed a little of the private man. He referred to Aly Khan as 'Daddy' and displayed awe of his grandfather ('Grandpa') and his inability as a young man to go against his wishes and attend the university of his choice. But he preferred to talk about the Aga Khan Economic Development Fund and the work it was doing to encourage individual enterprise in the Third World.

Despite a fast-receding hairline and a tendency toward middle-aged portliness, he was extremely youthful-looking. A handsome man by most standards, it was more the enthusiasm he displayed, the intensity of his beliefs, that gave him such an appearance of youth. While listening he would lean forward, his dark eyes fixed upon the speaker, making instant eye contact. When thinking, creases would furrow his high forehead. He would respond with characteristic zeal whenever a question excited his interest.

One subject sure to ignite his fervour is the need for the Third World to nurture private enterprise and creativity. 'We are talking here,' he explained emotionally to the *Life* interviewer in 1981, 'about the way in which people across the complete spectrum of endeavour can be much more effective than they have been in the past . . . This is a moment of opportunity for fresh thinking about development and about the need for an enhanced private-sector role in the Third World. It is a moment of opportunity created by a number of forces . . . We must get a grip on the forces of change.'

Certainly he was doing his share of ushering in the necessary changes. He sponsored global conferences on health care and private enterprise in the development of the Third World and set up a news agency in Luxembourg to disseminate information about and to the Third World. With the combined resources of the Foundation, his private fortune and subsidies from the Pakistan government, a $300 million university and teaching hospital was built in Karachi. He invested $50 million of his own money in growth companies in the Third World. He is universally respected by statesmen and academics for his work on behalf of the Third World and in the field of Islamic architecture, and is the recipient of many honours.[1] Yet he remains better known by the general public for his enormous wealth, his private business ventures and his stable of prize-winning horses, which has been the chosen perception of him by the media.

He maintained his intense interest in Islamic architecture and established annual prizes and grants both for restoring old buildings and for designing new ones in Muslim countries. In 1987, when the awards were made in Cairo (they are presented in a different location each year), he led a contingent of the city's élite into some of the poorest, most neglected quarters but where there remained, often in a crumbling condition, ancient buildings of great architectural interest and others that he felt needed to be torn down to make way for better housing and to improve health conditions. This incident led to wide media coverage and controversy in Egypt (something he worked hard to avoid), as the occupants of the buildings he suggested be demolished believed they would lose their homes and businesses. These fears were overcome and three years later old dilapidated housing was torn down and new buildings erected to rehouse the former occupants, once again with Karim Aga Khan's financial assistance.

Since most Islamic architectural design has its roots in the pattern

---

[1] Karim Aga Khan has been awarded the Grand Croix, Order of Prince Henry the Navigator (Portugal), 1960; l'Ordre de la Côte d'Ivoire, 1965; l'Ordre du Croissant Vert des Comores, 1966; Grand Cordon, Order of the Taj (Iran), 1967; Nishan-i-Imtiaz (Pakistan), 1970; Cavaliere di Gran Croce della Repubblica Italiana, 1977; Grand Officer, l'Ordre National du Lion (Senegal), 1982; Grand Cordon, Ouissam-al-Arch (Morocco), 1986, among other honours. He has also been given the degree of Doctor of Laws at Peshawar University, Pakistan, 1967; Sind University, Pakistan, 1970; and McGill University, Canada, 1983.

of the mosque, it is considered sacrilegious to criticize it. Even in places like Cairo, where there is a free popular press to print such views, architecture is sceptically treated. Karim Aga Khan was ardent in his crusade to retain the classic Islamic design but, never forgetting his role as diplomat and religious leader, made concessions to popular taste. In 1986, for example, an award went to the Bhong mosque in Rahim-Yar Khan in Pakistan. The mosque is elaborately decorated with ivory, coloured glass, gold leaf, artificial stone, wrought iron and imported bathroom tiles; a giant Broadway-style illuminated sign proclaims 'Mohammed'. Islam's growing group of architectural critics considered that aesthetics had been sacrificed on the altar of populism; the Aga Khan's jury felt rather that the mosque is 'the sort of construction which the masses can adore no matter how much the architects may loathe it'.

But his seminars on Islamic architecture harked back to a pure Islamic standard of building exemplified by the al-Azhar and al-Aqmar mosques in Cairo, presumed long lost, and supported the notion that Western modernism (which is appearing with great frequency in many Islamic countries) was a style that had to be avoided.

However, the architecture in Karim Aga Khan's private real estate ventures was almost invariably in the European tradition. He was a billionaire by 1980, far richer than his grandfather had been, and it seemed his wealth was still on the ascent. He had invested $770 million by now in the Costa Smeralda, which would soon be able to offer 504 hotel rooms. In early 1985 he extended his hotel interests in the mainland of Italy and beyond. The CIGA hotel group was facing liquidation. Karim became the major shareholder in a blue chip consortium, Fimpar, formed to buy out CIGA, which owned in Venice alone the Gritti, Danielli, Europa Excelsior and Des Bains hotels.

He had made a close friend of the dashing, grey-haired Gianni Agnelli, the scion of Italy's richest family, owners of Fiat, and the man who had once lured Pamela Churchill from Aly Khan's bed to his own. Agnelli was a partner with him in CIGA, although Karim Aga Khan had control of the company. With five of the leading hotels in Venice, their idea was now to expand further and they chose as their next project the historic fortress-like Arsenale.

About 80 of the Arsenale's 114 acres covered docking areas. These Karim Aga Khan and Gianni Agnelli were negotiating to buy from the Italian navy to convert into what they planned would become Europe's largest marina to replace the city's inadequate docking facilities. Venetians, whose space is limited, were up in arms over the Arsenale's future. The navy had originally agreed to turn it over to the civil authorities to construct much needed low-rent housing inside its long-standing stone walls. In the end, CIGA lost this contest to civic outcry. But the company went on to buy more hotels – the grand old Excelsior in Rome and fourteen others (to make a total of twenty) in Italy and sixteen others throughout Europe – including the historic and luxurious Palace Hotel in Madrid and the Hotel Imperial in Vienna. To do this, CIGA and Fimpar borrowed $616 million from Italian banks and another $100 million from a German-led bank consortium. This was a time when European travel was enjoying a tremendous upsurge. CIGA hotels were geared to tourists who were able to pay $300–400 a night for a room. Business travellers were not a priority, a great mistake when a descending economy discouraged tourism.

Karim Aga Khan had misjudged an investment – and one of over a billion dollars. But, staunchly confident in his own acumen, he turned to his primary concern – his entrepreneurial leadership of the Ismailis.

His association with Agnelli and CIGA, however, had great impact on his marriage. The Begum did not accompany him on his frequent business trips and they were more often apart than together. In 1984 he appeared to have fallen in love with Pilar Goess, a beautiful 27-year-old Austrian and the former fiancée of Spyros Niarchos. She was soon seen wearing a dazzling $500,000 pink diamond ring, said to be a gift from Karim. While Pilar moved into a luxurious Paris apartment, the Begum leased a magnificent $25 million estate overlooking Lake Geneva and left the house in France which she had shared with Karim and their children (all three of whom were in boarding schools).

None of this was known to the press. Whatever their personal problems were, Karim was determined to keep them private. The Begum was guaranteed an enormous sum of money to withdraw to her new villa and Karim conducted his romantic affair with great discretion: he and Pilar were never seen together in public. His father's flamboyant and very public love affairs and divorces had been greatly responsible for Aly Khan's having been by-passed in the succession. The old Aga Khan had known how important it was for Ismailis to have respect for their religious leader and Karim had learned this lesson early in life.

Rita Hayworth lay dying in 1985, remembering nothing of her past glory, her Hollywood stardom, her marriage to Aly or her other numerous stormy marriages. (She once said, 'Every man I married had fallen in love with Gilda and awakened with me.' Not entirely true, for she had been married and divorced twice before the film was made.) Although she was terribly frail, her once famous red hair faded to grey and showing the pinkness of her scalp in several places, there was enough of her past beauty lingering in her gaunt but strongly marked face as she rested back on a bank of pillows in her well-appointed New York bedroom to remind one that the dying woman had once been a celebrated movie star, and one of Hollywood's great sex symbols. With her memory of events gone, she seemed never to have forgotten she was a beautiful woman: the slim hand would sweep back the grey hair with poignant grace and she would ask for lipstick more frequently than food.

Yasmin was with Rita as often as possible, devoting herself to making sure her mother was well-cared-for. In 1980 she founded the Alzheimer Foundation for research into the disease and to help its victims. She had given up any idea of a professional career. Almost all her efforts were devoted to raising money for, and publicizing the work being done on behalf of, Alzheimer's disease. Then, at the age of thirty-five, Yasmin fell in love with Basil Embiricos, an old Etonian and member of a rich Greek shipping family.

Embiricos, at thirty-six, was suavely handsome with a flashing smile, merry eyes and great charm. Following in the footsteps of other well-known Greek shipping tycoons like Aristotle Onassis and Spyros Niarchos and of her father, Aly Khan, Embiricos also had an eye for beautiful women. This did not deter Yasmin who felt secure in the handsome Greek's love. Her world had been so circumscribed by Rita and her illness that she desperately needed to break out of the restraint she was feeling. Embiricos brought youth and joy into her life. Despite the groom being of Greek Orthodox faith, she obtained Karim Aga Khan's permission for them to marry and the date was set for August 1985.

They were married first in a civil ceremony in Paris which was followed by a reception for 500 guests at the Ritz Hotel, hosted by her half-brother, Karim Aga Khan. Yasmin wore a spectacular white Valentino gown with large puffed sleeves and something like thirty yards of fabric in the skirt and train. There was a gasp when she entered the room. Her resemblance to her mother was striking; her thick, dark auburn hair worn loose and to her shoulders, the wide smile and expressive dark eyes so reminiscent of Rita.

The reception was every bit as ostentatious as when Hollywood's love goddess had married Aly Khan, although Yasmin did not cut her wedding cake with a sword as her mother had done. She was attended by her niece, Karim Aga Khan's fourteen-year-old daughter, the beautifully maturing Princess Zahra. The Begum Andrée had died several years back, but the Aga Khan III's widow, whom Yasmin was very close to, was present along with Karim Aga Khan, his wife and sons, Prince Sadruddin, Prince Amyn and a galaxy of the brightest stars in international society. Rita was of course too ill to attend.

A few months later, Yasmin became pregnant. By then the marriage was falling apart, the difference of religion and culture too wide to bridge. She and Embiricos were divorced before the birth of their son Andrew ('the most wonderful thing that ever happened to me – my son,' Yasmin replied when asked if there had been any up-sides to her brief first marriage of less than a year).

Rita died in 1987. It had been fifteen years since she had appeared on the screen in *The Wrath of God*, an offbeat film that co-starred Robert Mitchum. But her name still conjured an image of Hollywood during its golden years. She represented an era and she remains, whenever her old films are shown, for ever young, for ever beautiful. That would have greatly pleased Rita Hayworth, just as it had filled her with much pride that her daughter was a Princess.

In February 1989, Yasmin married for the second time in a gala society wedding that again included her father's family members. Her new husband was an American, Christopher Jeffries, head of the powerful General Atlantic Realty Corporation. He was a brilliant businessman, financially independent, attractive, a keen sportsman and anxious to be a good father to Andrew. Yasmin was certain that she had found true happiness. They had been living together for two years before their marriage and knew each other better than she and Embiricos had at the time of their wedding. But somehow this marriage also fell apart and in December 1993 they were divorced after Jeffries accused his wife of abandoning him.

'I think it's very hard to maintain a relationship with someone and grow together over a long period of time,' Yasmin, who had recently celebrated her forty-third birthday, told a reporter at that time. 'It really is difficult to find a formula for growing in the same direction and ageing together.'

A week later she was in Switzerland with Andrew. She had decided to base herself in Geneva, flying back to the States regularly to continue her work on behalf of the Alzheimer Foundation (there were now chapters in 32 countries but the central office was in New York). Her father's family were the only family she knew and she clung to these relationships. She frequently saw the Begum, who was nearly blind now and lived in Geneva a short distance from the house Yasmin was having built for herself. Yasmin, in fact, became one of the few people the Begum would let visit her. ('Please, don't come see me,' she pleaded to Laurence Moschietto Sihol, one of her oldest, dearest friends. 'I see nothing and cannot even know how terrible I must look.')

'I think everyone has something in their lives,' Yasmin has said philosophically. 'Life isn't easy. There are wonderful moments and hard times. It's a learning process . . . It's important to focus on other people and not just on yourself. And it's difficult to strike a balance: helping others and surviving yourself. I don't have the answers, but I think that as long as you know and like yourself, you realize that life isn't a bed of roses! You have to adapt and see things in a positive way, as challenges.'

That outlook was very much the Ismaili way of looking at life, as was Yasmin's dedication to helping others. She remained rich enough to do whatever she wanted. What she wished to do was please herself by pleasing the Imam who guided her and had given her strength in her spiritual life. For Karim there was no person to look to. His strength had to come from within and from God.

By the time of his Silver Jubilee in 1982, Karim Aga Khan ('His Highness' to the 250,000 employees in his innumerable private enterprises)
was one of the world's wealthiest men. Estimates varied, but all placed
his personal fortune well over several billion dollars. (When asked if
he differentiated between his personal holdings and those of the
Imamate, he quickly responded, 'Absolutely. Investments are made
by the Imam for the purpose of development. The returns are reinvested [for the welfare of the Ismailis], not brought back to me
personally.')

His twenty-fifth anniversary as Imam was celebrated with parades
and fireworks in the Ismaili communities, but there was no attempt
to organize a *tula-vidhi*, or weighing ceremony, to mark this special
year of his reign. Such old ways and customs no longer had a place
in Karim Aga Khan's 21st-century approach to his sect. He had become
the Imam that his grandfather believed he would – taking the Ismailis
into a new century equipped to compete with the Western world,
better educated and with more advantages than the majority of
Muslims in the Third World where most of his people still lived.

But the image of his grandfather's spectacular jubilees had created
the impression that all the money raised by the Imam's followers went
directly into his pockets. This has been a constant source of irritation
to Karim. 'I have some institutional expenses [paid by the Ismailis],'
he explains. 'If I didn't occupy the office of Imam, I wouldn't fly on
a private aircraft. I wouldn't have a secretariat of some 100 people.
You really should apply to the Imam the same criteria you would apply
to any public office. But that's never been done, because there has
been a sort of inheritance of gloss. Maybe I should have addressed
that issue more quickly. I have felt that the area of the world I work

in has not had that misperception; that's much more a Western misperception . . . [more specifically it is] the Western perception of Orientals. When you think of Orientals all your cultural exposure is linked to that concept [that Imams and Oriental potentates take money from their subjects]. In your literature, it is an extraordinary perception. And it is a specifically Western perception.'

'A lot of our culture,' he adds, 'came through the eyes of people who were travellers, struck by things they had never seen anywhere else. They sent back a perception without understanding what it meant. And that has stuck in Western traditions even today; it's extraordinary.'

What Karim Aga Khan does not address is the lack of knowledge as to the workings and financial structure of his Imamate, information kept extremely secret. A great deal is known about the economic set-up of established Western religious groups, like the Catholic Church and the Mormon Church, which have central governments. Except for the relatively small groups which have emigrated to England and Canada and the even less-populated communities in France and the United States, the Ismailis live mainly in the East. Their two most recent leaders, Karim Aga Khan and his flamboyant grandfather before him, have lived for a century as Western representatives of Ismaili culture and ways.

Most Europeans are also prone to confuse the Ismailis with the other Shiite and Sunni Muslims who have been more in the public eye; the sensational offshoots of those faiths – the militant fundamentalists and terrorists – hold beliefs that are in direct opposition to the Ismaili religion. They are a pacifistic sect who have not been known to engage at any time in the twentieth century in acts of terrorism, political rioting or mayhem, and who have managed to live peacefully, side by side with people of dramatically different beliefs. They do not believe in the accumulation of riches for the sake of increasing personal power or possessions, although it is not in the Ismaili tradition to question how the Imam uses his wealth. If an Ismaili is fortunate enough to amass more than what is needed for a comfortable life, then his duty is to share that over-abundance with others less fortunate. Of course, individual views of what is comfortable to them could well vary. One thing is certain, very few Ismailis – if any – would complain that their current Imam retains too much or lives too well. Despite their varied citizenship, he has been responsible for their general welfare since his succession in 1957 and he has seen to it that they are the best-educated, most health-conscious and self-sufficient sect in the Third World.

But Karim Aga Khan, despite the great love of his followers, all the luxuries of his great wealth – the grand estates, private jet plane, yacht, numerous cars, the incomparable stable and a valuable art collection – has not been without personal trials. In 1983 his multi-million-dollar stallion Shergar was kidnapped by Irish Republic Army terrorists in an apparent effort to win worldwide attention and to cripple Britain's greatest sports attraction, horseracing. Shergar was never seen again and is presumed dead. There were unsubstantiated rumours in the racing world that the IRA demanded a million-pound ransom which Karim Aga Khan refused to pay. Whatever the truth, and he has categorically refused to discuss the incident with the press, he appeared quite shaken at the time over Shergar's unknown fate and that a horse carrying his colours had been singled out by a terrorist organization.

In 1989, Karim Aga Khan's Gold Seal Oaks winner Aliysa was disqualified directly after the race when the horse was tested and found to have drugs in its urine. At this time the Horseracing Forensic Laboratory at Newmarket conducted drug tests on all horses entered into English races and was the sole arbiter, unlike in Ireland and France where cross-testing by more than one laboratory was the normal procedure. Karim Aga Khan was satisfied that the small trace of drugs found in testing Aliysa came from a camphor substance (said to be illegal by the Jockey Club's disciplinary committee) used on the filly's sore foreleg.

Staunchly believing that no horse of his could have been drugged intentionally, Karim stated flatly a few months later that he would not race again in Britain until effective measures were taken to correct 'flawed equine drug-testing procedures'. A bitter row with the Jockey Club ensued and he resigned, withdrew his string of ninety horses from British horseracing altogether and sent those which had been trained in Great Britain to France and Ireland. But he agreed to compensate his former British trainers for a period of six months, or until his horses had been replaced by those of other owners.

In 1991 he launched a High Court fight to challenge the Jockey

Club's decision to strip Aliysa of her classic win. The case failed, but it did bring about new rules in British racing that required that drug testing of horses must be carried out by more than one laboratory. Two years later, with new rules in effect, Karim Aga Khan re-established his British stable and entered Massyar, which ran fifth, in the Irish Derby, paving the way to end his boycott in Britain.

These were small crises compared to the financial blow he received in 1993 when CIGA found itself over £680 million (considerably over a billion dollars) in debt. *Ricco come l'Aga Khan* ('rich as the Aga Khan') is a phrase frequently heard in Italy. But the astronomical size of the CIGA losses questioned the stability of his legendary wealth. Could the Aga Khan have come unstuck? the press asked when, on 20 May, creditor banks moved to seize the assets of CIGA after it missed a payment on its escalating debt. In 1993, CIGA was forced to suspend interest payments on loans owed to Italian banks. A court order was issued, CIGA assets frozen and their shares plummeted. The Sheraton Hotel Group, with 24 per cent of the shares, acquired a controlling interest at a bargain price. Karim was down, but far from out.

'The Aga Khan has made a series of bad business decisions in recent years, ploughing investment into luxury hotels at a time when fewer and fewer people had the money to stay in them,' said Isidoro Albertini, a veteran broker at the Milan Stock Exchange, 'and now he is paying the price.'

As the largest investor, he is reported to have personally lost over £500 million in the CIGA fiasco (none of the Imamate's money was involved), and at the time of writing has to settle another £20 million in the group's debt between CIGA and Fimpar. Despite biting press coverage which might have dimmed his lustre, it did not appear to have affected his status as one of the world's richest men; the boom times of the eighties had greatly bolstered his other private holdings such as the Costa Smeralda enterprise, his stables and his investments in public stocks and bonds.

Wisely, moderately-priced hotel rooms had been built on the Costa Smeralda along with luxury accommodation and the resort had captured a loyal clientele. But such had not been the case with CIGA hotels. The nineties brought recession with them, especially among American tourists who had been the greatest source of revenue in the previous decade. Travellers were now unwilling to spend $300 a night and more for a hotel room, while American firms were cutting over-heads and tightening the budgets for trips made by their representa-tives. CIGA was a name that stood for extravagant luxury in hotels, as do Cartier, Tiffany's and Van Cleef & Arpels in jewels. Tourists and business people became nervous of the ancillary costs in such establishments – room service, tips and so on. With 22 of their 36 hotels in Italy, an overvalued lira made a difficult situation worse. For many travellers, Italy had simply become too expensive.

Perhaps to help to balance his CIGA losses, Karim Aga Khan turned to his flourishing investment in Sardinia. Plans were put into place to develop a massive new resort area a few miles south of Porto Cervo with apartments, villas and more hotels geared for middle income families. The foundations were about to be laid when, in the autumn of 1991, the Sardinian government blocked the project on environmental grounds. The claim was based on the fear that waste matter would leak into the sea and endanger the fish population.

The failed expansion plan could have been a devastating blow to Karim Aga Khan, but he was a great deal more prescient than reports of his huge financial losses indicated. Always a shrewd businessman, perhaps one of the keenest in Europe, he had protected himself during the boom times of the eighties. None of his own money (other than his original investments) was put into an attempt to shore up CIGA, and instead he had sought to sell all or part of the hotel chain while they were still solvent (the Venice and Rome hotels had not been as severely hit as others in the chain). He had also sold personal assets, land and other holdings, to CIGA in the eighties for $136 million, which, in effect, reimbursed him for a healthy chunk of his losses.

Then, in October 1993, a deal was negotiated with ITT to take control of the CIGA hotels, with their agreement to invest £158 million in the group. This was a bitter pill for Karim Aga Khan, whose shareholding in CIGA had been blocked by the Italian courts to enable them to push through a restructuring plan to enable the company to pay back its creditors. Karim still retained his original 50.01 per cent of the shares, now of course greatly diminished in value (although the asset value – the buildings and the land on which they stood, the expensive antiques with which many of them had been furnished – remained higher than the group's debts and could, at auction, have more than cleared the deficit).

Despite these personal business setbacks, Karim Aga Khan seems as self-confident as he ever did. His main objective has always been, as he has said repeatedly, 'the welfare, good life and continuing belief in their faith of the Ismailis'. In contrast to the financial losses he had suffered in his private dealings, the Aga Khan Foundation is a most successful and stable organization benefiting his followers in the quest for a better standard of living.

The Aga Khan Program for Islamic Architecture at Harvard University and the Massachusetts Institute of Technology has become world-renowned. At present the Program is helping to formulate a plan to accommodate the growth while preserving the historic buildings of Karimabad, a village that was once the capital of a fiefdom 8000 feet high in the Karakoram range of the Himalayas in northern Pakistan, overlooking the Hunza River. The opening in 1986 of the Khunjerab Pass on the border with China brought the outside world and a large influx of tourists to the village of 600 families. With no planning laws, buildings were being erected – small hotels, restaurants and guest houses – without consideration for the considerable ecological damage from increased water use and the lack of a town sewerage system.

This is exactly the kind of scheme that Karim Aga Khan likes to set in motion. The Aga Khan Cultural Services, collaborating with the Aga Khan Program for Islamic Architecture, are directing the development in Karimabad to supply designs for new buildings, to renovate older houses, and to establish an organized pattern of growth. Blending the historic with the new has been an important part of his character since his succession. In dynastic terms he will have one more momentous task to complete – choosing his successor.

'Have you made that decision?' an interviewer asked him in the mid-eighties when his three children were still quite young.

'It would be very, very foolish of me not to,' he laughed. 'Life is no more eternal for me than for anyone else.'

'You have two sons [Rahim, the elder, and Hussain, four years younger; Princess Zahra, by Ismaili law, could not become Imam] –

one of them will succeed you, the other one will not. Yet, as a father, you obviously want to treat these two sons as equally as possible. What will you do?' the interviewer inquired.

'Well, during my lifetime, I will treat them absolutely identically. They must have the same education, same exposure, same understanding of their father's work. I would not want to make any differentiation between them, any more than my grandfather made a differentiation between my brother and myself.'

There is a close parallel between the relationship of Rahim and Hussain and that of Karim and Amyn. Rahim has always been protective of his younger brother. All three children had their early education in Switzerland and then went on to attend American universities. Princess Zahra, the oldest, graduated magna cum laude from Harvard in May 1994 with an AB. She also received a special citation for her work in Islamic studies and has decided to work by her father's side towards the development of the Third World. Unlike the wide coverage given Karim Aga Khan's American university education, there has been little media exposure of the three young Khans. Requests by the press for interviews or photographs are uniformly rejected. Their security certainly plays a part in this, but also their parents had been determined that their two sons and daughter would have as normal a life as it was possible for them to have.

Princess Zahra has become the only one of the three to place herself in the public eye as she stepped into a sad family breach and, in late 1994, began to act as a kind of 'first lady', dressed in saris as she accompanied her father on Third World visits. For the most painful personal crisis that Karim has experienced has been the disintegration of his marriage which began in 1982 and greatly affected the children.

Zahra, the oldest, was just thirteen and her brothers still quite young when their parents formally separated. The breakdown of the marriage was in the main kept out of the press (there were items printed in one or two gossip columns), but the children were well aware of the difficulties of their mother's position. For the past ten years the Begum had been almost cloistered in her rented estate near Geneva as part of an agreement she made with Karim at the time of their estrangement that would give her a cash settlement of about £20 million exclusive of gifts of property, investments and jewels which she received during their married life. Apart from infrequent visits to London to see her mother, or formal occasions when her presence was required, she maintained a secluded life while Karim had a succession of companions including the exotic Egyptian-born Ariana Soldate, widow of a wealthy Argentine businessman. The Begum's dignity and discretion have been impressive. From the time of her marriage she has seemed the perfect Begum, drawing no attention to herself and remaining out of the limelight. But while she withdrew into her separate and more private world, her husband was leading a vital, exciting life. So their interests grew further apart. The Aga Khan, as he grew older, turned to other women for reassurance and, though now paunchy and balding, readily received it.

Karim Aga Khan did spend more time with his sons than either Aly Khan or the old Aga Khan had spent with theirs. As a young boy, because of his father's service activities in the Second World War, Karim Aga Khan hardly knew his father. And then he had gone straight into boarding school (along with Amyn) for the next nine years while Aly Khan was cutting a dashing swathe through the bedrooms of society on both sides of the Atlantic. He saw his parents separately, his father more infrequently than his mother. Then came Harvard and further distancing, this time from his mother, and it appears history is repeating itself with his sons. (Karim's mother, Princess Joan, was remarried in 1986 to Viscount Camrose, a former director of the *Daily Telegraph*.)

Rahim and Hussain also attended boarding school as young boys, but they came home as often as their school schedule permitted and their family life was close. There were family meetings in which they discussed their problems, views and aims. Despite the separation, Karim Aga Khan remained an approachable parent, but one who had very little private time. His work on behalf of education has kept him in touch with young people. He prides himself on his ability to bridge the generation gap in discussions. He has respect for the ideas of youth. A charismatic man, he is none the less an Imam for this century, a modern man, not an icon of the past nor the flamboyant figure of the old Aga Khan, whom Karim appears to have chosen as his paternal figure above his own father. ('Well, it's funny,' he said about this, 'you see I actually knew my grandfather much better than I knew my father.')

Both brothers have studied economics and languages (Urdu and

Arabic among them). Zahra, slim and fair with gold-brown hair that she mostly wears drawn back from her high forehead, is strikingly beautiful and a good athlete (as children the three siblings all took lessons in marksmanship, swimming, skiing, gymnastics and rowing). Along with Zahra, Rahim and Hussain have also visited Ismaili communities and taken an active interest in youth projects sponsored by the Aga Khan Foundation. But as of 1995, neither of the two sons has played a major role in the Imamate. Hussein attends Williams College in Massachusetts and Rahim, at twenty-three, after graduating from Brown University in Rhode Island, moved to San Diego to live a freer, more casual life. He is described by his sect as the 50th descendant of the Prophet Mohammed. But Karim Aga Khan may still reign many more years as Imam and it is as yet too early to know if Rahim will be able to avoid the dangers of being young, good-looking, rich and without a career to give him stability.

In a commencement address to the 1994 class of MIT, Karim Aga Khan told graduands that the world must be prepared to draw upon the wisdom of three different cultures – those of the ex-Communist world, the Muslim world and the Western world – in solving the problems of modern society.

> The Islamic world is . . . a rich and changing tapestry, which the West would do well to understand. The economic power of the Islamic world is increasing, not so much because of Middle Eastern oil but because of the rapid growth of newly industrializing countries like Malaysia and Indonesia. Its population is increasing, and already represents nearly one-quarter of the world's total. It is remarkably diverse – ethnically, economically, politically and in its interpretations of its own faith. The Muslim world no longer can be thought of as a subset of the developing world. Islam is well represented in the United States, Canada, the United Kingdom and Western Europe – and that presence is growing.
>
> The religious diversity of Islam is important, and misunderstood by most non-Muslims . . . for many in the West, the first awareness that there were two major branches of

Islam – Shia and Sunni – came only with the Iranian revolution [1979]. That represents a superficiality of understanding that would be as though we Muslims only just learned that there were two branches of Christianity – Protestant and Catholic . . . or as though we thought that most Americans were Branch Davidians.

He gave his thesis on how to bring a solution to the better understanding of the three cultures he had outlined.

> The West has many strengths, but prominent among them are science and democracy . . . and also private institutions, liberal economics, and a recognition of fundamental human rights. The Muslim world offers deep roots in a system of values, emphasizing service, charity and a sense of common responsibility, and denying what it sees to be the false dichotomy between religious and secular lives. The ex-Communist world, although it failed economically, made important investments in social welfare, with particular emphasis on the status of women . . . These are a powerful array of strengths and goals. Just how to combine them . . . is not clear. But if the outcome is to be sustainable, it seems necessary to concentrate resources on the development of private institutions, of accountable public institutions and of human potential.

Karim Aga Khan was the first Muslim to speak to an MIT graduating class since it was founded in 1865. He has several speech-writers but he first makes full notes on what he wants to say and always edits the final draft before presenting a speech. Possessing an unexpected shyness for a man who has been a public figure for so long, he does not like to speak to large audiences (there were 1824 seniors, graduate students, faculty and guests at the MIT commencement). In the beginning of an address, his voice is usually soft even with the use of a microphone. But as he gets into the main text of a speech, he becomes more the vital and enthusiastic speaker he is before small groups and in private conversation.

No one can foresee what will happen twenty or thirty years hence.

So far, the Ismaili sect has not had its independence threatened by the rise in the numbers of Islamic fundamentalists. The very nature of the Ismailis and what is practised by them precludes danger from within the communities. Karim Aga Khan has heeded his own advice in his leadership of his Imamate. He has incorporated Western, Muslim and Communist ideals in his approach; the emphasis on science, health and democracy, private institutions and liberal economics in the West, the Muslim dedication to service and charity, and Communist principles concerning the equal status of women. It is advice that has worked for Ismailis in the twentieth century and it stands a good chance of helping them to remain safe from outside pressures as they enter the twenty-first century.

The Ismailis possess an Imamate that has been in the hands of Karim Aga Khan and his forefathers for over fourteen centuries. It has been brought to the end of the twentieth century by two quite different but equally dedicated men: Sultan Mohammed, Aga Khan III, and Karim Aga Khan IV, who turned his grandfather's throne of gold into a vehicle for modern times and one would hope for the unknown future.

APPENDICES

APPENDIX I

Classic winners from the racing stables of Aga Khan III

Horses that Aga Khan III bred, raced or sold won at least once nearly all of the most coveted races in England, Ireland and France and the horses he bred and owned have influenced racing and breeding the world over. Among his most notable exports to the United States for breeding purposes were the Derby winners Blenheim II, Mahmoud and Bahram, and for this he was sharply criticized in Europe.

Two Thousand Guineas
        1924 Diophon*
        1935 Bahram
        1950 Palestine

One Thousand Guineas
        1929 Taj Mahal†
        1957 Rose Royale II

Derby Stakes
        1930 Blenheim II*
        1935 Bahram
        1936 Mahmoud (by Blenheim II)
        1948 My Love*
        1952 Tulyar

Oaks Stakes
        1932 Udaipur
        1948 Masaka (by Mahmoud)

St Leger
        1924 Salmon Trout*
        1932 Firdaussi
        1935 Bahram
        1940 Turkhan (by Diophon)
        1944 Tehran
        1952 Tulyar (by Tehran)

Prix du Jockey Club
1924   Pot au Feu*

Grand Prix de Paris
1947   Avenger
1948   My Love*

Poule d'Essai des Poulains
1956   Buisson Ardent

Poule d'Essai des Pouliches
1957   Toro

Irish Two Thousand Guineas
1946   Claro (by Mahmoud)

Irish One Thousand Guineas
1942   Majideh (by Mahmoud)
1952   Nashua

Irish Oaks
1930   Theresina
1940   Queen of Shiraz
1942   Majideh (by Mahmoud)
1948   Masaka (by Mahmoud)
1953   Noory

Irish Derby
1925   Zionist*
1932   Dastur
1940   Turkhan (by Diophon)
1948   Nathoo
1949   Hindostan
1951   Fraise du Bois II

Irish St Leger
1951   Do Well

* Bred by another, won for the Aga Khan.
† Bred by the Aga Khan, won for another owner.

APPENDIX II

Business enterprises of Aga Khan III established at the time of his Diamond Jubilee in 1945

The Aga Khan established numerous trusts and investment companies at the time of his Diamond Jubilee in 1945. They are as follows:

Diamond Jubilee Investment Trust, Kenya
Diamond Jubilee Investment Trust, Uganda
Diamond Jubilee Investment Trust, Tanzania
Diamond Jubilee Investment Trust Service, Kenya
The Pak Ismailia Co-op Bank (which controlled ten industrial enterprises including jute mills and a marble factory)

The following article appeared in *The Times*, 26 July 1945

> Dar es Salaam, July 25
> Followers of the Aga Khan in East Africa have incorporated in Tanganyika an investment trust with a capital of £1,000,000. The Aga Khan is subscribing £250,000 in war bonds and the proceeds of his Diamond Jubilee – he is being offered his own weight in diamonds by his followers next year – to be added to the trust's capital at nominal interest. The shareholders are all Ismailis (followers of the Aga Khan), but the operations – savings or investment – are open to all.

NOTES

Chapter 1

p. 5 'On behalf of . . .' Frischauer, *The Aga Khans*, p. 139.

p. 5 'poor fields . . .' Naipaul, *An Area of Darkness*, p. 71.

p. 6 'never having . . .' William Shirer, personal interview.

p. 6n. 'Do you know the difference . . .' Somerset Maugham, Introduction to *World Enough and Time* (memoirs of Aga Khan III), ix.

p. 7 'If a man had . . .' Speech by Aga Khan III, 19 January 1936.

p. 8 'The Aga Khan . . .' Nehru, *Glimpses of World History*, p. 706.

p. 9 'He was condemned . . .' Obituary, *The Times*.

Chapter 2

p. 13 'gentleman officers . . .' Collins & Lapierre, *Freedom at Midnight*, p. 23.

p. 15 'A new class . . .' Nehru, *Glimpses of World History*, p. 435.

p. 17 'My mother is the only woman . . .' Frischauer, *The Aga Khans*, p. 44.

p. 17 'perfumed isolation . . .' *ibid*.

p. 17 'revealing a backside . . .' Naipaul, *An Area of Darkness*, p. 73.

p. 18 'the habits of Europe . . .' *ibid*, p. 75.

p. 18 'With a zest . . .' Khan, *World Enough and Time*, p. 16.

p. 18 'By a bigoted . . .' *ibid.*, p. 17.

p. 19n. 'The vast majority . . .' *ibid*.

p. 19 '"No," she replied . . .' Jackson, *The Aga Khans*, p. 21.

p. 21 'the esoteric truth . . .' *ibid*.

p. 22 'proceeding to break down . . .' *ibid*.

p. 23 'every man in his household cavalry . . .' *ibid.*, p. 46.

p. 24 'although seventy years of age . . .' *ibid*.

p. 25 'first big emotional . . .' *World Enough and Time*, p. 33.

p. 26 'Why are you looking so sad . . .' Greenwall, *The Aga Khan*, p. 68.

p. 27 'imprisonment of half the nation . . .' *World Enough and Time*, p. 38.

Chapter 3

The Aga Khan's first visit to Windsor Castle was reconstructed with the help of *World Enough and Time*, Lady Lytton's *Court Diary*, Longford, *Victoria RI* and *Louisa, Lady in Waiting*, Athlone, *For My Grandchildren*, Tschumi, *Royal Chef*.

p. 31 'unstrained social mixing . . .' Khan, *World Enough and Time*, p. 26.

p. 32 'there was frigidity . . .' *ibid.*, p. 27.

p. 34 'Tenderness and diffused affection . . .' *ibid.*, p. 36.

p. 36 'in what they were assured . . .' Lady Lytton's Court Diary, p. 36, Longford.

p. 37 'believed him to be . . .' *ibid*.

p. 37 'to make out that the poor good

Munshi . . .' Lady Lytton's Court Diary, p. 38.

p. 38   'some such awful frights . . .' Pope Hennessy, *Queen Mary*, p. 346.

p. 39   'they were distinctly . . .' *World Enough and Time*, p. 42.

p. 39   'I stared at the shop windows . . .' *ibid.*, p. 49.

p. 40   'who lends money . . .' Edwards, *The Grimaldis*, p. 167.

p. 42   'a most interesting man . . .' Warner, *India in Transition*, p. 16.

p. 42   'enfolded in voluminous . . .' *World Enough and Time*, p. 61.

p. 43   'By the educated, of course . . .' Lady Lytton, p. 39

p. 44   'his eyes . . . red . . . the pouches beneath them . . .' *ibid.*

p. 45   'How dared [he] say her Munshi . . .' *Louisa, Lady in Waiting*, p. 543.

Chapter 4

p. 46   'the sublime vision of peoples . . .' St Aubyn, *Edward VII*, p. 144.

p. 47   'as loyal to the English throne . . .' *ibid.*

p. 47   *et seq.* Descriptions of the Aga Khan III from various daily papers during the course of his stay in London.

p. 47   'swarthy, mostly bearded . . .' Townsend, *The Last Emperor*, p. 21.

p. 48   'Victoria in the course of . . .' *World Enough and Time*, p. 49.

p. 50   'a private purgatory . . .' *ibid.*, p. 50.

p. 52   'I was staying in Bagamoyo . . .' Shah, *The Prince Aga Khan*, p. 81.

p. 53   'went the Imperial virtue . . .' Morris, *Farewell the Trumpets*, p. 104.

Chapter 5

p. 59   'to approach the civilization of India . . .' Morris, *Farewell the Trumpets*, p. 105.

p. 60   'the bewhiskered Maharajas . . .', *ibid.*

p. 61   'old, tottering fellows . . .' Townsend, *The Last Emperor*, p. 21.

p. 62   'We all feel . . .' Lord Minto's Diaries, India Office Archives, India House.

p. 63   'a personal law to govern . . .' Frischauer, p. 43.

p. 64   'with hours of ritual ablutions . . .' Collins & Lapierre, *Freedom at Midnight*, p. 36.

p. 64   'a kind of spiritual shopping . . .' *ibid.*, p. 37.

p. 65   'The Aga Khan arrived . . .' Lady Minto's Diary, 9 February 1910.

p. 65   'Would the people of India . . .' Edwards, *Matriarch*, p. 119.

p. 68   'We little dancers . . .' Slater, *Aly*, p. 15.

p. 69   '[My father] was never rich . . .' *ibid.*, p. 14.

p. 69   'My sister was a pure . . .' *ibid.*, p. 8.

p. 69   'Well, it was very difficult . . .' Personal interview, March 1994.

Chapter 6

p. 72   'We sat on chairs in front of a raised seat . . .' Shah, *The Prince Aga Khan*, p. 93.

p. 73   'As regards the ladies . . .' *ibid.*

p. 75n.   'permanent form of marriage . . .' Khan, *World Enough and Time*, p. 321

p. 77   'All the long years of my reign . . .' Tuchman, *The Guns of August*, p. 12.

p. 78   'war in the air . . .' Morris, *Farewell the Trumpets*, p. 126.

p.000   'I . . . trust and believe . . .' Edwards, *Matriarch*, p. 123.

p. 84   'the permanent imprisonment and enslavement of half the nation . . .' Speech by the Aga Khan III, 13 December 1911.

Chapter 7

p. 85 'My way of life . . .' Khan, *World Enough and Time*, p. 29.

p. 87 'I will shed . . .' *ibid.*

p. 87 'Knowledge is the only . . .' *ibid.*

p. 90 'One of the nannies . . .' Young, *Golden Prince*, p. 42.

p. 90 'a very grand personage . . .' Slater, *Aly*, p. 22.

p. 92 'and ruled with a rod . . .' Young, p. 42.

p. 94 'a progressive, satisfied . . .' Khan, *Indian in Transition* p. 302.

p. 95 'a solid yet unchafing . . .' *ibid.*

p. 95 'It is imperative no stone . . .' Townsend, *The Last Emperor*, p. 26.

p. 98 'Why have so many magicians . . .' Jackson, *The Aga Khans*, p. 85.

p. 100 'There are well-known . . .' India Office, Private Files Aga Khan III.

p. 101 'I may remind you . . .' *ibid.*

p. 101 '[His claims] . . .' *ibid.*

p. 102 'I can assure you . . .' *ibid.*

Chapter 8

p. 107 'That woman . . .' Private interview, March 1994.

p. 108 'whether it is held . . .' India Office, Private Files Aga Khan III.

p. 111 'To the Aga Khan . . .' Mortimer, Onslow & Willett, *Biographical Encyclopedia of British Flat Racing*, p. 6.

p. 113 'pour the essence . . .' Frischauer, *The Aga Khans*, p. 114.

p. 115 'How much did you have on it?' *ibid.*, p. 117.

p. 116 'Herewith a new horror . . .' India Office, Private Files Aga Khan III.

p. 116 'a Muhammadan lady . . .' *ibid.*

p. 116 'Her Highness the Begum . . .' *ibid.*

p. 116 'If the new marriage . . .' *ibid.*

p. 116 'Her Highness the Lady Aga Khan . . .' *ibid.*

p. 118 'There he stood . . .' Gulbenkian, *Autobiography*, p. 146.

p. 118 'Andrée might have come from . . .' Private interview.

p. 119 'The doors were guarded . . .' Gulbenkian, p. 149.

p. 119 'the mood was so ugly . . .' Frischauer, p. 120.

p. 120 'God-obsessed . . .' Collins & Lapierre, *Freedom at Midnight*, p. 32.

p. 121 'What he now said . . .' Shirer, *Gandhi*, p. 192.

p. 121 'a rambling, antiquated . . .' Duke of Windsor, *A Family Album*, p. 73.

p. 123 'The King was wearing enough clothes . . .' Shirer, p. 166.

p. 123 'The British were not about to hand over . . .' *ibid.*, p. 193.

Chapter 9

p. 126 'entering a corridor . . .' Nicolson, *George V*, p. 523.

p. 128 'the poorest vying . . .' Greenwall, *The Aga Khan*, p. 138.

p. 128 'tangible recognition . . .' *ibid.*

p. 131n. 'One night she appeared . . .' Private interview.

p. 131 'a very handsome, very dashing . . .' Vanderbilt & Furness, *Double Exposure*, p. 294.

p. 132 'all this [attention] . . .' *ibid.*

p. 132 'I hear Aly Khan . . .' *ibid*, p. 295.

p. 132 'Are you jealous?' *ibid.*

p. 132 'steadily if imperceptibly . . .' Young, *Golden Prince*, p. 102.

p. 135 'Darling, will you marry me?' *ibid.*

Chapter 10

p. 138 'At the Opera . . .' Channon, *Chips*, pp. 158–9.

p. 139   'Thirty thousand pounds . . .'
          Khan, *World Enough and Time*,
          p. 242.

p. 139   'extremely naive . . .' Private
          interview.

p. 140   'all forms of democracy . . .'
          Nehru, *Glimpses of World
          History*, p. 915.

p. 140   'a Dictator *de facto* . . .' BBC
          Archives.

p. 142   'in order to give my heirs . . .'
          India Office Archives.

p. 145   'India is troubled . . .' *World
          Enough and Time*, p. 244.

p. 146   'be justified . . .' *ibid*, p. 264.

p. 146   'I stand before history . . .' *ibid*,
          p. 265.

p. 147   'For your personal
          information . . .' India Office,
          Private Files Aga Khan III.

p. 148   'Help Britain . . .' Young,
          Golden Prince, p. 71.

p. 149   'It was in uniform . . .'
          Frischauer, *The Aga Khans*,
          p. 162.

p. 149   'I was told by General
          Wavell . . .' Wintle, *The Last
          Englishman*, p. 224

Chapter 11

p. 153   'save on the basis . . .' India
          Office Archives, Private Files
          Aga Khan III.

p. 153   'The Khedive of Egypt . . .'
          ibid.

p. 154   'Although the Aga . . .' *ibid.*

p. 154   'We do not believe . . .' *ibid.*, 15
          June 1941.

p. 155   'The loyalty of the Indian . . .'
          Churchill, *The Hinge of Fate*,
          p. 182.

p. 155   'either actively hostile . . .' *ibid.*

p. 156   'If God wills it . . .' Fischer, *The
          Life of Mahatma Gandhi*, p. 393.

p. 159   'mutual dislike . . .' Swiss
          records of divorce, Geneva
          1943.

p. 161   'Not only was the whole . . .'
          Morris, *Farewell the Trumpets*,
          p. 477.

p. 161   'The British Commonwealth

          and Empire . . .' *ibid*,. p. 460.

p. 161   'There was something
          rotten . . .' *ibid.*, p. 477.

p. 161   'As long as we rule India . . .'
          ibid., p. 495.

p. 161   'the idea of a united . . .' India
          Office, Private Files Aga Khan
          III, 29 October 1942.

p. 162   'that it was impossible . . .'
          ibid., p. 92.

p. 162   'The scene here . . .' Collins &
          Lapierre, *Freedom at Midnight*,
          pp. 96, 180.

p. 162   'He would admit no . . .' Khan,
          World Enough and Time, p. 293.

p. 163   '[I] tried every trick I could
          play . . .' Lapierre & Collins,
          p. 118.

p. 163   'The first time Bertie . . .'
          Edwards, *Matriarch*, p. 312.

p. 163   'power over . . .' Jackson, *The
          Aga Khan*, p. 189.

p. 164   'In some quarters . . .' *ibid.*

p. 165   'probably a small amount . . .'
          India Office, Private Files Aga
          Khan III.

p. 167   'ear-cracking . . .' and (p. 168)
          'wash your hands . . .' Private
          interview with a member of the
          Aga Khan's party.

p. 168   'At such a time . . .' Young,
          Golden Prince, p. 162.

p. 170   'This is for me . . .' Private
          interview.

p. 172   'If only Aly . . .' Young, p. 120.

Chapter 12

p. 173   'everything considered worth
          shooting . . .' *Life*, 11 May 1959.

p. 174   'People don't realize . . .'
          Young, *Golden Prince*, p. 121.

p. 174   'waddled off to . . .' Jackson,
          The Aga Khan, p. 182.

p. 174   'I was therefore amazed . . .'
          ibid.

p. 175   'Suddenly he jumped . . .' *ibid.*

p. 175   'most recent No. 1 . . .' *ibid.*

p. 175   'suddenly he began staring . . .'
          ibid.

p. 175   'The trouble with Aly . . .' *ibid.*

p. 177   'I have nothing to wear,'

Leaming, *If This Was Happiness*,
p. 154.

p. 177 'The Prince was . . .' *ibid*.

p. 178 'about to embark . . .' *ibid*.,
p. 157.

p. 180 'It was too overwhelming . . .'
ibid., p. 159.

p. 181 'I never saw the Prince as a sex
maniac . . .' *ibid*., p. 165.

p. 183 'to cease being like a
Hollywood . . .' *Life*, 11 May
1959.

p. 184 'Joan always knew more . . .'
ibid..

p. 185 'I couldn't get any plane . . .'
Leaming, p. 189.

p. 186 'This was a fantastic . . .' Khan,
World Enough and Time, p. 312.

Chapter 13

p. 188 'At noon precisely . . .' Korda,
Charmed Lives, p. 196.

p. 190 'looked upon her marriage . . .'
Khan, *World Enough and Time*,
p. 313.

p. 191 'Miss Hayworth somehow got
it . . .' *ibid*.

p. 191 'Had Miss Hayworth . . .' *ibid*.

p. 192 'there is no way . . .' *ibid*.

p. 192 'I can only hope . . .' *ibid*.

p. 193 'Being a gentleman . . .' Korda,
p. 211

p. 193 'in ski trousers . . .' *ibid*.

p. 199 'There's a false notion . . .'
Speech by the future Aga Khan
IV, July 1954.

Chapter 14

p. 200 'which spectacularly . . .'
Young, *Golden Prince*, p. 15.

p. 201 'With my grandfather . . .' *Life*,
April 1983.

p. 202 'I was too young . . .'
Frischauer, *The Aga Khans*,
p. 216.

p. 202 'He could extract more
from . . .' *Life*, April 1983.

p. 203 'was dressed casually . . .' *This
Week Magazine*, 10 November
1957 (Harvard Archives)

p. 204 'drumming on anything

available . . .' *ibid*.

p. 204 'He was lean but too
stocky . . .' *ibid*.

p. 205 'His ski clothes were a
sight . . .' *ibid*.

p. 205 'Since he had . . .' *ibid*.

p. 205 'They say his grandfather . . .'
Boston Globe, 14 July 1957.

p. 206 'an extremely remarkable
resemblance . . .' *Boston
Sunday Herald*, 14 July 1957.

p. 208 '"That!" she cried . . .' Private
interview with member of Aga
Khan III's staff.

p. 208 'I think it was Bettina . . .'
Private interview.

p. 210 'He should never . . .' *Life*, 11
May 1959.

p. 210 'Yassy . . .' Private interview.

p. 213 'The Imam is dead . . .' Private
interview with member of Aga
Khan III's staff.

Chapter 15

p. 218 'He had a strong sense . . .'
Frischauer, *The Aga Khans*,
p. 291.

p. 219 'My grandfather dedicated . . .'
Published press statement.

p. 220n. 'On this sad occasion . . .'
Published press release.

p. 225 'Karim Aga Khan . . .' *ibid*.

p. 225 'In the first months after . . .'
ibid.

p. 227 'The old Aga Khan . . .' Private
interview.

p. 228 'The Queen was having a
spot . . .' *ibid*.

p. 230 'Listening to him making . . .'
Frischauer, p. 293.

p. 230 'He had the look . . .' Private
interview.

Chapter 16

p. 236 'the only player on either
side . . .' *Life*, 11 May 1959.

p. 236 'People all over . . .' *Life*, 11 May
1958.

p. 236 'the way the light hits the
trees . . .' *ibid*.

p. 237 'to hit the books . . .' *ibid*.

p. 237 'Many of the soccer
spectators . . .' *Boston Globe*, 22
November 1958.

p. 239 'He smelled of lemon and
talc . . .' Private interview.

p. 239 'All of them, in relation to
the . . .' Records, United
Nations.

p. 239 'He was European . . .' *The
Economist*, 14 November 1987.

p. 241 'As Imam I insist . . .'
Frischauer, *The Aga Khans*,
p. 298.

p. 242 'Prince Karim did not
want . . .' *ibid.*

p. 244 'He died . . .' *Daily Mail*, 19
May 1960.

Chapter 17

p. 247 'What am I going to do . . .'
Frischauer, *The Aga Khans*,
p. 301.

p. 247 'You don't remember . . .'
Leaming, *Rita: If This Was
Happiness*.

p. 253 'The advantage of being . . .'
Private interview.

p. 255 'You know what thrills me . . .'
Daily Mail, 20 September
1961.

p. 255 'The Aga Khan is a
perfectionist,' *ibid.*

Chapter 18

p. 258 'We are tough about our
standards . . .' Boston, *Sunday
Herald Traveler*, 21 April
1968.

p. 259 'except that he has never been
beset . . .' *ibid.*

p. 260 'I used to drive a lot . . .' *ibid.*

p. 261 'I didn't realize racing . . .'
ibid.

p. 263 'Karim Aga Khan has an
aura . . .' Private interview.

p. 263 'Anyone who prays . . .' *Life*,
April 1983.

p. 263 'I want to build a house
here . . .' Frischauer, *The Aga
Khans*, p. 354.

Chapter 19

p. 274 'Our people . . . feel the pain
of . . .' Wolpert, *Zulfi Bhutto*,
p. 128.

p. 279 'I don't see Yassy much . . .'
Life, September 1972.

p. 281 'If I am ever Queen . . .'
Edwards, *Royal Sisters*, p. 41.

p. 281 'Sometimes . . . she would
whisper . . .' *ibid.*

p. 281 'it was such an honour . . .' *ibid.*

p. 282 'had no interest in them . . .'
Life, April 1983.

p. 283 'Oh, you know . . .' Coleridge,
Paper Tigers, p. 386.

p. 283 'Well, Mr Curtis . . .' *ibid.*

p. 284 'to rub his finger . . .' *ibid.*

p. 284 'It was the official opening . . .'
ibid., p. 389.

p. 285 'There are certain things . . .'
Life, April 1983.

p. 285 'African and Western
society . . .' *ibid.*

Chapter 20

p. 289 'because spectacles are difficult
to ski in . . .' *Life*, April 1983.

p. 292 'Being Ismaili is more than a
religion . . .' *Forbes*, 17
November 1986.

p. 292 'I see my people more than the
Pope . . .' *ibid.*

p. 296 'Nationalization of private . . .'
ibid.

p. 296 'creases would furrow . . .' *Life*,
October 1981.

p. 296 'We are talking here . . .' *ibid.*

p. 302 'Please don't come see me . . .'
Private interview.

p. 302 'I think everyone has
something . . .' *Hello*, August
1993.

Chapter 21

p. 304 'Absolutely . . .' *Life*, August
1985.

p. 304 'I have some institutional . . .'
ibid.

p. 305 'A lot of our culture . . .' *ibid.*

p. 307 'The Aga Khan has made . . .'
ibid.

p. 309 'Have you made that decision . . .' *ibid.*

p. 311 'Well, it's funny . . .' *ibid.*

p. 312 'The Islamic world . . .' Commencement Speech MIT Class of 1994 by Karim Aga Khan, MIT Archives.

BIBLIOGRAPHY

Athlone, Countess of (HRH Princess Alice), *For My Grandchildren*, Evans, London, 1966.

Beaton, Cecil, *Self Portrait With Friends*, ed. R. Buckle, Times Books, New York, 1979.

Bence-Jones, Mark, *The Viceroys of India*, Constable, London, 1982.

Bose, Mihir, *The Aga Khans*, World's Work, London, 1984.

Channon, Sir Henry, *Chips*, ed. R. R. James, Weidenfeld & Nicolson, London, 1967.

Churchill, Winston S., *The Second World War*, Cassell, London, 1948–56. Vols I–VI: *The Gathering Storm, Their Finest Hour, The Grand Alliance, The Hinge of Fate, Closing the Ring, Triumph & Tragedy*.

Coleridge, Nicholas, *Paper Tigers*, Heinemann, London, 1993.

Collins, L., & Lapierre, D., *Freedom at Midnight*, Simon & Schuster, New York, 1975.

Cooper, Diana, *The Light of Common Day*, Rupert Hart-Davis, London, 1959.

Daftary, Farhad, *The Ismailis – Their History and Doctrine*, Cambridge University Press, 1990.

Damasia, Navaroji Mankji, *The Aga Khan and His Ancestors*, Calcutta, 1939.

—— *A Brief History of the Aga Khan* (including writings and speeches of Aga Khan III), Calcutta, 1903.

Donaldson, Frances, *Edward VIII*, J. B. Lippincott, New York, 1975.

Edwards, Anne, *Matriarch, Queen Mary and the House of Windsor*, Hodder & Stoughton, London, 1984.

—— *Royal Sisters*, HarperCollins, London, 1990.

Fischer, Louis, *The Life of Mahatma Gandhi*, Harper & Brothers, New York, 1950.

Fisher, W. B., *The Middle East* (7th edn), Methuen, 1978.

Frischauer, Willi, *The Aga Khans*, Hawthorn Books, New York, 1971.

Gandhi, Mohandas K., *An Autobiography*, trans. M. Desai, Beacon Press, USA, 1957.

Graves, Charles, *None But the Rich*, Cassell, London, 1963.

Greenwall, Harry J., *The Aga Khan*, Cresset Press, London, 1952.

BIBLIOGRAPHY

Gulbenkian, Nubar, *The Autobiography of Nubar Gulbenkian*, Hutchinson, London, 1965.

Hastings, Selina, *Nancy Mitford*, Hamish Hamilton, London, 1985.

Hill, James, *Rita Hayworth*, Simon & Schuster, New York, 1983.

Jackson, Stanley, *The Aga Khan*, Odhams, London, 1952.

Kesavji, Habir Velsi, *The Aga Khan and Africa*, London, 1949.

Khan, Aga, *India in Transition*, 1918

—— *World Enough and Time*, Cassell, London, 1954.

Korda, Michael, *Charmed Lives*, Random House, New York, 1979.

Lacey, Robert, *Majesty*, Hutchinson, London, 1985.

Leaming, Barbara, *If This Was Happiness*, Viking, New York, 1989.

Longford, Elizabeth, *Louisa, Lady in Waiting, the Personal Diaries and Albums of Louisa, Lady in Waiting to Queen Victoria and Queen Alexandra*, Jonathan Cape, London, 1979.

—— *Victoria RI*, Weidenfeld & Nicolson, London, 1964.

Lyle, Robert C., *The Aga Khan's Horses*, London, 1938.

Lytton, Edith (Villiers), Bulwer-Lytton, Countess, *Lady Lytton's Court Diary*, ed. Mary Lutyens, Hart-Davis, London, 1961.

Malick, Qayyum A., *His Royal Highness Prince Aga Khan*, London, 1954.

Moraes, Dom, *Indira Gandhi*, Little, Brown, Boston, 1980.

Morella, Joe, & Epstein, Edward Z., *Rita*, Delacorte Press, New York, 1983.

Morris, James, *Farewell the Trumpets*, Harcourt, Brace, Jovanovitch, New York, 1978.

Mortimer, Roger, Onslow, Richard, & Willett, Peter, *Biographical Encyclopaedia of British Flat Racing*, Macdonald & Jane's, London, 1978.

Mullally, Frederic, *The Silver Salver, The Story of the Guinness Family*, Granada, London, 1981.

Naipaul, V. S., *An Area of Darkness*, Macmillan, New York, 1964.

Nanji, Azim, *The Nizari Ismaili Tradition*, Vantage, USA.

Nehru, Jawaharlal, *Glimpses of World History*, John Dary, New York, 1942.

Nicolson, Harold, *Diaries*, Collins, London, 1966.

—— *King George V: His Life and Reign*, Constable, London, 1952.

Oaksey, Lord, *Queen (The Queen's Horses)*, Penguin, Harmondsworth, 1977.

Payne, Robert, *Gandhi*, Dutton, New York, 1969.

Potocki, Count Alfred, *Master of Lancut*, W. H. Allen, London, 1959.

Sahgal, Nayantara, *Indira Gandhi*, Frederick Ungar, New York, 1982.

St Aubyn, Giles, *Edward VII*, Atheneum, New York, 1979.

St John Nevill, Barry, *Life at the Court of Queen Victoria 1861–1901*, Webb & Bower, Exeter, 1984.

Sale, George, *A Preliminary Discourse on The Koran*, translated into English from the original Arabic, Frederick Warne, London, 1920.

Shah, Sirdar Ikbal Ali, *The Prince Aga Khan*, John Long, London, 1933.

Shirer, William L., *Gandhi, A Memoir*, Simon & Schuster, New York, 1979.

Slater, Leonard, *Aly, a Biography*, W. H. Allen, London, 1966.

Spear, Percival, *India*, Univ. of Michigan Press, Ann Arbor, 1972.

Townsend, Peter, *The Last Emperor*, Weidenfeld & Nicolson, London, 1975.

Tschumi, Gabriel, *Royal Chef*, William Kimber, London, 1954.

Tuchman, Barbara, *The Guns of August*, Macmillan, New York, 1962.

Vanderbilt, Gloria, & Furness, Thelma, Lady, *Double Exposure*, Frederick Muller, London, 1959.

Warner, Philip Lee, *India in Transition*, London, 1918. [Not to be confused with the book of the same title by the Aga Khan III].

Windsor, Duke of, *A Family Album*, Cassell, London, 1960.

Wintle, Lt. Col. A.D., *The Last Englishman*, Michael Joseph, London, 1968.

Wintle, Justin, *A Family Album*, Michael Joseph, London, 1968.

Wolpert, Stanley, *Zulfi Bhutto of Pakistan, His Life and Times*, Oxford University Press, New York, 1992.

Young, Gordon, *Golden Prince, The Remarkable Life of Prince Aly Khan*, Robert Hale, London, 1955.

Ziegler, Philip, *Mountbatten*, Knopf, New York, 1985.

Periodicals, papers and pamphlets

An Open Letter to His Highness The Aga Khan (the Aga Khan and the Khoja Community), Khoja Reformers Society, Karachi, 1927.

An Open Letter to His Excellency Sir Lancelot Graham . . . Governor of Sind (A criticism of the Aga Khan's government of the Khojas by Karim Ghulam Ali), 1937.

Genealogical Table of the [Aga Khan III], Sulaiman Ghulam Husain Hadji, 1905.

His Highness The Aga Khan: a sketch of his life. Madras, 1917.

A Voice from India: An appeal to the British Legislature against the oppressive domination of Aga Khan I.

Forbes Magazine, New York, 17 November 1986; 13 June 1987.

The Economist, New York, 4 November 1987; 9 January 1988.

Life, 16 May 1949; 30 May 1949; 6 June 1949; 3 April 1950; 4 December 1958; 11 May 1959; 11 December 1967; August 1985.

Quest, December/January 1993–4

The Blood Horse

Archives

India House, London

India Office, London

Ismailia Centre, London

Royal Archives, Windsor

The library of Churchill College, Cambridge

United Nations, New York

Academy of Motion Picture Arts and Sciences, Beverly Hills, California

Time/Life, New York

Harvard University, Cambridge, Mass.

Kentucky Archive of Horse Racing and Breeding, Lexington, KY.

BIBLIOGRAPHY

Massachusetts Institute of Technology, Cambridge, Mass.
Aga Khan Program
British Broadcasting Corporation (BBC)
Islamic Architecture
Roach Visual Library, Cambridge, Mass.

INDEX

The Khan family and their wives are indexed as follows: Aga Khan I to III as such; Aga Khan IV and other members and their wives under their first names, as preferred in the text. See Begum Aga Khan for references to Begums. As far as practicable, sub-headings are in chronological order.